Almighty God Created the Races

Almighty God Created the Races

CHRISTIANITY, INTERRACIAL MARRIAGE, & AMERICAN LAW

Fay Botham

The University of North Carolina Press Chapel Hill

© 2009 The University of North Carolina Press
All rights reserved

Designed by Michelle Coppedge
Set in Scala and Scala Sans Types
by Tseng Information Systems, Inc.
Manufactured in the United States of America

The paper in this book meets the guidelines for permanence
and durability of the Committee on Production Guidelines for
Book Longevity of the Council on Library Resources.

The University of North Carolina Press has been a member of
the Green Press Initiative since 2003.

Library of Congress Cataloging-in-Publication Data
Botham, Fay, 1968–
Almighty God created the races : Christianity, interracial marriage,
and American law / Fay Botham.
p. cm.
Includes bibliographical references and index.
ISBN 978-0-8078-3318-6 (cloth : alk. paper)
1. Interracial marriage — Law and legislation — United States —
History. 2. Religion and law — United States — History. I. Title.
KF511.B68 2009
346.7301'6 — dc22
2009024330

13 12 11 10 09 5 4 3 2 1

To those who have inspired the thinking—
Judge Leon M. Bazile, Daniel G. Marshall,
and Tahlia Fischer

Contents

Tables

Acknowledgments

So very many individuals have supported me during this project during the nearly eight years that it has evolved into a book; I am sure to omit someone important, so I will begin at the beginning with the many extraordinary mentors who have guided my journey. My interest in interracial marriage originated in Robert Dawidoff's "Intellectual History of the American South" course at Claremont Graduate University. I owe a profound debt to Robert for raising the questions that led me to embark on an initial exploration of the topic. Robert, together with Ann Taves, Janet Farrell Brodie, Lori Anne Ferrell, and Peggy Pascoe, taught me, at times with great resistance on my part, what it meant to think like a historian. They trusted my sense that religion did play a significant role in American antimiscegenation cases and that the primary sources were, in fact, out there somewhere. I feel very blessed to have had such a terrific team of individuals guiding my learning and shaping my thinking to have whatever merits it may have. And I am very thankful for the mentoring I continue to receive from these scholars.

My hunt for primary sources was long, somewhat arduous, but ultimately satisfying. I visited many libraries and archival collections, including the California State Archives in Sacramento; the Caroline County Clerk's Office, Bowling Green, Virginia; the Colorado State Archives in Denver; the Denver Public Library, Western History Division; the Special Collections of the Georgetown University Library, Washington, D.C.; the Los Angeles County Law Library; the Los Angeles Public Library; the archives of the *Richmond Times-Dispatch* in Richmond, Virginia; the Virginia Historical Society; and the Library of Virginia. I am especially grateful to several librarians and archivists who helped me locate materials: Vincent Sansone of the Archives of the Diocese of Richmond, Virginia; Kevin Feeney and Monsignor Francis J. Weber of the Archival Center of the Archdiocese of Los Angeles; Tony Amodeo of the Loyola-Marymount University Library in Los Angeles; Betty Clements and Elaine Walker of the Claremont School of Theology Library, and Adam Rosenkranz of Honnold Library at the Claremont Colleges; and Beth Beretta and Joseph Chmura, librarians of Hobart and William Smith Colleges. I am also extraordinarily grateful to Sandy Satterwhite and Maurice Duke, relatives of the late Judge Leon M. Bazile of Hanover County, Virginia. Sandy and Maurice took me—a complete stranger—on a tour of Hanover County, and they shared with me their love for the intelligent, complex man who inspired this book in the first place. I owe a deep debt to Sandy and Maurice for any insights I may have offered about Judge Bazile and his famous statement.

No book is written without significant financial assistance along the way. I am grateful for several Graduate Theological Education Fellowships from the Evangelical Lutheran Church; for Claremont Graduate University's Hillcrest Transdisciplinary Research Fellowship, the John MacGuire Presidential Fellowship, and the Claremont Graduate University Dissertation Grant; and the National Endowment for the Humanities Summer Stipend in 2006.

Many, many friends and colleagues have read and commented upon draft upon draft of chapters and on seemingly endless versions of this book. My writing group, consisting of Dan Cady, Karen Linkletter, Glenn Mitoma, and Sara M. Patterson, at Claremont, offered much support and initial feedback. My students have also read early versions, and I owe a special thanks to University of Iowa graduate student Sarah Dees, who assisted with the final manuscript revisions and with the index and who good-naturedly tolerated my disorganized, last-minute, Gemini self. Katie Oxx, Laura Ammon, Randy Reed, Anna Creadick, Alison Redick, and Holly Rine, and my supersmart, awesome nephew, Thad Botham, have read various incarnations of my ramblings and patiently told me to keep going. Jennifer Glancy and Darryl Caterine took time from their excruciating schedules to read the entire book and to offer kind and helpful suggestions. In addition, Leslie Schwalm, Kim Marra, Paul Finkelman, and Martha Hodes provided critical advice and commentary along the way. I am especially grateful to Tracy Fessenden and Peter Wallenstein, who reviewed drafts of the manuscript and offered feedback that has made the final product so much stronger. And my editor, Elaine Maisner, who saw something promising in the project even when I had completed only one very early chapter, has been encouraging, patient, and gently persistent throughout my long revision process—precisely the combination that worked for me.

To my family and extended family of dear friends, I cannot adequately convey my gratitude for being there during the most difficult—and the most joyous—moments: Katie Oxx and Rick Jacobsen: Laura Ammon and

Randy Reed; Sara M. Patterson; Mary Hess; Lauren Alleyne; Susan Henking and Betty Bayer; Stephanie Sleeper and Geoff Spady; Sara Moslener; Holly Rine; Farha Ternikar and Travis Vande Berg; Jennifer Glancy and David Anderson; Sue Tallon and Linda Beaton; Don Snodgrass; Zoe Fischer Shillcock and Paul Shillcock; Donna and Clare Fischer; and David Chase and Adikus Sulpizi. For countless conversations, bottles of wine, encouraging words, sage advice, and Deep Thoughts, thank you, thank you, all. To my mom and dad, who thought the book would never be done, thank you for your patience and never-wavering confidence. And Tahlia Fischer, thank you for being my arch-defender, and the funniest, smartest, and most productive conversation partner, without whose thoughts this book—and a whole lot of other good things—would never have sprung into being.

Almighty God Created the Races

Introduction

In early June 1958, eighteen-year-old Mildred Delores Jeter and twenty-four-year-old Richard Perry Loving drove from their hometown of Central Point, Virginia, to Washington, D.C. Sweethearts for some six years, Mildred, who was part black and part Cherokee with a light brown complexion, and Richard, who was of English-Irish descent, had decided to get married in the District of Columbia. Once their union was legalized there, they returned home to Central Point and began to build their life together.

The Lovings' matrimonial bliss ended abruptly about five weeks later. During the wee hours of a sultry July morning, three Caroline County police officers entered the Lovings' home through their unlocked front door. Sheriff R. Garnett Brooks and his two deputies found their way into the couple's bedroom, shined a flashlight in their faces, and demanded to know what they were doing in bed together. When Mildred answered, "I'm his wife," and Richard directed the officers to the District of Columbia marriage certificate that hung on the wall, Sheriff Brooks curtly informed them that their marriage was invalid in the State of Virginia.[1] He then arrested the bewildered young couple and hauled them off to jail. There they were charged with having violated Virginia Code 20-54, which prohibited interracial marriage, and Code 20-58, which prohibited "any white person and colored person" from leaving Virginia to evade Code 20-54.[2]

A few months later in January 1959, a Caroline County grand jury indicted Mildred and Richard for having "unlawfully and feloniously go[ne] out of the State of Virginia, for the purpose of being married, and with the intention of returning to the State of Virginia," and for "cohabiting as man and wife against the peace and dignity of the Commonwealth."[3] The Lovings pleaded guilty to the charges, and the Honorable Judge Leon M. Bazile sentenced each to one year in the Caroline County Jail. A compassionate man, the judge suspended the jail sentence, sparing the couple from an experience behind bars and from time away from their new baby boy, born in 1958. But he did so only on the condition that they agree to leave Virginia and not return together for twenty-five years.⁴ The heartbroken couple, effectively banished from their own state, then went to live with relatives in Washington, D.C.

In 1963, Mildred learned that Congress had begun debating a civil rights bill (which would become the Civil Rights Act of 1964). Hoping that her and Richard's convictions might be challenged as a civil rights issue and that they might be able to return to Virginia with their three children, Sidney, Donald, and Peggy, she wrote to then–U.S. attorney general Robert Kennedy. Kennedy's aides forwarded her letter to the American Civil Liberties Union, and attorney Bernard S. Cohen eagerly agreed to take the case. (ACLU attorney Philip J. Hirschkop joined the case later.) The attorneys filed motions with the Caroline County Circuit Court to vacate the 1959 convictions and sentences, contending that Virginia's antimiscegenation statutes violated the couple's constitutional rights to due process and equal protection.⁵ Fifteen months later in January 1965, Judge Bazile, a lifelong Catholic, reaffirmed the validity of both Virginia antimiscegenation statutes and his original decision and sentence. He concluded his remarks with the following words: "Almighty God created the races white, black, yellow, malay, and red, and he placed them on separate continents. And but for the interference with his arrangement there would be no cause for such marriages. The fact that he separated the races shows that he did not intend for the races to mix."⁶ Their motion having thus been denied, Cohen and Hirschkop then appealed to Virginia's highest court, which one year later affirmed the constitutionality of the statutes but deemed the Lovings' sentences "unreasonable." The couple was ordered back to Caroline County to be resentenced.

Meanwhile, Cohen and Hirschkop took the case, aptly named *Loving v. the Commonwealth of Virginia*, to the U.S. Supreme Court.⁷ "Mr. Cohen," Richard Loving implored as the attorneys prepared their arguments, "tell the Court I love my wife, and it is just unfair that I can't live with her in Virginia."⁸ On 12 June 1967, after nine years of fighting for the legality of their marriage, Mildred and Richard Loving at last received the news they had awaited: The Court ruled that Virginia's antimiscegenation laws violated Americans' Fourteenth Amendment rights to due process and equal protection of the law, and that such laws were therefore unconstitutional. Chief Justice Earl Warren delivered the Court's unanimous opinion. "Under our Constitution," he stated, "the freedom to marry, or not marry, a person of another race resides with the individual and cannot be infringed by the State."⁹ Affirming the civil rather than the religious right to marry, the decision ended the nation's three-hundred-year history of laws prohibiting marriage across the color line. And for perhaps the first time in American history, a federal court held the individual's right to choose a spouse above the state's right to create and enact marriage laws.

In all the years of legal wrangling and media attention in the Loving case, religion appeared explicitly in only two places: in Judge Bazile's now-famous statement about God having created the races, and in an amicus curiae brief that a group of Catholic ordinaries filed on behalf of the Lovings. When the case went to the U.S. Supreme Court, a coalition of two Catholic organizations and sixteen Catholic bishops from the South filed the brief, arguing that antimiscegenation laws unconstitutionally restricted the couple's free exercise of religion, insofar as the right to marry was a religious one.[10] In both of these places where religion appears, interesting questions arise. What are the historical origins of Judge Bazile's strange statement about God having "separated the races"? Did it have anything to do with the fact that he was Roman Catholic? How did such a notion make its way into American law? Why did the coalition of Catholics file a brief on behalf of the Lovings, who were Protestant? And more broadly, what do these two instances reveal about the historical relationships between Christianity, race, and marriage law?

On the other side of the continent, about twenty years prior to the U.S. Supreme Court ruling in Loving, a young Catholic couple encountered legal obstacles to their marriage in a case that posed similar questions about religion. In 1941, Lockheed Aviation hired Sylvester Davis Jr., a Catholic African American man and graduate of Los Angeles City College. Soon after, he became smitten with Andrea Perez, a brown-skinned woman of Mexican descent who worked with him on the assembly line at Lockheed, and who shared his Catholic faith. After serving overseas in the U.S. Army during the Second World War, Sylvester returned to the City of Angels and asked Andrea to marry him. She happily agreed.[11] The couple approached their pastor at St. Patrick's Catholic Church and expressed to him their wish to get married. St. Patrick's was a racially mixed parish, and the priest had encountered such requests before. He knew he had no choice but to give the couple sad news. He informed them that the state of California prohibited marriages between whites and persons of color. Although Andrea did not necessarily identify herself as "white," the priest expected that Sylvester would be categorized as "black" and that their request for a marriage license would thus be denied.

Desperate for a solution that would allow them to marry in the parish,

Andrea and Sylvester then turned to fellow Catholic Daniel Marshall, a prominent Los Angeles civil rights attorney and president of the local Catholic Interracial Council, and a member of their church. In Marshall, they found far more than a sympathetic ear. They obtained the services of a talented lawyer who earnestly desired to help Andrea and Sylvester marry in the church. But even more important, Marshall—a committed integrationist—viewed the prohibitions against interracial marriage as a pet issue. So when Andrea and Sylvester approached him with the problem, he enthusiastically agreed to assist them.

Upon Marshall's counsel, in August 1947 the couple applied for a marriage license with the Los Angeles county clerk Joseph Moroney. As Marshall expected, Moroney took one look at them, designated Andrea as "white" and Sylvester as "Negro," and flatly rejected their application. Marshall then filed a petition with the California Supreme Court, requesting that the court issue an order compelling Moroney to grant the couple a license. A shrewd and skillful thinker, Marshall employed an innovative plan through which to structure his arguments. Rather than disputing the racial identities assigned the couple by Moroney—the approach taken by most attorneys in such cases—he strategically framed his case around the couple's *Catholic* identity. In the Catholic Church, he argued, marriage was a sacrament, and since the church did not bar interracial marriage, California's antimiscegenation laws impeded the couple's ability to participate in this most sacred of Catholic rituals, and thus violated their First Amendment right to practice their religion freely. Andrea Perez and Sylvester Davis waited for one year until the Court handed down its decision in the *Perez v. Lippold* case.[12]

In 1948 the couple received good news. The California Supreme Court declared the state's antimiscegenation laws unconstitutional—the first such ruling in the twentieth century—and Andrea and Sylvester married at St. Patrick's Church a few months later. Although the Court ultimately reached its decision based upon Fourteenth rather than First Amendment considerations, Marshall's choice to structure his argument on First Amendment issues raises many questions about the significance of religion in the *Perez* case. What role did religious freedom play in the right to marry the person of one's choosing, and did it have some special relationship to Catholic belief? As in the Lovings' case, why were Catholics active in advocating on behalf of an interracial couple? Did the Catholic affirmation of the sacramental nature of marriage have some bearing on Catholic views on interracial marriage? Does not the very assertion of Catholic beliefs about intermarriage imply the existence of non-Catholic views on intermarriage? If so, what might these non-Catholic beliefs be?

Religious Belief and the Right to Marry Interracially

The answers to these questions lie in a long and fascinating history of conflicting religious beliefs about race and marriage, and of interpretations of legal and religious texts and doctrines. Like contemporary same-sex couples, interracial couples of the American past asserted the legitimacy of their relationships, and they fought for the right to marry the person of their choosing in courts often hostile to those rights. Just as the constitutional issues faced by today's same-sex couples in many ways parallel those in antimiscegenation cases, religion similarly played a critical, though far less apparent, role in historical interracial marriage cases.[13] Interracial couples faced religious censure in American courts just like same-sex couples. Judges pronounced interracial couples' relationships "unnatural" and "evil," deemed such unions "corruptions" of what God had intended for human relationships, and claimed that God had made black and white persons morally and socially unequal and thus unsuitable for marriage. Yet despite the evidence for the strong correlation between religious beliefs and historical attitudes toward intermarriage, no historians or legal scholars have analyzed this issue in a book-length study. Indeed, scholars have given very little attention to the role of religion in American antimiscegenation cases or in the history of interracial marriage more generally.[14] Although historians have recently begun to investigate this topic, they have not yet fully addressed the connections between Christianity and American beliefs about intermarriage.[15] In short, of all the vast historical literature on marriage, interracial marriage, and antimiscegenation cases, very little devotes sustained attention to the ways that religious beliefs influenced American marriage law, antimiscegenation law, conceptions of marriage and race, or attitudes toward intermarriage. And none attempts to compare different types of Christian beliefs about interracial marriage or examine their influences upon antimiscegenation cases.[16]

My book, *Almighty God Created the Races*, begins to fill this void in the scholarship on religion and interracial marriage and antimiscegenation law. Contending that the *Perez* and *Loving* cases function as windows into the cultural history of interracial marriage and its legal regulation, I analyze the ways that religious beliefs and regional differences about race and marriage underlie the two cases. Tracing the historical development of religious ideas about race and marriage requires analysis of a wide variety of historical sources over a long period. I therefore examine Reformation-era writings on marriage; papal encyclicals; nineteenth-century articles from newspapers and religious periodicals; post–Civil War writings by Catholic and Protestant clerics and canon law specialists; the available legal and non-legal documentation of the *Perez* and *Loving* cases; and relevant historical cases on interracial sex and marriage from several state supreme courts and the U.S. Supreme Court. Reading these materials together reveals the connections between Catholic and Protestant beliefs about marriage and race, and between race, religion, and American law. By enhancing our understanding of the means through which religious beliefs constructed American ideas about interracial marriage, we see more clearly the role of religion in *Perez* and *Loving*, in antimiscegenation history, and in the legal regulation of marriage.

A cultural history of law more than a legal history per se, *Almighty God Created the Races* advances the view that Christian beliefs about race and marriage exerted a powerful and enduring ideological influence on anti-miscegenation law and litigation and on American attitudes toward race, intermarriage, and segregation. I contend that there were, in fact, divergent Catholic and Protestant theologies of marriage and race in the United States, and that these established the bases for differences of opinion between Catholics and Protestants over the cultural and religious legitimacy of interracial marriage. The Roman Catholic Church alone affirmed the doctrine of the sacramental nature of marriage—the rite of matrimony as an instrument that conferred divine grace upon the couple. Understanding marriage as a conveyor of sanctification, the church consequently proclaimed sole authority to adjudicate marriage law—and, especially, to oversee legal regulations regarding the formation and dissolution of Christian marriages. More to the point, the church denied the authority of the secular state to determine such laws, particularly after Protestant reformers made this very claim during the sixteenth century. From the Catholic perspective, American bans on interracial marriage could thus be viewed as unwarranted and illicit barriers to otherwise legitimate marriages, particularly for Catholic couples.

I also argue that the Vatican ultimately proclaimed what may be called a theology of race, though it did not fully emerge until the twentieth century—hundreds of years later than its theology of marriage. A response to both religious and nonreligious theories of racial separateness articulated by non-Catholics, and particularly by the Nazi regime, the Catholic theology of race affirmed the unity of the human family, created by God, united in Christ, and subjected to the universal authority of the holy catholic and apostolic church. Emphasizing common origins in Eve and Adam, the Catholic position implied—at least in theory—racial equality and the acceptance of interracial marriage, as well as the rejection of racial segregation and white supremacy. The Roman Catholic theology of race, together with the sacramental theology of marriage, thus created the theological bases on which Catholics might oppose laws restricting or banning interracial marriage.

Not surprisingly, white American Protestants expressed very different ideas. From the earliest moments of the Reformation, Protestant reformers—in direct contradiction to Catholic doctrine—insisted that marriage was sacred, but not a sacrament. Therefore, since marriage was an earthly rather than heavenly institution, civil rather than ecclesiastical authorities should oversee marriage law. According to this theological view, the state held all responsibility for the legal regulation of marriage, including the determination of impediments that might preclude marriage. These notions dominated American legal conceptions of marriage since early in the formation of the British colonies. And with legal authority thus located, it fell well within the purview of the state to establish legal impediments to marriages between whites and persons of color.

Early in the colonial period, a Protestant theology of race also began to develop as whites made slavery a perpetual, inheritable status for African peoples. Consistent with their belief in the Bible as the authoritative guidebook for all things, white Protestants turned to the Good Book—and especially to the book of Genesis—for answers to questions about racial origins. Increasingly, white American Protestants came to associate Noah's grandson Canaan with Africa and with blackness, which, combined with the fact that in the story of Genesis 9 Noah had cursed Canaan to perpetual enslavement, functioned to create the biblical justification of racial slavery.[17] Though the story of "Noah's curse" remained an important and familiar explanatory paradigm for racial hierarchy after the Civil War, white Americans revised their interpretations of the Genesis stories once the peculiar institution ended and enslaved persons were emancipated. Indeed, following the Civil War, a localized strain of white southern Protestantism emerged that offered an explicitly biblical rationale for racial segregation. These whites asserted that in Genesis 10–11, God had "dispersed" the human races to separate continents, thus demonstrating God's desire for racial groups to remain separate.

Protestant beliefs about the state's right to regulate marriage—combined with the theology of separate races—appeared frequently in post–Civil War antimiscegenation cases. In case after case, white judges reiterated the biblical basis for laws prohibiting interracial marriage, inscribed religious biases against interracial (and particularly, black-white) marriage in American law, and upheld the legalized segregation of whites and blacks more generally. Similar to today's religious rhetoric against same-sex relationships, historical notions of God having created separate and hierarchical races resonated with white Christians, due to their claims that such notions were "biblical." The assertion of the purportedly biblical basis for segregation thus rooted their views in what they understood to be the unchanging authority and will of God.

While the analysis of primary source materials reveals clear distinctions in Catholic and Protestant theologies of marriage and race, it is far too simple to conclude that all white American Protestants expressed hopelessly racist views, or that all white Catholics regarded their black sisters and brothers as equals worthy of respect. Official theological doctrines often do not correspond precisely to the beliefs of the Catholic or Protestant believer sitting in the pew. Yet the Catholic Church's emphasis on racial unity is significant in that it posed a challenge to the white, post–Civil War notion of "separate races," and during the twentieth century, the Catholic theologies of race and marriage contributed to the demise of American antimiscegenation laws and racial segregation at the marriage altar. Correspondingly, courts arguing in favor of antimiscegenation laws proclaimed the "states' right to regulate marriage" as one of the key arguments about the constitutionality of antimiscegenation statutes, though the Protestant origins of this notion had largely disappeared from public view. Likewise, the Protestant theology of separate races, articulated most forcibly among white southerners, found vivid expression following the U.S. Supreme Court's *Brown v. Board of Education* decision of 1954 and provided the religious basis for intense white southern hostility toward desegregation.

Like many other doctrinal differences between Catholics and Protestants, Catholic and Protestant theologies of marriage and race were rooted in historic tensions over ecclesiastical authority and biblical hermeneutics. As we will see, the very issues that divided Catholics and Protestant reformers during the sixteenth century mirrored the differences between Catholics and Protestants over interracial marriage and its legality. Disputes over the appropriate location of spiritual and temporal authority, over the role of the Bible and who possessed the authority to interpret it, and over the nature of marriage imbued Catholic-Protestant disagreements about marriage and race. Catholic and Protestant beliefs about the church as a universal or local institution also functioned to underscore differences over interracial marriage, for the Catholic emphasis on the universal authority of the church came into sharp relief with Protestant localism, particularly as it developed among white southerners following the Civil War. As historian Mark Noll has noted, most white Protestants "felt free to take up, modify, discard, or transform inherited ideas and institutions as local circumstances dictated." Their insistence on the Bible as the sole source of spiritual authority, coupled with their freedom to interpret biblical passages differently—according to individual congregations or denominational traditions—thus allowed for the development of local beliefs, such as the theology of "separate races."[18] While most mid-twentieth-century white southern Catholics were hardly proponents of social equality for their African American neighbors, they would not likely have articulated an explicitly biblical basis for racial inequality.

Several hundred years of doctrinal differences thus shaped the development and outcomes of American Catholic and Protestant thinking on race, marriage, and interracial marriage. Ultimately, a few progressive American Catholics took up the task of eradicating what they perceived as unjust infringements on couples' religious liberty to marry individuals of another race.

Almighty God Created the Races examines these extraordinarily complex issues by telling a segment of the story of the *Perez* case in each chapter and allowing it to direct our attention to a specific aspect of my analysis. *Perez* exemplifies the conflicts of theological beliefs, constitutional interpretations, and regional values in antimiscegenation cases. By beginning with specific issues of religion in this case and the underlying questions that these issues raise, we follow a path that enables us to discover the many ways that Christian beliefs historically shaped American notions of race and interracial marriage. Indeed, I suggest that it is precisely in the instances where religion does appear in *Perez* and *Loving* that points to the ways that Christianity functioned underneath the surface of antimiscegenation history and—more generally—marriage law.

Each chapter, then, begins with the *Perez* case, highlighting a particular aspect of religion. Chapter 1 explores *Perez* in detail, including the Los Angeles context and the specifically interracial Catholic context of the parish in which Andrea Perez and Sylvester Davis wished to marry, their attorney's civil rights activism, and his legal strategy. I contend that these issues affirm the centrality of Catholic Christianity to the *Perez* case, which in turn points to the necessity of considering Catholic and Protestant beliefs together when analyzing other antimiscegenation cases and American attitudes toward interracial marriage. Chapter 2 provides an overview of the historical development of American laws against interracial sex and marriage, highlighting some of the reasons why antimiscegenation laws did not develop in Spanish Catholic regions of the United States. Chapters 3 and 4 examine Catholic and Protestant theologies of marriage and race and their implications for the legal regulation of interracial marriage. Chapter 5 demonstrates how these theologies appeared in nineteenth- and twentieth-century antimiscegenation cases and how they played out regionally. Chapter 6 brings the book full circle by returning to the *Loving* case and offering an explanation for Catholic Judge Leon M. Bazile's famous "Almighty God" statement.

[1] Catholic California The Historic Junction of Religion, Region, and Law in *Perez v. Lippold* (1948)

In his essay on everyday life in California during the Second World War, historian Arthur Verge observes that during this tumultuous period, a spirit of cooperation prevailed among the American people. "Haunted by the carnage of World War I and hardened by the ten long years of the Great Depression," he writes, "the American people entered this war without frivolity. Resignation, determination, and an attitude of 'we're all in this together' became the prevailing spirit upon entering the Second World War." Despite, or perhaps because of, the unprecedented atrocities of this war, Americans rallied together, united in the face of human tragedy. By the end of the war when the magnitude of the Nazi genocide campaign had been disclosed to the world, a small glimmer of light appeared on the horizon of racial understanding. Glimpsing the potentially deadly relationship between biological notions of racial identity and the eugenic policies epitomized in Hitler's "final solution," Americans slowly began to revise their long-held ideas about race, particularly in jurisprudence.[1]

For people of color and proponents of civil rights and racial equality, several developments gave cause for new hope, in spite of the dire events in other parts of the world. Fighting for American-style "freedom," African American servicemen experienced social equality in other parts of the world and then returned home, hopeful for change in their own nation. At the behest of A. Philip Randolph, African American leader of the Brotherhood of Sleeping Car Porters, President Franklin D. Roosevelt in 1941 at last appointed the Fair Employment Practices Committee to ensure that defense industry employers did not discriminate against workers "because of race, creed, color, or national origin."[2] Increasingly, groups such as the NAACP and ACLU challenged issues of racial inequality in the nation's courts.

In 1944 in *Smith v. Allwright*, the U.S. Supreme Court outlawed all-white political primaries, thus expanding the voting power of people of color.

After the war ended, the promise of a brighter day continued. In 1946, President Truman established the President's Commission on Civil Rights, a body charged with developing measures to protect minorities' rights to employment, education, and housing. The Supreme Court issued several decisions suggesting a significant shift in attitudes toward the constitutionality of racial discrimination. It banned segregation in interstate travel in 1946 and racial restrictions in property laws in 1948.[3] In 1948, President Truman integrated the armed services, and in 1949 he announced his "Fair Deal" program, in which he advocated health insurance, minimum wage increases, and the guarantee of equal rights to all Americans. Having witnessed in the Third Reich one of the most brutal racial regimes in history, pensive Americans demanded a humane, egalitarian understanding of race and racial differences.

Residents of multicultural California perceived the hope for racial equality perhaps even more strongly than other parts of the country. Although the state had coped with the deportation of Japanese American citizens to internment camps after the bombing of Pearl Harbor and the Los Angeles "Zoot Suit Riots" of 1943, signs of a new era in race relations began to appear. World War II brought dramatic increases in shipping and aircraft manufacturing, creating new jobs and higher wages for people of all colors in southern California. In 1941, Douglas Aircraft listed 10 African Americans out of 33,000 workers; out of 3,000 employees at Bethlehem Shipbuilding 2 were black; and at Lockheed Aircraft and Vega Airplane, 54 of its 48,000 workers were black. But by 1943, thanks in large part to FDR's Fair Employment Practices Committee, these companies reported thousands of African American employees on the payroll.[4] Moreover, by 1944, Mexican Americans composed 10 to 15 percent of Lockheed's employees and almost 1,300 members of the California Shipbuilding Corporation's workforce.[5] The injection of "massive amounts of federal dollars" into California for the creation of military bases and defense industries resulted in an economic windfall for many, especially for the record numbers of women and minority workers in the workplace.[6] The future also looked hopeful for racial minorities with respect to legal developments. In 1947, California governor Earl Warren, the future chief justice of the U.S. Supreme Court and author of *Brown v. Board of Education* (1954), signed a bill repealing the state's school segregation policies against Mexican American students.[7] A year later, the Japanese American Citizens' League brought *Oyama v.*

State of California to the U.S. Supreme Court, which declared unconstitutional California's alien land laws—statutes that had restricted the ability of "alien[s] ineligible for naturalization" to lease and purchase real estate properties.[8]

As the fault line in American racial segregation policy began to crack open, legal restrictions on interracial intimacy also began to loosen in southern California. Shortly before Christmas in 1948, *Tidings*, the official newspaper of the Los Angeles Catholic Archdiocese, casually announced that a young couple, Andrea Perez and Sylvester Davis, would be married "shortly after the New Year in St. Patrick's Church." Although news of the Catholic couple's marriage had thrust them into the national spotlight, *Tidings* offered scanty details, noting simply that "a civil action" over California's antimiscegenation laws had precipitated the marriage.[9] In fact, the Perez-Davis marriage had sparked controversy not only because the groom was "black" and the bride "white," but also because the couple had won the right to marry in California's Supreme Court.[10] And while the *Tidings* article credited the Los Angeles Catholic Interracial Council for its work on the couple's behalf, it made no mention of the uproar that the council's advocacy of the marriage had generated within the Catholic Archdiocese of Los Angeles or of the church's reluctance to assist Perez and Davis. These details—the Catholic Interracial Council, the Catholic background of Perez, Davis, the attorney who argued on their behalf, and even the attorney's legal arguments—underscore the many ways that Christianity influenced the case. They also begin to highlight the importance of regional differences in attitudes toward interracial marriage.

Religion appears in *Perez v. Lippold*—the California Supreme Court case in which Perez and Davis won the right to marry—in two critical but very different ways. First, *Perez* took place wholly within the multiracial Catholic context of California, and specifically, within a progressive interracial Catholic parish in Los Angeles. This context begins to reveal the critical significance of Catholic Christianity within American antimiscegenation history. Second, as the couple's desire to marry became a legal matter, their Catholic attorney, Daniel Marshall, inserted Catholic belief directly into his legal arguments. He developed an explicitly religion-based legal strategy that made religious freedom—and specifically, religious freedom for Catholics—the basis of his case. Analysis of religion in *Perez* thus underscores, on the one hand, Christianity and region, and on the other, Christianity and law. Both of these issues in turn underline the centrality of Catholic Christianity in *Perez*. Together these issues raise additional questions about the relationship between Christianity and prohibitions against interracial marriage elsewhere, and they hint at the even deeper ways that religious beliefs influenced American antimiscegenation history.

Region and Religion:
The Cultural Background of the *Perez* Case

California's multiracial character and Catholic history established the context for the *Perez* case, long before it even went to court. Journalist Carey McWilliams astutely noted in 1945 that California's inhabitants were racially unlike those in other regions of the country. "Here, in this one region," he observed, "are represented important groupings of all the racial strains that have gone into making the American people."[11] Perhaps nowhere in the state was the population more colorful than in Los Angeles. Founded in the early 1780s as El Pueblo de Nuestra Señora la Reina de los Angeles del Río de Porciúncula, and composed of Native American tribes and Spanish priests and soldiers, the City of Angels exemplified the mix of cultures that occurred after the European "discovery" of the New World.

During the years following California's statehood in 1850, Los Angeles transformed from a "Hispanic pueblo to an Anglo-American city" and from a strongly Catholic to a Protestant religious culture.[12] But by the 1920s, more than 100,000 people each year were moving into southern California, and many of them were people of color. Mexico's Revolution of 1910 spurred many of its citizens to go north. According to George M. Sanchez, in 1920 Mexicans—a racial category added to the U.S. Census that year—numbered about 30,000 of Los Angeles residents, but by 1930 that figure had increased to 97,000 (of 1,238,048 total residents).[13] During that same period, Japanese, Chinese, and African Americans all began to make Los Angeles their new home. The number of African American Angelenos grew from 15,500 to 39,000. Similarly, the Japanese population nearly doubled, from 11,600 people in 1920 to more than 21,000 in 1930. By 1930, 14 percent of Los Angeles was "nonwhite" (including Mexicans), making Los Angeles second only to Baltimore for having the largest nonwhite population. This trend continued into the next generation. In 1940, the U.S. Census listed 64,000 African Americans, 23,000 Japanese, and 219,000 Mexicans out of the total Los Angeles population of 1.5 million; just six years later, a special census reported that the black population had more than doubled to 133,000.[14]

Kevin Allen Leonard's analysis of Los Angeles in the 1940s argues that not only was the overall population more diverse than other cities, but also there was a high likelihood of interaction between racial groups. Communities of different racial and ethnic groups were often adjacent to one other, and in some neighborhoods, those of black, Mexican, Asian, and European descent lived next door to one another. Leonard maintains that "in 1940, significant numbers of Mexican, European, and African Americans lived in Watts, and the West Jefferson district west of downtown was home to many middle-class blacks and Japanese."[15] Although residential patterns increasingly tended to segregate by 1950, during the 1940s when Andrea Perez and Sylvester Davis met, Los Angeles neighborhoods and their institutions were relatively integrated.

One such institution was St. Patrick's parish, where Perez and Davis sought to be married. During the 1940s St. Patrick's exemplified the interracial, multicultural character of Los Angeles. Located at Thirty-fourth Street and Central Avenue, it was one of several Catholic churches in Los Angeles at which African Americans and Mexican Americans attended mass together.[16] Founded in 1908 during the bishopric of Thomas J. Conaty, St. Patrick's began as a largely Irish parish. But from 1917 to 1947 when socially progressive Bishop John J. Cantwell led the diocese, the membership at St. Patrick's, like much of Los Angeles, began to change.[17] Italian and German, and then Mexican and black families moved into the area, so that the parish became known as an interracial church.[18]

"About 65 percent Negro, 15 percent Mexican, the rest a little of everybody," St. Patrick's embodied the spirit of interracial and interethnic cooperation gently urged by Bishop Cantwell.[19] Cantwell, viewed as "one of the great benefactors of Mexicans in the United States" and "one of the few Catholic prelates to maintain friendly relations with the NAACP," actively promoted goodwill toward the nonwhite members of his see and encouraged his priests to do the same.[20] He admitted at least one African American student into a San Franciscan seminary, established schools and churches for Mexican parishioners, and required Anglo-American diocesan priests to learn to speak Spanish.[21] As early as 1921, Bishop Cantwell addressed the NAACP, asserting the need for a "strong alliance" between blacks and whites and decrying white bigotry. During his prelacy, he organized an Immigrant Welfare Department within the Associated Catholic Charities, served as general chairman of the executive board of the Bishop's Committee for the Spanish Speaking, constructed a large "social center" for African American Catholics at Sixteenth and Essex Streets, and founded a Chinese Catholic Center in 1942.[22] Under Cantwell's leadership, Los Angeles Catholics thus experienced, for a time at least, a religion-based culture of benevolent inter-racialism and of tolerance for non-Anglo cultural traditions.

St. Patrick's typified this interracial culture not only in its demographic composition, but also in its relationship with the Catholic Interracial Council of Los Angeles (CIC), a short-lived but influential organization. The CIC played a central yet behind-the-scenes role in the story of Andrea Perez and Sylvester Davis, for it was there that their attorney, Daniel Marshall, had undertaken his vision of racially integrating Los Angeles, starting with the Catholic Church. In 1944, Marshall, along with his friends Ted LeBerthon and African American physician Thomas Peyton—a vocal and very progressive trio of advocates of racial equality—decided to create a Los Angeles chapter of the Catholic Interracial Council. St. Patrick's Church offered to provide the CIC with space to hold its meetings, and so the group invited Father John LaFarge to Los Angeles to discuss the best way to go about establishing a local council. LaFarge, a Jesuit priest, graduate of Harvard University, and gentle champion of socioeconomic justice for American blacks, had founded the original Catholic Interracial Council in New York City.[23]

Father LaFarge agreed to come to Los Angeles. His deferential relationship with the New York hierarchy—most notably with future Los Angeles archbishop J. Francis McIntyre—had earned him the consternation of progressive Catholics, who viewed him as a gradualist. All the same, the priest advised Marshall's group to avoid seeking official archdiocesan approval for the council, because, he warned, "'such approval was a liability, not an asset, inasmuch as it would result in Chancery Office control.'" "'Prudential bishops,'" the long-suffering LaFarge counseled, often insisted, "as 'the price of official approval,' that a CIC remain interminably a study club, completely foregoing any stand or action on concrete instances of social prejudices or discrimination."[24]

As Marshall and the other members of the group intended to shape the Los Angeles council as an intrepid advocate of interracial justice, they heeded LaFarge's advice. The group set up the Los Angeles CIC in 1944 without archdiocesan approval. Composed of mostly "whites and Negroes," along with a "few Chinese, Filipinos and Mexican [sic] and even two converts from Judaism," the young CIC drafted a mission statement, establishing as its foremost goals "oppos[ing] all forms of discrimination directed at minority groups . . . and . . . mak[ing] known the Catholic viewpoint on both legal and extra legal practices of segregation on account of race or color."[25] An article published in October 1945 in the *Interracial Review*, the New

York–based Catholic monthly magazine edited by LaFarge, demonstrates more clearly the rather insistent tone taken by the Los Angeles CIC. Penned by journalist and council member Ted LeBerthon, who acknowledged the group's "adamant platform," this article stated that the council's mission called for "integration as against segregation; free and uncondescending social mingling as against friendship for non-Caucasians at a safe distance; and the cleaning of our own houses by some of us white Catholics before we start ridding others of racism." Although LeBerthon clearly shared these views, he attributed the council's no-nonsense, antigradualist tenor to Daniel Marshall, who, LeBerthon candidly noted, "thinks gradualism is intellectual dishonesty when it isn't plain stupidity."[26] Marshall's leadership thus helped to push the Los Angeles CIC in a progressive and perhaps somewhat confrontational direction.[27]

The Los Angeles CIC also perceived itself as being different from CICs in other cities, in part because of the multiracial character of Los Angeles. In his 1945 article entitled "Council of All Races," LeBerthon noted that at its first meeting in 1944, the council realized that "the Los Angeles interracial picture was different" from that of New York. According to the article, "unusual conditions" existed in Los Angeles that were especially pronounced "during a global war" in which Los Angeles ranked as "the nation's second greatest war production center."[28] In addition, the CIC recognized that in Los Angeles, "numerically, the major races on the scene were the Caucasian, Indo-Latin, and Negro, in that order." The council's members consequently aimed to structure its leadership to reflect the unique local racial composition, which LeBerthon contrasted with LaFarge's New York City CIC. Whereas, LeBerthon wrote, "the New York Council alternates the offices of president and vice-president from term to term, so that a Negro president is followed in office by a white president, the Los Angeles Council tentatively plans to rotate a white, Mexican and Negro in the presidency, and have the offices of vice-president, secretary and treasurer each filled, when possible and feasible, by a member of a different race."[29] The multiracial character of Los Angeles thus played a significant role in the council's leadership strategy, as well as in the makeup of its membership.

After establishing its mission and organizational principles, the Los Angeles CIC began its work immediately, focusing on segregation in local Catholic organizations and institutions. LeBerthon reported that from its inception in the summer of 1944 to the publication of LeBerthon's article in October 1945, the CIC had urged two Los Angeles Catholic schools and the Knights of Columbus to admit blacks, attempted to procure a position for black cic member Thomas Peyton on the staff of "a leading Catholic hospital in Los Angeles," campaigned against "residential race restriction covenants, and worked for the constitutional rights of Japanese-Americans and their return from concentration or relocation camps." According to LeBerthon, the council also "held meetings concerning the treatment of Jews, Mexicans and Filipinos, and has denounced unfair attitudes by courts and law enforcement officers towards minorities. The Council in resolutions, has condemned both expressions of racism and the soft-pedaling of race issues by specific newspapers and specific radio programs. It has inveighed against racial stereotypes in motion pictures, against segregation in the armed forces and against Jim Crowism in Washington, D.C."[30] In less than a year and a half, then, the Los Angeles group took action on a variety of significant and potentially explosive issues, suggesting a well organized and strongly committed leadership.

Although LeBerthon did not specify which cic members engaged in its activities, in those areas involving law and labor relations, Daniel Marshall played a central role. Marshall drew upon his knowledge as a lawyer to agitate actively against all kinds of civil infringements. A cic press release of April 1947, for example, tells of the organization's legal intervention— presumably led by Marshall—on behalf of a "Catholic Indian family" (composed of an "Indian" wife, her Canadian husband, and their three children) whom white residents had ordered to vacate their home, which was located in a white neighborhood.[31] Another one of Marshall's personal crusades included his push to persuade the Los Angeles Bar Association to admit black attorneys. In 1950, he joyfully reported to LaFarge that the association had at last voted to "abandon the Jim Crow membership policy." And in a letter that same year to Marshall from LaFarge, the priest expressed his interest in "hearing of [Marshall's] legal contest with regard to the restrictive [housing] covenants," confirming that Marshall had directed his attention to that problem as well.[32]

Moreover, Marshall had earned the opprobrium of local conservative politicians due to his efforts on behalf of progressive causes. According to a 1949 letter from Ted LeBerthon to Father LaFarge, Marshall's campaign for the establishment of a Fair Employment Practices Committee in California earned him the accusation of being "associated with the 'Communist Front.'" While awaiting confirmation as chairman of the state senate's Social Welfare Board, Marshall was accused by "hysterical" California state senator Jack B. Tenney—longtime chairman of California Committee on Un-American Activities—of "subversive activities."[33] Tenney had denounced in no uncertain terms the 1941 Fair Employment Practices Act signed into law by President Franklin D. Roosevelt, pronouncing the proposition "a Communist bill" and its supporters "a group of termites indoctrinated with an atheistic, totalitarian foreign ideology."[34] Marshall explained in a letter to LaFarge that Tenney had accused him of being a "Communist, Communist dupe and fellow-traveler, and a Communist masquerading as a Catholic." Marshall stated that he could not "have contrived for [him]self a better position in which to be hit by fifteen or twenty bricks, hurled by as many different hands."[35] In another letter to LaFarge, Marshall lightheartedly remarked that he had "recently received [his] annual 'un-American' citation." While Tenney had bestowed the "citation" the year before, he joked, this time it came "from His Excellency, the Archbishop [McIntyre]." "I am sure," he wrote, "it is a last desperate effort to save the writer [i.e., Marshall] from the Marxists."[36]

For Marshall, civil rights work was so important that he continued to engage in it even though it threatened both his career and his standing with the Los Angeles hierarchy. Part of the reason activism was so critical to him was that his activities were intimately bound up in his Catholic identity. He could not be a Catholic without being an activist, and vice versa. Even apart from the *Perez* case, Marshall's work on the CIC indicates that he viewed his civil rights labors as efforts to implement his conception of Catholic theology, and his campaign to legalize interracial marriage represented the practical application of his beliefs. Andrea Perez and Sylvester Davis could not have asked for a more committed attorney to fight California's anti-miscegenation laws.

Within this broad context of multicultural community, interracial activism, and Catholic service on behalf of the oppressed, Andrea Perez and Sylvester Davis fortuitously acquired the legal talents of Daniel Marshall. In 1947 when the young couple decided to marry, they were unaware of California's antimiscegenation law. But their pastor, a "most militant member" of the CIC, had evidently encountered the situation before, and this time, he sought outside assistance.[37] He contacted the Los Angeles Archdiocese to see if it might be able to help, explaining that "many interracial couples, being unable to have a legal marriage, nevertheless wished to receive the sacrament of marriage."[38] But the church turned him away, refusing him "on grounds of the law" and insisting that it held no power against the state's laws. Undeterred, the priest then turned to the CIC to see if it might be able to take legal action against the antimiscegenation statutes. Meanwhile, Perez, who had during high school worked as a babysitter for a couple in her church—Daniel and Dorothy Marshall—contacted the Marshalls to see if they might be able to help.[39]

Daniel Marshall readily agreed to take the couple's case. In consultation with Perez and Davis, and with the CIC, Marshall developed a plan to test the case in the California courts. In April 1947 the CIC announced in a press release its intention to challenge the state's antimiscegenation laws.[40] The section "Interracial Marriage Ban to Be Attacked" stated that legal "Counsel for the Catholic Interracial Council of Los Angeles is continuing research to ready an attack upon the California statute prohibiting interracial marriage of Caucasians." According to the statement, a recent U.S. Supreme Court decision had ruled that a public school requirement that students pledge an oath of allegiance to the country violated a sect's religious freedom.[41] An "attorney engaged in the project" suggested that if the Court deemed the school requirement a violation of the U.S. Constitution then "a law which forbids a Catholic couple to participate in the full sacramental life of the religion of their choice . . . must likewise be invalid." On this basis, the statement continued, California's antimiscegenation statute constituted "the expression of a heresy" insofar as the law violated a 1938 Vatican declaration that had "condemned" efforts to "'preserve and promote racial vigor and the purity of the blood.'"[42]

One of the most explicit articulations of the CIC's theology of interracial marriage, the press release ended by noting that a bishop would be asked to testify "concerning the dogma of the Church on marriage and race."[43] Although Marshall and the CIC were delighted to take the case, they would soon learn that the Los Angeles Archdiocese was less than eager to take a public stance advocating the Perez-Davis marriage. Marshall's plan to attack the antimiscegenation statute on religious freedom grounds necessarily involved the archdiocese in the case, in that it might require Catholic officials to substantiate Marshall's theological claims—a public legal battle the church had no interest in supporting. Marshall anticipated that that the Los Angeles county clerk would request that Marshall "prove that the dogma and teachings of the Church are as alleged in the petition," so in April 1947, the same month the CIC issued its press release, and four months before Andrea Perez and Sylvester Davis officially applied to the Los Angeles county clerk for a marriage license, Marshall sent a letter to Auxiliary Bishop Joseph McGucken. Marshall's letter explained his intention to make religious freedom the linchpin of his argument, which hinged upon several key points of Catholic doctrine: first, that Jesus Christ is the "founder of the Roman Catholic Church"; second, that marriage is a sacrament "instituted by Jesus Christ"; third, that the Catholic Church has no law forbidding "the intermarriage of a nonwhite person and a white person"; and fourth, that the Church "respects the requirements of the State for the marriage of its citizens as long as they are in keeping with the dignity and Divine purpose of marriage."[44]

To ward off any argument from McGucken, Marshall, whom his friend Ted LeBerthon described as a "New Deal type Democrat and a profound student of the Papal social encyclicals," then appealed to the highest source of Catholic authority: the Holy Father himself.[45] Citing Pope Pius XI's 1937 encyclical to the church in Germany, *Mit brennender Sorge*, Marshall pointed out that the "Church has condemned the proposition that 'it is imperative at all costs to preserve and promote racial vigor and the purity of blood; whatever is conducive to this end is by that very fact honorable and permissible.'" He explained to McGucken that he planned to have the couple "present themselves to your Excellency" so that McGucken might satisfy himself that they were "in all respects eligible to receive conjointly the Sacrament of marriage," and that the sacrament "would be administered to them in this city were it not for the prohibition of the civil statute." Last, and most maddening to McGucken, Marshall requested that McGucken testify in court as to the veracity of the doctrine that Marshall had spelled out.[46]

Three days later, McGucken dispatched a brief but surly response to Marshall. He remarked that Marshall's theology, particularly with regard to his fourth point, was "not quite accurate," though he did not explain its errors. McGucken then tersely addressed Marshall's request that he testify. "I cannot think of any point in existing race relations," he snapped, "that will stir up more passion and prejudice than the issue you are raising," and "I want to make very clear that I am not at all willing to be pulled into a controversy of this kind."[47] Suggesting that the "chief success" of Marshall's case would be only in "promoting the class struggle that some of our neighbors are so anxious to provoke," McGucken expressed his concern for "fairness and justice for all groups." Yet, experience had taught him, he continued, that becoming "'a Don Quixote' gets us nowhere" and that "the problem you have so much at heart is not to be solved by any shortcuts." He advised Marshall to "consult with some older heads before attempting this issue, particularly since you are planning to involve the Church in it."[48]

Marshall's antigradualist approach, and his desire to connect the issue to the Catholic Church, clearly earned him McGucken's disapproval, as well as that of others within the archdiocese.[49] In October 1947, two months after Marshall had filed his petition with the California Supreme Court, Archbishop John Cantwell died, and McGucken was appointed interim bishop. But in February 1948, Archbishop James Francis McIntyre, Father LaFarge's adversary in the New York Archdiocese and a well-known "ultra-conservative," was named as Cantwell's permanent replacement.[50] It was only a matter of time before McIntyre and Marshall locked horns. In a letter to a colleague years later, Marshall's friend Ted LeBerthon recounted a rather amusing story of Marshall's relationship with McIntyre. Soon after the archbishop arrived in Los Angeles, he attempted to curtail Marshall's activities on the CIC.[51] According to LeBerthon, McIntyre invited Marshall and his wife for dinner at the episcopal mansion one evening "to 'set them right on their views.'" McIntyre also invited a handful of wealthy "right-wing" Catholics, whom he apparently desired to tutor Marshall in the ways of prudent politics. LeBerthon claimed that Marshall described the archbishop as a "'tough old rooster'" with whom he disagreed on "EVERYTHING except that Christ founded the Church on Peter." Marshall most "definitely aroused" McIntyre's "DISPLEASURE," his friend stated.[52]

The Perez-Davis case served to distance Marshall and the CIC from the Los Angeles hierarchy. LeBerthon conjectured that the "newspaper publicity given Dan [Marshall] as President of the Catholic Interracial Council for his success in overturning the law against interracial marriage was, in [LeBerthon's] opinion, one of the factors that made him [Marshall] *persona non grata* in the Chancery office about that time [1948] and from that time on."[53] Indeed, the Los Angeles CIC did not survive long after Archbishop McIntyre arrived in California.[54] And although the Perez-Davis case was only one of His Excellency's disagreements with the CIC, by publicly advocating the most intimate union of members of different races, and by forcing the church into the spotlight on this volatile issue, the CIC exemplified most strikingly McIntyre's trepidations about interracialism. For Marshall, however, "Catholic" and "interracial" could not be separated. In a November 1947 letter to Father LaFarge, Marshall observed that even if the *Perez* case did not succeed, "at least it can be said that Catholics, not communists, tried to knock out the law."[55] Indeed, for Marshall, Catholic belief and social activism together formed a core part of his personal and professional identity, and they deeply informed his legal strategy.

The Case Goes to Court:
Marshall's Religion Strategy

Daniel Marshall made religion a central strategy of the *Perez* case. Indeed, legal conceptions of religious freedom alongside Catholic Christianity formed the very basis for Marshall's legal arguments. In early August 1947 after Los Angeles county clerk Joseph Moroney had denied Perez and Davis's application for a marriage license, Marshall put the first part of his plan into action. He submitted a petition for a writ of mandamus to the California Supreme Court—a court order issued from a high-level court compelling an inferior agency, such as a county official, to perform an action specified in the writ, such as issuing a marriage license. Naming Andrea Perez and Sylvester Davis the "petitioners" and County Clerk Moroney the "respondent" in the case, the petition thus commenced the couple's battle over their right to marry.

Marshall explained that when Perez and Davis applied for a marriage license from Moroney, Moroney had "refused to grant petitioners such license to intermarry, on the ground that said first-named petitioner [Andrea Perez] being a white person and second-named person [Sylvester Davis] being a Negro person, Section 69 of [California's] Civil Code prohibited him from issuing to petitioners a license." Ignoring altogether Section 60 of California's Civil Code, which prohibited "all marriages of white persons with Negroes, Mongolians, members of the Malay race, or mulattoes," Marshall instead focused on Section 69, the statute that directly involved Moroney. Section 69 stipulated that "no license be issued authorizing the marriage of a white person with a Negro, mulatto, Mongolian, or a member of the Malay race."[56]

The petition then stated that each of the petitioners is "a member and a communicant of the Roman Catholic faith and belief," that "marriage is a sacrament instituted by Jesus Christ," that it "is and was at all times mentioned herein the teaching and discipline of said church, that a person of the white race and a person of the Negro race, if otherwise eligible, are entitled to receive conjointly said sacrament of matrimony and thus to intermarry." Further, Marshall asserted that "There is no rule, regulation or law of the Roman Catholic Church which forbids a white person and a Negro person from receiving conjointly the sacrament of matrimony and thus to intermarry." Marshall asserted that Perez and Davis "have the right under the belief, teaching and discipline of the Roman Catholic Church . . . to participate in the full sacramental life of said church by conjointly receiving the sacrament of matrimony." Further, the petition claimed that "said dogma, beliefs and teachings are universal among the members of said church and are and were applicable and in force of according to said dogma, belief and teachings."[57]

Having established the acceptability of interracial marriage among Roman Catholic believers, Marshall concluded his petition by asserting that Moroney's refusal to issue the couple a marriage license resulted in

(a) . . . denying to them . . . the right to participate fully in the sacramental life of the religion in which they believe . . . ; (b) prohibit[ing] the free exercise by petitioners of their said religion; (c) violat[ing] the guarantee . . . of the free exercise and enjoyment . . . of their religious profession and worship; (d) violat[ing] the First and Fourteenth Amendments of the Constitution of the United States.

In addition, the petition alleged that Moroney's action also violated the California State Constitution. Contending that his suit raised "important questions of constitutional law concerning the validity" of this statute, Marshall thus petitioned the California Supreme Court to order Moroney to issue Andrea Perez and Sylvester Davis a marriage license, "notwithstanding the provisions" of Section 69.[58] Hoping to bypass lower-level courts and to enable Perez and Davis to get married in a timely manner, Marshall asserted that the constitutional questions presented in his petition were of such "great public importance" that they warranted the immediate attention of the highest court in the state.[59]

As Marshall later noted in his reply brief, the *Perez* case was also one of first impression, that is, one that raises legal issues that a court has not examined previously.[60] Had Marshall employed the conventional Fourteenth Amendment approach rather than his innovative First Amendment strategy to contest the state's antimiscegenation laws, the court could very well have chosen not to hear the case at all. A Fourteenth Amendment–based challenge to the statutes might have led the justices to invoke stare decisis, the principle compelling courts to stand by prior decisions on cases raising the same constitutional issues. Fortunately for Perez and Davis, however, asking the court to examine antimiscegenation laws in a way that no one had ever done before grabbed the justices' attention. Three weeks after Marshall filed the petition, the court issued an alternative writ of mandate, which commanded Moroney either to issue Perez and Davis a marriage license or to provide reasons why the court should not compel him to do so. Thus, the first success of Marshall's religion strategy was to get the case into the court and to cause the justices to examine afresh the constitutionality of California's antimiscegenation statutes.

Marshall's religion strategy also involved refusing to contest the racial identities that Moroney had assigned to the couple, accepting Moroney's categorizations of Perez as "white" and Davis as "Negro." Marshall's choice to ground the case in the couple's *religious* identity was a carefully considered strategy. In the petition for the writ, Marshall stated that as Catholics, Perez and Davis subscribed to the belief that marriage "is a sacrament instituted by Jesus Christ."[61] Although theoretically Marshall could have based his case on First Amendment issues had the couple been Protestant, he could not have invoked the doctrine of marriage as a sacrament, for that belief is specifically Roman Catholic. According to Catholic doctrine, the sacrament of matrimony is the means by which God confers grace upon the couple and sanctifies their offspring, and marriage symbolizes the union of God and humankind. The marriage sacrament is therefore a symbolically and theologically significant ritual that the church urges upon every communicant who chooses to marry, and thus represents a particularly important concern for Catholic believers. Indeed, the church expects all who choose to marry to receive this sacrament as a matter of personal holiness.

Catholic sacramental theology thus raised religious freedom issues in Marshall's case in a way that Protestant theologies could not. In contrast to Catholic belief, Protestant theology recognizes marriage as a sacred institution, but denies that it is a sacrament.[62] By barring interracial couples from receiving the sacrament of matrimony, California's antimiscegenation statutes could be viewed by Catholics as restricting those couples' access to Christ's redemptive power. The Catholic identity and beliefs shared by Perez and Davis thus created a theological problem not experienced by Protestant couples. Though the significance of specifically Catholic sacramental theology was not one that Marshall explicated in this way, the point was surely not lost on either Marshall or California Supreme Court justice Roger Traynor, who was also Catholic.

Marshall's religion strategy also entailed his reading of recent U.S. Supreme Court decisions as establishing a new standard of stricter scrutiny for cases involving individual liberties and specifically the right to religious freedom. Throughout the United States, previous couples who had challenged antimiscegenation laws most often based their cases on Fourteenth Amendment grounds of due process and equal protection. To understand the significance of Marshall's First Amendment strategy, it is necessary to examine the legislative history of the Fourteenth Amendment in relation to antimiscegenation cases and civil liberties more generally. Ratified in 1868 following contentious congressional debates over the Civil Rights Act of 1866, the first section of the Fourteenth Amendment stated: "All persons born or naturalized in the United States, and subject to the jurisdiction thereof, are citizens of the United States and of the State wherein they reside. No State shall make or enforce any law which shall abridge the privileges or immunities of citizens of the United States; nor shall any State deprive any person of life, liberty, or property, without due process of law; nor deny to any person within its jurisdiction the equal protection of the laws."[63] The amendment thus aimed, among other things, a) to guarantee fundamental human rights to "life, liberty and property," b) to reiterate the right to "due process," a clause first articulated in 1791 in the Fifth Amendment that emphasized a principle of fairness in law, most particularly for black citizens in the postwar South; and c) to guarantee citizens—particularly African Americans—the "equal protection of the laws," that is, the right to be treated equally in both the procedures and principles of law, such that the government must treat every person the same as it treats other persons in similar circumstances.[64] Moreover, in the postwar context of protecting blacks in the South from Black Codes, which some Republicans in Congress regarded as "having left too much of slavery in place," the Fourteenth Amendment specifically affirmed that "no State shall make or enforce laws" that violated these rights.[65] After the Civil War when a number of states enacted antimiscegenation laws, interracial couples began to challenge the statutes as violations of the Civil Rights Act of 1866 and/or of their concomitant rights to due process and equal protection. These couples typically claimed such statutes to be unfair and discriminatory insofar as they treated interracial couples differently than intraracial couples.

During Reconstruction, Republican-led supreme courts in three southern states briefly overturned their antimiscegenation laws, ruling them violations of the Fourteenth Amendment, the 1866 Civil Rights Act, or some combination thereof.[66] The reversal of these laws derived wholly from the context of Reconstruction. Because Republican judges controlled southern courts during this era, judicial decisions tended to favor values associated with Republicans, such as the political equality of blacks and whites. In the most well-known of these cases, *Burns v. State*, for example, the Alabama Supreme Court ruled in 1872 that the state's antimiscegenation law contravened interracial couples' rights to make contracts (in this case, a marriage contract) as guaranteed in the Civil Rights Act, and to equal protection and due process. But the ousted southern Democrats never regarded *Burns* as a legitimate ruling. Five years later when they returned to power, *Burns* was decisively overturned by *Green v. State*, which came to serve as the classic legal response to allegations that antimiscegenation laws violated an interracial couple's constitutional rights. In *Green*, the Alabama Supreme Court ruled that because antimiscegenation statutes prevented both blacks and whites from entering into interracial marriages, and because members of both races were punished equally, the laws did not therefore violate any constitutional rights. Furthermore, *Green* affirmed the state's exclusive Tenth Amendment right to regulate marriage law, which effectively made federal mandates for due process and equal protection inapplicable to state marriage laws.[67]

These three decisions thus constituted anomalies in the history of antimiscegenation laws.[68] The dismantling of Reconstruction and the return of southern Democrats to the courts put an end to this brief period of lawful marital unions between whites and blacks. By the end of Reconstruction, in all cases involving interracial marriage, courts consistently ruled that 1) laws pertaining to marriage were and had always been subject to the control of the state and it was therefore the state's right to enact legislation prohibiting intermarriage; 2) marriages contracted in another state between parties now living in the state would not be recognized if they had been prohibited under antimiscegenation laws of the current domicile (which thus allowed parties legally married in one state to be tried for fornication or adultery in another state); 3) antimiscegenation laws did not violate the equal protection clause because the laws applied equally to both races in their prohibitions and penalties; and 4) marriage did not constitute a contract as understood in the Civil Rights Act of 1866, and therefore such statutes did not violate the act's contract clause.

The *Green* decision is representative of the tendency of Reconstruction-era courts to construe clauses of the Fourteenth Amendment very narrowly.[69] Indeed, within just a few years of its ratification, the U.S. Supreme Court began whittling away at the constitutional protections newly afforded to African American citizens. In *The Slaughter-House Cases* (1873), the Court rendered a narrow interpretation of the "privileges and immunities" clause of the Fourteenth Amendment in a case brought by a group of independent white butchers from New Orleans. The butchers contended that a local law giving one slaughterhouse an exclusive franchise created a monopoly and thus deprived them of their livelihood, and that the resulting situation created the "involuntary servitude" for the white butchers. They thus also claimed that ordinance violated the Thirteenth Amendment. The Court upheld the New Orleans law, asserting that the "sole purpose" of the "privileges and immunities" clause "was to declare to the several States that whatever those rights . . . neither more nor less, shall be the measure of the rights of citizens of other States within your jurisdiction." In other words, it essentially deferred the power of protecting civil rights and liberties back to the states, thus contradicting the very purpose of the Fourteenth Amendment, insofar as it sought to guarantee African Americans protection from unjust state laws.[70]

In 1883, the Court issued another decision on the Fourteenth Amendment, this time curtailing its equal protection clause. In *The Civil Rights Cases* (1883) the Court assessed and rejected the constitutionality of the Civil Rights Act of 1875, in which Congress guaranteed that "all persons within the jurisdiction of the United States shall be entitled to the full and equal enjoyment of the accommodations, advantages, facilities, and privileges of inns, public conveyances on land or water, theaters, and other places of public amusement; subject only to the conditions and limitations established by law, and applicable alike to citizens of every race and color, regardless of any previous condition of servitude." The 1875 act had made any violation of these rights a federal crime.[71] The Court ruled that Section 5 of the Fourteenth Amendment, which gave Congress the "power to enforce, by appropriate legislation, the provisions of this article," constrained only state actions.[72] As legal scholar David M. O'Brien notes, in the Court's reading of the Fourteenth Amendment, Congress could only enact legislation that prohibited any racial discrimination that had resulted from a state law or state action.[73] Congress, in the Court's view, was authorized neither to enact the Civil Rights Act of 1875 nor to forbid racial discrimination by individuals and corporations in public accommodations. Legal bans on racial discrimination by private individuals or corporations fell beyond the purview of Congress or the courts.

The Court's narrow reading of the Fourteenth Amendment in these cases continued in litigation involving the right to marry a person of another race. In the same year as *The Civil Rights Cases* ruling, the Court also heard *Pace v. Alabama*, a case involving Tony Pace, an African American man, and Mary Cox, a white woman, who were convicted of "living together in a state of adultery or fornication."[74] Here the Court ruled that a state law punishing interracial adultery more harshly than intraracial adultery was constitutional. According to Justice Stephen J. Field, Alabama's law was entirely consistent. The one prescribes, generally, a punishment for an offence committed between persons of different sexes; the other prescribes a punishment for an offence which can only be committed where the two sexes are of different races. There is in neither section [of the State Code] any discrimination against either race. . . . Whatever discrimination is made in the punishment prescribed in the two sections is directed against the offence designated and not against the person of any particular color or race. The punishment of each offending person, whether black or white, is the same.[75]

Though this decision addressed adultery rather than marriage, *Pace*, along with *Green*, became the most important precedents for cases challenging antimiscegenation statutes. The Court's narrow-construing logic—that such laws were constitutional because there was no discrimination against either race, insofar as both parties were punished equally—became the prevalent interpretation of the Fourteenth Amendment in subsequent antimiscegenation cases in state courts, as well as in state and federal cases involving racial discrimination and civil liberties. By the time the U.S. Supreme Court heard *Plessy v. Ferguson* in 1896, as Peter Wallenstein notes, the "antimiscegenation regime had consolidated its hold on the southern states."[76] And by the turn of the twentieth century, southern *and* northern legislatures and courts consistently viewed individuals' Fourteenth Amendment rights to marry and to receive equal protection and due process as subordinate to the states' Tenth Amendment rights to enact marriage law.

Such was the legal history of race and rights with which Daniel Marshall had to contend as he pondered the best means to champion the right of Andrea Perez and Sylvester Davis to marry. Judging from the legal precedents, the couple's hopes for a wedding looked bleak. But Marshall's familiarity with more recent U.S. Supreme Court rulings enabled him to envision a new basis on which to challenge California's antimiscegenation statutes: the free exercise clause of the First Amendment. Moreover, he perceived that this new basis would compel the California Supreme Court to review his case with a stricter standard of scrutiny, since the U.S. Supreme Court had begun to establish this standard for cases involving fundamental liberties. To explain Marshall's reasoning, it is necessary to look briefly at the relationship between the due process clause and the First Amendment (and the Bill of Rights, more generally), and between fundamental liberties and strict scrutiny.

Prior to 1940, there had been considerable controversy as to whether any of the individual rights articulated in the first nine amendments to the U.S. Constitution were binding upon the states, and it was not until the twentieth century that the Supreme Court applied the Bill of Rights of the states, thus limiting the states' power to restrict individual liberties.[77] Though it is beyond the scope of my analysis to explore this history at length, a brief discussion is necessary to establish the jurisprudential context in which Daniel Marshall created his 1947 case against California's antimiscegenation laws.[78] Prior to 1868, the "prevailing view of the Bill of Rights" and its application to the states derived from *Barron v. The Mayor and City Council of Baltimore*, an 1833 U.S. Supreme Court decision in which Justice John Marshall opined that the guarantees enunciated in the first ten amendments "contain no expression indicating an intention to apply them to the State governments. This court cannot so apply them."[79] This perspective remained the dominant interpretation into the 1920s, and even to this day *Barron* has not been "expressly overturned."[80]

With the ratification of the Fourteenth Amendment in 1868, however, the debate over incorporation intensified considerably, for it offered a new legal basis by which the Bill of Rights might be applied to the states. By specifying that "no State shall" restrict the rights and liberties guaranteed in its provisions, the amendment inherently limited states' power and thus possessed the potential to thrust state and federal governments into conflict, for the Tenth Amendment guaranteed that "those powers not delegated to the United States by the Constitution, nor prohibited by it to the States, are reserved to the States respectively, or to the people."[81] As we have seen with *The Slaughter-house Cases* (1873) and *The Civil Rights Cases* (1883), the Court's rendering of the Fourteenth Amendment had effectively allowed the states to ignore the individual rights and liberties guaranteed by the Constitution. But as the Court's composition changed, and more cases involving these rights and liberties were filed, the justices had to create standards by which they could determine whether state laws violated Fourteenth Amendment guarantees.[82] Following the First World War when the Court heard a number of free speech cases, its interpretive schema on the applicability of the Bill of Rights to state laws began to shift. As David O'Brien notes, "by the 1940s, the other First Amendment freedoms were construed to be so fundamental as to constrain the states" as well as the federal government.[83]

Thus the Court increasingly came to view the free exercise of religion as one of several fundamental liberties protected through the due process clause of the Fourteenth Amendment. During the 1920s, the Court's reading of state laws on religion began to embrace a standard of "fundamental religious liberty" as a basis for determining the constitutionality of state laws. In a number of cases beginning with *Meyer v. Nebraska* (1923), the Court connected individuals' religious liberties to the due process clause of the Fourteenth Amendment.[84] In this case, which involved a Nebraska law that prohibited instruction of grade school students in any language other than English, the Court also noted that the amendment's guarantee that no state deprive a citizen of "life, liberty, or property without due process of law" included, among other things, the rights "to marry, establish a home and bring up children, to worship God according to the dictates of his own conscience, and generally to enjoy those privileges long recognized at common law as essential to the orderly pursuit of happiness by free men."[85] So the Court's rulings began to hint at the inviolability of rights and liberties explicitly mentioned in the U.S. Constitution, as well as others—including the rights to marry and procreate—that it perceived as implicitly "essential to the orderly pursuit of happiness."

Moreover, in the 1940 *Cantwell v. Connecticut* decision, the Court explicitly incorporated the religion clauses of the First Amendment into the due process clause of the Fourteenth Amendment, thus applying them to the states.[86] As Justice Owen J. Roberts stated in the *Cantwell* opinion, "the fundamental concept of liberty embodied in that [Fourteenth] Amendment embraces the liberties guaranteed by the First Amendment. The First Amendment declares that Congress shall make no law respecting an establishment of religion or prohibiting the free exercise thereof. The Fourteenth Amendment has rendered the legislatures of the states as incompetent as Congress to enact such laws."[87] Daniel Marshall saw within this shift in judicial reasoning the hope to bring down California's antimiscegenation statutes and win Andrea Perez and Sylvester Davis the freedom to marry. If the free exercise clause of the First Amendment did apply to state legislation, then the California Supreme Court might declare the state's antimiscegenation laws unconstitutional on that basis. Prior to the *Cantwell* decision, Marshall's argument would not have been possible. Marshall recognized an open window post-*Cantwell*—one that might allow his clients a new pathway to marry interracially.

And as Marshall well knew, *Cantwell* was the first time that the U.S. Supreme Court "applied a heightened level of scrutiny in its application of the free exercise clause."[88] This factor was perhaps even more important to Marshall's strategy, for in reviewing individual liberties cases, the Court had begun to develop stricter standards of judicial scrutiny. In a 1938 case, *U.S. v. Carolene Products Co.*, Justice Harlan F. Stone penned what became perhaps "the most famous footnote in Supreme Court history," in which he suggested that cases having to do with individual liberties might be subject to a strict standard of scrutiny. "There may be," he wrote, "a much narrower scope for operation of the presumption of constitutionality when legislation appears on its face to be within a specific prohibition of the Constitution, such as those of the first ten amendments."[89] Although his comments did not employ the terms "fundamental rights" or "strict scrutiny," Justice Stone thus "planted the seed for the modern Court's equal protection analysis" and for the heightened scrutiny of laws "based on 'suspect classifications,' such as religion and race, or which impinged on 'fundamental rights.'" As the strict scrutiny theory developed over time, the justices applied a test to these "suspect classifications," upholding legislation only if they could discern "a compelling state interest" for the classification specified in the law.[90] Justice Hugo Black's 1944 opinion in *Korematsu v. United States*, the case that, paradoxically, upheld the constitutionality of Japanese American internment camps during the Second World War, explicitly formulated the concept of "strict" or "rigid scrutiny:" "all legal restrictions which curtail the civil rights of a single racial group are immediately suspect. That is not to say that all such restrictions are unconstitutional. It is to say that courts must subject them to the most rigid scrutiny."[91] In other words, rather than presuming that state legislation "rests upon some rational basis" and thus requiring the claimants to prove that a statute is unconstitutional, the standard of strict scrutiny compels the state that enacted the challenged statute to bear the burden of proving that the law is constitutional.[92]

To Daniel Marshall, these new developments in constitutional law, coupled with the Court's affirmation in *Meyer v. Nebraska* (1923) that one of the liberties guaranteed under the due process clause included the right to marry, afforded a new basis for challenging California's antimiscegenation statutes.[93] In his petition he cited several recent cases that established his reasons for why his case called for a standard of strict scrutiny. In *West Virginia State Board of Education v. Barnette* (1943), the U.S. Supreme Court ruled on the constitutionality of compulsory flag saluting in public schools. In contrast to *Minersville School District v. Gobitis*, decided just three years earlier, the justices this time ruled that regulations compelling school children who were members of the Jehovah's Witnesses to salute the flag violated the First and Fourteenth Amendments. According to Justice Robert Jackson, who wrote the majority opinion:

Much of the vagueness of the due process clause disappears when the specific prohibitions of the First [Amendment] become its standard. The right of a State to regulate, for example, a public utility may well include, so far as the due process test is concerned, power to impose all of the restrictions which a legislature may have a "rational basis" for adopting. But freedoms of speech and of press, of assembly, and of worship may not be infringed on such slender grounds. They are susceptible of restriction only to prevent grave and immediate danger to interests which the State may lawfully protect.[94]

As we will see later in the oral arguments between Daniel Marshall and his opponent, Marshall perceived that the state's argument for the "grave and immediate danger" presented by interracial marriage was extremely weak. In Marshall's estimation, if the State of California was thus compelled to prove that its antimiscegenation statutes were constitutional, the chances of its success were very slim.

Similarly, Marshall cited another federal case to bolster his claim about why a strict standard of scrutiny should be applied in the *Perez* case. In *Busey et al. v. District of Columbia* (1943), a U.S. Court of Appeals for the District of Columbia reversed a decision of a lower court in which two Jehovah's Witnesses had been convicted of selling religious magazines without holding the appropriate license or paying a required tax. The appeals court affirmed, first, that First Amendment freedoms fall within the protected liberties of the due process clause. "Freedoms of speech, press, and religion are entitled to a preferred constitutional position because they are 'of the very essence of a scheme of ordered liberty.' . . . Because they are essential, the guarantees of free speech, press, and religion in the First Amendment, though not all constitutional guarantees, are within the 'liberty' which is protected by the due process clause of the Fourteenth Amendment." Further, the justices claimed, such cases demanded a strict standard of scrutiny, because "essential" human freedoms were at stake "when legislation appears on its face to affect the use of speech, press, or religion, and when its validity depends upon the existence of facts [i.e., the presumed rational basis of legislation] which are not proved, their existence should not be presumed; at least, when their existence is hardly more probable than improbable. . . . The burden of proof in such a case should be upon those who deny that these freedoms are invaded."[95] The precedents that Daniel Marshall cited in his case, and particularly *Cantwell, Barnette,* and *Busey,* demonstrated his belief that it was the state's responsibility to prove to the California Supreme Court justices that an interracial marriage posed a danger that the state must prevent or restrict. Combining the *Barnette* and *Busey* cases, Marshall argued that California's antimiscegenation statute indeed appeared "on its face to affect the use of religion," insofar as it prevented Perez and Davis from participating in the Catholic sacrament of marriage. Consequently, Marshall reasoned, the stricter scrutiny and individual liberties bases would compel Moroney's attorney to defend California's antimiscegenation statutes and to demonstrate that the Perez-Davis marriage presented a danger to state "interests."[96]

Marshall's Opponent Responds

Los Angeles county counsel Charles Stanley, attorney for Clerk Joseph Moroney, disputed Marshall's claims that the antimiscegenation statutes burdened his clients' freedom of religion and his interpretation of the applicability of the strict scrutiny test. Stanley thus promptly took steps to assail the validity of Marshall's argument. In response to Marshall's petition, Stanley submitted two briefs. The first served as Moroney's official reply to the court's writ requiring him either to grant the marriage license to Perez and Davis or to state why the court should not compel him to do so. Moroney, of course, opted to explain the grounds upon which he refused to issue the license. In this brief, Stanley agreed that the Catholic Church did not impose any impediment on interracial marriages.[97] However, he refuted Marshall's allegation that support for interracial marriage constituted a "dogma" that was "universal" among Catholics.[98] Stanley located a particularly nettlesome source on which to base this claim: the writings of Marshall's old friend, Father John LaFarge.

Stanley attempted to depict LaFarge's views, rather than Marshall's allegations, as orthodox Catholic doctrine, contending that the imprint "Permissu Superiorum" on the flyleaf of each of LaFarge's books indicated the church's official sanction of his writings. The remainder of Stanley's brief quoted a long passage from one of LaFarge's books, showing that LaFarge himself—forward-thinking laborer on behalf of racial justice—advised against interracial marriage. According to LaFarge, Stanley claimed, Catholic pastors should counsel interracial couples to follow state laws regarding intermarriage. And potentially even more troubling for Marshall, Stanley quoted LaFarge as stating that there were "*grave reasons* against any general practice of intermarriage between the members of different racial groups," and that together these reasons "amount[ed] to a moral prohibition of" interracial marriage.[99] In light of the wisdom of this foremost Catholic authority on race, Stanley requested that the court rule in favor of Moroney and deny Marshall's petition.

Stanley also filed a "Return by Way of Demurrer," a type of brief that essentially asks a court to dismiss a case based upon the opposing side's failure to demonstrate adequate grounds for its argument. The demurrer thus alleged that Marshall's petition did not "state facts sufficient to constitute a cause of action against this respondent, or at all," or in other words, that Marshall had failed to demonstrate adequate grounds for his First Amendment argument.[100] Stanley drew heavily upon two U.S. Supreme Court rulings, *Reynolds v. United States* (1878) and *Cantwell v. Connecticut* (1940). *Reynolds*—the decision ruling that the right to religious freedom excluded the Mormon practice of polygamy—acknowledged the sacred nature of marriage, but it affirmed that it was "nevertheless . . . a civil contract, and usually regulated by law." Further, *Reynolds* and other cases affirmed the right of state legislatures to declare certain types of marriages, such as polygamous and interracial unions, "inimical to the peace, good order, and morals of a society" (6). *Cantwell*, Stanley pointed out, distinguished two implicit freedoms within the concept of religious liberty: the freedom to believe and the freedom to act. "The first," the decision stated, "is absolute, but, in the nature of things, the second cannot be."[101] While a person had the right to believe that a polygamous or interracial marriage was valid based upon religious doctrine, a person did not have the right to act upon that belief. Attempting to force Marshall to address the "true issue" of the case—that is, that due process and equal protection, rather than religious freedom, was at stake in *Perez*, and that the case thus had to be argued "under the rules applicable to the Fourteenth Amendment"—Stanley's brief therefore argued that religious freedom was "a false issue in this case" (9). As with the first brief, the demurrer requested that on these grounds, the court rule in favor of Moroney.

After receiving a copy of these documents in mid-September 1947, Marshall flew into action. He quickly airmailed a letter to Father LaFarge, requesting that he elaborate upon the quotations Stanley had cited, though Marshall noted in the letter that he did not see how the priest's statements "impeach[ed] in any way the basic allegations of the petition."[102] A week later, LaFarge wrote back, praising Marshall for having prepared the brief convincingly and "with the greatest of care," and explaining his intentions in the passages Stanley had quoted. The main point of his remarks on interracial marriage, LaFarge claimed, was to distance himself from individuals who erroneously viewed calls for racial justice as a de facto "campaign for interracial marriage." Intermarriage was not a question of as "immediate and practical importance" as other elements of social justice for African Americans. Yet, he continued, urging priests to respect the law did not necessarily mean "that one approves of the laws or considers them either just or equitable." Rather, LaFarge had merely intended to bid ministers to exercise "pastoral prudence" by counseling couples to be fully aware of the difficulties an interracial marriage might pose.[103]

LaFarge closed his letter by remarking—rather surprisingly for one labeled a "gradualist" by racial progressives—that since only the couple could ultimately choose how best to exercise prudence, "it is altogether improper and immoral for the State to lay down a regulation on a matter over which it has no competence." Changing social conditions and the present push for racial justice "would seem to make it equally the part of prudence to see that such laws are done away with and to register a protest against them."[104] Thus armed with LaFarge's blessing for challenging California's unjust laws, Marshall finished preparing his oral arguments, which the court had scheduled for the first week of October—less than a week after he received LaFarge's response.

On 6 October, Marshall and Stanley appeared at the California Supreme Court before Chief Justice Phil S. Gibson and Justices Jesse W. Carter, Douglas L. Edmonds, B. Rey Schauer, John W. Shenk, Homer R. Spence, and Roger J. Traynor. Marshall apparently initiated the proceedings by reading his statement, which interestingly did not mention religion until page 4. In response to Stanley's allegation that the First Amendment grounds on which Marshall had argued were insufficient, Marshall instead focused on the inconsistency of the section of the Civil Code that prohibited marriages between white persons and Negroes, mulattoes, Mongolians, or member of the Malay race.[105] This statute, Marshall rather comically stated, allowed whites to marry "red" persons, and tolerated "any combination of yellow, black, red and brown," but forbade "every interracial marriage which consists of a combination of white and any other color, except red."[106] Spotlighting the arbitrary and ludicrous nature of the prohibitions, he asserted that in light of the fact that the State of California tolerated intermarriage "between the darker groups, and between the white group and one of the darker groups," there was no truth to Stanley's claim that interracial marriage "is an evil to be legislated against." In order to support the statute, Stanley would have to establish its constitutionality on the "much narrower ground that only a certain kind of interracial marriage is wrong" (2).

Having assailed the statute's lack of internal logic and the irrationality of the "dogma that it is imperative at all costs to preserve the purity of the blood," Marshall then turned to the issue of his clients' religious freedom to marry (3). After summarizing the religious issues in the case and briefly remarking that Father LaFarge's statements did not refute the allegation that the statute violated Perez and Davis's religious liberty, Marshall attacked the idea that interracial marriage was as inimical to Christian morality as bigamy and polygamy. Citing the two cases he had drawn upon in his writ, *West Virginia State Board v. Barnette* and *Busey v. District of Columbia*, he argued that "these decisions support these petitioners because what they seek to do conforms with the teaching of Christian life throughout the world, a teaching not restricted to the sect to which they belong" (9).

Marshall then addressed the unconstitutionality of the statute in relation to the Fourteenth Amendment. In his demurrer, Marshall asserted, Stanley had cited nearly twenty cases involving interracial sex or marriage, all of which upheld the state's right to enact marriage laws and to promote public morals and welfare. Observing that seventeen of the cases directly or indirectly cited *State v. Tutty* (1890), an influential Georgia case, Marshall contended that *Tutty* "stated the motivation which led to the validation of the statute," implying that the rationale behind *Tutty* undergirded the other sixteen cases. He then read an excerpt from *Tutty*, in which he found particularly troubling and outmoded ideas about race.[107] "'The amalgamation of the races," he read,

'is not only unnatural, but it is always productive of deplorable results. Our daily observations show us that the offspring of these unnatural connections are generally sickly and effeminate, and that they are inferior in physical development and strength to the full blood of either race. It is sometimes urged that such marriages be encouraged for the purpose of elevating the inferior race. The reply is that such connections never elevate the inferior race to the position of the superior, but they bring down the superior to that of the inferior. They are productive of evil, and evil only, without any corresponding good.'[108]

Launching his most stinging rebuke yet, Marshall declared that the same "doctrine and beliefs espoused by this opinion . . . were reiterated in another place." He read yet another passage that expressed similar views on race-mixing. The quotation ended with the assertion that "there is only one most sacred human right, and this right is at the same time the most sacred obligation, namely, to see to it that the blood is preserved pure, so that by its preservation of the best human material a possibility is given for a more noble development of these human beings." Marshall then dramatically revealed the source of these statements: Adolph Hitler. Coming a mere three years after the end of World War II, Marshall's theatrics must have had a substantial effect on the courtroom. The "choice," he proclaimed, "must then be between the dogma of the Tutty case, the decisions which have followed it and the concepts of those leaders who adopted that dogma . . . and the sublime expressions of our national aspiration forever imbedded in our constitutional documents" (13). After dramatically making the connection between antimiscegenation statutes and racial genocide, Marshall rather anticlimactically discussed and dismissed a California case Stanley had cited in his demurrer as irrelevant to the case at hand, and then closed his statement by briefly reasserting that "the prevention of race crossing is not a permissible objective of legislation" and that the court should thus issue the writ (14–15).

Marshall's compelling presentation was a difficult act to follow, and Stanley did not fare very well in the oral arguments. Stanley began his remarks by observing that it was "quite obvious why the petitioners would like to bring their case under the first amendment": the "recent cases in the United States Supreme Court have indicated that if the first amendment is involved, it is necessary for the state to establish that there is a clear and present danger, or else that the legislation affects religious liberty." The "clear and present danger" test Stanley then dismissed as "a very extreme rule."[109] He then turned to claim that *Reynolds v. United States* served as a stare decisis decision for denying marriages the protection of the First Amendment,[110] Justice Roger Traynor—a liberal on the court and well-informed reader of social science literature on race—sharply interjected, "What about equal protection of the law?" Traynor's query appears to have momentarily stopped Stanley in his tracks, as he began to utter a few disjointed phrases about *Pace v. Alabama*. But before he could complete his sentence or clarify his thoughts, Traynor interrupted him again, this time inquiring what "legitimate social purpose" an antimiscegenation statute served, and why such a law would not violate the "privileges and immunities" provision of the Constitution.[111] Before Stanley could respond, Traynor demanded that Stanley first explain California's statute, and specifically, what it meant by "Negro."[112]

With that question, a lively discussion over race commenced. Stanley found himself floundering both to define race and to establish a "clear and present" basis for California's statute. Stanley admitted to Justice Traynor that "we have not the benefit of any judicial interpretation" with regard to racial definitions. Traynor then jumped on the vague legal definition of "mulatto" and refused to let go. "If there is ⅛ blood," he insisted, "can they marry? If you can marry with ⅛, why not with ¹⁄₁₆, ¹⁄₃₂, ¹⁄₆₄? And then," he continued, "don't you get in the ridiculous position where a negro cannot marry anybody? If he is white, he cannot marry black, if he is black, he cannot marry white" (3). Stanley agreed. It "would be better for the Legislature to lay down an exact amount of blood," he admitted, "but I do not think that the statute should be declared unconstitutional as indefinite on this ground" (4).

Traynor pushed Stanley to admit that the concept of race eluded definition—by lawyers, legislators, and anthropologists alike. The last group, Traynor stated, "say generally that there is no such thing as race." At this statement, Stanley hesitated, observing, "I would not say that anthropologists have said that generally, except such statements for sensational purposes." "Would you say," Traynor cut in, "that Professor Wooten [sic] of Harvard was a sensationalist? The crucial question is how can a county clerk determine who are negroes and who are whites?"[113] Unsatisfied with Stanley's response that clerks determine race "by taking a statement" as to a couple's racial identities, Traynor relinquished the issue and returned to an earlier line of questioning, repeating his inquiry about what legitimate social purpose an antimiscegenation statute served.[114]

Already treading on thin ice with Traynor, Stanley attempted to remind the court that if there were any evidence to support a basis for the law, its constitutionality had to be upheld. Traynor, unimpressed, reminded Stanley that the statute did not prevent all "miscegenous marriages" but only those between whites and "Mongolians, Malays, and Negroes." Stanley's task, therefore, was to establish a basis for this particular aspect of the statute. So Stanley summoned all the classic biological and medical supports for antimiscegenation laws, citing the "detrimental biological results" of mixing between members of "widely divergent races," such as the "loss of vitality and fertility" and the "certain disharmonic [social] conflicts" that result. "I do not like to say it or to tie myself in with 'Mein Kampf,'" he continued, "but it has been shown that the white race is superior physically and mentally to the black race, and the intermarriage of these races results in a lessening of physical vitality and mentality in their offspring" (6).

At this point, Traynor jumped in once again. "Are there medical men in this country today who say such a thing?" he asked. Stanley mentioned an encyclopedia entry on sickle-cell anemia as afflicting only the black race, and he cited evidence from intelligence tests that concluded whites were superior to blacks.[115] He contended that it has been the "unanimous opinion," of whom he did not indicate, that couples "who enter into miscegenous marriages are usually from the lower walks of both races . . . generally people who are lost to shame."[116] As to the question of sexual relationships between unmarried interracial couples, which California, unlike certain other states, did not prohibit, Stanley admitted that these were "impossible to control," but again, such generally occurred among "only the lower classes who will accept the consequent ostracism." Citing Father LaFarge as an "eminent Catholic authority," Stanley reasoned that if the "social evils attendant upon miscegenetic marriages are so great that in some circumstances the church itself will place an impediment to the marriage," then surely it was "also within the competency of the Legislature to say that these evils exist." Finally, Stanley offered the "most important thing—the troubles their children are going to have—and those considerations may be deemed by the Legislature as so serious that it would be most selfish, and therefore, immoral for those persons to enter into such a marriage" (7). The "strain on the marital relation and family times" and concomitant placement of "the offspring in such an unfavorable condition" thus constituted the "principal reason" for justifying antimiscegenation laws (8).

Throughout this explanation, Traynor and the other justices had listened quietly to Stanley's rationales, not saying a word. Then Traynor broke in again, asking how Stanley would "answer the argument that the statute in reality amounts to a 'carfare statute,'" that is, since California recognized interracial marriages that had been legalized elsewhere, did not the law merely encourage interracial couples to go out of state to get married?[117] Stanley responded that "there [was] a great deal of evidence that such marriages [were] not recognized," although he offered no substantiation for his claim. The state did, however, recognize marriages of non-California residents who had legally married in another state and subsequently moved to California. Stanley then suddenly dropped the issue and began to refute Marshall's allegation that most of the cases cited in the demurrer had relied upon the *Tutty* decision. He claimed that other cases also offered "a sound basis" for antimiscegenation statutes, and he believed that basis to be the "strain on the marital relation which can make such a marriage improper." "Who can estimate the evil," he began, quoting from *Green v. State of Alabama*, "of introducing into their most intimate relations, elements so heterogeneous that they must naturally cause discord, shame, disruption of family circles and estrangement of kindred? While with their interior administration, the State should interfere but little, it is obviously of the highest public concern that it should, by general laws adapted to the state of things around them, guard them against disturbances from without."[118] Stanley then suggested that this "language sounds almost like the Mormon [*Reynolds*] case," intimating that interracial marriages, like polygamous marriages, were morally repugnant. There the oral arguments abruptly end.

On that same day, Stanley filed a 121-page supplemental brief that offered additional oppositions to Marshall's petition for the writ of mandamus. One month later, in early November 1947, Marshall submitted his 55-page reply and also sent a copy to Father LaFarge. Between this time and October 1948, when the court announced its final decision, there was no further correspondence about the case between Marshall and LaFarge, and no more legal documentation. And Andrea Perez and Sylvester Davis had to wait for the court's decision.

The Final Decision and the Religious Right to Marry

In October 1948, nearly one year to the day that Daniel Marshall and Charles Stanley had presented their oral arguments to the Supreme Court of California, the justices finally issued their decision on the *Perez* case—a ruling that one legal scholar deems "far more remarkable" than even the U.S. Supreme Court's 1967 *Loving* decision.[119] By a 4–3 majority, the court ruled, among other things, that "legislation infringing on the right to marry must be based on more than prejudice and must be free from oppressive discrimination to comply with the constitutional requirements of due process and equal protection of the laws." Explicitly construing the right to marry as a fundamental human right, the majority further stated that "since the essence of the right to marry is freedom to join in marriage with the person of one's choice, a segregation statute for marriage necessarily impairs the right to marry."[120] Of the seven justices on the court, three resurrected all the traditional legal arguments in support of antimiscegenation laws, contending that such statutes posed no threat to the couple's religious freedom and that judges are to presume the constitutionality of a law's "purpose and application" (42). Justice Roger Traynor authored the twelve-page primary opinion of the majority. Chief Justice Phil Gibson concurred with Traynor, but Justices Jesse Carter and Douglas Edmonds wrote separate concurring opinions. All together, then, the majority issued three opinions. Traynor and Gibson based their statements on the irrationality of racial categories, and Carter on antimiscegenation laws as affronts to American values of freedom and equality.

Justice Edmonds cast the deciding vote that granted victory to Andrea Perez and Sylvester Davis. A Christian Scientist for whom religious freedom mattered deeply, Justice Douglas Edmonds was the only judge fully persuaded by Marshall's First Amendment argument: he based his five-paragraph opinion entirely upon the right to marry as a religious liberty. One historian speculates, in fact, that Marshall might have taken the religious affiliations of the justices into consideration as he formulated his religion-based arguments. "Marshall may have considered Traynor sympathetic to his clients because, like them, Traynor was Catholic. Marshall may also have tailored his religious freedom argument to appeal to Justice Douglas Edmonds. Justice Edmonds generally voted with socially conservative justices on the Court, Shenk, Shauer [sic], and Spence; Court watchers expected him to vote with them in *Perez*. Edmonds was, however, a devoted Christian Scientist who felt strongly about religious liberty."[121] Given Marshall's attention to detail, this claim is plausible. But whether or not Marshall considered the justices' religious views as part of his grand strategy, what is clear is that Edmonds's opinion shifted the entire outcome of the case.

Justice Traynor, who was appointed to the court in 1940 and became chief justice in 1964, structured his opinion in *Perez* around the central questions and answers posed by the case: 1) did the right to due process include the freedom to marry, 2) could the state restrict that freedom on the basis of race without violating the equal protection clause, and 3) did antimiscegenation laws aim at preventing a clear and present danger to the state's residents. Religious freedom, then, did not even make a "blip" on Traynor's "radar screen" in terms of having any real importance to the case. Although the religious right to marry formed the first topic of debate in his opinion, Traynor concluded there that it was secondary to the right to marry more generally. Devoting a mere two paragraphs of his twelve-page decision to religious freedom, he asserted that "if the miscegenation law under attack in the present proceeding is directed at a social evil and employs a reasonable means to prevent that evil, it is valid regardless of its incidental effect upon the conduct of particular religious groups. If, on the other hand, the law is discriminatory, it unconstitutionally restricts not only religious liberty but the liberty to marry as well" (18). Although Traynor's position suggests that he did not view religious freedom as entirely relevant in the case, he did allow that if the law was unconstitutional, then it did in fact violate both religious liberty and the freedom to marry.

In Traynor's view, the more critical issue was whether or not the statute prevented a "social evil." Having established that marriage is a "fundamental right of free men" and that there could be "no prohibition of marriage except for an important social objective and by reasonable means," he analyzed what "social evil" such a law might curtail. As in his debate with Stanley during the oral arguments, Traynor addressed the medical and sociological grounds offered in support of antimiscegenation statutes. Arguing that the law "condemn[ed] certain races as unfit to marry with Caucasians on the premise of a hypothetical racial disability, regardless of the physical qualifications of the individuals concerned," Traynor asserted that if "this premise were carried to its logical conclusion, non-Caucasians who are now precluded from marrying Caucasians on physical grounds would also be precluded from marrying among themselves on the same grounds. The concern to prevent marriages in the first category and the indifference about marriages in the second category reveal the spuriousness of the contention that intermarriage between Caucasians and non-Caucasians is socially dangerous on physical grounds" (24).

Turning then to the legitimacy of the allegation that the statute prevented race tensions, he observed that it "is no answer to say that race tension can be eradicated through the perpetuation by law of the prejudices that give rise to the tension." Restrictions on the marriage rights of the Negroes, mulattoes, Mongolians, and Malays differed from legal decisions upholding the segregation of public facilities, for in those, states were required to provide equal facilities. But antimiscegenation laws offered "no redress" for an individual "barred by law from marrying the person of his choice, and that person to him may be irreplaceable. Human beings are bereft of worth and dignity by a doctrine that would make them as interchangeable as trains" (25). Rather than limiting a "social evil," Traynor thus intimated that antimiscegenation statutes perpetuated other evils: intolerance and lack of respect for human dignity. Traynor ended this discussion by concluding that the statutes lacked a valid legislative purpose.

Traynor then began his most innovative analysis, challenging for perhaps the first time in the history of American law the very notion of race. As a writer for the black-owned *Los Angeles Sentinel* observed, Traynor's opinion in *Perez* "cut under all the customary myths trotted out by those who defend the marriage ban and other discriminatory statutes."[122] Having asserted earlier that "the right to marry is the right of individuals, not of racial groups," he explored the statute's vagueness with regard to racial identities, contending that a "certain precision is essential in a statute regulating a fundamental right" (20, 27). He applied his knowledge of social science literature on race, highlighting both the historical changes in perspectives on how many races there actually were and the lack of scientific agreement therein.

Traynor then observed that the California legislature had "made no provision for applying the statute to persons of mixed ancestry." This problem, Traynor declared, underscored the unconstitutionality of the statute, for it restricted the law in accomplishing its purpose, which, he stated, was to "discourage the birth of children of mixed ancestry within this state" (27). If the statute did not explicate the rules for marriages involving mixed race persons—establishing who they were or what procedures they were to follow—then it could be declared unconstitutional on the basis of its indefiniteness. Furthermore, Traynor contended, enforcing the statute would place the burden of ascertaining a couple's racial identity, and the "task of determining the meaning of the statute," on government officials, who could ascertain mixed-race individuals only on the "basis of conceptions of race classification not supplied by the Legislature," resulting in a subjectivity not tenable in law (28). Traynor thus concluded that California's antimiscegenation statutes were "not only too vague and uncertain to be enforceable regulations of a fundamental right, but that they violate[d] the equal protection of the laws clause of the United States Constitution by impairing the right of individuals to marry on the basis of race alone and unreasonably discriminating against certain racial groups" (29). On this basis, the statutes must therefore be deemed unconstitutional.

Justice Jesse Carter concurred with Traynor's ruling, but he based his reasoning on equal protection issues. Well-known for his dissents and for his strongly worded opinions, Carter contended that the statutes violated the concepts of human equality articulated in such foundational American documents as the Declaration of Independence and the U.S. Constitution, as well as the Gettysburg Address, the Charter of the United Nations, and the Bible. Carter quoted a verse from the biblical book of Acts that was subsequently cited by segregationists and integrationists alike in support of both sides: "God . . . hath made of one blood all nations of men for to dwell on the face of the earth, and hath determined the times before appointed, and the bounds of their habitation." He provided no further comment on this verse. Carter also offered an interesting analysis of *Plessy v. Ferguson*, observing that although that case had affirmed the right of the state to enact legislation "'in good faith for the promotion of the public good,'" the authors of *Plessy* also insisted that laws must be "reasonable," which "left the door open" for reinterpretation of a "future, more enlightened generation." In "the light of future developments," Carter wrote, "all the reasonableness may have been lost and the regulation may have reduced itself to a mere tool of oppression," and that "what once may have appeared reasonable has become an absurdity."

Carter contended that "the constitutionality of a statute is not determined once and for all by a decision upholding it." Rather, "a change in conditions may invalidate a statute which was reasonable and valid when enacted." According to *Plessy*, "the reasonableness of the regulation is therefore the decisive factor."[123] Further, he reasoned, recent cases such as *Korematsu* had established the rule that made laws restricting the rights of racial groups immediately suspect; this standard was "sufficient to overcome the presumption of validity and constitutionality normally present when a statute is attacked as unconstitutional" (33). Last, Carter explored sociological and medical rationales against racial mixing. Echoing Marshall, he concluded that such views merely gave credence to the views of Hitler—a "madman, a rabble-rouser, a mass-murderer" whose ideas no American should tolerate (34). Carter's statements made no mention of religious freedom, which suggests that he shared Traynor's view that First Amendment freedoms had little bearing on the constitutionality of California's antimiscegenation statutes.

In response to the majority opinions, Justice John W. Shenk authored the dissent on behalf of Justices B. Rey Schauer and Homer R. Spence, unapologetically citing, as Randall Kennedy notes, the "Negrophobic postulates of white supremacists in America and abroad."[124] Shenk's twelve-page opinion repeated the same justifications for the statutes that virtually every antimiscegenation case in American history had affirmed: the long tradition of such statutes, the state's constitutional right to regulate marriage, and the idea that the judiciary had no business interfering with the right of the legislature to enact laws. Shenk asserted that antimiscegenation statutes had "never been declared unconstitutional," that such legislation did have "a valid legislative purpose," and that in the face of that purpose, "it is entirely beyond judicial power, properly exercised, to nullify them" (35).[125] Shenk did examine the First Amendment issues that the case raised but contended that "the attitude of the church has no particular bearing on the asserted rights of the petitioners," and that in fact the church's "attitude," which he conflated with that of LaFarge, "is one of respect for local laws and an admonition to her clergy to advise against their infringement" (36). Moreover, he reiterated the ruling of *Cantwell*, asserting, as Stanley had, that religious freedom entailed two concepts—the freedom to believe and the freedom to act—the latter of which necessarily involved restrictions. Shenk's conclusions about religious freedom thus resembled those of Traynor: religious belief was just not relevant to the constitutionality of California's antimiscegenation statutes.

Shenk argued at length for the state's right to regulate marriage, and he retold the history of antimiscegenation cases in the United States. The lack of harmony in the majority's written opinions struck a nerve with Shenk, who scolded Traynor and the others for having arrived at their ruling "not by a concurrence of reasons but by the end result of four votes supported by divergent concepts not supported by authority and in fact contrary to the decisions in this state and elsewhere."[126] He then listed the rules a court was supposed to follow, and what it could not do in regard to legislative enactments, intimating that the majority had not obeyed the rules. In language foreshadowing the 1956 "Southern Manifesto" issued by southern congressmen in reaction against *Brown v. Board of Education* (1954), the *Perez* dissenters charged the majority justices with having deviated from their responsibilities as servants of the judiciary. Among other things, the responsibilities of the judicial branch were to presume the constitutionality of a statute, to resolve "in favor of and not against the validity of a statute," to presume that the "Legislature acted with integrity and with a purpose to keep within the restrictions and limitations laid down in the fundamental law," and "when the constitutionality of a statute depends on the existence of some fact or state of facts," to allow the legislature to address the problem (41–42). "These presumptions," Shenk asserted, "apply with particular emphasis to statutes passed in the exercise of police power" (42). It was simply not "within the province of the courts to go behind the findings of the legislature and determine that conditions did not exist which gave rise to and justified the enactment" (43).

Shenk then turned to the sociological rationales for antimiscegenation laws and insisted that though they were inconclusive, they formed an adequate "background for the legislation." Once again he reiterated that those "favoring present day amalgamation of these distinct races irrespective of scientific data . . . should direct their efforts to the Legislature in order to effect the change in state policy which they espouse" (43, 46). He concluded with the issue of the alleged "vague and uncertain" nature of the laws, asserting that "after almost one hundred years of continuous operation of the present and pre-existing similar laws, the claimed obstacles to the application of the statute are more theoretical than real," since neither Perez nor Davis had claimed any vagueness in their racial identities and, rather, had affirmed that Perez was white and Davis black. The dissenters thus concluded that all things considered, the "alternative writ should be discharged and the peremptory writ denied" (47).

For the dissenters as well as for three of the majority justices, the question of religious freedom played little role in the overall resolution of the case, as issues involving due process, equal protection, definitions of race, and the state's right to regulate marriage occupied center stage. Despite their differences on these matters, Justices Traynor, Gibson, Carter, Shenk, Spence, and Schauer seemed to agree that had the court ruled California's antimiscegenation statutes constitutional, those statutes remained constitutional even if they infringed the religious right of Perez and Davis to marry. Justice Edmonds, however, disagreed with this assessment. Edmonds tended to vote with the "socially conservative justices on the Court," but his opinion in *Perez* surprised the "Court watchers."[127] In concurring with the broader judgment that "the challenged statutes [were] discriminatory and irrational," Edmonds insisted that marriage was more than a fundamental right of free human beings. In his view, the right to marry was also "grounded in the fundamental principles of Christianity," and was by implication protected under the First Amendment (34).

Unlike his peers, Edmonds accepted Marshall's First Amendment argument. He read the opinions given in *Cantwell* and *Barnette* and analyzed them in regard to their conclusions on cases involving both the First and Fourteenth Amendments. Edmonds reiterated Marshall's claim that in *Cantwell*, the U.S. Supreme Court had ruled for the first time that "through the due process clause of the Fourteenth Amendment, a state statute may be declared invalid if it violates the specific guarantees of religious freedom as stated in the First Amendment." The Court's opinion in *Cantwell*, Edmonds noted, was even more "forcefully" articulated in the 1943 *Barnette* case. Quoting at length from that decision, he expressed the significance of the criteria for cases based on First and Fourteenth Amendment grounds even more pointedly than Marshall had. According to *Barnette*, it was necessary for courts to "'distinguish between the due process clause of the Fourteenth Amendment as an instrument for transmitting the principles of the First Amendment and those cases in which it is applied for its own sake.'"

Edmonds quoted the same passage that Marshall had cited in his petition, asserting that First Amendment freedoms may not be infringed on the "rational basis" test but, rather, are "'susceptible of restriction only to prevent grave and immediate danger to interests which the state may lawfully protect'" (34–35). Like Marshall, Edmonds thus concluded that the "reasonable classification" standard was "not the test to be applied to a statute which interferes with one of the fundamental liberties which are protected by the First Amendment." Rather, he continued, "the question is whether there is any 'clear and present danger' justifying such legislation," and "the burden of upholding the enactment is upon him who asserts that the acts which are denounced do not infringe the freedom of the individual." In Edmonds's opinion, then, when enacting legislation that curtailed those freedoms, the state indeed had the responsibility to demonstrate what the danger or social evil was. In the *Perez* case, the state of California had failed to establish any clear and present danger and had merely confirmed that there was some factual basis for the statutes. In Edmonds's view, attorney Charles Stanley's arguments thus fell short of the standards set forth in *Cantwell* and *Barnette*, as well as *Busey v. District of Columbia* (1943) and *Schenck v. United States* (1919).

Justice Edmonds's opinion also dismissed Stanley's citation of *Reynolds v. United States*, claiming that it was irrelevant to the *Perez* case. In contrast to Stanley's suggestions that *Reynolds* provided a stare decisis principle restricting the exercise of religious freedoms in respect to marriage, and that it upheld the state's right to pronounce certain types of marriage as contrary to the good order of a society, Edmonds maintained that cases upholding state statutes against polygamy fell into a different category than *Perez*. In *Reynolds* the U.S. Supreme Court had proclaimed polygamy as "contrary to the spirit of Christianity and of the civilization which Christianity has produced in the Western world." Edmonds did not fully elaborate upon how he understood the principles of *Reynolds* to differ from those of *Perez*, but it appears that he believed that because not all states of the union upheld laws against interracial marriage, and because even California's statutes did not in fact prohibit *all* interracial marriage, then it did not pose the same threat to Christian society as polygamy. Edmonds concluded that in contrast to antimiscegenation statutes, *Reynolds* and *Mormon Church v. United States* (1890) "rest[ed] on the principle that the conduct which the legislation was designed to prevent constituted a clear and present danger to the well being of the nation and, for that reason, the statute [against polygamy] did not violate constitutional guarantees" (35). In Edmonds's view, then, interracial marriage posed no such threat to the social order, and the state had no right to restrict an individual's choice of marriage partners.

Perez was won on Justice Edmonds's opinion, making the entire case pivot on the axis of religious liberty. Swayed neither by the reproach of the dissenting justices nor by the divergent bases forming the majority opinions, Edmonds based his statement solely on the relevance of the religious liberty to marry. As the only justice to vote this way, his decision tipped the otherwise divided court to rule in favor of Perez and Davis, highlighting once again the centrality of the religious right to marry both as a legal strategy and as a Catholic position in this case.

HAVING WAITED ON pins and needles as to the future of their relationship for a whole year, Andrea Perez and Sylvester Davis were overjoyed to learn the outcome of the case. It did not matter to them that when the final decision was publicized, the panel of judges—with one exception— had summarily dismissed Marshall's religious freedom argument, or that six of the seven justices depicted the religious freedom issue in such a way that readers of the decision could easily conclude that the First Amendment claims were but a foolish ploy on the part of a naive or not terribly astute attorney.

Yet it is clear that religion played a critical part in the *Perez* story in several different ways. The story behind *Perez*—the multiracial composition of Los Angeles and of St. Patrick's parish, the development and demise of the Catholic Interracial Council, and the activities of Daniel Marshall as a Catholic advocate of racial justice—demonstrates the central part played by both region and Catholic beliefs in the case. Indeed, *Perez* arose precisely from the multicultural and religious context of 1940s Los Angeles and cannot be understood properly apart from it. The multiracial character of California, and most especially of Los Angeles, coincided with an era of progressiveness within the Catholic Archdiocese of Los Angeles, which not only allowed Andrea Perez and Sylvester Davis to meet at their workplace and to worship together at the same parish, but also to locate progressive thinkers who took up their cause within the Los Angeles CIC. Moreover, the wave of U.S. Supreme Court decisions involving First Amendment rights and their connections to the Fourteenth Amendment enabled Daniel Marshall to construct an innovative argument for the couple's right to marry as both a fundamental human liberty and a religious freedom.

Religion's role in this case enables us to catch a glimpse of other ways that Christianity functioned in the broader history of laws on interracial marriage. To understand the deeper role of Christian beliefs in this history, we must examine the colonial development of laws on interracial sex and marriage in the Americas and their relationship to racialized slavery. By comparing the laws in British, French, and Spanish colonies, important differences emerge that once again point to the critical significance of Protestant and Catholic beliefs.

[2] The Historical Origins of American Laws on Interracial Sex and Marriage

The Role of Religion and Region

The United States is one of a few countries in the world to have enacted laws restricting and prohibiting sex and marriage between whites and blacks or other persons of color. Nazi Germany and South Africa share most famously in this dubious distinction.[1] Under Hitler's regime, obsession with *Rassenschande* ("race defilement") was codified into the Nuremberg Laws of 1935. The "Law for the Protection of German Blood and German Honor" categorized Germans into Jews, *Deutschblütiger* ("of German blood"), or *Mischlinge* ("mixed blood") and forbade both sex and marriage between "Jews and citizens of German or some related blood."[2] Faced with the question of defining who was German, Jewish, and *Mischlinge*, the Nazis created charts to elucidate these categories, using white figures to represent Germans, black figures to represent Jewish people, and gray figures to represent *Mischlinge*. The Nuremberg Laws ended with the arrival of the Allies in 1945.

In South Africa laws regulating interracial sex and marriage began much earlier. The parliament prohibited sex between white prostitutes and black men in 1902 but broadened this law in 1927 to include sexual intercourse between all whites and "Africans." During a 1949 House of Assembly debate over the Prohibition of Mixed Marriages Act, which proposed to declare marriage between "a European and a non-European" illegal, supporters of apartheid appealed to the judicial wisdom of American States that had banned interracial marriage. "Look at the experience of other countries in this very same sphere of mixed marriage," demanded one assembly member. "Is it not something for the other side to think about that in thirty out of the forty-eight States of the United States they have legislation on similar lines to this? Is it not an argument to show that it is no reason for discarding such legislation, because it is not so effective as one would like it to be? I take it the difficulty is as great there as it is here, but thirty states have decided on legislation on these lines; thirty states have found it necessary to take legislative steps to keep down this social evil."[3] The assembly passed the act in 1949, and the law remained on the books until 1985.

The bans in Germany and South Africa began and ended during the twentieth century. But American prohibitions against interracial sex and marriage began in the 1600s—almost as soon as white Europeans and black Africans set foot together on the shores of the New World—and persisted, in some cases, until the turn of the millennium. Even in colonies where slavery did not become the basis of the socioeconomic system, some legislatures enacted laws on interracial sex and marriage. Among the original thirteen colonies, all except Connecticut, New Hampshire, and New Jersey enacted laws punishing sex and marriage across the color line.[4] (See table 2-1.) Most of the colonies that did establish such laws had them in place by 1750. Maryland and Virginia enacted the earliest statutes during the 1660s, and the laws from these two colonies seem to have provided a blueprint for those enacted elsewhere. In each colony, the prohibitions were directed at whites and "Negroes or mulattoes," and in some cases, between whites and Native Americans, but the matter of which behaviors were prohibited varied greatly from colony to colony. As of 1700, Delaware and South Carolina forbade bastardy and/or fornication but not marriage, while Rhode Island prohibited marriage only, Georgia and Massachusetts outlawed illicit marriage *and* sex, and the other colonies proscribed some combination of fornication, bastardy or marriage.[5] And by 1800, in every colony that banned interracial sex and/or marriage, all except Delaware, Georgia, and South Carolina also punished ministers or magistrates for solemnizing a marriage ceremony between a white person and a person of color.[6] (See table 2-2.) Ten of the thirteen original colonies thus enacted bans or restrictions on intermarriage within one hundred years after settlement.

In the history of the American colonies and states, only eight never restricted or banned interracial relations: Alaska, Connecticut, Hawaii, Minnesota, New Hampshire, New Jersey, Vermont, and Wisconsin. Following the Civil War and the emancipation of slaves, such laws burgeoned, particularly in the West, where some legislatures prohibited relations between whites and Native Americans, Chinese, Mongolians, Japanese, Filipinos, or "Hindoos" as well as those between whites and African Americans. For a brief period after the war, Mississippi lawmakers went so far as to make marriage between white and black persons a felony punishable by life im-

TABLE 2-1. Dates of Laws on Interracial Sex and Marriage
in the Original Thirteen Colonies

Colony	Date Laws Enacted	Date Laws Repealed (or Omitted)
Connecticut	Never enacted a law	—
Delaware	c. 1726	Post-*Loving*
Georgia	1750	Post-*Loving*
Maryland	1661	March 1967 (3 months before *Loving*)
Massachusetts	c. 1705	1843
New Hampshire	Never enacted a law	—
New Jersey	Never enacted a law	—
New Amsterdam (later New York)	1638 (one year only)	Omitted from subsequent statutory books (while still under Dutch colonial rule)
North Carolina	1715	Post-*Loving*
Pennsylvania	c. 1725	1780
Rhode Island	c. 1798	1881
South Carolina	1717	Post-*Loving*
Virginia	1662	Post-*Loving*

Note: Dates are approximate, as there are a number of discrepancies among the sources that discuss these laws. The materials used to assemble these data come from several sources having internal omissions and discrepancies; there are also inconsistencies and contradictions from one source to another. These materials include Doherty, *Moral Problems*; Fowler, *Northern Attitudes*, 336–439; Hurd, *Law of Freedom*; Johnson, *Development of State Legislation*; Mangum, *Legal Status*; Martyn, "Racism in the United States"; May, *Marriage Laws and Decisions*; Stephenson, *Race Distinctions*. Martyn's citations are the most complete and recent. The sources tend to focus on the development of antimiscegenation laws after 1865, so the data for earlier periods are sketchy, especially for 1607–1725, although Martyn's work is comprehensive. Most of the others focus on the period from 1865 to the time of publication, which was usually 1910–1920.

prisonment.[7] In the thirty years following the war, six southern states—Alabama (1865), Tennessee (1870), North Carolina (1875), Florida (1885), Mississippi (1890), and South Carolina (1895)—even amended their state constitutions to include bans on intermarriage.[8] And in two of these six states, the prohibitions did not officially end until 1998 and 2000—some thirty years after the U.S. Supreme Court had declared them unconstitutional.[9]

TABLE 2-2. Contents of Laws on Interracial Sex and Marriage in the Original Thirteen Colonies through 1850

Colony	Who	What	Penalty
Connecticut	Never enacted a law	—	—
Delaware	c. 1726 — Whites/Negroes or mulattoes	Bastardy and fornication (abolished in 1796); marriage not prohibited until 1806	Fine, whipping, and pillory for white woman with child; 39 lashes, pillory, and cropping of ear for black/mulatto man; 21 lashes and 20 pounds fine for white man; black woman not penalized. 1796 — All fines and corporal punishments abolished for bastardy and fornication. 1850 — No penalty for intermarriage, but white women, white men, and black men fined for begetting bastards. 1852 — Marriage becomes misdemeanor with fine of $100 for each person.
Georgia	1750 — Whites/Negroes or mulattoes	Marriage and sexual relations	For whites, forfeit 10 pounds sterling or corporal punishment at discretion of court; for blacks, corporal punishment at discretion of court
Maryland	1664 — Freeborn English women/Negro slaves (whites/Negroes specified in 1692)	Marriage (bastardy added in 1692)	1661 — White woman to serve slave-husband's master during life of husband. 1692 — Whites who married Negroes to serve seven years, and free Negroes were to become slaves for life. Whites and free Negro men convicted of bastardy to serve seven years. 1717 — If bastards born of white women, to serve seven years; if born of black women, to be slaves for life.
Massachusetts	1705 — White English or Scottish subjects or subjects of any Christian nation/ Negroes or mulattoes (Indians added in 1786)	Marriage and fornication	No punishment for marriage. For fornication, white man to be whipped, fined, and ordered to maintain any child of relationship; white woman ordered to maintain child, but if unable to do so, sold into service for court-ordered term; Negro or mulatto man or woman sold out of province. 1786 — Penalties for fornication or adultery omitted. 1843 — All provisions repealed.
New Hampshire	Never enacted a law	—	—
New Jersey	Never enacted a law	—	—

		Adulterous intercourse	Violators subject to correction and punishment.
New York	1638—Whites/heathens, blacks, or other persons	Adulterous intercourse	
North Carolina	c. 1715—Whites/Negroes, mulattoes or Indians	Marriage and bastardy	Marriage: for whites, fine of 50 pounds. Bastardy: for free white woman, fine of 6 pounds or 2 years of service; for white servant woman, fine of 6 pounds or, in default, 4 extra years of service, 2 for benefit of parish; for colored women if child is begotten by her master, to be sold for 2 years of service. 1741—Whites who married Indian, Negro, mustee, mulatto, or any person of mixed blood to the third generation, bond or free, fine of 50 pounds. 1830—Marriage or cohabitation merits fine and imprisonment or whipping at court's discretion. 1854—No penalties specified for marriage.
Pennsylvania	c. 1725—Whites/Negroes	Marriage, cohabitation, adultery, fornication	Free Negroes intermarrying become slaves for life; whites cohabitating with Negroes fined 30 pounds or sold as servant for 7 years. For adultery or fornication, Negroes to be sold for seven years of service, whites punished as law directs in cases of adultery or fornication. 1780—Entire law repealed.
Rhode Island	1798—Whites/Negroes, mulattoes, or Indians	Marriage	No punishment specified. 1872—Fine of 50 dollars assessed for all persons marrying without proceeding according to law. 1881—Entire law repealed.
South Carolina	1717—Whites/Negroes	Bastardy (marriage added 1865)	Whites and free Negro men to serve seven years. Law does not appear to change until after Civil War.
Virginia	1662—Christians/Negroes (English or other whites/Negroes, mulattoes, or Indians added in 1691)	Bastardy and fornication (marriage added in 1691)	Fine for Christian doubled for fornication with member of own race. 1691—For marriage, whites forever banished from dominion. Free white woman with bastard child to be fined and sold for five years of service; if a servant, to be sold for five years after completing her original term. 1705—Fine and prison for whites. 1753—Prohibition of marriage between whites and Indians omitted. 1819—Whites fine and jailed.

Note: Compiled from Fowler, *Northern Attitudes*; and Martyn, "Racism in the United States."

How did these laws on interracial sex and marriage originate? Why did they appear so early in American history, and why did they last more than one hundred years after slavery ended? How might a comparison of laws on interracial sex and marriage in British Protestant and Spanish and French Catholic regions deepen and complicate the answers to these questions? Might religion have some bearing on the development of laws regulating interracial sex and marriage? The answers to these questions are complex, and they point to race-based slavery and conceptions of gender as well as to the significance of Catholic and Protestant beliefs. This chapter examines the origins of laws on intermarriage in the British colonies, paying particular attention to slavery and gender. Then we turn to French and Spanish colonies to consider how laws on interracial sex and marriage differed from those in the British colonies, and to assess the role of religion in influencing those differences.

The British Colonies: Slavery, Gender, and Laws Regulating Interracial Sex and Marriage

Two factors begin to account for the origins of prohibitions of interracial sex and marriage in the British colonies: race-based slavery and notions of gender. In part, laws on interracial sex and marriage originated from the unprecedented development in the Americas of race-based slavery.[10] To be sure, every culture that legalized slavery faced the problem of clarifying the legal status of children born from sexual and marital unions between enslaved and free persons: were such children "free" or "enslaved"? But the shift to race-based slavery significantly complicated the issue in that one's legal status as "free" or "enslaved" potentially became visible in one's body. Whereas the enslavement of persons having similar phenotypes did not readily demarcate "enslaved" and "free" according to physical appearance (for example, Roman enslavement of Greeks), the advent of racial slavery presented a new way to identify members of each group. Or rather, race-based slavery presented a new way for people to make assumptions about who was who: an "African" would always be "enslaved," and an English person would always be "free."[11] A child born from one English parent and one African parent thus represented a mixed category—called "mulatto"—that was neither "white" nor "black," which confused the legal status of "free" and "enslaved." Colonists thus attempted to eliminate the possibility of "mixed-race" individuals by enacting laws that punished white-black couples for having children or attempted to prevent the union altogether. As historian Winthrop Jordan observes, "the separation of slaves from free men depended on a clear demarcation of the races, and the presence of mulattoes blurred this essential distinction. Accordingly, [the white colonist] made every effort to nullify the effects of racial intermixture. By classifying the mulatto as a Negro he was in effect denying that intermixture had occurred at all."[12] Laws punishing interracial unions therefore theoretically aimed to discourage the birth of mixed-race children in order to retain racial distinctions as a means of preserving the legal status of "slave" and "free"—to keep these most discrete categories separate.

British colonial laws on interracial sex and marriage were also intertwined with colonial notions of gender. Early colonial laws especially targeted English women for having sexual relations with African men, both in and out of wedlock. Children born to unmarried, indentured white women presented troubling financial and legal problems for early colonists.[13] If the father was unavailable to provide for the child's upbringing, was the woman's master then required to support her children, and if so, how was he to be compensated for that support? And what of a child born to an indentured English woman and an enslaved African man? Certainly an enslaved father receiving no compensation for his labors could not support his child. Early colonial laws resolved the financial aspect of illegitimate children born to indentured women by requiring the mother to labor for additional years beyond her original term of indenture, and also by consigning her children to serve until they reached adulthood. Maryland was one of the first colonies to address the situation of mixed-race babies born to unwed parents.[14] The colony resolved both issues—the compensation of the master and the legal status of the child—by enacting a law that punished indentured English women both for their marriage to enslaved African men and for any resulting offspring. Although the 1664 law did not expressly prohibit intermarriage, it did make it an unappealing option: "whatsoever freeborne woman shall intermarry with any slave," the statute declared, "shall serve the master of such slave during the life of her husband; and . . . all the issues of such freeborne women, so married, shall be slaves as their fathers were."[15]

Such laws reveal underlying cultural presumptions, including the dependency of English women, who were deemed unable to care for their children without a man's financial support, and also the expectation that, if not threatened with punishment, women were likely to make foolish choices, such as consorting with enslaved men. Further, Maryland's law reinforced colonial conceptions of the appropriateness—and the natural-ness—of white male dominance, thus reflecting English legislators' joint mission to retain dominance over English girls and women as well as over all Africans—enslaved or free. White male beliefs about race and gender, as well as belief in their own right to rule, thus formed the central assump-tions behind, as well as the goals of, laws regulating interracial sex and mar-riage. And these laws empowered English males to fulfill these aims. They enabled English slaveholders to benefit from the labor both of the inden-tured English woman, at least throughout her enslaved husband's lifetime, and of her offspring, who were demarcated as nonwhite and condemned to slavery in perpetuity. And as with all other laws pertaining to slavery, these regulations gave white men absolute control over black men.

Changes to slave law further ensured white male racial and gender dominance. Maryland's 1664 law remained consistent with the traditional English law, in which the children arising from unions between enslaved men and free women inherited the legal status of their fathers.[16] But else-where, colonial legislators turned traditional slave law on its head. In 1662 the Virginia legislature contravened centuries of slave law by ruling that "Children got by an Englishman upon a Negro woman shall be bond or free according to the condition of the mother."[17] With this one seemingly small change, colonial legislators reshaped slave law to benefit forever the white slaveholder, condemning the child to lifelong slavery, and reserving the privilege of parenting for free whites. Further, the change not only ab-solved the slaveholder from all sexual relations—even rape—with African girls and women, but it also made unions with them all the more attractive to slave-owning English men, for any resulting offspring became the man's property. This transformation in law, in which the legal status of offspring derived from the mother's status, replaced centuries of legislative tradition, and it became the standard practice in American slave law from the colonial era through Emancipation. The consequences for girls and women of both races were far-reaching and formidable. English women having children by enslaved men lost these children to slavery, and African women were stripped of any protections from the predations of white or enslaved men.

Intersecting notions of race and gender—including both masculinity and femininity—thus influenced legislation on interracial sex and marriage and contributed to the intensity of English hostility toward these unions. At every turn, laws on interracial sex and marriage reinforced the emerging ideology of separateness—not only the notion of the disparateness of the categories of enslaved and free, but also that of the distinct and radical difference between English and African. Early statutes punishing interracial sex and marriage thus anticipated what would later become a far more elaborate ideology of racial separateness or, put another way, an ideology of the perverseness of interracial—and especially, black-white—unions.[18] A 1691 Virginia law conveyed well the emergent animosity toward the unions between English and African persons, and most especially toward their hybrid offspring. The statute famously stated:

> And for the prevention of that abominable mixture and spurious issue which hereafter may increase in this dominion, as well by negroes, mulattoes, and Indians intermarrying with English, or other white women, as by their unlawful accompanying with one another, Be it enacted by the authoritie aforesaid, and It is hereby enacted, That for the time to come, whatsoever English or other white man or woman being free shall intermarry with a negro, mulatto, or Indian man or woman bond or free shall within three months after such marriage be banished and removed from this dominion forever, and that the justices of each respective countie within this dominion make it their particular care, that this act be put in effectuall execution.[19]

Deeming interracial children as an "abominable mixture and spurious issue," and forever banishing their white parents from the colony, Virginia legislators left no doubt about their revulsion for race-mixing and their desire to keep separate categories separate.

Although Virginia's law theoretically punished white women and white men for intermarriage with black persons and Native Americans, early civil laws on interracial sexuality did not generally condemn or penalize nonmarital relationships between white men and African women.[20] Implicit in the failure to punish such unions and to denounce them with the same vehemence as those between white women and black men are several key colonial assumptions about gender. Underlying the legislature's hostility toward racial hybridity was an almost neurotic anxiety about white femininity: the law implied that white girls and women were dependent, sexually untrustworthy, and in need of the protection of white males. And perhaps most troubling, black girls and women were so insignificant as to merit no attention at all.[21] The statute thus inscribed gender inequalities in law: black females were not worthy of protection by white men in the way that white females were, for sexual availability was the hallmark of black femininity. Sexual domination and exploitation of African girls and women was thus expected and assumed. In addition, the law implied that although white girls and women might make foolish sexual choices, they possessed a level of virtue that black females never had and were therefore worthy of white male protection. Black girls and women, on the other hand, deserved no such protection and were in fact available for any male sexual advances. For both black and white females, these laws sanctioned and maximized white male freedom and dominance and female dependence.

The law also conveyed colonial notions of masculinity. According to this paradigm, white men were independent and dominant over all women and nonwhite males, and black men threatened the safety of white females and thus needed to be kept in check by white men. As Kathleen M. Brown observes, such statutes "aimed at severing the ties of masculinity that bound enslaved and servant men together." In addition to protecting white girls and women from African male sexuality, these laws also endeavored to limit African men's "access to white women," and to deny "to enslaved men a component of white masculinity that brought with it patriarchal status and privileges."[22] Laws punishing or prohibiting sex and marriage across the color line conveyed the white male colonial right to establish and assert supremacy over all of their charges.

In the British colonies laws banning and punishing interracial sex and marriage emerged in the context of race-based slavery. The laws purported to retain racial and legal distinctions between "African" and "English," and "enslaved" and "free," though as we have seen, this aim was more rhetorical than actual. Moreover, the laws directly connected to English notions about gender and, most especially, about the dependence and sexual purity of white girls and women. Yet, this pattern of laws regulating interracial sex and marriage was not universal throughout the Americas. On the contrary, a very different situation developed in Spanish colonies. Spanish, French, and Portuguese cultures in the Americas, in fact, were rumored to tolerate and even encourage interracial marriage. Analysis of the Catholic colonies highlights the role of religion in laws on interracial marriage and, more specifically, the differences between Protestants and Catholics in laws and attitudes on intermarriage.

The French and Spanish Colonies: Intermarriage Restrictions and Catholic Protest

In his 1918 article "The Beginnings of Miscegenation," African American historian Carter Woodson called upon a belief long held among Americans that the Spanish, Portuguese, and French possessed a greater tolerance for marriages between whites and blacks than the English. The peoples of Spain, Portugal, and France freely mixed with African-descended persons in the New World, he contended, and "miscegenation had its best chance among the French." But "among the English the situation was decidedly different." "It was not that miscegenation occurred less frequently among the English," Woodson insisted, but rather, unlike the Spanish and Portuguese, with the English "there remained the natural tendency so to denounce these unions as eventually to restrict the custom."[23] A considerable body of scholarship further substantiates Woodson's observations.[24] Yet despite the purported proclivities of the French to take non-European lovers, in 1724—around the same time that the last of the thirteen British colonies had banned intermarriage—France enacted its *Code Noir*. Historian Sue Peabody describes the *Code* as a French legal system developed in 1685 that was "designed to bring Catholicism to the heathen and curb abuses of cruel masters across the sea" in French colonies.[25] The *Code* banned marriage between "white subjects of either sex from contracting marriage with blacks," and this law was applied in, among other regions, Louisiana.[26] Spain retained this tradition even when it governed Louisiana during the eighteenth century.

In addition, although Spain, during more than two hundred years of governance, never enacted its own laws explicitly prohibiting concubinage or marriage between whites and blacks, mulattoes, or Indians in North American regions, Spanish colonies did impose nonracial restrictions on marriage that effectively limited interracial marriage. In 1776 the Spanish Crown issued the *Pragmática Sanción*, a decree aimed at curbing "unequal" marriages between persons of different social classes within Spain. Since the late Middle Ages, "unequal" marriages had posed a problem in European countries, due to the Catholic Church's emphasis on the individual's freedom to choose a marriage partner, and the state's conflicting interest in preserving the assets of wealthy families.[27] The edict attempted to prevent such marriages by penalizing violators with disinheritance and by requiring parental consent for parties under the age of twenty-five and for those whose parents lent them financial support. Two years later, Spain extended the law to its overseas possessions.[28] Although the decree did not expressly restrict interracial marriage—indeed, it excluded "Mulattoes, Negroes, Coyotes and other Castas and similar races"—in actuality it functioned to do precisely that.[29] Because the decree aimed at restricting marriage across class lines, interracial marriages were inevitably affected, for in the Americas social classes tended to divide along racial lines. Historian Patricia Seed observes that the "tripartite division" of Spaniard, Indian, and black in Spanish colonial culture within the Americas "echoed the peninsular division of status among nobles, plebeians, and slaves. Only in the New World, however, did all ethnic Spaniards consider themselves noble, see the Indians as plebeian, and the blacks as slaves. Thus in the New World, without fundamental alteration, Spanish categories of status came to represent racial difference."[30] Among the enslaved or laboring classes, Africans and Native Americans had few financial assets, while "whites" tended to be wealthier and to rank among the higher classes. Limits on interclass marriages thus invariably constrained interracial unions.

In 1805 the Council of the Indies imposed an additional law that more deliberately endeavored to restrict interracial marriages. The council declared that couples in which one party was "of known nobility or known purity of blood" must request permission from a civil official to marry "negroes, mulattoes and the other castes."[31] The Cuban government reiterated the council's decree in 1806, and four years later, the viceroy of Mexico similarly declared that all whites, regardless of socioeconomic position, must seek permission to marry members of the castas or nonwhite races. Yet it is important to emphasize that under these laws, marriage between whites and persons of color did require special approval, but it was not prohibited in the Spanish colonies as it was in the French and British colonies.[32]

Also important to note are the actions of certain Catholic priests who married interracial couples in spite of legal bans or restrictions, or who advocated intermarriage to civil authorities. Historian Martha Hodes's analysis of court records in colonial Maryland reveals that in 1681, nearly twenty years after the assembly had enacted its law punishing white women who married and bore children to enslaved African men, a Catholic indentured servant woman named Irish Nell—servant of the third Lord Baltimore—married a slave known as Negro Charles. A Catholic priest by the name of Hubbert presided over the wedding ceremony, and Nell, Charles, and their children lived out their lives as slaves to a Catholic family.[33] Although the priest's marriage of Irish Nell and Negro Charles did not contravene the law (since the marriage was not prohibited), his action is significant in that he performed the marriage at all. Hubbert's actions raise questions—to which we later return—about why he would have agreed to marry a couple who, in accordance with the law, could have been penalized for their marriage.

Louisiana also offers an example of a priest acting contrary to the law. In his lectures on French colonial Louisiana history, nineteenth-century historian Charles Étienne Arthur Gayarré noted that one of the reasons that French Creoles ousted Spanish governor Don Antonio de Ulloa from New Orleans in 1766 had to do with allegations as to his and his chaplain's disregard for this law. According to Gayarré, the Creoles claimed that Ulloa "had the sacrament of marriage conferred under his own roof by his chaplain, on a white man and a black female slave, without the permission of the curate, without any of the forms or solemnities established by the church, in contempt of the decrees of the Council of Trent, and against the precise directions of the civil and canon laws which governed the colony."[34] In this case, the priest's marriage of the couple did violate Louisiana's civil laws, which were enacted under French colonial rule. Similarly, historian Charles Edwards O'Neill observes in his meticulously documented study of church-state relations in early Louisiana, that in several Louisiana towns in the early 1700s, "missionaries gave the Church's blessing to unions between Frenchmen and Indian girls, even though in certain cases the latter were not Christian. Nevertheless, these interracial marriages in Louisiana were against the express will of the secular authority."[35] Such situations not only point to a greater tolerance of interracial marriage among Catholics, but, as with the marriage of Irish Nell and Negro Charles in the previous century, also raise the question of why Catholic priests would agree to marry interracial couples in the first place.

Across the continent in Spanish California, another interesting situation arose involving clerical advocacy of intermarriage. Historian Antonia Castañeda observes that during California's early colonial period, interracial marriage became a "political strategy and an instrument of conquest promoted by Church and State."[36] When Spanish soldiers and missionaries arrived in California in 1769, soldiers perpetrated relentless sexual assaults against Native American women. In direct contradiction to the theological and moral values articulated by priests, the soldiers' attacks threatened to destroy the soul-saving efforts of Catholic missionaries. An escalating conflict between missionaries and governors over who held the authority to punish the rapists finally led Father Junipero Serra to travel to Mexico City in 1773 to discuss the matter with the viceroy. Serra proposed a novel remedy to the problem. Appealing to what Castañeda terms a "colonial tradition" of intermarriage between Spaniards and Native "noblewomen," Serra suggested that soldiers be rewarded for marrying neophyte Native women.[37] This policy, he contended, would protect Native Americans, promote Catholic sexual morality, develop and stabilize sparsely populated regions, and resolve the conflict of authority between church and state.

The Mexican viceroy agreed and established a policy whereby a Spaniard would receive an animal upon marrying a female Native neophyte, two cows after laboring on the mission for a year, and a parcel of land thereafter. Interracial marriage thus became a Catholic strategy for ending sexual violence and promoting settlement.[38] The intermarriage policy served larger ends as well. Serra envisioned interracial marriage as a strategy for both Christianizing and Hispanicizing Native Americans. By making Catholic marriage a religious and political tool for conversion, Spanish missions shaped Indian sexual and marital practices to reflect Christian and Spanish values: male control of women, female virginity before marriage, monogamy, marriage "without divorce, and a severely repressive code of sexual norms."[39] Although Serra's intermarriage policy did result in a few marriages, by 1795—little more than a generation after Serra's journey to Mexico City—the church "reversed its position" and stopped granting land to soldiers who married Christianized women.[40] Despite its overall failure and the small number of marriages resulting from the policy, the fact that the intermarriage strategy originated in the mind of a Catholic priest and became the policy of a Catholic state demonstrates how interracial marriage could serve both ecclesiastical and civil needs. Moreover, it highlights a tradition of Catholic advocacy of and tolerance for interracial marriage.

One final example presents a compelling story of a cleric's somewhat ambivalent activism on behalf of an interracial couple. In 1852 Archbishop Antonio Maria Claret of the Archdiocese of Havana penned a heartbreaking letter to Jose G. de la Concha, governor of Cuba. Claret explained to the governor that he knew of whites who had lived for many years in concubinage with "mulattas," with whom they had several children. The conflicted archbishop lamented the situation: "I would say that those who are from distinct classes and [who] do not have any compelling reason [such as previous children or a pregnancy] should not [be allowed to] marry. But if they have lived together many years in peace, and having eight or more children, and are so upset that they threaten to commit suicide if they are not permitted to marry, to impede them from doing so is an intolerable thing for a Prelate who wants to comply with the law; this is tyranny, as they say." Archbishop Claret pleaded with Governor la Concha to make an exception to the law in situations such as this, and he threatened to take the matter up with the superior governor of Madrid. "I am certain that he will accommodate me," the archbishop wrote, "for he has many times offered and has given me very clear proof of the sincerity of his promises."[41] The case eventually went before the Supreme Tribunal of Havana, which decreed that the law restricting interracial marriage would apply only to noblepersons who desired to marry a person of another race.

After considering the evidence of greater tolerance for interracial marriage in Spanish regions, which had no explicit bans on intermarriage, we are still left with unanswered questions. What accounts for the differences between British and Spanish colonies in laws on intermarriage? Why did Catholic France impose laws banning interracial marriage, while Spanish Catholic colonies restricted but did not ban it? And why did some Catholic priests flout the local restrictions or customs and marry interracial couples or advocate for their marriage? What connection might any of this have to Catholic beliefs? The explanations lie in a larger historical drama between church and state, and in the concomitant Catholic theologies of marriage. In short, in Catholic colonies there was a conflict between ecclesiastical and civil powers over the legal authority to regulate marriage and to impose marital impediments. In the eyes of the church, the question of authority to establish marriage law rested on the very nature of marriage itself, which explains why some priests insisted on celebrating marriages between racial groups, and why civil authorities sometimes resisted it.

Reformation-Era Precedents for Conflicts over Interracial Marriage in the Americas

Frank Tannenbaum's 1944 book *Slave and Citizen*, a comparison of the treatment of blacks under the slave regimes of the American South and Latin America, provides a useful structure for framing these issues. Tannenbaum examines ideas about the moral value of the enslaved persons in these regions, contending that "wherever the law accepted the doctrine of the moral personality of the slave and made possible the gradual achievement of freedom implicit in such a doctrine, the slave system was abolished peacefully. Where the slave was denied recognition as a moral person and was therefore considered incapable of freedom, the abolition of slavery was accomplished by force—that is, by revolution."[42] While many of his claims have, for a number of good reasons, been soundly challenged, Tannenbaum's analysis recognizes the significance of religious differences between the United States and Latin America on the development of each region's laws.[43] His question about the implications of the moral value of enslaved persons, and the ties of such ideas to religious belief, are instructive for my analysis. He observes that "Spanish law, custom, and tradition were transferred to [Spanish] America and came to govern the position of the Negro slave," and that "the Catholic doctrine of the equality of all men in the sight of God" influenced Spanish law, particularly its openness toward. manumission. In contrast, Anglo U.S. law tended to restrict the possibility of manumission and the rights of slaves more generally. Moreover, he contends, "the contrast between the United States and British West Indian slave law, on the one hand, and the Spanish and Portuguese, on the other, was further heightened by the different role of the church in the life of the Negro. The slaves in the British West Indies were almost completely denied the privileges of Christianity."[44]

The Catholic-Protestant and Latino-Anglo distinctions that Tannenbaum highlights reveal a theological framework underlying the Catholic clerical support of interracial marriages, as well as the laws against intermarriage in Catholic regions. He recognizes that theological differences between Catholics and Protestants had a considerable effect on the underlying notions of humanity and human worth that were written into law in Catholic and Protestant regions. In French Louisiana and the Spanish colonies, the legal restrictions on marriage exemplified a political tug-of-war between the Catholic Church and the Catholic state, and this conflict centered on *which* institution held the authority to establish marriage law. During the eighteenth-century in Europe's Catholic nations, the church's authority was dwindling in the competition with the state for temporal power, and this trend was transmitted to the Americas. As historian Charles Cutter notes, although the church's influence remained strong in the Spanish colonies throughout the colonial era, still, "the eighteenth century was a time of slow but inexorable growth of secular over religious aspects of colonial administration." Significantly, Cutter suggests the ways that law functioned as a principal area of contention between secular and ecclesiastical authority. He remarks: "Legal administration mirrored the general trend, and in many ways it became the vehicle for the crown's attacks on the prerogatives of the church. Particularly important was the curtailment of a special legal jurisdiction that had long been one of the traditional sources of autonomy, and through a series of decrees the church lost many of its privileges during the course of the century."[45] Increasingly, civil authorities in the Spanish Americas emerged as the victors in the tug-of-war with the church. Marriage became one of the principal places in which this conflict played out, and as anthropologist Verena Stolcke notes, interracial marriages became in effect "the direct province of the civil authorities."[46]

Historian Patricia Seed confirms this trend. According to her study of marriage in sixteenth-century Mexico, the Catholic Church initially played the role of defender of "matrimonial liberty." In some cases the church aided young couples who wished to marry when their families attempted to halt their marriage, and in other cases priests and ordinaries advocated on behalf of one party who did not wish to marry whomever the family had chosen to be his or her spouse. Based upon formulations developed at the Council of Trent, the church promoted freedom in the choice of marriage partners and strongly opposed "parental vetoes" in their children's spousal choices. However, when "faced with a decline in their authority to enforce its traditional marriage practices, officials of the Catholic Church in Mexico gradually began to modify the ways they intervened in marriage conflict cases." By 1769, "depriving a child of the liberty required by marriage was no longer treated by church courts as unreasonable conduct," and consequently, force acquired a greater role in resolving marital disputes. During the eighteenth century "as interracial marriage increased . . . more and more church officials came to favor preventing socially unequal marriages—those that were racially mixed as well as those between Spaniards of different status." Moreover, with the crowning of Charles III in Spain in 1759, "curtailing the independence of the Catholic Church in the New World became a royal project."[47]

The Spanish government in the New World—like that of France—thus sometimes took a stance over the regulation of marriage that was decidedly in conflict with Catholic marriage doctrine. The Maryland priest's marriage of Irish Nell and Negro Charles, the decision of Louisiana governor Don Antonio de Ulloa allow a priest to celebrate an interracial marriage under his own roof, Father Serra's plea for intermarriage in California, and Archbishop Claret's plea to the Cuban governor all point to a deepening conflict between church and state over the right to control the institution of marriage. More important, these situations hint at the role of theological doctrine in explaining differences in both laws on and attitudes toward interracial marriage in Catholic and Protestant regions. Theological understandings of marriage entailed serious consequences for its governance: namely, was it the right of the state or the right of the church to determine legal impediments to marriage?

Indeed, church-state conflicts over interracial marriage in Catholic colonies having race-based slavery have everything to do with the Catholic theology of marriage and, most especially, with the pronouncements on marriage from the Council of Trent in 1563. As the first comprehensive articulation of Catholic doctrine and administration of marriage, the twenty-fourth and final session of the council articulated two key statements that served potentially to put the Catholic Church and Catholic states (and later, Protestant states) into conflict with one another over the legal regulation of marriage. First, its fourth canon pronounced anathema on anyone who affirmed that "the Church could not establish impediments dissolving marriage; or that she has erred in establishing them." Second, the council stated that certain "temporal lords and magistrates" had compelled men and women under their jurisdiction, "especially such as are rich, or who have expectations of a great inheritance, to contract marriage against their inclination with those whom the said lords or magistrates may prescribe unto them." The council therefore forbade secular rulers, "under pain of anathema to be ipso facto incurred, that they put no constraint, in any way whatever, either directly or indirectly, on those subject to them, or any others whomsoever, so as to hinder them from freely contracting marriage."[48] More important, while the council did affirm its impediment of marriages proposed between Christians and the unbaptized, it did not impose any impediment on marriages between members of different races.

AS WE WILL SEE, this situation was very different for Protestants. Moreover, theological differences over marriage doctrine accounted in part for the theological schisms that separated Protestants from Catholics during the Reformation. To understand the Catholic Church's position on ecclesiastical versus civil regulation of marriage law, we must first be familiar with its sacramental theology of marriage, for the "sacred character" of marriage is key to grasping the Catholic conception of the relationship of marriage to church and state. Moreover, Protestant theologies of marriage resulted in the possibility of an entirely different position on the legal regulation of interracial marriage. As a result, both groups found themselves potentially at odds over legal restrictions or bans on interracial marriage.

[3] Church Authority or States' Rights?
Protestant and Catholic Theologies of Marriage

Several months before he filed a petition with the California Supreme Court, Catholic attorney Daniel Marshall explained his intention to make Catholic doctrine the basis of his legal challenge against California's antimiscegenation statutes. In his April 1947 letter to Los Angeles auxiliary bishop Joseph McGucken, Marshall stated that "the Church recognizes the right of the State to legislate in certain respects concerning marriage, on account of its civil effect, e.g., alimony, inheritance and other like matters. When the State enacts laws inimical to the laws of the Church, practically denying her right to protect the sacred character of marriage, she cannot allow her children to submit to such enactments. She respects the requirements of the State for the marriage of its citizens as long as they are in keeping with the dignity and Divine purpose of marriage."[1]

Marshall's letter boldly proclaimed the church's right to oppose civil marriage laws should they violate in some way "the sacred character of marriage." Although he excluded this assertion in the final briefs that he filed, his statement in fact pointed to an important distinction between Protestants and Catholics. Protestant and Catholic believers disagreed over the nature and regulation of marriage. Protestants viewed it as a sacred institution to be subject to civil laws. Catholics, on the other hand, believed marriage to be a holy sacrament, a spiritual union between a woman and a man. As a supernatural institution, marriage therefore had to be carefully regulated by the church. The church granted secular governments control over the civil aspects of marriage, but on issues such as impediments, it claimed authority. In the United States where there was no national church, did the Catholic Church have the right to determine legal impediments to marriage? And was not the individual's freedom to choose whom to marry a critical aspect of the "sacred character" of marriage?

Marshall's legal opponent, Los Angeles county counsel Charles Stanley, proclaimed the states' right to enact and regulate marriage law. While recognizing that the individual's freedom to marry "undoubtedly" constituted "one of the liberties guaranteed by the Fourteenth Amendment," Stanley, like virtually all the attorneys and judges before him who argued for antimiscegenation laws, asserted that "the State has full control over the subject of the marriage of its citizens, including the determination of who may enter into that relationship."[2] Stanley's briefs cited nearly twenty legal precedents that declared the states' right to regulate marriage. His arguments against a white person's right to marry someone of another race were thus consistent with the position historically offered by his legal predecessors. Moreover, this response exemplified the traditional Protestant position on marriage, namely, the view that the state—and not the church—held the right to enact and enforce laws on marriage and to adjudicate disputes over its laws.

This chapter examines Catholic and Protestant theologies of marriage in order to demonstrate how they historically placed Catholics and Protestants at odds over the authority of church or state to impose marital impediments and regulate marriage law. The Catholic Church's sacramental theology of marriage granted the church jurisdiction over marriage and marital impediments, and it elevated the importance of the individual's freedom to choose a marriage partner. American Protestants, on the other hand, vested the state with the primary authority to establish marriage law. Indeed, these differences made it possible for Catholics and Protestants to hold contradictory positions with regard to interracial marriage. This chapter explains how these differences evolved in the American context, from the creation of colonial marriage law to nineteenth-century debates over polygamy. When finally during the twentieth century American Catholics increasingly began to proclaim the right of the individual to choose whom to marry, they thus found themselves in conflict with Protestants—particularly white southern Protestants—over antimiscegenation laws.

Catholic Theology of Marriage

In the fifth chapter of the letter to the church at Ephesus, the writer—usually thought to be Saint Paul—offered one of the most important pronouncements on marriage and the proper relationship between husband and wife in all of Christian texts. After prescribing that wives be subject to their husbands and that husbands love their wives, the writer likened the marital relationship to that of Christ and the body of believers in the church. Quoting the famous passage from Genesis in which the writer characterized the relationship between Adam and Eve—the prototype of all marriages—as the two becoming "one flesh," the writer then offered a statement that has been the subject of debate ever since: "This is a great sacrament," the Catholic version of Ephesians 5:32 reads, "but I speak in Christ and in the Church."[3] The "sacrament" to which he refers, and which the King James Version translates as "mystery," is the sacrament of marriage.[4]

From this statement and from some of Christ's statements in the Gospels originate the Catholic theology of marriage.[5] Soundly denounced by Protestant thinkers, the sacramental theology of marriage established two concepts of significant consequence to later Catholic perspectives on interracial marriage. First, it made an individual's freedom to marry the person of her or his choosing a paramount value; second, it established the church as the sole entity with the authority to determine which circumstances might impede one person from marrying another. Analysis of the Catholic theology of marriage demonstrates how this is so. This section first describes what, according to Catholic theology, constitutes a sacrament, and how and why marriage is understood as such, particularly within the shifting context prior to the Second Vatican Council. It then explores how the individual's freedom to choose a spouse and the church's authority to regulate marriage factor into this theology. Last it considers the implications of these two elements for Catholic perspectives on interracial marriage.

Although the church formally recognized marriage as a sacrament in the Middle Ages, it began to clarify its marriage doctrines and procedures during the mid-sixteenth century. During the same era that European nations encountered new peoples on faraway continents, thereby commencing some of the most formative clashes of cultures in history, the Roman Church experienced cultural skirmishes at home, where questions about marriage loomed large in the conflicts. Inconsistent application of marriage rules, clandestine marriages, the doctrine of clerical marriage among the rebel Protestants, and the contest between England and the Vatican over Henry VIII's scandalous marriages and divorces forced the sixteenth-century church to establish clear policies on holy matrimony. The Council of Trent (1545–1563) clarified the church's position on Protestant beliefs about marriage—pronouncing anathemas upon "heretical" views of marriage—and proposed a number of reforms to address problems within the church's marriage procedures. The council upheld the traditional definition of sacraments as "outward signs of inner grace, instituted by Christ for our sanctification," and also reaffirmed the church's view that matrimony was one of the seven sacraments.[6]

According to the 1910 *Catholic Encyclopedia* entry on the sacrament of marriage—perhaps one of the clearest explications of sacramental theology, and an appropriate source for twentieth-century marriage doctrine prior to the Second Vatican Council—the "following elements belong to a sacrament: it must be a sacred religious rite instituted by Christ; this rite must be a sign of interior sanctification; it must confer this interior sanctification or Divine grace; this effect of Divine grace must be produced, not only in conjunction with the respective religious act, but through it." Although the church regards God as the creator of the institution of marriage, it also views matrimony as a rite instituted by Christ, for Jesus's condemnation of divorce and characterization of marriage as a lifelong monogamous union elevated marriage to the level of a sacrament. In the church's view, the intimation in Ephesians that marriage symbolized the union between Christ and the church further imbues it with sacramental significance. Perhaps the most important aspect of a sacrament, however, is the idea that it confers grace, or sanctification, to baptized recipients. The *Catholic Encyclopedia* described matrimonial grace as that which "gives the graces necessary for those who are to rear children in the love and fear of God" and which "sanctifies the procreation and education of children."[7] Intimately connected to the notion of original sin—which the *Encyclopedia* defines as "the consequence" of Adam's sin, "the hereditary stain with which we are born"—marriage doctrine prior to the Second Vatican Council (1962–1965) emphasized the idea that divine grace is necessary for couples in order to atone for the transmission of sin and death from one generation to the next, which occurs through procreation.[8] One writer contends that marriage is "intended primarily by the Author of life to perpetuate His creative act and to beget children of God; its secondary ends are mutual society and help, and a *lawful remedy for concupiscence*."[9] As the only legitimate venue for sexual expression, then, Christian matrimony confers grace by pardoning parents for the transmission of sin to their child.[10]

In these ways, Catholic doctrine depicts marriage as holy and sacramental. And because marriage between baptized Christians is a sacred institution, it is the responsibility of the Catholic Church to regulate it, protecting it from the inapt laws of the worldly state, although, as we see later, the church does admit the states' authority over certain aspects of marriage.

Sex, State, and Catholic Marriage

Although the Council of Trent clarified many procedural issues relating to matrimony and affirmed marriage as a divinely inaugurated, indissoluble contract made by two freely consenting, baptized parties, the full explication of the Catholic theology of marriage has unfolded since Trent in canon law and papal encyclicals.[11] With the state's increasing control over marriage in Europe and North America during the late nineteenth and early twentieth centuries—and the rise of eugenics laws, civil marriage, and divorce—canonists and popes alike endeavored to explain and clarify the church's views on marriage. Two papal encyclicals were particularly significant in articulating the Catholic position: Leo XIII's 1880 *Arcanum* and Pius XI's 1930 *Casti Connubii*. Further, the church revised its canon marriage law in 1917. Two key points expressed in *Arcanum* played a special role in the eventual Catholic position on interracial marriage: the individual's freedom to choose a marriage partner, and the church's authority to regulate impediments to marriage. Both of these issues bore implications for private and public matters: the individual's sexuality and personal choices, and the church's relationship with the state.

The consensual nature of the contract—that is, an individual's consent to marry the person he or she chooses—constitutes a critical aspect of the Catholic theology of marriage. Moreover, the pre–Vatican II Catholic vision of sexuality—marriage as a "lawful remedy for concupiscence"—necessitates this free choice. American priest and moral theologian Joseph Francis Doherty summarized the issue in this way. In marriage, a man and a woman "mutually confer and accept the perpetual and exclusive right to the use of each other's body for the purpose of performing acts which are in themselves suitable for the begetting of children. To determine freely one person as a marriage partner to the exclusion of all others is what is known as freedom of choice. From the very nature of the marriage contract this is necessary if the parties concerned are to be held responsible for fulfilling the burdens of marriage." The "concession of rights over one's body for the performance of conjugal acts" must therefore be a primary consideration in choosing a marriage partner, and it required that the individual's choice be his or her own. Indeed, Doherty stated, it "demands unimpeded freedom." Mutual sexual attraction—or at least, consenting to sexual intercourse with that particular person after marriage—is necessary to ensure both (sexual intercourse for) procreation and lifelong fidelity. Individuals must be free to choose a marriage partner whom they find sexually attractive. "No other human power," Doherty asserted, "can supply this necessary element of the marital consent except the parties themselves."[12]

Louis J. Nau, canon law specialist on marriage, confirmed Doherty's assertions and offered two additional reasons for the free choice of spouse: the responsibilities of parenthood and the lifelong character of marriage. The "indissolubility of the marriage bond," he stated, "demands that freedom of choice of a life partner be fully protected." Because Catholic doctrine obliges the couple to remain together until death, their individual and joint commitment requires that they freely select the person with whom they would spend their lives. In addition, the spiritual and domestic lives of a couple's children demand that both parents freely choose to be together. The "eternal happiness of married people" and of their family relate closely to the careful choice of spouse. As such, Nau observed, the decision to marry a specific individual constituted "a distinct matter of conscience for Christians." Accordingly, he contended, "such supernatural considerations cannot be left to the play of politics" in the secular state.[13] Sexuality, the indissolubility of marriage, the happiness of the couple, and the future harmony of the family, then, require Catholics' unfettered freedom of choice in marriage partners.

Liberty to choose a marriage partner implies that individuals freely select a specific person. Indeed, in *Casti Connubii*, Pius XI stated that consenting to marry a specifically chosen person was necessary for a marriage to be legitimate. Quoting from canon marriage law, the pontiff wrote that marriage "arises only from the free consent of each of the spouses; and this free act of the will, by which each party hands over and accepts those rights which are proper to the state of marriage, is so necessary to constitute true marriage that the place of it cannot be supplied by any human power." However, he continued, this freedom "regards only the question whether the contracting parties really wish to enter upon matrimony or to marry this particular person."[14] Free consent signified a person's consent to marry a specific person. According to Joseph Doherty, Pius's assertion made the freedom to marry that particular person as important as the freedom to choose whether or not to marry at all.[15]

The concept of free consent bears consequences for the state as well as for the individual. It suggests not only that no outside party may compel one person to marry another, but also that no external party may prohibit a marriage between two eligible individuals who wanted to marry each other.

So long as "the laws of God and of the Church are not violated," Doherty declared, no one should be either forced into a marriage or impeded from a marriage with a chosen person. "To impede unjustly the marriage of a person with another person of his own choice," he insisted, "is to violate a right that this person has to make the proper disposition of his whole life according to the dictate of his reason and in conformity with the Divine and Natural laws" (42).[16] The Catholic position on a person's free choice to marry thus raised significant questions about the church's views on civil marriage law and especially the authority of the state to restrict individuals' choices of spouse. As we saw earlier in the chapter, the church might balk at state restrictions on marriage, for it constituted part of what Nau referred to as the "supernatural order."

The "supernatural" character of marriage required the church's exclusive authority over the institution.[17] In its intimate connection to earthly and heavenly happiness, as well as to sin and redemption, the sacramental theology of marriage thus bears profound theological, if not soteriological, weight for the Catholic couple and their family. The church recognizes several legitimate vocations for Christians with regard to marital status: ordination (celibacy), religious life (membership in a religious order that may or may not allow the person to be married), marriage, or single life. For those who choose to marry, the human implications of Catholic marriage doctrine are considerable, for the salvation and righteous living of a significant portion of the body of Christ is at stake. In light of the theological significance of matrimony, the church has insisted on its authority to regulate marriage, specifically in regard to any legal restrictions that the secular state may seek to impose on Catholic citizens. Only the church may establish impediments to marriage.

The Council of Trent's session on marriage elaborated at length on the church's authority to regulate marriage over and against that of the state, especially in regard to individuals' free choice of spouses. "Temporal lords, or magistrates," the council declared, "shall not attempt anything contrary to the liberty of marriage," such as compelling wealthy citizens under their jurisdiction to marry someone "against their inclination with those [individuals] whom the said lords or magistrates may prescribe unto them." To "violate the liberty of matrimony" is "a thing especially execrable"; therefore, the council "enjoins on all . . . under pain of anathema," to "put no constraint, in any way whatever, either directly or indirectly, on those subject to them, or any others whomsoever, so as to hinder them from freely contracting marriage." If this declaration did not adequately proclaim the church's position, the twelfth canon certainly did: "If any one saith, that matrimonial causes do not belong to ecclesiastical judges; let him be anathema."[18]

Three centuries after the last session of the Council of Trent, Pope Leo XIII reaffirmed the church's authority over marriage in his 1880 encyclical, *Arcanum*. Writing in response to the French government's efforts to make marriage a civil institution, Leo observed that "all nations seem, more or less, to have forgotten the true notion and origin of marriage." Secular leaders, he lamented, "endeavor to deprive [marriage] of all holiness, and so bring it within the contracted sphere of those rights which, having been inspired by man, are ruled and administered by the civil jurisprudence of the community." Decrying the secular state's refusal to let the church have jurisdiction over matrimony, Leo proclaimed the sacred nature of marriage and the church's authority to regulate it: "Since marriage, then, is holy by its own power, in its own nature, and of itself, it ought not to be regulated and administered by the will of civic rulers, but by the divine authority of the Church, which alone in sacred matters professes the office of teaching. . . . [T]o decree and ordain concerning the sacrament is, by the will of Christ Himself, so much a part of the power and duty of the Church, that it is plainly absurd to maintain that even the very smallest fraction of such power has been transferred to the civil ruler."[19] Perhaps Leo overstated the Catholic position, for historically the church has recognized the rights of the state to administer certain legal aspects of marriage, such as the licensing and recording of marriages, restrictions of marriages between certain relatives, and settlement of property disputes. Canonist Louis Nau asserted that canon law specialists and theologians alike recognized the state's authority to regulate marriages of "the unbaptized," and the "joint control" by church and state over marriages between baptized and unbaptized persons.[20]

Yet the issues of joint control of church and state over marriage, and the secular authority over marriages of the "unbaptized," are complicated. "In practice," Nau observed, "the Church seems to concede to the State the right to place diriment impediments [i.e., those that render a marriage invalid] on the unbaptized."[21] But the very theology of marriage itself generates a certain degree of ambivalence on the church's position on secular authority over marriage. The ambivalence stems from two issues: the church's beliefs in the human right to marry, and in the sanctity of all— even non-Christian—marriages. The church affirms the right of all persons to marry, regardless of religious affiliation, regardless of state interests.

Canonists assert that "the right to marry is a natural right, not to be denied unless a valid prohibition of natural or ecclesiastical law can be proved." They mention only two impediments to marriage established by natural law: impotence/sterility, and mental deficiency.[22] Leo XIII expressed this same view in Rerum Novarum, his 1891 encyclical on labor and the secular state's responsibilities to its citizens. "No human law," he declared, "can abolish the natural and original right of marriage, nor in any way limit the chief and principal purpose of marriage ordained by God's authority from the beginning: 'increase and multiply.'" Leo went on to note that because the family unit flowing out of the matrimonial union preceded the secular state, "it has rights and duties peculiar to itself which are quite independent of the State."[23] Although his larger point had to do with the family's right to private property and the limits of the state in restricting those rights, Leo's statement articulated the underlying Catholic beliefs that all humans— even the unbaptized—possess the right to marry, that this right exists independently of any state-instituted rights, and that the state can restrict that right only for reasons supported by natural or ecclesiastical law.

Consequently, on the one hand, the church grants the state a limited authority to prohibit marriages, even those of Christians. On the other hand, it asserts a limited authority over marriages of non-Christians, for the church affirms the sanctity of all marriage. While it denies that marriages between non-Christians are vested with sacramental grace, it does concede their general sacredness and on this basis lays claim to regulating them. "Marriage," Leo XIII wrote, "has God for its Author," and "therefore there abides in it a something holy and religious." Leo then asserted that earlier popes had thus "affirmed not falsely nor rashly that a sacrament of marriage existed ever amongst the faithful and unbelievers."[24] Leo's comments suggest, then, that because marriage is sacred in and of itself, even marriage between the unbaptized should not be wholly subjected to civil regulation. Rather, canon law affirmed that marriage, as a "natural institution," was "subject to the divine natural law, whether the parties are Christians or not." Moreover, "Christ, with divine authority, restored marriage to its pristine purity, as regards unity and indissolubility, not for Christians alone but for all men." Indeed, the church claims "control of the contract, even when it is not a sacrament, provided one of the parties is baptized."[25]

The church's view of its authority to oppose state-imposed impediments to marriage, as well as its theology of the individual's freedom to choose a spouse, left the door open for Catholic intervention on behalf of couples whom secular governments prohibited from marrying. But its doctrines put it into conflict with non-Catholic nations. What right did the church have to insist on its authority over marriage in the United States—a nation that not only rejected its authority, but also historically viewed the Roman Church as the epitome of tyranny and whose understanding of marriage and its legal regulation had derived explicitly out of resistance to that church?

The Protestant Theology of Marriage

In its 1563 session on matrimony, the Council of Trent condemned the heretics and "impious men of this age" who rejected the sacramental theology of marriage. In its very first canon, the council decreed: "If any one saith, that matrimony is not truly and properly one of the seven sacraments of the evangelic law, (a sacrament) instituted by Christ the Lord; but that it has been invented by men in the Church; and that it does not confer grace; let him be anathema."[26] When the council issued this statement, the "impious men" included Protestant reformers representing a broad variety of theological perspectives. Despite differences on biblical interpretation, most early modern Protestants agreed that baptism and the Eucharist were the only sacraments. Marriage, though sacred, did not constitute one.[27]

Martin Luther proclaimed in 1520 that the notion of marriage as a sacrament was "without the least warrant of Scripture" and was instead "invented by men in the church who [were] carried away by their ignorance of both the word and the thing."[28] Several years later John Calvin similarly pondered, "what man in his sober senses" could regard marriage as a sacrament? "Marriage is alleged to be a good and holy ordinance of God," he continued, "so agriculture, architecture, shoemaking, and many other things, are legitimate ordinances of God, but they are not sacraments."[29] In England, marriage reforms came much more slowly than on the Continent. Yet by the time of the 1571 formulation of the Thirty-Nine Articles of Religion, English theologians affirmed that holy matrimony was "not to be counted for Sacraments of the Gospel."[30]

By stripping marriage of its sacramental status, European and English Protestants accomplished something that would bear directly upon the legal regulation of marriage and upon later conflicts with American Catholics over laws banning interracial marriage: if marriage was not a sacrament, then the Christian church did not possess the authority to establish marriage law. No church could determine the circumstances that might impede one person from marrying another. Rather, the Protestant theology of marriage relegated the legal jurisdiction over marriage to civil authorities. According to this perspective, the state, and only the state, was authorized to establish, enforce, and alter laws pertaining to marriage.

How specifically did the Protestant theology of marriage shape American marriage law? To what extent was civil government "secular" in the early colonies, insofar as Protestant magistrates made up the leadership of early American governments? What bearing did shifts in American conceptions of both the "state" and the state's authority to regulate marriage have upon marriage law? How did these issues affect interracial marriage?

Civil Authority, Protestant Marriage, and American Law

In the century following the Protestant reformations in Europe and England, British colonists in North America began to apply the Protestant theology of marriage to colonial marriage law. Although marriage law was far from uniform in the various colonies, yet from its earliest moments it assumed a Protestant perspective on marriage: the idea that marriage—at once a sacred and civil institution—was to be regulated by civil rather than by religious authorities. Colonial governments therefore claimed the right to stipulate, among other things, which marriages might be prohibited, including those between white and nonwhite persons. Indeed, the transfer of marriage law to civil authorities was so smooth that the uniqueness of the civil regulation of marriage has gone virtually unnoticed by colonial observers, historians, and legal scholars. University of Chicago marriage historian George Elliot Howard remarked in 1904 that the "causes which determined the establishment of civil marriage in the New England colonies" were difficult to pinpoint, and that "already in the middle of the eighteenth century colonial historians were at a loss to account for it."[31]

Although the process by which marriage became subject to American civil law has escaped the attention of most scholars, the fact of the matter is that from the beginnings of the British colonies, Protestants granted legal authority over marriage to the civil government, thus subtly fixing Protestant beliefs about marriage in American law. In his classic three-volume history of marriage published in 1904, George Elliott Howard devoted over six hundred pages to the historical development of marriage in the United States. Howard discovered that in the New England colonies, the "process of secularization in legal functions proceeded with rapid strides." Nowhere was this process more evident, he maintained, than "in the administration of matrimonial law and in the conception of the marriage contract." Unlike the confusing marriage laws of post-Reformation England, which retained a pre-Tridentine system of ecclesiastical regulation until the nineteenth century, marriage laws and procedures of in New England strived to "prevent the manifold evils growing out of a lax or uncertain law." In the New England colonies, the "conception of wedlock which existed there from the beginning was identical with" the contractual theories of marriage that appeared [in England] under Cromwell. In other words, New England colonists specifically aimed to establish marital procedure that both clarified English law and vested the state with jurisdiction over marriage. Yet they also viewed marriage as a sacred institution. In Howard's words, the "early establishment of civil marriage in New England . . . was required by the spirit of Protestantism." This "spirit" enabled the colonists to reject religious marriage ceremonies in favor of civil proceedings, and to "emphasize its secular character" so much that they seldom applied "the words 'holy' or 'sacred'" to the institution.[32] Nonetheless, they still admitted that marriage derived from God and had a religious character. The Protestant theology of marriage—a sacred institution regulated by civil authorities—thus imbued New England colonial marriage law from its earliest moments.

The southern colonies similarly vested the state with the authority to regulate marriage law from a relatively early period. From time to time its regulation shifted, depending upon which religious group retained control and upon the extent to which the law was enforced. In Virginia, for example, the Church of England administered the colony until 1794. Thus, in keeping with the church's marriage policy, Virginia law prescribed religious marriage ceremonies until that date. However, according to Howard, the regulation of marriage was "gradually intrusted to the county officers and the local courts," such that marriage had become "in effect a civil contract long before it [was] squarely acknowledged to be such by the law." Similarly, in North Carolina, authorities rarely enforced its regulations on marriage, despite the fact that the Church of England was established there in 1669. For the next fifty years or so, "there was in practice full toleration as to the form of the marriage celebration."[33] In 1715, however, the Vestries Act allowed civil authorities to marry couples only if there was no minister available, and in 1741 a new law prohibited dissenters from performing marriages.

The situation was similar in South Carolina and Georgia, where the legal regulation of marriage shifted back and forth between civil and ecclesiastical authorities. Even Maryland—founded by English converts to Catholicism—legalized the civil ceremony in 1658, but this policy was repealed in 1692 with the establishment of the Church of England. In 1777 the Maryland legislature enacted a law permitting only ministers—Anglicans, dissenters, Catholics, and Quakers—to perform marriage ceremonies. However, despite the shifts in which institution claimed the authority to regulate marriage, Howard concluded that "throughout the southern colonies matrimonial legislation was tending in the same direction [i.e., toward being a civil institution]. Everywhere, except in Maryland, the optional civil ceremony was legally or practically recognized, though under various restrictions. Marriage was already a civil contract of mutual partnership. . . . In short, in its principal elements, throughout the South matrimonial law had reached or was strongly tending toward the existing American type."[34] Howard's study of the southern colonies thus supports the idea that the influence of the Protestant theology of marriage on American marriage law was ubiquitous. In the South, as in New England, Americans recognized the sacred character of marriage while granting full legal authority over it—including the imposition of marital impediments—to civil officials.

Howard confirmed that in the middle colonies also, religious toleration "in the main prevailed," which increased the openness toward the civil regulation of marriage. In the New Netherlands, both civil and ecclesiastical marriage was legal, and couples could choose to be married by either a magistrate or a minister. Similarly, in 1668, New Jersey—composed of a number of religious groups—established a law allowing either a minister or a justice of the peace to celebrate the ceremony. Although the Church of England was established in New Jersey during the 1730s, Howard asserted that the "attempt to force the rites of the English church . . . on the people of New Jersey proved a failure."[35] And Pennsylvania law also allowed both civil and ecclesiastical marriage ceremonies, and it permitted Quakers to celebrate marriage as they wished.

Even when ecclesiastical marriage was the prescribed form of ceremony, Howard's account indicates that civil authorities were the primary source of law. Thus, from the beginning of American history, even in regions having significant Catholic populations, marriage was regarded as a sacred institution and yet regulated by civil law. In addition, after the founding of the United States and the disestablishment of religion, marriage everywhere became subject to civil law, administered by the individual states. Whether Catholic, Quaker, Congregationalist, Baptist, Methodist, or Episcopalian, Americans by and large agreed that while marriage had a sacred element, the state held primary jurisdiction over its legal regulation. What had commenced as a Protestant theology of marriage had evolved into an American conception of marriage—one might say a secular theology of marriage—that had lost its Protestant identity.[36]

General agreement as to the sacred character of marriage and the civil authority to establish and regulate marriage law did not, however, end conflicts about specifically which state institution had the right to enact and enforce law. In fact, in the century following the American War for Independence and the First Amendment guarantee of the individual's right to exercise freely his or her religious beliefs, there were shifts in the civil understanding of marriage. In the context of disestablishment, what had once been a sixteenth-century struggle between civil and ecclesiastical authorities over control of marriage law became a contest between federal and state authorities. Rather than asserting the authority of the civil government to enact marriage law—which had by now been established—Americans now began to weigh the question of *which* civil government held that right: the federal or the state government.

The Collision of Federal and State Governments over the Regulation of Marriage Law

By the early nineteenth century, Americans of all religious stripes—including Catholics—accepted the secular state's legal authority to control marriage and impose marital impediments. Where in previous eras, the battle over the legal regulation of marriage had been waged between civil and ecclesiastical authorities, in the later nineteenth century, the contest turned in an entirely new direction: between that of federal and state authority. This contest played out most vividly in the controversy over polygamy in the Utah Territory. Following the 1844 murder of Joseph Smith, the Latter-day Saints journeyed west in 1847 to the Great Salt Lake Basin to found the New Zion. In 1850 Congress organized the region, which the United States had recently acquired from Mexico in the Mexican-American War, into the Territory of Utah. Almost immediately, the Mormon-controlled territorial legislature incorporated the church and granted it jurisdiction over Mormon marriages. After the church's 1852 announcement that confirmed the long-rumored practice of "celestial" or "plural" marriage, the national debate over polygamy commenced. In 1862 Congress enacted the Morrill Anti-Bigamy Act, which made bigamy a federal crime. The act stated that "every person having a husband or wife living, who shall marry any other person, whether married or single, in a territory of the United States, or other place over which the United States have exclusive jurisdiction, shall . . . be adjudged guilty of bigamy, and, upon conviction thereof, shall be punished by a fine not exceeding five hundred dollars, and by imprisonment for a term not exceeding five years."[37] Twelve years later, the federal government stepped in once again to assert its authority in Utah Territory. The Poland Act of 1874 eliminated offices held by territorial officials and transferred their duties to federally appointed officials. In essence, the act permitted federal courts to try federal crimes, including bigamy, and allowed these courts to appoint juries of which at least half the members could be non-Mormon.[38]

The legitimacy of federal authority in Utah Territory came into question most explicitly just four years later when a low-level Utah court convicted George Reynolds, a Mormon bookkeeper, of having contracted marriages with two women. Reynolds appealed to the Supreme Court of the Utah Territory, which reversed the decision. Federal prosecutors then indicted and tried Reynolds a second time, and the court ruled that the original conviction should be upheld. In 1878 the case reached the U.S. Supreme Court, where it raised a number of constitutional issues, one of which was the authority of Congress to legislate over a U.S. territory. Reynolds's attorney argued that while Congress could "undoubtedly" legislate territorial governments, its laws could be "neither exclusive nor arbitrary." "There is always," the attorney declared, "an excess of power exercised when the Federal government attempts to provide for more than the assertion and preservation of its rights over such a territory, and interferes by positive enactment with the social and domestic life of its inhabitants and their internal police."[39] The dispute over the right of the federal government, as opposed to that of the territorial state, thus commenced.

U.S. Supreme Court Chief Justice Morrison Waite barely paused to consider the attorney's claim. "In our opinion," Waite stated, "the statute immediately under consideration is within the legislative power of Congress." Indeed, he continued, "it is constitutional and valid as prescribing a rule of action for all those residing in the Territories, and in places over which the United States have exclusive control. This being so, the only question which remains is, whether or not those who make polygamy a part of their religion are excepted from the operation of the statute."[40] The power of Congress—qua the federal government—to regulate territorial law was so clear to the Court as to be inarguable, a given. Thus, with regard to restrictions on polygamous marriages, the Court's decision declared territorial laws against polygamy to be constitutional—a legitimate function of the federal government. *Reynolds* thus strongly affirmed the authority of the federal government to enact marriage law.

In 1882, Congress passed yet another bill aiming to curb polygamy in the Utah Territory. The Edmunds Anti-Polygamy Act, proposed by Senator George Edmunds of Vermont, "criminalized bigamous 'unlawful cohabitation'" and "deprived anyone who practiced it of the right to vote and to hold public office." Mormon men who were thus denied the right to vote challenged the Edmunds Act, proclaiming their "'right and religious duty to continue in violation of the law their polygamous relation,'" and denying "'the authority of Congress to regulate and interpose any restriction as to the marital relation.'"[41] In 1887 Congress imposed the even more stringent Edmunds-Tucker Act, which repealed the 1851 incorporation of the Mormon Church and assigned jurisdiction over criminal adultery, incest, and fornication to Utah's federal courts. In 1889, the Saints brought a suit before the U.S. Supreme Court, *Mormon Church v. United States* (1890), claiming that the disincorporation of the church was unconstitutional. The Court ruled that because the incorporation had taken place in order to aid a religious institution, and because this particular institution not only promoted the practice of polygamy—"a crime against the laws, and abhorrent to the sentiments and feelings of the civilized world," a practice "contrary to the spirit of Christianity"—but also persevered "in defiance of law, in preaching, upholding, promoting, and defending it," the Mormon Church was essentially not a religious institution and thus not deserving of incorporation. Congress therefore proclaimed its authority to enact the Edmunds-Tucker Act to dissolve the corporation of the Mormon Church.[42]

Although Mormon polygamy best exemplified the tug-of-war between federal and territorial/state claims to legal authority over marriage law, the contests played out elsewhere as well. The year following the Edmunds-Tucker Act of 1887, the U.S. Supreme Court once again ruled on the constitutionality of territorial marriage law in *Maynard v. Hill* (1888)—which, as Peter Wallenstein observes, along with *Pace v. Alabama* (1883), "proved vital to the constitutional history of miscegenation laws."[43] The *Maynard* case involved a probate dispute between two women who each claimed to be the rightful heirs of property in the Oregon Territory. Both women had been married to the same man, who had deserted the first woman in another state and then, without her knowledge, divorced her after he moved to Oregon. Because Oregon was subject to territorial laws enacted by Congress, the divorce proceedings transpired through an act of the territorial legislature, rather than through a state court. The man then acquired some land and married the second woman. The first wife claimed that her divorce was not valid because a) she had not known about it, and b) it was granted by the legislature, which was not the appropriate body to make such decisions. Therefore, she claimed, she was the rightful heir to the Oregon property. The second woman contended that the divorce was indeed valid and that she was therefore the lawful claimant to the land. Consequently, the central question in *Maynard* was whether Oregon's territorial legislative assembly held the legal authority to grant a divorce.

The Court ruled in favor of the second wife, affirming that although the husband's actions were reprehensible, the divorce from the first woman was valid because the territorial legislature rightfully held the authority to dissolve marriages. Whether determining which parties might lawfully marry or the procedures by which a marriage might be dissolved, the civil government alone held full rights to establish marriage laws. In a passage frequently cited in subsequent marriage cases, the Court proclaimed, "Marriage, as creating the most important relation in life, as having more to do with the morals and civilization of a people than any other institution, has always been subject to the control of the legislature."[44] That body, it continued, held the responsibility of determining the appropriate age at which parties might marry, the procedures, duties, and obligations constituting marriage, and the means by which it could be dissolved. The civil government—in this case, the territorial legislature acting as an arm of the federal government—held the right to regulate all marriage law.

The *Reynolds* and *Maynard* cases encapsulated the nineteenth-century dispute over which civil body—state/territory or federal government—was entitled to regulate marriage law. This debate represented the first shift in American modifications of what had been the Protestant theology of marriage. Moreover, it foreshadowed the coming of another debate over the right to regulate marriage. *Reynolds* and *Maynard* served as important precedents in late nineteenth- and twentieth-century antimiscegenation cases, and the next shift in this debate thus focused on interracial marriage. In subsequent antimiscegenation cases, attorneys and judges frequently cited the *Reynolds* and *Maynard* decisions as support for the states' right to enact and enforce antimiscegenation statutes.[45] In its most frequently quoted passage, for example, *Reynolds* declared: "Marriage, while from its very nature a sacred obligation, is nevertheless, in most civilized nations, a civil contract, and usually regulated by law. Upon it society may be said to be built, and out of its fruits spring social relations and social obligations and duties, with which government is necessarily required to deal."[46]

But over and against this affirmation of the states' authority to enact marriage law, twentieth-century interracial couples increasingly began to assert their right to marry the person of their choosing. Thus the new conflict emerged. The state/federal dispute over polygamy was supplanted by a struggle between states and individuals: did the states' right to regulate marriage trump the individual's human right to marry whomever he or she wished? Antimiscegenation cases thus symbolized the next transformation in the American understanding of marriage. In these cases, states proclaimed—over and over again—their right to establish marriage law and to maintain the "purity" of the white race, thus thwarting the wishes of those individuals who deigned to proclaim their right to marry across the color line.

American Catholics and Interracial Marriage: The Twentieth Century

The Catholic Church's theology of marriage, including both the doctrine of its authority to oppose state-imposed impediments to marriage as well as its theology of the individual's freedom to choose a spouse, created a ready space for Catholics to protest against antimiscegenation laws and to intervene on behalf of interracial couples whom American states prohibited from marrying. Indeed, these beliefs formed the theological bases for Catholic clerical opposition toward civil laws against interracial marriage in the colonial Americas. And they continued to do so during the twentieth century, when American courts witnessed interracial couples' fights for the right to marry. As we have seen, progressive American Catholics such as California attorney Daniel Marshall carried high the banner in this battle.

Yet Marshall was not alone in his effort. Two years after the California Supreme Court issued its ruling in *Perez*, Joseph Doherty, a priest and recent graduate of the Catholic University of America with a doctorate in Sacred Theology, published his dissertation, *Moral Problems of Interracial Marriage*. In this book Doherty aimed to explore these problems "in the light of Catholic moral teaching." Doherty painstakingly analyzed scores of documents—Christian teachings on race, statements of popes and findings of ecclesiastical councils, and writings of twentieth-century Catholics who had explored the same questions, including canonist Louis Nau and progressive Father John LaFarge. Although Doherty's tone was more resolute than the others before him, his conclusions were nevertheless very similar to theirs. The writings of these Catholics, Doherty contended, make up a corpus of texts teaching "with uniformity on interracial marriage involving white persons. It may be concluded on their combined authorities, on the silent consent of the Church, and on the fact that to enter an interracial marriage is the exercise of a natural right, that . . . the entrance upon such a marriage in itself retains the primary morality of entering properly upon marriage in general; namely, it is a morally good act." Catholic doctrine, he concluded, could not and did not support civil laws prohibiting interracial marriage.[47]

Doherty's reasons for making this assertion arose from his understanding of the Catholic theology of marriage: the exclusive authority of the church to establish impediments to Christian marriage, the natural right of all humans to marry, and the sacred and sacramental character of marriage. According to the priest,

> Outside of the very limited sphere encompassed by civil effects allowed to the State, the civil power has absolutely no competence over any matters which affect the essentials of setting up or dissolving the marital bond for the baptized. Consequently, as far as the baptized are concerned, these laws are not just laws. They offend against commutative justice because they impose an obligation on baptized persons who are not subjects of the State as to Matrimony. Only the Church founded by Christ and entrusted by Him with authority over res sacrae for the baptized can impose laws on baptized persons in matters pertaining to the sacraments.[48]

As strongly worded as the statements of ecclesiastical councils, canon law specialists, and popes before him, Doherty's declaration reiterated the church's historic position on state-imposed marital impediments for the baptized. But unlike these earlier figures, he attached his claim specifically to interracial marriage.

Also unlike his predecessors, Doherty affirmed not only the ecclesiastically sanctioned right, but also the natural right to marry a member of another race. "As far as nature is concerned," he declared, "the right to marry interracially is a corollary of man's natural right to marry." The state "usurps competence if it directly abolishes the right to marry," for individuals possess this right "independently of the State."[49] Affirming the right of all competent humans—even the unbaptized—to freely select the spouse of their choosing, Doherty especially proclaimed that right for Christians.[50] For the baptized, he insisted, desiring to receive the sacrament of marriage "constitutes a motive of such a high order as to transcend the considerations of a social nature militating against entrance upon an interracial marriage." Doherty believed that the simple fact of one person's love for another constituted sufficient reason both to request the sacrament of matrimony and to contract an interracial marriage. "It is the love of the unique goodness of this particular person that makes merely human love sufficient reason for contracting interracial marriage," he stated, and it is a "goodness which . . . is unshared by others. It is in this sense that the person chosen is irreplaceable."[51]

Doherty's analysis of the Catholic theology of marriage in relation to interracial marriage was rather unusual for an American Catholic. Citizenship in a country proclaiming the constitutionality of "separate but equal" did not alert most American Catholics to possible inconsistencies between their faith and their nation's conceptions of civil rights. Yet Doherty makes it clear that the church's theology of marriage made legal prohibitions of interracial marriage very problematic for the Catholic faithful. In fact, in the decade prior to the publication of his book, the question of *how* problematic became painfully clear. Events in 1930s Europe compelled the Vatican itself to denounce civil bans on interracial marriage.

The Vatican Takes a Stand

The clash over state and individual rights in antimiscegenation cases first foreshadowed, and later mirrored, a new disagreement developing between American Catholics and southern white Protestants, and between American and European Catholics. While some progressive American Catholics such as Bishop John Ireland began to advocate for racial equality in the late nineteenth century, the rest of the white church remained unconcerned by racism and racial injustices. Meanwhile, events in Europe began to force the church in Rome to take an active stance against legal bans on interracial marriage there. Despite the church's ambivalence toward Hitler and fascism, as Nazi racial doctrines permeated Italy during the 1930s, the Vatican declared antimiscegenation laws incompatible with the Catholic theology of marriage. In November 1938, during the midst of the Kristallnacht pogrom in Germany and Austria, the Italian government, under the leadership of Benito Mussolini, enacted a new law "prohibit[ing] and declar[ing] null any and whatsoever marriage between Italian citizens of Aryan race and persons belonging to other races."[52] Within three or four days, *L'Osservatore Romano*, the official newspaper of Vatican City, issued a response to the law.

Noting the Italian state's assertion that no exceptions to the law were to be tolerated, the *L'Osservatore* statement made a sharp "contrast between the very recent Italian law and Canon Law." The contrast between civil and ecclesiastical laws was not so stark when secular prohibitions mirrored impediments already imposed by the church, such as in the case of marriages between baptized and unbaptized persons, the statement said. But "when two Catholics of different races are concerned," the law placed the church and state into conflict. While the church might dissuade a couple from marrying if their union might "put the offspring at a disadvantage," the church merely "suggests, admonishes, persuades; she does not impose or forbid" such marriages. But "when two Catholics of diverse races have decided to contract marriage and present themselves to her, free from any canonical impediments, the Church cannot, just by reason of the diversity of race, deny her [official] assistance. This is demanded by her sanctifying mission and by those rights which God has given and the Church recognizes for all her children without distinction. Thus, on this point, a general and absolute prohibition of marriage is in opposition to the doctrine and laws of the church."[53]

The statement in *L'Osservatore Romano* is the most direct—as well as the most official—articulation of Catholic belief about interracial marriage. As the color line increasingly hardened during the 1940s and 1950s in the American South, where white Protestants denounced intermarriage and proclaimed the "separation of the races" as God's divine plan, the Vatican proclaimed such views as un-Catholic.[54] Although the Vatican never specifically denounced American antimiscegenation laws, the statement effectively articulates the church's position on both interracial marriage and antimiscegenation legislation, whether in the United States, South Africa, or Italy.

The *L'Osservatore Romano* statement hints at yet another theological difference between Catholics and American Protestants, especially white southern Protestants. In addition to articulating the Catholic theology of marriage, the statement portrayed antimiscegenation laws as incompatible with a Catholic theology of race. Throughout the 1950s the American hierarchy remained reluctant to admit black students to Catholic colleges and seminaries, and lay white American Catholics quite adamantly opposed black Catholics' attendance at their parish churches and black priests saying Mass.[55] Yet in a variety of papal letters and statements, the Vatican firmly proclaimed the catholicity and unity of the human family, and the more progressive wing of the American church challenged its fellow believers to love their black neighbor. So although there were deep differences in beliefs about race among American Catholics, and between American Catholics and the Vatican, with the *L'Osservatore Romano* statement, the church in Rome had embarked on a journey to articulate once and for all a Catholic doctrine on race. In so doing, the church hinted at the vast differences between American Catholics and white evangelical Protestants, especially those in the South. By the early 1940s, there were cultural and theological differences between Catholic and American Protestant understandings of interracial marriage—understandings that were deeply embedded in each group's theologies of marriage and race.

As seen earlier in this chapter, one Roman Catholic, Daniel Marshall, astutely perceived that there existed in Catholic theology a different understanding of marriage than that traditionally expressed in American anti-miscegenation cases. Perhaps more remarkable, Marshall also recognized in these cases a profoundly different conception of race from the one he understood as a Catholic. While he did not explicitly designate that conception of race as Protestant, Marshall seems to have been hinting at a Protestant-Catholic divide over notions of race and interracial marriage, and that these differences were distinct and embedded enough in Christianity to constitute "theologies." Exploring these Catholic and Protestant theologies of race reveals yet another factor in the cultural history of interracial marriage and antimiscegenation laws.

[4] Noah's Sons and Common Origins in Adam and Eve Protestant and Catholic Theologies of Race

In the 1947 legal arguments between Daniel Marshall and Los Angeles County attorney Charles Stanley, both attorneys addressed the role of religion in prohibitions of interracial marriage. "It is interesting to note," Stanley remarked, "that the Bible is not silent upon the question of the mingling of races." He cited a story from the book of Genesis in which Abraham made his son swear not to take a wife "of the daughters of the Canaanites," and another, from the book of Nehemiah, in which the writer claimed to have cursed and "smote" Hebrew men who had married non-Hebrew women. According to Stanley, the Bible stories, along with his "ample evidence of sociological conditions," together proved that "marriages between Negroes and Whites" placed "such a strain upon the family relations" and "such unfortunate social conditions for the offspring of such a marriage as to justify the legal prohibition of such marriages."[1] In other words, to Stanley, the biblical evidence provided a viable basis for California's antimiscegenation statutes. Stanley also cited three legal cases as support for California's antimiscegenation laws, all of which mentioned the idea that God had created separate or dissimilar races. One case, *Green v. Alabama* (1877), proclaimed not only that had God made the races "dissimilar," but also that both natural and divine law forbade intermarriage and racial mixing.

Daniel Marshall strongly denounced the religious ideas represented in *Green*, especially the notion that biblical passages constituted a legitimate foundation for antimiscegenation statutes. The "quoted language of the *Green* case," he declared, was "only a veneer to hide the theological basis upon which the decision is based." A great number of citizens, Marshall continued, including the Perez-Davis couple "and their [Catholic] co-religionists, do not subscribe to the theology expressed in the *Green* case."

Quoting from a passage from *Green* that Stanley had excluded from his brief, Marshall offered the following passage as the "theology" to which Catholics did not subscribe: "Why the Creator made one white and the other black, we do not know; But the fact is apparent and the races are distinct, each producing its own kind, and following the peculiar law of its constitution. Conceding equality with natures as perfect, and rights as sacred, yet God has made them dissimilar. . . . *The natural law which forbids their intermarriage and that amalgamation* which leads to a corruption of the races, is a clearly divine as that which imparted to them different natures." Clearly rattled by the religious ideas expressed in *Green*, Marshall protested the right of any court to "impose this theological conception, regarded by vast numbers of citizens as the rankest error, as support for a statutory enactment" against interracial marriage.[2]

Marshall stated that these religious claims explicitly affirmed "the same racism" embodied in California's antimiscegenation statutes—a racism that, in Marshall's opinion, Stanley viewed as the constitutional right of the state. Rather than attempt to "rebut" such a foolish view, Marshall said, he thought it would be "better" that he end his own brief with a passage from the first book to the Corinthians: "For as the body is one, and hath many members; and all the members of the body, whereas they are many, yet are one body, so also is Christ. For in One Spirit were we all baptized into one body, whether Jews or Gentiles, whether bond or free; and in one Spirit have we been all made to drink. . . . But now there are many members indeed but one body."[3] Thus Marshall concluded his brief by lifting up an alternative biblical passage that emphasized the spiritual unity, rather than the dissimilarity, of humankind.

In these citations of legal cases and Bible verses offered by Stanley and Marshall, we witness perhaps the most interesting and significant discussion of race and religion in the history of American antimiscegenation cases. One side, arguing for the legitimacy of laws prohibiting interracial marriage, located a history of racial restrictions on marriage in biblical tradition—a tradition that posited the notion of God having created "separate" or "dissimilar" races. The other side opposed such a perspective, viewing it as the "rankest error," and proffering an alternative position rooted in Christian scriptures: the unity of the human races in Christ. This second perspective—coming as it did from a Catholic believer—proclaimed that the idea of "dissimilar races" represented a theological perspective wholly different from that found among Catholics. This claim thus implied the existence of both Catholic and non-Catholic theologies of race.

What, then, were these theologies of race? What evidence suggests that the "theologies" divided along Catholic and Protestant lines, or that Catholics and Protestants held different views on race at all? Where did Catholic and Protestant theologies of race come from historically, and from which biblical sources and hermeneutical traditions? How did they shape perspectives on the legitimacy of interracial marriage? Drawing upon a variety of primary source materials, this chapter explores these questions. Building upon Mark Noll's observation about Protestants' historical tendency "to take up, modify, discard, or transform inherited ideas and institutions as local circumstances dictated," and upon the Protestant emphasis on the Bible as the sole source of spiritual authority, I argue that white Protestants, particularly southerners in the years following the Civil War, derived a theology of divinely created "separate" races from a variety of biblical stories and hermeneutical traditions.[4] White post–Civil War southern Protestants interpreted Genesis 10–11 to indicate a divine mandate for racial segregation, most especially in marriage. In contrast, Catholics—or at least official church doctrine—emphasized the unity of the human family, based upon biblical traditions of Adam and Eve as the progenitors of all races and upon the notion of humankind being united in Christ. Catholics—in theory, at least—thus posited the unity of the races as the underlying approach to interracial relations and thus the social and theological legitimacy of interracial marriage.

The Sons of Noah and the Origins of Theologies of Race

Several key narratives from the book of Genesis purport to recount the lives of the earliest humans, including Adam, Eve, and their children as well as the righteous patriarch Noah and his sons, Shem, Ham, and Japheth. Although none of the stories directly mentions anything that modern readers would identify as "race," interpretations of these passages have made deep and enduring connections between the Bible and the understandings of human racial origins.[5] Genesis 4, for example, tells the story of how God cursed Adam and Eve's son Cain for having murdered his brother, Abel, and how God then placed a "mark" upon Cain. Although the story makes no reference to racial identity or skin color, some interpreters contended that this enigmatic "mark" was that of black skin. Another passage commonly cited as an explanation for racial differences was Genesis 11, which contains the Tower of Babel story. According to this narrative, all the people of the world spoke a common language until, swollen with pride, they attempted to build a tower that reached up to heaven. God, angered at their effort, then "confounded their language" so that they could not communicate and "scattered them abroad from thence upon the face of all the earth." Some interpreters understood this story as the explanation of human racial differentiation—something, they pointed out, that God inflicted as a punishment for pride.

Most influential in the historical Christian hermeneutics of race, and particularly in American interpretations, were the stories of Noah's sons in Genesis chapters 9 and 10. In Genesis 9:18–27, Noah, the righteous patriarch whose sons peopled the entire earth, cursed Canaan, his grandson through Ham, to perpetual slavery after Ham observed his inebriated father naked.

> And the sons of Noah, that went forth of the ark, were Shem, and Ham, And Japheth: and Ham is the father of Canaan. These are the three sons of Noah: and of them was the whole earth overspread. And Noah began to be an husbandman, and he planted a vineyard: And he drank of the wine, and was drunken; and he was uncovered within his tent. And Ham, the father of Canaan, saw the nakedness of his father, and told his two brethren without. And Shem and Japheth took a garment, and laid it upon both their shoulders, and went backward, and covered the nakedness of their father; and their faces were backward, and they saw not their father's nakedness. And Noah awoke from his wine, and knew what his younger son had done unto him. And he said, Cursed be Canaan; a servant of servants shall he be unto his brethren. And he said, Blessed be the LORD God of Shem; and Canaan shall be his servant. God shall enlarge Japheth, and he shall dwell in the tents of Shem; and Canaan shall be his servant.[6]

Interpreters paired this enigmatic story with the "dispersion" story of Genesis 10, in which Noah's three sons and their descendants scattered across the earth in three different directions from their homeland. Canaan thus became associated with black skin and Africa, since interpreters believed his descendants to have relocated to Africa. In the context of American slavery, American Bible readers interpreted this story of "Noah's curse" and the dispersion of Noah's sons as a justification and explanation for racial slavery.

Since the earliest days of the Common Era, Jewish, Christian, and Muslim readers and scholars have attempted to unravel the meanings of these mysterious passages, often coming up with some rather negative interpretations, particularly of the figures Ham and Canaan of Genesis 9–11.[7] In his influential *Antiquities of the Jews*, first-century Jewish historian Josephus claimed that upon discovering his nude, drunken father asleep in his tent, Ham "came laughing, and showed him to his brethren."[8] According to religious studies scholar Stephen Haynes, the idea that Ham's laughter served as the reason for his punishment subsequently became a "leitmotif in the history of interpretation" of the story. The Babylonian Talmud, however, postulated that Ham's transgression against Noah might have been sexual assault or even castration of Noah, while another rabbinic text suggested that Ham had observed Noah and his wife having sex, which led Ham to try and castrate Noah.[9]

Among early Christian interpreters, Augustine asserted that Ham represented heresy and disruption of Christian peace: "what does he [Ham] signify but the tribe of heretics, hot with the spirit, not of patience, but of impatience, with which the breasts of heretics are wont to blaze, and with which they disturb the peace of the saints?"[10] Clement of Alexandria associated Ham with sorcery and depicted him as the first magician.[11] Like Josephus, Ambrose of Milan attributed Noah's condemnation to Ham's ridicule of his father's nakedness. Significantly, several early Christian commentators also depicted Noah—in contrast to the sinful Ham—as a pillar of moral rectitude and forerunner of Christ. Justin Martyr, for example, likened Noah and Christ in that Christ "regenerated" himself "through water, and faith, and wood," while Noah "was saved by wood when he rode over the waters with his household."[12] Augustine speculated that Noah's misfortune "elegantly intimate[d] that Jesus was to suffer the cross and death at the hands of His own household, His own kith and kin, the Jews."[13] Among this tradition of thinkers, Noah's curse acquired a quasi-divine significance, as if in condemning Ham's posterity to slavery, Noah spoke on God's behalf, while Ham became "the church fathers' archetype of human depravity."[14]

The connection between Ham, Canaan, and slavery is clear—Noah cursed Ham's progeny to be "a servant of servants to his brethren" (Genesis 9:25). What is less clear, however, is how Ham came to be associated with dark skin or blackness. Haynes contends that Ham was "rarely racialized before Europeans' exploration of West Africa in the fifteenth century."[15] Yet premedieval interpretations occasionally connected the legend of Ham and blackness. Even as early as the second century BCE, *The Book of Jubilees*, an anonymous Jewish rendering of the history of creation up through Moses, linked Ham and Africa. The writer suggested that as his blessing to his sons, Noah apportioned the earth into three parts, and that the sons subsequently divided their land among their own sons. Ham's sons purportedly received Ethiopia, Egypt, Libya, and the region from Libya to the Atlantic Ocean.[16] Other interpreters offered different ways of associating Ham and his descendants with blackness. Some asserted that Ham had married a black woman, a descendent of Cain, thus having mixed-race offspring, while the Jerusalem Talmud proposed that Ham had emerged from Noah's ark "charcoal colored."[17] The *Babylonian Talmud Tractate Sanhedrin* elaborated on this last theory, suggesting that because Ham had misbehaved on the ark during the Great Flood—allegedly having sex with his wife, in violation of Noah's command—he received dark skin and his father's subsequent curse as punishments.[18] Yet another explanation for the association between Ham and blackness derived from the fact that the name "Ham" was linguistically related to the Hebrew word for "dark, black, or hot."[19]

Ham and Canaan became associated more closely with Africa and blackness by the late fifteenth or early sixteenth centuries, when European Christian interpreters commonly interpreted the Genesis 10 account to mean that Ham had dispersed to Africa, Shem to Asia, and Japheth to Europe. Thus by this period, the "dispersion" story sometimes referenced what twenty-first century observers might call racial differentiation, insofar as Ham, Shem, and Japheth had—through generations of interpretation of the stories—come to represent racially distinct groups. Moreover, as some thinkers from this period associated Ham and blackness with slavery, increasingly the story of Noah's curse served to rationalize the enslavement of Africans, though not until after the Reformation, the European "discovery" of the New World, and the subsequent enslavement of African and Native American peoples did the "racialization" of the Genesis stories begin in earnest. At this time, readers turned to the biblical accounts of human origins and dispersion to explain the physical and cultural differences between human beings, which signaled some new interpretive innovations in the Genesis stories, including that of Cain as well as of Ham. French Calvinist Isaac de la Peyrère, for example, who was deemed a heretic by his contemporaries, developed a "pre-Adamite" theory of human origins, in which he posited that there were human beings prior to Adam and Eve. Subsequent generations adopted and adapted Peyrère's polygenetic theory to suggest that whites were the Adamites and all other groups were the pre-Adamites, thus establishing a biblically based racial hierarchy with whites at the top.[20] Other early modern interpreters viewed black skin as the punishment meted out to Ham's descendants, explaining Africans' skin color as well as the deviant sexuality, dishonor, and paganism that European Christians perceived among African "heathens."[21]

By the turn of the eighteenth century, the hermeneutical traditions surrounding the Genesis stories had crossed the Atlantic and taken up residence along the shores of Boston's Charles River. In a 1703 sermon seeking to understand the origins of slavery, Puritan Samuel Willard proclaimed, "all Servitude began in the Curse."[22] During the subsequent decades of the eighteenth century, as British and American thinkers began to debate the morality of chattel slavery and its relationship to republican ideals of liberty and equality, defenders of slavery regularly called upon the strange tales of Ham, Shem, and Japheth, first, to justify slavery, and later, to justify the enslavement specifically of Africans. By the time the young United States began inching toward sectional crisis in the 1830s, proslavery advocates appealed so frequently to the story of Ham as a rationale for their arguments that abolitionist Theodore Dwight Weld famously remarked in 1837, "this prophecy of Noah is the *vade mecum* of slaveholders, and they never venture abroad without it."[23] More recent scholars confirm Weld's assertion. The Ham story, according to historian H. Shelton Smith, formed one of the "major bulwarks" of proslavery defenses, and Richard T. Hughes and C. Leonard Allen argue that the story of Noah and his sons "became the soul of the civil theology of the South."[24]

Yet careful analysis of the sources reveals very interesting interpretive developments in the United States. First, although the hermeneutical history of biblical racial stories is common to both Catholics and Protestants, interpretations of the Genesis myths developed a remarkable significance and endurance particularly among American Protestants. After the Reformation, what had historically been a broadly *Christian* history of interpretation increasingly became a *Protestant* one. Second, after the Emancipation of African Americans during the 1860s, the white American Protestant hermeneutics of the "sons of Noah" stories began to downplay the origins of slavery and Genesis 9 and to emphasize, instead, the "dispersion" of Noah's sons in Genesis 10–11. This shift signaled the culmination of a theology that justified the segregation of "Hamitic" Africans and their descendants from the "white" descendants of Japheth. Indeed, the development of biblical racial origins myths in segregationist literature reveals an increasing emphasis on the notion of the divine "separation of the races." Moreover, by 1900, some American Catholics were beginning not only to reject the notion of "separate races" outright, but also to designate it as "Protestant."

In these shifts, we witness not only an example of a local form of racial doctrine developing among southern white Protestants, but also the biblical basis for laws against interracial marriage. On the Catholic side, we see both a reiteration of the traditional view that ecclesiastical doctrine originates in the church universal, rather than in local congregations, and the doctrinal basis for opposition to laws banning intermarriage.

"God, the Original Segregationist": The Southern White Protestant Theology of Race

In his examination of the Genesis stories as the biblical justification for American slavery, Stephen Haynes observes that the "American reliance on Genesis 9–11 as a source for discerning God's will in racial matters is responsible for significant continuities between the proslavery and prosegregation arguments."[25] Indeed, the "dispersion" story of Genesis 10–11 began to replace the "Noah's curse" story of Genesis 9 as the religious basis for understandings of race, because it offered an explanation and justification for the social and political inequality of black persons. With the demise of the "peculiar institution," white Americans no longer needed to explain slavery. But they did need to justify sociopolitical inequality, the political and economic disfranchisement of African Americans, and the "separation" or segregation of whites from persons of color. Increasingly, some white southerners—the primary mouthpieces of these views—sought to rationalize Jim Crow laws and attitudes with appeals to Genesis 10–11.[26] Interpreting the "dispersion" story as one of racial separation, proponents of this theology of separate races—as we will see—came to view Genesis 10–11 as God's mandate for racial segregation, most especially in marriage.

As proslavery and antislavery debates became increasingly heated during the antebellum period, Protestant ministers authored a number of treatises that appealed to Genesis 9 as support for the enslavement of Africans. Baptist preacher Thornton Stringfellow of Virginia cited the story in 1841 as proof of God's approval of slavery.[27] John Leadley Dagg, a Baptist and president of Mercer University, asserted that "as the sons of Adam are bound to submit patiently to the curse which requires them to earn their bread in the sweat of their face, so the sons of Ham are bound to submit patiently to the curse which has doomed them to bondage."[28] Other diverse figures also called upon the Genesis stories to explain racial slavery and the subordination of blacks to whites. Brigham Young, for example, cited the story of Cain both to rationalize slavery in the Utah Territory during the 1850s and to exclude blacks from the Mormon priesthood.[29] Senators and political figures also helped to popularize the association of Ham with blackness.[30] Harriet Beecher Stowe's *Uncle Tom's Cabin* included references to the curse narrative.[31] Even abolitionists and those who opposed the enslavement of black peoples sometimes accepted the notion that Africans had descended from Ham.[32]

But as the possibilities of civil war and emancipation loomed ever closer during the 1840s and 1850s, Protestant proslavery advocates began to make a subtle shift in their thought—a shift that ultimately distinguished them from Catholics. A few years before the Civil War, Protestant interpreters' emphasis on the biblical story of slavery began to transition to the biblical story of racial "dispersion" of Genesis 10–11, thus signaling the development of a white southern Protestant theology of "separate races." In his influential 1843 book, *Slavery as It Relates to the Negro, or African Race*, New York harness maker and adventure writer Josiah Priest noted, for example, that God had divided the human family into racial groups. The popular book, which was reprinted five times in eight years, affirmed that "among men reckoned in classes, as belonging to distinct families or nations, the earth has also been divided by the operation of the Divine hand, and suited to their several natures. To the white race, the descendants of Japheth, the northern regions of the earth were given. To Shem and his descendants, the red or copper colored race, the middle regions or temperate clime, north of the equator, was allotted. But to Ham and his race was given the burning South."[33] Although his purpose in making this point was to proffer evidence for physiological differences in blacks that suited them to slavery, Priest's words are representative of the slight shift in language that would be taken up by white southerners after 1865. The notion of "distinct" races created and "divided" by God forms a recurring theme in the literature from Priest onward.

In the next decade, the idea of "distinct" or "separate" races idea gained momentum—and briefly, scientific credibility—among scientists and others willing to suspend belief in the historicity of biblical accounts of human origins. Two physicians published works that disseminated the short-lived scientific theory of polygenesis. Focusing less on slavery and more on the physiological reasons for the sociopolitical subordination of black persons, internationally renowned scientist Dr. Josiah Nott of Mobile, Alabama, proposed that the biblical record of racial origins was not quite accurate. In fact, in his controversial 1854 book *Types of Mankind*, which by

1871 had gone through ten editions, Nott claimed that racial groups had descended from more than one original pair. Building upon the work of other scientists, Nott asserted that blacks had originated not from Adam and Eve, but from other parents; they were therefore a separate species and thus rightly subjected to whites.[34]

According to historian Reginald Horsman, while polygenesis remained controversial, by the middle of the nineteenth century, "the most important American ethnologists accepted it as scientific fact." New Orleans physician Samuel Cartwright was one who agreed. In an 1857 essay, he argued that the "species of the genus homo are not a unity, but a plurality," and though he regarded Negroes as "more like the monkey tribes and the lower order of animals than any other species of the genus man," he did not believe them to be "brutes," as some later thinkers did. To Cartwright, the Bible together with science verified the separate or plural origins of the human races: "Aside and apart from Scripture authority," he wrote, "natural history reveals most of the same facts, in regard to the negro that the Bible does. It proves the existence of at least three distinct species of the genus man, differing in their instincts, form, habits and color."[35] Though more subtle in its notion of divinely separated races than Nott, and though most Christians rejected his plural origins theory, Cartwright's thought still captured the essence of the transition toward a theology of separate races. The separateness and distinctiveness of each race served to indicate that the racial characteristics native to each group should be preserved, as God intended.

The concept of God having made distinct or separate races began to appear more and more frequently. In his 1857 book in defense of slavery, James A. Sloan, a Presbyterian minister from Mississippi, located human inequality in God's design, although he stopped short of Nott and Cartwright's argument for the separate or plural origins of the races. To those who argued against slavery on "'the claim that the Gospel makes no distinction between men on the ground of color, or race,'" Sloan contended that such an assertion was "a very silly thing, for this [racial or color] distinction was made immediately after the flood and long before the Gospel dispensation commenced." He addressed Acts 17:26, which stated that God "hath made of one blood all nations of men for to dwell on the face of the earth, and hath determined the times before appointed, and the bounds of their habitation," a verse that abolitionists often cited in support of the "no distinction" claim. This text, Sloan continued, "simply proves that all men of all nations are descended from the same original stock, or what is usually called 'the unity of the race.' This we have admitted and are prepared to sustain. But the *unity* and *equality* of races is a *distinction* with a *difference*, and that difference has been made by the Creator himself. . . . The *unity* of the race would prove its *equality* also, provided there had been nothing to disturb this equality. Sin has disturbed this *equality*, while it has not interfered with its *unity*."[36] To Sloan, God had thus created distinct races, and sin had made them unequal. Although he did not specifically cite Genesis 10 — the dispersion story — as the biblical support for his assertion, Sloan's reference to the distinction of the races having been created "after the flood" alludes to the passage. It also signals the shift away from Genesis 9, offering Genesis 10–11 as the biblical bases for white dominance of black peoples, even free black peoples.

These views recur in the literature published on the eve of the Civil War and Emancipation. Samuel Davies Baldwin, a Methodist preacher in Tennessee, published an influential book in 1858 called *Dominion; or, The Unity and Trinity of the Human Race with the Divine Political Constitution of the World, and the Divine Rights of Shem, Ham, and Japheth.* As the title suggests, the book refuted the "ethnological infidelity" posed presumably by Nott. Baldwin argued that the human race had been "united" by its origins in Adam and Eve, but that through Noah's three sons God had created a "trinity of races" and reinforced their differences via linguistic and geographical barriers, once again hearkening back to Genesis 9–11. Of the writers discussed thus far, Baldwin was the first to mention interracial marriage as a divinely prohibited act and as the logical conclusion of a theology proclaiming "triune" yet divinely separated races. Moreover, like many of the writers addressed here, Baldwin claimed that a "project of the fusion of the races" during the time of Noah constituted a "bold rebellion against the Divine order for dispersion." This "rebellion" resulted in a divine "judgment alike perpetual and profluent of evil." Indeed, Baldwin argued, "by miraculously dividing the nations" God "intended to prevent fusion," and because "color, as a natural badge of race, was needful to perpetuate separateness, its primordial institution must be recognized as among those great landmarks divinely and universally impressed, as was the diversity of language, the elevation of mountains, and the separation by waters, deserts, and climate, and at the same epoch."[37]

As the threat of black emancipation loomed closer, the theme of racial separateness occurred again and again. In addition, proslavery writers addressed interracial "fusion" more frequently, and more anxiously, than they had in the literature of the 1830s and 1840s. In his 1863 publication *Pictures of Slavery and Anti-Slavery*, Methodist pastor John Bell Robinson of Pennsylvania penned 388 pages against abolition and "disunion" (although by the time the book was published, President Lincoln had already liberated enslaved persons in most southern states). Robinson emphasized the Genesis 9 passage, going so far as to assert that "Ham's crime [against Noah] was one thousand times more flagitious" than Adam's crime against the human race. He also noted that "the confusion of tongues, and the separation of the human family" had originated in the "building of Babel" in Genesis 11. And it was precisely in his discussion of "spurious mixtures" of the distinct racial groups that Robinson's language included the "distinct" races rhetoric. Apparently blind to the existence of mixed-race individuals, Robinson suggested that the inability of interracial couples to reproduce underscored the inherent and divinely created separateness of the races. He claimed that "mulattoes are a forbidden race," and that "to prohibit a mixture of blood with the negroes by the white people, our great Creator has made these laws of nature to prohibit a new race of men being formed between those two very distinct races of mankind."[38]

Other writers, though far from representative of the postwar Protestant mainstream, expressed another influential strand of southern white Protestant thought on intermarriage—one that would recur forcefully among twentieth-century segregationists, even as late as the 1990s. In 1867 a self-proclaimed Bible scholar and theologian from Ohio named Buckner Payne (using the pseudonym, Ariel) published a pamphlet called *The Negro: What Is His Ethnological Status?* In it, Payne offered an argument that most of his contemporaries viewed as extreme and even unbiblical. Following a line of thought similar to Nott's, though decidedly less erudite and far more outlandish, Payne asserted that Negroes were not humans. Rather, black peoples were beasts that had survived the great flood by having been brought aboard Noah's ark along with the other animals.

Although advocating a very different notion of God having created distinct races than other writers, Payne's pamphlet is important because it contains a theme common in later segregationist thought: the notion that the biblical flood constituted God's punishment for miscegenation. Basing his view on the strange passage from Genesis 6 in which the "sons of God" are stated to have taken wives from the "daughters of men," Payne charged that these "sons" were human men, and the "daughters" were Negro females— "beast[s], without soul[s]—without the endowment of mortality." This, he opined, was the reason that God "drowned the world." This bestial amalgamation constituted "a crime *in the sight of God,*" one that "can not be *propiti-ated* by any sacrifice or by any oblation, and can not be forgiven by God."[39]

Declaring that God hated all attempts to "elevate" the Negro "to *social, political* and *religious* equality with the white race," Payne interpreted virtu-ally the entire book of Genesis as a diatribe against interracial mixing and the social equality of blacks. He claimed, for example, that "the first attempt at the social equality of the negro, with Adam's race, brought the flood upon the world—the second, brought confusion and dispersion—the third, the fire of God's wrath, upon the cities of the plain—the fourth, the order from God, to exterminate the *nations* of the Canaanites—the fifth, the inhibition and exclusion, by express law of God, of the *flat-nosed* negro from his altar. Will the people of the United States now furnish the sixth? Nous verrons."[40] Because the tone of the pamphlet leads the reader to believe that the writer was more than a little mad, it could be dismissed as a worthless expres-sion of extremism. Yet, as we will see, the recurrence of such notions in the thought of subsequent segregationists suggests that Payne's eccentric speculations cannot be wholly discounted as fanaticism.

Following the Civil War, the theology of separate races began to develop in earnest, largely as the hermeneutics of white southern Protestants. In 1873, for example, *Harper's Weekly* published an article noting that Richmond's *Christian Herald,* "the organ of the white Baptists," had given the following reason for not receiving their "colored brethren" into white churches: "God has made the two races widely different not only in complexion, but in their instincts and social qualities. We take it for granted it was not the purpose of the Creator that they should be blended. Nature abhors the union."[41] Similarly, in 1887 another northern-inflected remark about the theology of separate races appeared in *Harper's.* The writer depicted the southern newspaper the *Montgomery (Alabama) Dispatch* as a most "ferocious and unreasonable opponent of equality in American citizenship," stimulating "ill-feeling and hostility" among Alabama citizens. Though the writer did not indicate any details, apparently he was responding to a discussion in the *Dispatch* of an antimiscegenation law that called upon the divine separation of the races as justification for the law. "Even assuming with the *Dispatch,*" the writer stated,

which claims to be very familiar with the Divine counsels, that God made a distinction between the races, and He never intended that there should be an amalgamation between the whites and blacks—

assuming this natural antipathy, why not leave it to its own operation? If there be such an antipathy there need be no fear of the races trying to associate in schools and elsewhere, and the individual instances of such attempted association will be of no importance. If there be no such antipathy, a law prohibiting their coeducation is as stupid as one forbidding Baptists and Methodists to go to the same school.[42]

In this case, the northern writer depicted the theology of separate races not merely as a justification for prohibitions against intermarriage, but also as a belief system existing among white southerners.

By the turn of the twentieth century, the theology of separate races had gained wide currency among white southern Protestants as the religious justification for Jim Crow policies and intraracial marriage. In 1903, the Reverend W. S. Armistead authored *The Negro Is a Man*, an outraged reply to Charles Carroll's 1900 pamphlet, *The Negro Is a Beast*. Carroll, a white supremacist extremist minister from Missouri who was denounced as a crackpot, appears to have lifted his ideas wholesale from Payne's pamphlet.[43] Armistead, a Baptist, deemed Carroll's rants as "Bible perversions." Against Carroll's claims, Armistead asserted, among other things, that Adam and Eve were not white, as Carroll claimed, but red, which thus made the lineage of Christ himself red or perhaps even mixed. Adamantly disputing Carroll's allegations that black people were nonhuman brutes, Armistead argued throughout the 542-page book that there was no such thing as amalgamation as Carroll defined it—that is, as the "carnal association of human beings and beasts"—for the fact that no offspring resulted from such unions proved that no amalgamation had occurred. In fact, Armistead boisterously proclaimed, "race intermingling" was nowhere prohibited in the Bible.[44] He went on to contend that

If amalgamation had been of so vile a character—a crime of such soul-destroying, soul-damning a nature—as to justify God in drowning the whole antediluvian population [as Carroll claims], it would certainly have been not only mentioned, but it would have been pointed out and specified, branded and denounced, in unmeasured terms as "the sin of sins," as "the sum of abominations." The very fact that amalgamation is not mentioned in the arraignment at all, coupled with the fact that the true causes are specified and particularized, renders it absolutely certain that amalgamation was not "a" cause, or "the" cause of the deluge! (137)

Although his views come across as unexpected or even radical—especially considering the fact that Armistead hailed from Georgia—the book is well organized, draws upon scholarly sources, and gives no indication of being tongue-in-cheek or otherwise disingenuous. Yet the writer concludes his book by declaring "without a moment's hesitation" that he is not an advocate of racial equality. While his book did "pull down every barrier" to racial equality, Armistead continued, the reader must remember that his stated purpose in writing the book was to refute Carroll's ideas and his artificial creation of racial barriers that the Bible in fact repudiated. Armistead claimed to be "writing in defense of the *Bible,*—showing why race intermingling was not unscriptural,—showing that God had drawn no such line as that of *color and pilious system*; that the divine line was one of Morals and Religion" (536).

After all these words about how no biblical injunction against intermarriage existed, Armistead nevertheless insisted that "God Himself" objected to the marriage of blacks and whites, for although God "interposed no *scriptural* barrier on *physical differences,*" in "'scattering the race upon the face of the whole earth,' and interposing *continental barriers*, [God] signified, aye, expressed in no uncertain terms, His *willingness*, aye, His *imperative desire*, that *race intermingling* or *intermarriage, should* not *take place*. Else why separate the nations by such natural, and withal, formidable barriers to such intermingling" (537). And even more unexpected, Armistead's final pages reflect ideas that Buckner Payne and Charles Carroll would have supported: his preference for "*digging deeper the foundations and building higher the walls that intervene Racial Social Equality.*" Indeed, Armistead declared, "God has drawn the line—a continental one. To remove it would be to reflect on the wisdom of God; to remove it would be the ruin of the negro race; to abolish it would be to destroy the white race morally and religiously" (539).

Not at all the open mind that he appeared to be earlier in the book, Armistead closed with a sinister warning to black men who might prey upon white women: "*Let the blacks beware!* As sure as there is a God in heaven, a *continuation* of such outrages on Southern females, is *digging the grave of their race*. To continue such practices is to *invite* and *make certain their extermination!* None but fools handle fire in a magazine!" (541–42). In its allusions to Genesis 10–11, its concomitant rhetoric of continental barriers and divinely separated nations, and its logically following interdiction against interracial marriage, Armistead's book conveys, in its final pages, the southern Protestant theology of separate races, par excellence.

The list of proponents of the Protestant theology of race continues. In his 1907 book, William M. Brown—an Ohio native–cum–bishop of the Episcopal Church of Arkansas and self-proclaimed "southernized Northerner"—called for the creation of a color line in the parishes of Arkansas. Alluding to the notion of God having differentiated the races as the basis for such a policy, Bishop Brown admitted that biblical principles implied that the church should welcome persons of any color in to worship. Yet, he contended, God himself "drew the Color-Line, and the failure to recognize it is irreligious, because it is disobedience." Refuting religious detractors, Brown insisted that the "hypothesis that the Christian religion does away with human distinctions in the religious realm will not stand, because it denies the unity of nature, and such denial involves the rejection of the fundamental doctrine of Christianity, the Divinity of Christ, for God is the author of nature; and if Christ was Divine, He could not have disregarded its unity."[45] Brown seems to have been arguing that churches separated by race were necessary to preserve God's racial distinctions, which ultimately and ironically retained the unity of God's purpose.

Preventing the amalgamation of the races was therefore the central reason for establishing the color line in the church. Brown contended that if the black race were "absorbed" and the white race "ruined as a result of intermarriage," then "God's plan in the creation of the two races, so far as America is concerned, would be defeated." From "inasmuch as God made yellow, black and white people, instead of only black or yellow, or white when He could have made all any one of these colors, it must be concluded that He had some great purpose to accomplish in doing so. Hence, the amalgamation of the races, or the aping of one by the other, must be wrong because it thwarts God's plan."[46] The theology of separate races thus mandated racial segregation to prevent racial mixing, and intermarriage therefore constituted an abomination in the eyes of God.

Another Episcopalian bishop—a Mississippian of more progressive ilk—observed in his essay on the education of southern blacks that the concept of racial equality was "an anachronism belonging to a medieval period of Reconstruction history, which is long ago gone to its reckoning." Moreover, he claimed, the "purpose of race distinction is known only to God," which implies his belief that God had created race distinctions in the first place.[47] In an 1899 essay published in the progressive Boston-based magazine, Arena, D. W. Culp of Georgia affirmed that, "if it is a fact (and there is no question as to that) that the distinct racial types are the result of a providential ordering, then that fact is so far forth a revelation of God's purpose as to the final disposition of the races." Culp then offered his historical assessment, alleging that history offered no instance "in which two races, as dissimilar as the whites and the blacks of this country, have fused," and that God had a "distinct mission for each distinct race to fill." Indeed, he continued, it was "God's wise purpose to keep the races separate that they may fulfill their respective missions."[48] Not surprisingly, the Knights of the Ku Klux Klan also expressed similar views in their literature. In the *Kloran*— the ritual book of the "Invisible Empire"—published in Georgia in 1916, the Klan's "Kreed" affirms: "We avow the distinction between the races of mankind as same has been decreed by the Creator, and we shall ever be true in the faithful maintenance of White Supremacy and will strenuously opposed any compromise thereof in any and all things."[49] Southern bishops and Klansmen alike thus shared in the southern white Protestant theology of separate races and the accompanying animosity toward interracial marriage.

Yet they were not the only figures to articulate such views. At least two additional bishops and two southern Protestants in the U.S. Senate expressed similar notions about God having created distinct races. In 1899 before a congressional committee, Confederate veteran, conservative Democrat, and internationally acclaimed legal scholar John Warwick Daniel of Lynchburg, Virginia, proclaimed his opposition to the ratification of a treaty that would annex the Philippines as an American territory. Uncharacteristically arguing against imperialistic actions on the part of the U.S. government, he claimed that ratifying the treaty would unleash hordes of Asian immigrants into the United States, such that the country would become "the United States of America and Asia." Dismissing the view that education of Asians could improve the situation, the senator observed, "You may change the leopard's spots, but you will never change the different qualities of the races which God has created in order that they may fulfill separate and distinct missions in the cultivation and civilization of the world."[50] Although he misquoted the notion from Jeremiah 13:23, which stated that the leopard could in fact not change its spots, Senator Daniel did convey the central idea of the southern white Protestant theology of separate races: that God had created separate and distinct races and intended them to remain that way.

Alabama senator James Thomas Heflin held similar views. The son of a prominent slaveholding family in Alabama, Heflin was notoriously antiblack—one source deems him "virulently Negrophobic"—and reputed to be a Klansman.[51] A defender of lynching as an appropriate punishment for black men who reportedly assaulted white women, Heflin caused a commotion in the Senate in 1930. He read aloud a letter he had written to a man who had inquired about his views on the marriage of a black man and white woman in New York City, which took place in a Catholic, New York City parish the previous fall. Heflin's letter stated his belief that "God had a purpose in making four separate and distinct races. The white, the red, the yellow, and the black. God intended that each of the four races should preserve its blood free from mixture with other races and preserve race integrity and prove itself true to the purpose that God had in mind for each of them when He brought them into being. The great white race is the climax and crowning glory of God's creation."[52] Like Senator Daniel, Heflin articulated the classic postwar white southern Protestant theology of race. Unlike Senator Daniel, however, Senator Heflin's assertion implied that interracial mixing represented a betrayal of God's plan for humanity.

Six and a half months before the California Supreme Court issued its decision in the *Perez* case, Presbyterian pastor J. David Simpson of Newton, Mississippi, published an essay unambiguously titled "Non-Segregation Means Eventual Inter-Marriage." In this brief 1948 article, Simpson admitted that although neither blacks nor whites desired "social intermingling," there was, however, an "affinity, the like [*sic*] of which many people are strangely unaware, between the negroes and whites." He boldly asserted that "the Scriptures teach Segregation, and most positively do not teach the pattern of non-segregation" being urged by non-southerners.[53] Like many segregationists before him, he called upon Genesis 11 and Acts 17:26 as the bases for his claims.

Yet Simpson's essay demonstrates an interesting modification in segregationist exegesis—one that would appear in much of the literature from this point onward. Simpson interpreted the phrase "bounds of their habitation" from Acts to indicate that there was "no doubt that God did not want the racial bounds separating the races broken down into hybrid races which will most certainly eventuate if all races move in and out among themselves with non-segregation and free social inter-mingling." By including the words "separating" and "segregation" in the same sentence, he subtly conflated and interchanged the two terms. Connecting the Acts verse to Genesis 11, he then asked: "What do you think the 'Tower of Babel' confusion story in the Scriptures meant if it did not mean that even the races should for the most part establish even their territorial boundary lines for their habitation, as well as racial? . . . Marriage between sharp racial lines of color and characteristics such as is found in the *Red, Brown, Black, White and Yellow* races is Unscriptural."⁵⁴ As the nation inched into the civil rights movement, the southern white Protestant theology of separate races became an explicit theology of segregation, and the marriage altar was the place where God's mandate had to be most vigorously enforced.

The Reverend G. T. Gillespie, president emeritus of Belhaven College of Jackson, Mississippi, made similar remarks as he addressed the Synod of Mississippi of the Presbyterian Church of the United States five months after the momentous May 1954 *Brown v. Board of Education* ruling. His speech, "A Christian View on Segregation," cited the Genesis stories as one of the bases for racial segregation. Noah's sons, he asserted, "became the progenitors of three distinct racial groups." According to Gillespie, the Genesis record was consistent with that of Acts 17:26, for the Genesis 9 passage, "while affirming the unity of the race, also implies that an all-wise Providence has 'determined the times before appointed, and the bounds of their habitation.'" This same Providence, he continued, "is thereby equally responsible for the distinct racial characteristics which seem to have become fixed in prehistoric times, and which are chiefly responsible for the segregation of racial groups across the centuries and in our time." Like Simpson, Gillespie also admitted that the "chief reason for segregation is the desirability of preventing such intimacies as might lead to intermarriage and the amalgamation of the races."⁵⁵ While conceding that "the Bible contains no clear mandate for or against segregation as between the white and negro races," Gillespie's pamphlet implied that those who upheld the southern white Protestant theology of separate races perceived therein a divine mandate for racial segregation in marriage.

Two years later in 1956, Baptist minister Kenneth Kinney echoed the claims of both Simpson and Gillespie. Equating "separation" and "segregation" even more explicitly than Simpson, Kinney asserted that "God ordained, for the period of man's life on earth, the segregation (which term is the equivalent of the familiar Biblical term 'separation') of the three lines which descended from the sons of Noah. . . . Noting that each of these three groups was to keep to its own tongue and family and nation, do we not face the fact that God drew the lines of segregation (or separation) according to His purpose?" Because God intended each group to retain its racial integrity, he continued, "there should be no crossing of the line by way of intermarriage between those of Japhetic (European), Shemitic (Oriental) and Hamitic (African) groups." Moreover, the "only way to comply with God's order, as we understand it, is to separate (segregate) schools, churches and families, since co-mingling . . . will lead inevitably to intermarriage, wherein God's law of separation is totally voided, hastening the day of judgment."[56] While Kinney stopped short of putting his views as baldly as the Dallas pastor who deemed God as the "original segregationist" and "Satan as the original integrationist," his claims that intermarriage would merit divine punishment were but a tiny step away.[57]

Less virulent versions of the theology of separate races occasionally appeared elsewhere than the country churches of the American South as a seemingly knee-jerk response to the subject of interracial marriage. One memorable instance involved a former U.S. president. In 1963 the *New York Times* reported a brief exchange between a reporter and Harry S. Truman in which Truman, a progressive and supporter of integration, remarked that interracial marriage "ran counter to the teachings of the Bible."[58] Truman did not specify *which* biblical passages—perhaps he would have been hard-pressed to provide them, even if he had been asked specifically. But the fact that the former occupant of America's highest political office uttered this statement suggests the extent to which the southern white Protestant theology of race saturated the thinking of even well-meaning, well-educated, and otherwise progressive white Americans. Although as David L. Chappell notes, "the southern church in the mid-twentieth century gave no significant support to segregation," much less to biblical justifications thereof, among a significant segment of the American population—ranging from local segregationist ministers like Gillespie, to state judges like Leon M. Bazile, to at least one U.S. president—a sense of God frowning upon interracial marriage influenced their beliefs about the cultural validity of marriage across the color line.[59]

Long after Truman's remark, the enactment of the Civil Rights Act of 1964, and the overturning of antimiscegenation laws in the U.S. Supreme Court, the theology of separate races continued to lodge deeply within the imagination of conservative white southern Protestants. In 1998, South Carolina residents prepared to vote on removing the ban on intermarriage from the state constitution, which had remained in place even though the state's antimiscegenation laws had been unenforceable since the 1967 *Loving* decision. The referendum sparked the old debate about whether interracial marriage violated the divine racial order. One public figure, Republican state representative Lanny Littlejohn, explained his opposition to intermarriage as a matter of his Southern Baptist upbringing. While Littlejohn admitted that "you're not going to die and go to hell for" intermarriage, he did state that interracial marriage "is an example of how humanity has fallen since they lived in the Garden of Eden."[60] Littlejohn's remarks and the South Carolina referendum later became the subject of discussion on a National Public Radio program in which reporter Phillip Martin interviewed the beleaguered politician. In the interview, Littlejohn reiterated that interracial marriage was "not what God intended when he separated the races back in the Babylonian days."[61] Littlejohn's remarks capture the postsegregation theology of separate races: no longer implying legal segregation of the races, it continues to depict racial mixing as contrary to the divine plan for humanity.

Historian I. A. Newby observes that there "seems to be no evidence to refute the conclusion of historians and social scientists, as well as church leaders and racists, that organized Protestantism [from 1900–1930] was a segregated and segregating force in the South and in the nation at large."[62] American Protestants, particularly white southerners, located the basis for segregation in scripture, and in fact they derived a theology of separate races largely from the story of the dispersion of Noah's sons in Genesis 10–11. This theology has deeply imbued southern culture from just before the Civil War through the present day. In various ways—some subtle, some overt—this theology established the religious and biblical bases for American views on interracial marriage. Moreover, it existed in contradistinction to Catholic views of race, which began to circulate after Reconstruction.

Humani Generis Unitas: The Catholic Theology of Race

John McGreevy's 1996 study of the "Catholic encounter with race" in twentieth-century northern urban parishes posits, among other things, that from the 1891 publication of Leo XIII's *Rerum Novarum* to the 1958 pastoral letter from American bishops "Discrimination and the Christian Conscience," the Catholic Church created a body of teachings on race that emphasized unity, integration, and wholeness. By 1960, McGreevy contends, "interracialism equaled orthodoxy."[63] Based on several Catholic doctrines and dispersed through several encyclicals and in the writings of several American priests and prelates, the Catholic theology of race proclaimed as its foundations unity in Christ, monogenism in Adam and Eve, and the committed quest for justice in the earthly world. The Catholic theology of race stood in contrast—indeed, in marked opposition—to theories that accentuated separate races. Indeed, the Catholic emphasis on human and racial unity resulted, it seems, from white supremacists' attention to racial separateness and especially their reliance on the Genesis stories as the basis for such views.

The Catholic theology of race thus enabled—required, even—American Catholics to hold a radically different perspective from white southern Protestants on the legitimacy of interracial marriage. If the Vatican proclaimed racial unity and common origins in Adam and Eve, then there was no doctrinal, biblical, or cultural basis for racial inequality, segregation, or legal prohibitions of interracial marriage. Although a terrible chasm loomed between theory and praxis—between what the church taught and how American Catholics behaved—Catholics never condemned marriage across the color line or cited biblical rationales for segregation.[64] Indeed, by 1940, the racial theories emanating from Europe's fascist regimes and the verification of the Nazi death camps compelled the church to address decisively the issue of racial separatism and to take an explicit stance against such views. By this time, the Roman Church had begun to articulate a theology of race explicitly emphasizing the biblical bases for racial unity, and it had condemned civil prohibitions of interracial marriage.

Yet the seeds of progressive American Catholic thinking on race began much earlier. In the South following Reconstruction, as segregation began to permeate southern thinking, customs, and institutions, progressive Catholics began to posit theological alternatives to the nascent theology of separate races. The Reverend John R. Slattery was among the first to posit human unity as the basis of the Catholic understanding of race. Slattery was the outspoken first American superior general of St. Joseph's Society of the Sacred Heart in Baltimore, or the Josephites, the only religious order devoted solely to ministry among African American Catholics. He devoted years of his life to converting and ministering to black Catholics, and he urged the American church to create a black clergy.[65] In 1883 Slattery published an essay in *Catholic World* in which he somewhat self-righteously declared:

> Wherever a Catholic missionary will appear among the colored people they will behold a personification of the Christian doctrine that all men are brethren. That doctrine does not, indeed, level men in the human sense, does not deprive wealth or family of social station, does not break down those barriers that are the metes and bounds of the gifts of Providence in the natural and civil order. But it elevates men so completely above the whole natural and civil order by regeneration into a

divine brotherhood and equality that the petty distinctions of this life are quickly forgotten. Catholicity antagonizes no truth or legitimate distinction.[66]

Notwithstanding the deep-seated reluctance of the American hierarchy to admit black men into seminaries, much less to ordain them and place them into parishes, Slattery's words foreshadowed subsequent Vatican doctrine on race. His emphasis on the unity in the familial bond of all humanity, and the assertion that catholicity admits no "legitimate distinction," stood in direct contradiction to the burgeoning white southern Protestant emphasis on divinely created racial divisions.

Five years after Slattery's essay was published, Pope Leo XIII offered one of the earliest intimations of Catholic racial doctrine. In his 1888 encyclical *In Plurimis*, Leo celebrated Brazil's decision that year to abolish slavery. Noting that the word "slave" did not appear in the Bible until "'the just man Noe branded with it the sin of his son,'" Leo asserted that those who had enslaved members of other races were "forgetful of the original brotherhood of the race." Consequently, they "began to think of other men as their inferiors, and to hold them as cattle born for the yoke."[67] "In this way," he wrote, "through an absolute forgetfulness of our common nature, and of human dignity, and the likeness of God stamped upon us all, it came to pass that . . . those who were the stronger reduced the conquered into slavery; so that mankind, though of the same race, became divided into two sections, the conquered slaves and their victorious masters" (4). The sin of "forget[ting] our common nature" was reversed, however, through Christ, whose merits lifted enslaved persons "out of the Slough and the distress of slavery" and restored "their high dignity as the sons of God." "Our common nature" had originated in the "likeness of God" (6).

Leo quoted three verses from the Pauline epistles that emphasized color-blind human unity in Christ.[68] The ideas expressed in these verses, he stated, were "golden words, indeed, noble and wholesome lessons, whereby its old dignity is given back," and humanity "of whatever land or tongue of class are bound together and joined in the strong bonds of brotherly kinship" (6). Leo then declared:

now through the new Adam, who is Christ, there is established a brotherly union between man and man, and people and people; just as in the order of nature they all have a common origin, so in the order which is above nature they all have one and the same origin in salvation and faith; all alike are called to be the adopted sons of God and the Father, who has paid the self same ransom for us all; we are all members of the same body, all are allowed to partake of the same divine banquet, and offered to us all are the blessings of divine grace and of eternal life (7).

Although slavery might have originated in Noah's curse upon his son, Christ had restored the original unity of the human race and made all persons equal and one once again. *In Plurimis* thus expressed the Catholic doctrine of human racial equality, of common human origins in Adam and Eve, and of unity in Christ—a stark contrast to white southern Protestants' vision of divine segregation.

Three years after the publication of *In Plurimis*, an Irish-born American ordinary continued Leo's theme of racial unity.[69] The Afro-American League in St. Paul, Minnesota, invited their local prelate, Archbishop John Ireland, to give an address in January 1891 commemorating the twenty-eighth anniversary of Emancipation. In his speech, Ireland proclaimed the unity and common origins of humankind. His speech, "Let There Be No Barrier against Mere Color," affirmed, "Men are all of the same race, sprung from the one father and the one mother. Ethnology and Holy Writ give the same testimony." Advocating the obliteration of the color line and the equality of black people before the law, Ireland—deemed a "consecrated blizzard" by some who felt his outspokenness to be frosty—addressed explicitly the issue of interracial marriage.[70] "In many states," he wrote, "the law forbids marriage between white and black—in this manner fomenting immorality and putting injury no less upon the white whom it pretends to elevate as upon the black for whose degradation it has no care. Let the Negro be our equal in the enjoyment of all political rights of the citizen."[71] Ireland's remarks, far from representing the views of American Catholics of his generation, are important because they proclaimed that racial separation—including separation at the marriage altar—was not compatible with Catholic doctrine. His words also foreshadowed the position on race and interracial marriage that the church would ultimately take.

Nearly fifty years after Archbishop Ireland's provocative statements, the Holy See took pains to affirm the unity of the human races. Amid the swirl of rumors and conjectures about the murders of Jewish people under Hitler, in March 1937 Pope Pius XI issued *Mit brennender Sorge*, an encyclical to the German hierarchy that took a fairly confrontational stance toward Germany's totalitarian regime. Anyone who "exalts race, or the people, or the State, or a particular form of State, or the depositories of power, or any other fundamental value of the human community . . . above their standard value and divinizes them to an idolatrous level," the document declared, "distorts and perverts an order of the world planned and created by God." Indeed, Pius continued, such a person "is far from the true faith in God and from the concept of life which that faith upholds." Rather, a "true faith in the Church" affirmed that the "Church founded by the Redeemer is one, the same for all races and all nations." Beneath the dome of the mother church "there is but one country for all nations and tongues," yet there was ample room "for the development of every quality, advantage, task and vocation which God the Creator and Saviour has allotted" to both individuals and "ethnical communities." But the church would tolerate only so many affronts to ecclesiastical unity. "Whoever tampers with that unity and that indivisibility wrenches from the Spouse of Christ one of the diadems with which God Himself crowned her; he subjects a divine structure . . . to criticism and transformation by architects whom the Father of Heaven never authorized to interfere."[72] Pius thus intimated that the church would intervene if Hitler's regime imposed restrictions on German Catholics or proclaimed any teaching counter to that of human unity.

The following year, Pope Pius XI took another step toward confrontation with racist and totalitarian governments. In April 1938 he invited Catholic priests and intellectuals to begin "forg[ing] the intellectual weapons required to refute" racism and totalitarianism, "validly and scientifically."[73] Two months later while traveling in Europe, American Jesuit John LaFarge received a summons to the pope's summer residence for an unexpected and private meeting. The pontiff had apparently been impressed with the book LaFarge had published the year before, *Interracial Justice: A Study of the Catholic Doctrine of Race Relations*. Pius appreciated LaFarge's use of Catholic teachings "to show that racial division within the human community [was] contrary to natural and revealed truth."[74] Pius was so impressed that he decided that LaFarge must immediately and secretly prepare an encyclical attacking racism and anti-Semitism and emphasizing the unity of the human family. That summer, LaFarge drafted the sections of the document on racism and anti-Semitism while two other priests worked on other parts.

Written in 1938, the year following Italy's enactment of the statute banning marriage between "Aryans" and "non-Aryans," the document commented on these laws in the section "Recommendations on race relations." "Just as there are unwritten matrimonial impediments arising from differences of age, education, social conditions and origin, and even from bodily conditions," the writers asserted, "so there are also such actual . . . circumstances in the relations of the races." Members of different races usually observe, "in their own interest," social restrictions and customs on such marriages. Such "unwritten matrimonial impediments between races are preferable to written ones, particularly if written impediments would attack the personal rights of individuals and the institution of matrimony as a Sacrament instituted by Christ and exclusively subject to the Church." The writers then bemoaned the inconsistency of sexual morality, noting the "degradation of humanity [that] is committed when marriage between members of different racial groups is systematically prohibited yet none take offense at unlawful sexual intercourse between members of different groups!"[75]

LaFarge submitted the draft to his superior in September 1938. The encyclical was to be titled *Humani Generis Unitas* (*The Unity of the Human Race*), and it constituted perhaps the most explicit and unified effort to create a Catholic doctrine on race and human unity, going even so far as to condemn—however tepidly—laws against interracial marriage.[76] But the encyclical was never published. Pius XI died in February 1939 before it could be issued, and it is not certain whether he even read the statement before his death. Moreover, the encyclical mysteriously disappeared until 1972, when a series of articles in the *National Catholic Reporter* announced: "Unpublished Encyclical Attacked Anti-Semitism."[77] In 1997, two writers gathered all the documents surrounding the creation and disappearance of *Humani Generis Unitas* and published their findings—including a draft of the encyclical—in their book, *The Hidden Encyclical of Pius XI*. According to the authors, a number of historical factors accounted in part for the disappearance of the draft, including tensions early in Pius XII's pontificate, the "deterioration of relations between the Fascist government and the Vatican," and the increasingly tense situation in Europe.[78]

Although the encyclical was never issued, Father LaFarge included "sometimes the letter, sometimes the spirit" of sections of *Humani Generis Unitas* in his later writings, and according to Passelecq and Suchecky, excerpts of it were included, "virtually unchanged," in the first encyclical of Pius XI's successor.[79] Writing to commemorate the fortieth anniversary of the Feast of Christ the King, the new Pope, Pius XII, emphasized human unity.[80] On Sunday, 20 October 1939—seven weeks after Germany had attacked Poland and nine days after President Franklin D. Roosevelt had received a letter signed by Albert Einstein urging the United States to develop the atomic bomb—Pope Pius XII issued *Summi Pontificatus* (*On the Unity of Human Society*). What a "marvelous vision" the church offered, he declared—a vision that "makes us see the human race in the unity of one common origin in God."[81] Against anti-Semitism in Nazi Germany—and, by extension, against all dogmas advocating superior and inferior, separated and segregated races—the pontiff proclaimed the historical position of the Roman Catholic Church. According to Catholic teachings, God had created all humanity in God's own image, united the human family in Adam and Eve, and redeemed it through Christ.

Pius first reminded the faithful that all humans had been created in the image of God, as stated in Genesis 1:26–27. He noted that the scriptures told "how other men took their origin from the first couple," and how their offspring subsequently divided into different groups and dispersed into various regions. But unlike southern Protestants, Pius did not then declare that God intended that the races be forever separated from that moment forward, or that the dispersion was evidence that God prohibited marriage between the races. Instead, he proclaimed that despite this division, God "did not cease to regard them as His children, who . . . should one day be reunited once more into His friendship" (10). The holy father then cited Acts 17:26, one of the same verses that some white Protestants employed to argue for the divine segregation of the races. Pius declared that in this verse the Apostle Paul had heralded the "truth which associates men as brothers in one great family," and that Paul had also portrayed "mankind in the unity of its relations with the Son of God" (10–11). In a phrase directed toward Germany, Pius stated that "despite a difference of development due to diverse conditions, of life and of culture," the nations were "not destined to break the unity of the human race." Rather, they were to "enrich and embellish it by the sharing of their own peculiar gifts." In contrast to doctrines of racial superiority, he continued, the church of Christ "cannot and does not think of deprecating or disdaining the particular characteristics which each people . . . cherishes and retains as a precious heritage. Her aim is a supernatural union in all-embracing love . . . and not the unity which is exclusively external and superficial and by that very fact weak" (11). Although veiling the Vatican's own ambivalent stance on anti-Semitism, *Summi Pontificatus* offered a marked contrast to the hermeneutics given by white southern Protestants and became one of several significant Catholic pronouncements on racial doctrine and human unity.

There were other elements of Catholic theology that facilitated an emphasis on unity as well. Pius XII issued *Mystici Corporis Christi* in 1943 and

Humani Generis in 1950, in which he explained the doctrine of the Mystical Body of Christ—a depiction of the church, comprising the faithful, and its union with and through Christ. Deriving primarily from Romans 12:4–5, *Mystici Corporis Christi* emphasized the spiritual and corporate nature of the church and the responsibilities of its members to nurture one another.[82] A body entails a "multiplicity of members," Pius stated, "which are linked together in such a way as to help one another. And as in the body when one member suffers, all the other members share its pain, and the healthy members come to the assistance of the ailing, so in the Church the individual members do not live for themselves alone, but also help their fellows, and all work in mutual collaboration for the common comfort and for the more perfect building up of the whole Body." Coinciding with the liturgical renewal movement of the 1930s and 1940s, during which time the church had begun to understand itself in new ways, *Mystici Corporis Christi* "gave papal approval" to an emergent theology of the church that emphasized community and spiritual connection to the human family through the person of Christ. Similar to *Summi Pontificatus*, the doctrine of the mystical body of Christ elevated the importance of the "divinely-given unity" of the church, through whom Christian persons "of every race are united to Christ in the bond of brotherhood," and Christ as the "perfect model of love," which all Christians are called to imitate. While not focusing on racial unity, yet *Mystici Corporis Christi* noted that the "charity of Christ" could not be diminished by "the diversity of race or customs."[83]

Humani Generis, on the other hand, coming as it did after the atrocities of Nazi Germany had been made public, took a more insistent tone on race. In it Pius XII condemned outright the theory of polygenesis, as well as inappropriate renderings of the Genesis stories. "The faithful cannot embrace that opinion," he declared, "which maintains that either after Adam there existed on this earth true men who did not take their origin through natural generation from him as from the first parent of all, or that Adam represents a certain number of first parents. Now it is in no way apparent how such an opinion can be reconciled with that which the sources of revealed truth and the documents of the Teaching Authority of the Church."[84] Again, then, the church proclaimed unity as the foundation of the Catholic theology of race.

Together these encyclicals at last signaled the orthodoxy of such views for the Catholic faithful.[85] Although certain figures in the American hierarchy resisted the church's teachings until well into the 1950s, and the

American laity even longer, there was little room to dispute the orthodoxy of racial unity, monogenism, and charity toward members of all races. The various theological bases offered as Catholic doctrines against racism and segregation underscore the fact that the church had articulated no official racial doctrine until *Mit brennender Sorge*, nor had it made a concerted effort to impart that doctrine to the American laity. More important for my analysis, despite the resistance of some Catholics in America and abroad to the church's pronouncements on racial unity, there is no getting around the fact that by 1950, the Vatican had taken a definitive stance against alternative biblical interpretations that promoted racial separation. It was becoming increasingly obvious both to proponents of the theology of separate races as well as to some American Catholics that the Catholic Church—which was slowly emerging as a less culturally suspect, Americanized institution—would likely find itself in deep conflict with those who preached a gospel of segregation. And when the U.S. Supreme Court issued the *Brown v. Board of Education* decision in 1954, there was no more volatile issue than marriage across the color line.

Catholic and Protestant Perceptions of Different Theologies of Race

Historian John McGreevy contends that the real evidence that interracialism—that is, the rejection of segregation and of biblical interpretations to support segregation—"equaled orthodoxy" for the American Catholic Church arrived in 1958 with the publication of "Discrimination and the Christian Conscience," a pastoral letter signed by American bishops. The letter proclaimed that racism was a moral and religious problem, one that must be overcome by recognizing that all humankind was equal before God. "By equal," the bishops declared, "we mean that [Negroes] are created by God and redeemed by His Divine Son, that they are bound by His Law, and that God desires them as His friends in the eternity of Heaven. This fact confers upon all men human dignity and human rights."[86] Although some bishops, particularly those in the South, were reluctant to release the statement, Pius XII secretly ordered that it be "issued at once."[87] In November 1958 the letter was printed in newspapers and magazines across the nation.[88] Although it emphasized racism as a moral issue, rather than human unity as a doctrinal issue, the fact that the church made its position public, even in the months during which Catholic John F. Kennedy's bid for the presidency was getting under way, suggests that by the late 1950s, opposition to segregation and racism had indeed become a theological doctrine not open for debate among Catholics.

Following the publication of the bishops' statement, an editorial in *U.S. News and World Report* cut to the heart of the statement's social implications. The writer acknowledged that it was "an eloquent defense of the rights of Negroes" but deemed it inadequate in its failure to address "the basic question . . . namely, intermarriage between white and colored." This issue, the writer insisted, formed "the root of the whole problem" with regard to integration.[89] The bishops' silence on this matter was strategic. As we have seen, the church's theologies of marriage and race implicitly—and sometimes explicitly—tolerated interracial marriage, but given the volatility of the issue, this was not a position the American bishops would openly support until the 1960s with *Loving v. Virginia*.

Throughout the 1950s and 1960s, Catholic bishops would, however, increasingly oppose racism and segregation, especially when white supremacists called upon Christianity to bolster their claims. As we have seen, from early in the Jim Crow era, progressive American Catholics, especially those who actually worked with black Catholics in the South, were aware of and opposed to the theology of separate races. While some preferred to address the notion of separate races by instead emphasizing racial unity as the Catholic doctrine, others explicitly rejected the very idea of "separate" races. Meanwhile, Protestant thinkers began to link Catholic doctrine with interracialism, depicting Catholics as advocates of the social equality of black persons as well as of interracial marriage. The late nineteenth-century development of these oppositional and accusatory strands of thought with regard to interracial marriage and "race-mixing" portended civil rights–era differences between Catholics and southern white Protestants on the issues of segregation and intermarriage. In addition, these divisions underscore the longevity, depth, and distinctiveness of Protestant and Catholic theologies of race.

Progressive Catholics Blame Protestants for the Theology of Separate Races

In 1862, Bishop William Elder of Natchez, Mississippi, demanded that local priests condemn the "abominable idea of the plurality of the races."[90] Some thirty years later, Archbishop John Ireland similarly depicted the notion of divinely separated races as the hallmark of narrow-minded ignorance. "The notion that God by special interposition marked off the subdivisions of the human family, and set upon each one an indelible seal of permanence is the dream of ignorance or bigotry," he wrote in 1891.[91] Still other Catholics unambiguously blamed Protestants for the theology of separate races. A nascent American Catholic theology of race thus began to develop in the late nineteenth century in explicit contradistinction to the southern white Protestant theology of separate races.

Josephite John Slattery was among those to connect the notions of separate races with Protestants. As a Josephite, Slattery had labored for eleven years in Baltimore and Virginia, attempting to convert African Americans to Roman Catholicism. In an essay in *Catholic World* in the late 1880s, he observed: "For two and a half centuries the Reformation has had the colored race under its thumb; and the result is that the very thought of its black protégés controlling a few States sends a nightmare of horror, not throughout the land, but in the South, among the very Protestants who made them, mentally and morally, what they are."[92] While this statement reveals Slattery's own troubling assumptions about African Americans, it is nonetheless instructive in its insinuation that the Protestant faith was somehow to blame for the disturbing ideas white southerners held about black people. He did not specifically state that Protestant racial views were at the heart of the South's racial problems, yet to Slattery, Protestant beliefs about "the colored race" underpinned the southern culture of racism.

By 1900, other Catholics were beginning to go a step further and to locate the origins of the notion of "separate races" in Protestant belief. Around the turn of the nineteenth century, Joseph Anciaux, a Belgian priest working with the Josephites in Lynchburg, Virginia, sharply critiqued white southern Protestant beliefs about race. In 1902 Anciaux sent an irate letter to each member of the American hierarchy and to the Sacred Congregation for the Propagation of the Faith in Rome.[93] In the letter, Anciaux declared that the notion of "a radical and unchristian separation of races" was a "Protestant idea." He also claimed that this viewpoint had "invaded the Catholic minds of the Anglo Saxon race." Perturbed at Catholics for foolishly buying into the notion, Anciaux decried white American priests who shared an "un-christian negro-phobia." He chastised white seminarians for thinking with "horror" that a black student might sit next to them in class, "at the same desk or at the same table," or that a black priest might "consecrate and bless as any other priest."[94] Anciaux's letter focused on the failures of white Catholics to treat black Americans as full humans, yet his initial remarks about the Protestant notion of separate races and the Catholic acceptance thereof were incisive. His observations positioned American Catholic racism as the by-product of southern white Protestant culture. In addition, they implied his recognition of a Catholic position on race that differed markedly from the separate races theology he blamed on Protestants.

These early statements by progressive American Catholics connecting the theology of separate races to white Protestants are telling. On one level, they foreshadowed the theology of race that would eventually issue from the Vatican. By linking white southerners' conceptions of race with Protestantism, Slattery and Anciaux implied that such beliefs were incompatible with Catholic doctrine. These statements, in other words, suggested by negation a Catholic doctrine of race, a kind of apophatic Catholic racial theology. On another level, connecting Protestantism and separate races underscored the subsequent problems in praxis that the church would face once it articulated its racial theology to American Catholics. The church met with resistance from the American hierarchy as well as the laity, and in all regions of the United States. And in the South, many Catholics accepted the theology of separate races, not recognizing it as a "Protestant" belief system so much as a "southern" cultural tradition.

Yet as John McGreevy demonstrates so well, Catholics in the urban north were just as likely as southerners to affirm segregation, though in some instances there the church itself felt more compelled to deem segregationist views as non-Catholic, if not Protestant. A situation in New York City offers one such example. In October 1929 the Reverend William S. Blackshear, rector of St. Matthew's (Episcopal) Church in Brooklyn, requested that Negroes attend their own churches. The *New York Times* picked up the story, which led Monsignor John L. Belford, pastor of the (Catholic) Church of the Nativity, to publish an article a few days later in his parish newsletter, contending that Blackshear was well within his rights to express his views. In fact, Belford claimed, the Episcopalian deserved applause for his honesty. Although Negroes had always been welcomed at the Church of the Nativity, Belford wrote, should "we see symptoms of an invasion or should strange negroes become numerous, we would not hesitate one minute to tell them to go to their own church and to exclude them if telling them was not effectual." "When people intrude they deserve exclusion," the monsignor continued, and "negroes love to make their way into white neighborhoods, white schools and white churches."[95]

Not surprisingly, Monsignor Belford's statements triggered a response from the NAACP. In a letter to Patrick Joseph Cardinal Hayes, the NAACP requested that he clarify whether the Catholic Church in fact endorsed separate churches for black Catholics. The organization stated that it "had not believed that any Catholic priest would express such sentiments" as Monsignor Belford had, and that it was "loath to believe that [Msgr. Belford's statement] represents the attitude and spirit of the Catholic Church."[96] The cardinal instructed Monsignor Thomas O'Keefe, pastor of the black Catholic Church of St. Benedict the Moor, to write to the NAACP, expressing the Catholic position on segregated churches. In his letter to the NAACP, Monsignor O'Keefe declared, "Every Catholic Church is wide open for any one who wishes to enter it for devotional purposes." Belford's publication "does not represent the attitude nor the spirit of the Catholic Church," and indeed, he continued, "it is the very opposite not only of that attitude and spirit but of the very doctrine of the Catholic Church."[97] Although O'Keefe's letter did not explicitly blame Protestants for segregation—indeed, the whole incident had been sparked by prosegregationist remarks by a Catholic—the perspective he offered clearly rejected religious-based affirmations of the legitimacy of segregated churches. O'Keefe depicted Catholic teaching as diametrically and unapologetically opposed to viewpoints that proclaimed a divinely sanctioned segregation of the races.

During the 1930s, as the racial theories of Nazi Germany became better known, and as the Vatican began proclaiming its theology of race in opposition to those theories, Catholic statements blaming Protestants for American racial problems became more pointed. Catholics specifically blamed Protestants for their role in perpetuating, and even inventing, the divisive, racialized interpretations of the Noah's curse story. In his 1934 manual on marriage law, canon law specialist Louis Nau asserted that there was absolutely no "foundation" for the "fable first introduced into Scriptural Exegesis in the eighteenth century by Protestant writers, namely, that the curse of Cham rests on the Negro."[98] Apparently unaware of the long interpretive history of the Noah's curse story that predated the eighteenth century and Protestantism itself, Reverend Nau had come to believe the whole hermeneutical tradition had originated with the Reformation. And he was not alone in his belief. In fact, accusing Protestants of depicting Ham as black formed a common theme in Catholic literature discussing American racial problems.

In 1940, for example, Canadian missions scholar Albert Perbal, O.M.I., wrote an influential article in the *Revue de l'Université d'Ottawa* in which he blamed the racialized interpretation of the curse of Ham squarely on Protestants. Perbal stated that there was "no trace" of the "curious theory" that Negroes had descended from Ham in the writings of the church fathers. He stated that some thinkers had suggested that Martin Luther—that most infamous Protestant—had first proposed the notion in his commentary on Genesis. However, this was a false assertion. "In reality," Perbal claimed, it was "the Lutheran Hannemann who, in 1677 in Kiel, openly and for the first time taught the proposition according to which Africans, Indians and Malays—all people with black skin—were the descendants of Ham and cursed with this fact, which is to say condemned to slavery for a million generations." In addition, he continued, "another Lutheran, Jean Pechlin, tried to refute him, but Hannemann claimed to rely upon Luther and on scripture; [thus] the proposition remained."[99] Catholics, Perbal admitted, had unfortunately done their share of perpetuating the story. But it was the Protestants who had linked blackness with the curse of Ham in the first place.

Perbal also offered a brief but poignant anecdote supporting his view that Catholics, unlike Protestants, rejected biblical bases for racial oppression. Catholics, he contended, had eventually recognized how the connection between blackness and slavery via Ham had hurt black peoples, and these Catholics proposed a solution. At the First Vatican Council in 1869–1870, "a group of bishops, moved by compassion and animated by a holy zeal, laid a postulatum upon the deliberations table [of the Council], [which] requested that the famous curse of Ham at last be lifted from the African peoples." Although the Council did not have time to discuss the issue, the bishops drew up a prayer from the postulatum, which was made an indulgence.[100]

Like his Catholic predecessors who had sought an official end to the curse of Ham, Perbal maintained a perspective entirely different from that of white southern Protestants on the lasting significance of Noah's curse. Even if the curse on Ham's descendants had been permanent, he reasoned, the Redemption would have interrupted and abolished it. "Every curse ceased at Calvary, and it would be reckless to place limits on the universal efficacy of the sacrifice of the Cross." Perbal closed his essay by remarking that "the destruction of this odious legend, the fruit of Lutheran lucubrations, should thus be a concern of Catholics. That it has been introduced into the Catholic world is already unfortunate; it is right that we get working to abolish it forever and expel it from our memory, so that soon one will no longer speak of the ridiculous error."[101] Only the Protestants, Perbal seems to have suggested, clung to the curse and foolishly denied the redemptive work of Christ. It was now up to Catholics to work to remove the stain of the Protestants' error.

Perbal's essay influenced at least two Catholics in the United States. A few months after its 1940 publication, an article appeared in John LaFarge's *Interracial Review* providing an abridged summary of Perbal's article in English for American readers. Claiming to be "largely indebted" to Perbal's essay, the writer began by noting that those "in believing circles" had been taught that black skin had originated with Noah's curse upon Ham's descendants. Although this "hoary tale" had suited well the antebellum American defenders of slavery, he continued, the biblical account made no mention of skin color, and "we can search in vain the Fathers of the Church and the medieval theologians for any trace" of evidence supporting the "Chamitic descent of the Negro." Following Perbal, the writer then asserted that the first person to have linked Ham and blackness "seems to have been an early disciple of Luther called Hannemann," who mistranslated the words "'foulest colors'" in Genesis 9 to state "'blackest'" or "'darkest colors.'" "Once launched, the doctrine spread far and fast," even among "distinguished [Catholic] Biblical scholars" and missionaries.[102]

Fortunately, the writer continued, "a reaction has now set in"—one supported by ethnological, exegetical, and theological evidence. Recent popes had condemned racism and proclaimed that "the Church recognizes no racial trait as a mark of Divine disfavor." The article ended in a manner similar to Perbal's, asserting that Christians "must so live and act that the canard of a curse on Negroes through a falsely alleged ancestor is buried under an avalanche of good deeds. Only then," he concluded, "can we be satisfied that we have properly interred a malodorous theory long since worthy of burial."[103] While the writer did not specifically emphasize the Protestant origins of the interpretation, he did continue to blame Protestants—and especially Luther's inept devotee—for the "malodorous theory."

Two years later, Lawrence Friedel of the Divine Word Missionaries in Bay St. Louis, Mississippi—an order originally established to prepare African American men for the priesthood—published an article in the *American Ecclesiastical Review*. Friedel cited Perbal's article, repeating his claim about the Protestant origins of the myth. Although Friedel admitted that the "belief that Negroes are Chamites has been traced to the twelfth century," he still affixed the blame for the dissemination of the belief upon Protestants, specifically upon Luther and his blundering henchman Hannemann. "There is . . . no doubt," Friedel declared, "that Luther unwittingly, and the Lutheran Hannemann, by misinterpreting a statement of Luther[,] have largely contributed to make the belief in the curse of the Negro race a household legend."[104]

Friedel also offered additional information on the postulatum presented at the First Vatican Council to remove the curse of Ham. He astutely observed that the first line of the prayer—"Let us pray for the most unhappy people of Africa, that God almighty may finally at some time remove the curse of Ham from their hearts"—appeared to "official[ly] sanction" the notion that black peoples had been cursed. Friedel then claimed that later versions of the prayer omitted the reference to the curse, thereby correcting that erroneous belief. Noting somewhat dourly that "it seemed to flatter [defenders of slavery] that they were executing God's will when they subjected Negroes to slavery," and that the "popular fable" explained Negro slavery "by the curse of God rather than by the malice of men," he argued that the evidence was inconclusive as to whether black peoples were descendants of Ham or Canaan. Even if they had been cursed, the curse surely did not continue past Christ. Friedel closed his essay by stating that "the anti-Negro Catholic cannot be a genuine Catholic," and that "we should respect all Negroes for what their race has suffered innocently." While he did not go so far as to blame all of African slavery on the Protestant hermeneutic of Genesis 9, Friedel's linking of black peoples' suffering due to misinterpretation of the story hints that the responsibility for their sufferings is related to a horrific Protestant error.[105]

As these examples illustrate, condemnations of the theology of separate races formed a theme in progressive American Catholicism following the Civil War and early twentieth century. Although many prelates remained resistant to pressures from the Vatican and from progressive American Catholics to denounce segregation and racism, and various Catholic groups formed to resist integration and desegregation, other Catholics—through words and actions—proclaimed a theology of race markedly different from that of white southern Protestants.[106] And almost as soon as progressive Catholics began to denounce segregation and "separate races" in the late nineteenth century, white southern Protestants reacted by dredging up the traditional accusations associated with racial progressivism: social equality and interracial marriage. Long before the Vatican had articulated a theology of race opposed to segregation or white supremacy, white Protestants, and especially southerners, perceived the Catholic Church as a potential seedbed of racial mongrelization.

Protestants Link Catholics with Interracial Marriage

In 1907, William Montgomery Brown, bishop of the Episcopal Church of Arkansas, explicitly linked Catholics with progressive, or at least non-southern, views on race. Brown had proposed something called the "Arkansas Plan," which called for the separation of Arkansas's parishes into black and white episcopates. He claimed that both Negroes and "the Catholic traditionalist white Churchmen" objected to the plan because it comprised "at once a denial of three doctrines, the Catholicity of the Church, the Fatherhood of God, and the Brotherhood of Man."[107] Though Bishop Brown did not elaborate, his statement suggests that he had encountered Catholic resistance to ecclesiastical segregation. Moreover, he recognized that Catholics opposed segregation on theological grounds.[108] Although Brown did not explicitly equate Catholic opposition to segregation with the advocacy of interracial marriage, it was but a small step to do so.

Two decades later, Alabama's outspoken Senator Thomas J. Heflin made precisely that claim. Following the marriage of a black NYU student and white woman in a New York City Catholic parish, Senator Heflin made incendiary statements about the Catholic Church as well as New York public officials. In a letter he read to Congress in early 1930 in which he first affirmed that God had created separate races, the Senator berated New York's Governor Franklin D. Roosevelt, Senator Royal Samuel Copeland, Alfred E. Smith, and New York City's Irish Catholic mayor, Jimmy Walker. Not only had these individuals failed to intervene in preventing the marriage, Heflin asserted, but also they had given their "hearty approval" to such marriages. The incident afforded Heflin the chance to portray Catholics as lusty aficionados of intermarriage and un-American compromisers of racial fidelity. "The fact," he declared, "that the Roman Catholic Church permits negroes and whites to belong to the same Catholic Church and to go to the same Catholic schools and permits and sanctions the marriage between whites and negroes in the United States is largely responsible for the loose, dangerous, and sickening conditions that exist in New York City and State to-day." With a flair for the melodramatic, Heflin, an alleged Klansman, observed that New York "would be a fine field for protection of white women by the Knights of the Ku Klux Klan." He then alleged that he had received "500 threatening letters" from Roman Catholics who disapproved of his statements against the pope and the Catholic Church. "Roman forces," Heflin claimed, had threatened "to put" him "out of 'their way.'" If anything were to happen to him, he wanted his "friends everywhere to know . . . that certain Roman Catholics are back of it and are responsible for it."[109] Resurrecting the tired Protestant cliché of the backwardness of all things Catholic, the senator depicted the church as wielding sinister mercenary forces ready to dispatch with dissidents and to destroy the hard-won Anglo-Saxon foundations of American democracy. As with Arkansas bishop Brown, Heflin perceived something in Catholicism that tolerated or even welcomed marriage across the color line.

Senator Heflin's assessment of Catholic doctrine was accurate. The church's theologies of race and marriage paved the way for support for interracial marriage, and there was historical evidence to prove it. There was the incident noted in Chapter 2 in which Cuba's archbishop in 1852 protested laws restricting interracial couples from marrying. Dutch archbishop Francis A. Janssens of New Orleans characterized Louisiana's 1894 antimiscegenation law as an injustice and "an infringement on human and religious liberty."[110] And during the decades following Senator Heflin's incendiary remarks to the U.S. Congress, progressive American Catholics began to oppose legal bans on interracial marriage more openly. In addition to canon marriage law specialist Louis J. Nau, theologians Joseph Francis Doherty and Francis Gilligan, and California attorney Daniel Marshall, several other Catholics affirmed the right to marry interracially as well.[111] In an article in the Negro Digest in 1943, Monsignor John A. Ryan affirmed the canonical right of Catholic interracial couples to request that their parish priest marry them.[112] During the 1950s, several southern prelates integrated Catholic schools—the first step to intermarriage, according to segregationists. And finally, a coalition of southern bishops and two Catholic organizations joined together in 1966 to advocate the legality of the marriage between Richard and Mildred Loving of Virginia.

White Protestants correctly perceived something within Catholic doctrine that allowed for the theological legitimacy of interracial marriage. But as racial tensions increased during the 1950s, some American Catholics resisted their church's stance on "political" issues such as segregation and interracial marriage. Moreover, just as some Catholics resisted Catholic doctrine, some white Protestants also resisted the southern theology of separate races. Far from indicating a simple bifurcation between racially progressive and thus "good" Catholics versus segregationist and thus "bad" Protestants, the analysis of Protestant and Catholic theologies of race reveals a most complex picture of human psychology in which believers demonstrate racial beliefs inconsistent with those of their congregational or regional cohorts. Indeed, the theology of race that shaped both American proslavery and prosegregation arguments emerged from the lips of white Catholics *and* evangelical Protestants.

Yet it was white southern Protestants who developed the dominant expressions of religious belief that shaped America segregationist arguments. White Protestants turned to the Genesis stories as the source for understanding race and human difference and perceived therein a rationale to explain southern cultural mores. The theology of separate races that derived from their interpretations of the stories of Noah and his sons permeated southern culture. According to Thomas V. Peterson, "when Ham, Japheth, and Shem became archetypes for the black, white, and red races in America, the story framed white Southerners' beliefs and value within a sacred history and therefore functioned as a myth. As myth the story of Ham symbolized the experiences of whites in the antebellum South; it unified their ancestral past with beliefs about the present and hopes for the future; it fused their racial ethos with their biblical worldview."[113] Having become blinded to the hermeneutical maneuvering needed to connect race to a text created during an era when no such concept existed, many white southerners—Protestant and Catholic alike—came to loosely regard "the Bible" as establishing the religious basis for the racial hierarchy that placed whites in positions of power over the "lesser" races.

During the one hundred or so years following the end of slavery, white southern Protestants' biblically inflected "racial ethos" mandated racial segregation in marriage. Indeed, the Protestant theology of separate races required legal action: if God had deemed racial separation as the divine plan, then humans must enact legal rules preventing any violation of that plan. Failure to uphold God's wishes constituted a direct affront to God. Antimiscegenation statutes and cases therefore functioned as the legal by-product of the theology of separate races. As Daniel Marshall astutely observed in the quotation early in this chapter, religious explanations for separate races permeated antimiscegenation cases. The next chapter examines the ways that Catholic and Protestant theologies threaded through nineteenth- and twentieth-century antimiscegenation cases, and how these shaped American perspectives on intermarriage and antimiscegenation law.

[5] States' Rights and the Southern White Protestant Theology of Race in Antimiscegenation Laws and Cases, 1867–1964

During the one hundred years following the American Civil War, several influential antimiscegenation cases offered Protestant theologies of marriage and race as legitimate bases for upholding antimiscegenation statutes. From district- and state-level courts to the U.S. Supreme Court, attorneys and judges who argued for the validity of antimiscegenation statutes affirmed the sacred status of marriage and the states' right to regulate marriage. In nearly every case—from *Scott v. State of Georgia* in 1869 to *Loving v. Virginia* in 1967—and in nearly every region of the country, the states' right argument formed the most commonly cited legal basis for antimiscegenation statutes.

From 1869 to 1967, legal arguments in antimiscegenation cases also appealed to the southern white Protestant theology of separate races. As we have seen, generations of educated white southerners—including judges, bishops and ministers, at least one college president, and U.S. congressmen—shared such views on intermarriage. Like the theology of marriage, the separate races theology threaded through antimiscegenation cases from after the Civil War through the civil rights movement. Indeed, Protestant theologies of marriage and race appeared in antimiscegenation cases from the Pennsylvania Supreme Court's *Philadelphia & West Chester R.R. Co. v. Miles* (1867) to the 1964 U.S. Supreme Court decision *McLaughlin v. Florida*, which at last foreshadowed the final demise of bans on intermarriage. The attorneys and judges who argued for antimiscegenation laws employed Protestant theologies of marriage and separate races to bolster their legal arguments. Moreover, comparison of antimiscegenation statutes in the West and the South demonstrates that there were significant differences between the two regions in terms of whether violations of the laws constituted felonies or misdemeanors and, consequently, differences in how violators were penalized. The evidence suggests that *Perez* influenced the abandonment of the laws in the West and that the Protestant theologies of marriage and separate races undergirded the harsher penalties and massive resistance toward intermarriage in the South.[1]

Theologies of Marriage and Race in Antimiscegenation Cases

In the years leading up to the American Civil War, Americans frequently and anxiously raised the specter of interracial marriages—particularly, those between black men and white women—as a frightening consequence of the liberation of enslaved black people. In the fall of 1863, prominent abolitionists across the nation received an anonymous pamphlet titled *Miscegenation: The Theory of the Blending of the Races, Applied to the White Man and the Negro*. The writer appeared to be an enthusiastic and radical abolitionist. He claimed that Lincoln's Republican party was the "party of miscegenation" and that Republicans would lead the United States to international dominance by granting social equality to blacks through the legalization of interracial marriage.[2] Within weeks of its publication, the pamphlet had become internationally known, but its author was suspected of writing under false pretenses. In October 1864, newspapers revealed that the little book was a hoax—a political satire written by two New York journalists, conservative Democrats David Goodman Croly and George Wakeman, who had hoped to cost Lincoln the presidency.[3] The hoax reflected white Americans' intense anxiety about the possibility of intermarriage following emancipation. And in the years immediately following the Civil War, southern states and western states and territories quickly enacted antimiscegenation statutes.

The enactment of the Civil Rights Act of 1866 and the Fourteenth Amendment in 1868 in turn led a number of interracial couples to challenge antimiscegenation statutes as violations of their constitutional rights to make contracts, and to receive equal protection and due process of the law.[4] Antimiscegenation laws, some couples contended, were unfair and discriminatory in that they treated interracial couples differently than intraracial couples. In other cases couples contested their criminal convictions for having unlawfully married or lived together, and still others involved the children or other relatives of interracial couples battling for inheritance rights in probate courts. Although three cases in Republican-led Texas and

Louisiana declared their antimiscegenation laws unconstitutional during Reconstruction, by 1894 all southern states had enacted or reenacted antimiscegenation statutes.[5]

American notions of marriage played out uniquely in postwar antimiscegenation cases. As we have seen, during the nineteenth century, the Protestant theology of marriage evolved into a civil conception of marriage, in which the disestablished civil government held the authority to establish and enforce marriage law, and which Americans of all religious affiliations accepted. Also, during that same century a new debate arose over whether the federal or state government should have jurisdiction over marriage law, and this controversy played out in the polygamy issue in the Utah Territory. We will now examine how antimiscegenation cases represent yet another dimension of the struggle between federal and state governments, and how during the twentieth century such cases initiated yet another contest between state authority and individuals' right to marry the person of their choosing. This final issue once again set progressive Catholics, who proclaimed the individual's right to choose (as well as the unity of the races), against southern Protestants. Immediately following the Civil War and the 1954 *Brown* decision, southern white Protestants were particularly adamant about the right of the state to determine its own laws.

Nineteenth-Century Cases

After the Civil War, and again following *Brown* (1954), courts affirmed the civil conception of marriage based on the notion of states' rights, and the southern white Protestant theology of separate races, as support for antimiscegenation statutes. In one memorable and influential instance, a court based its position entirely on the separate races theology. Oddly enough, marriage across the color line was not the subject matter in the case. Perhaps more surprising, it originated north of the Mason-Dixon line—in fact, in the City of Brotherly Love. Prefiguring the *Plessy* case of 1896, in 1867 the Supreme Court of Pennsylvania ruled constitutional the right of railroad companies to segregate passengers by race. In *Philadelphia & West Chester R.R. Co. v. Miles*, Chief Justice Daniel Agnew cited the Protestant theology of race as proof of the separate nature of the races and thus as the "reasonable ground" for separating the two groups. "Why the Creator made one white and the other black, we know not," he stated, "but the fact is apparent and the races distinct, each producing its own kind, and following the peculiar law of its constitution." Although the judge conceded that each race was equal insofar as its nature and its rights, "yet God has made them dissimilar, with those natural instincts and feelings which He always imparts to His creatures, when He intends that they shall not overstep the natural boundaries He has assigned to them."[6]

Justice Agnew could have ended his discussion there, having established a religious and, in his mind, historical basis for separating the races. Yet he continued on and claimed that racial "amalgamation" was precisely what social segregation aspired to avoid and what natural law utterly condemned. "The natural law, which forbids their intermarriage and that amalgamation which leads to a corruption of races," he stated, "is as clearly divine as that which imparted to them different natures. The tendency of intimate social intermixture is to amalgamation, contrary to the law of races. The separation of the white and black races upon the surface of the globe is a fact equally apparent." Justice Agnew refused to speculate on God's reasons for having scattered the black and white races in opposite directions of the earth. Yet, he asserted, "the fact of a distribution of men by race and color is as visible in the providential arrangement of the earth as that of heat and cold." That racial separation was a natural aspect of human life was thus "undeniable," and "all social organizations which lead to their amalgamation are repugnant to the law of nature."

Justice Agnew insisted that the separation of the races did not "declare inferiority in either." Rather, laws mandating racial separation simply indicated human compliance with "the order of Divine Providence." Consequently, when "we declare a right to maintain separate relations, as far as is reasonably practicable, but in a spirit of kindness and charity, and with due regard to equality of rights, it is not prejudice, nor caste, nor injustice of any kind, but simply to suffer men to follow the law of races established by the Creator himself, and not to compel them to intermix contrary to their instincts." Like the subsequent cases that presented the Protestant theology of race as support for antimiscegenation laws and racial segregation, the judge's analysis begged the question of why laws mandating racial separation were necessary if "intermixing" were in fact "contrary to their instincts." Yet what is significant is the fact that the theology of separate races is offered and accepted as a legitimate basis for a legal argument. In addition, several subsequent antimiscegenation cases cited *Philadelphia*—a clear indication of the case's influence, of the ubiquity of the separate races theology, and of the social sanction of the theology in courts of law.

Two years after Justice Agnew's decision, one of the most influential antimiscegenation cases to articulate the southern Protestant theology of race appeared before the Supreme Court of Georgia. In *Scott v. State*, the court upheld the conviction of Charlotte Scott. Scott, an "unmarried woman of color," had been convicted of "cohabiting and having sexual intercourse with one Leopold Daniels," who claimed to have been a Frenchman born in "Leon."[7] Addressing the question of whether or not whites and persons of color had the right "under the Constitution and laws of Georgia, to intermarry, and live together in this State as man and wife," the court affirmed that the antimiscegenation statute had been "dictated by wise statesmanship" and had a "broad and solid foundation in enlightened policy, sustained by sound reason and common sense." In what would become one of the most commonly cited passages of nineteenth-century antimiscegenation cases, the judge then stated:

The amalgamation of the races is not only unnatural, but is always productive of deplorable results. Our daily observation shows us, that the offspring of these unnatural connections are generally sickly and effeminate, and that they are inferior in physical development and strength, to the full-blood of either race. It is sometimes urged that such marriages should be encouraged, for the purpose of elevating the inferior race. The reply is, that such connections never elevate the inferior race to the position of the superior, but they bring down the superior to that of the inferior. They are productive of evil, and evil only, without any corresponding good. (323)

After declaring that the state legislature "had as much right to regulate the marriage relation by prohibiting it between persons of different races as they had to prohibit it between persons within the Levitical degrees, or between idiots," the judge went on for three pages, insisting that Georgia lawmakers had no authority to legislate the social status of the citizenry (324–25). A law allowing interracial marriage, in other words, would imply the social equality of blacks and whites. Any such law, in this judge's mind, would exceed both the scope of the legislature's power and the intention of constitutional guarantees. He then explained that moral and social equality between the races did not and could never exist, for the "God of nature made it otherwise, and no human law can produce it, and no human tribunal can enforce it" (326). Although the decision stopped short of stating that God had separated the races, the core elements of the white southern Protestant theology of race were present in this case. God intended for the races to be separate in all social relations and most definitely in marriage.

Antimiscegenation cases that went to court also proclaimed the states' right to regulate marriage. North Carolina's *State v. Hairston* (1869) was among the first of the post–Civil War antimiscegenation cases to offer the civil understanding of marriage as the rationale for the constitutionality of antimiscegenation statutes. In this case, defendants Wesley Hairston and Puss Williams—a black man and white woman—were convicted in North Carolina for having contracted an interracial marriage. Like the defendants in Alabama's 1868 *Ellis v. State*, Hairston and Williams appealed their convictions, claiming that North Carolina's antimiscegenation statutes violated their right to make and enforce contracts—a marriage contract—as guaranteed in the Civil Rights Act of 1866.[8] The court disagreed with the couple's argument and declared that the Civil Rights bill had "no application to the social relations."

In a classic postwar southern affirmation of the states' right to deny social equality to black citizens, the North Carolina court stated that although the bill did grant equality in business contracts, courts, property contracts, and such, it was not "intended to enforce social equality; but only civil and political rights." Marriage, as part of the social sphere, was most assuredly not what the bill was designed to regulate. For although marriage was in one sense a contract, it was also a "relation, an institution, affecting not merely the parties, like business contracts, but offspring particularly, and society generally." Every state, therefore, had "always assumed to regulate it and to declare who are capable of contracting marriage," including the specifications of the ceremony, the duties and privileges of marriage, and the means of its dissolution. "These things," the court proclaimed, "have never been left to the discretion of the individuals, but have been regulated by law."[9] Subtly denying the couple's free right to choose whom to marry, the court thus ruled Hairston and Williams's marriage to be "pretended" and invalid and declared them guilty of fornication and adultery. The state, and only the state, held the authority to deem a couple "married" or to prohibit them from marrying.

Two years later a Tennessee court similarly declared the right of the state to set and regulate marriage law. In *Lonas v. State*, a prisoner serving a sentence for having married a person of another race contested the constitutionality of the states' antimiscegenation statutes. The court waved away the defendant's claim that the federal government could lawfully exert some authority over the state laws. The judge asserted: "That this [marital] relation is subject to the law of the State, without any restriction from the Constitution of the United States, is too clear for argument."[10] Still reeling from the losses of the war, the southern judge reiterated his argument, appealing directly to the Tenth Amendment of the U.S. Constitution for the states' authority to establish its own laws: "it is well to look back upon our [legal] landmarks which our fathers have set, and ascertain what rights the States have not been bereft of as the result of the late unhappy civil war. And prominent and paramount among these, is the provision that 'the powers not delegated to the United States by the Constitution, nor prohibited by it to the States, are reserved to the States respectively, and to the people.' Art. 10. Con. U.S." (304). The court seemed to have been saying, How could anyone—including the federal government—be so obtuse as to refute the constitutional right of a state to proclaim its own marriage law?

The *Lonas* decision also explicitly denied that the right to marry constituted a legal privilege held by all citizens. "Marriage is in no sense a privilege which the citizen has, as a citizen, of the United States," the court stated. Such privileges were "not claimed or held of the United States, but of the State" (293–94). And in the state of Tennessee, black and white citizens did not have the right to marry each other. In this court's view, the states' duty to regulate marriage law irrefutably trumped the individual citizen's freedom to choose a marriage partner. *Lonas* thus affirmed a principle in direct contradiction to that of the Catholic theology of marriage, which extolled the free right of the individual to choose a spouse.

Lonas also called upon the white southern Protestant theology of race to justify antimiscegenation laws. The decision first noted that black and white persons were forbidden from marrying due to the "distinction between them in race and color, made by nature." Tennessee's antimiscegenation law, the court stated, "recognize[d] and assert[ed] that distinction, and ma[de] it a bar to intermarriage" (288). Although the writer cited no biblical passage, he did mention that the "Mosaic law" had forbidden "the Jews to gender animals of a diverse kind together." This mandate, he claimed, was no more rooted in discrimination than the antimiscegenation law, which merely aimed to "prevent the production of this hybrid race" and to "prevent violence and bloodshed which would arise from such cohabitation, distasteful to our people, and unfit to produce the human race in any of the types in which it was created" (299–300).

Several pages later, the writer resumed his discussion of biblical injunctions against intermarriage. "The discrimination as to race and people, in this most important institution [marriage]," he stated, "has been observed, even from the days of the patriarchs, and even as to different people of the same race." Citing a passage in Genesis 24 in which Abraham instructed his son not to marry a Canaanite woman, he moved on to claim that the "laws of civilization" required that "the races be kept apart in this country" (310–311). Although he did not explicitly state that God's law necessitated segregation or that God had separated the races, the judge's appeals to the Bible strongly suggest that his beliefs stemmed from Christian beliefs about race.

The same year that the Tennessee court handed down the Lonas decision, an Indiana court affirmed the states' right to prohibit certain marriages. In fact, this case boldly asserted this right against that of the federal government. The appellees in *State v. Gibson* challenged the validity of the laws based upon the Civil Rights Act of 1866, and the court denied that the contract clause of the Civil Rights bill applied to marriage. In a passage that would frequently be quoted in subsequent antimiscegenation cases, the Indiana court rather querulously proclaimed, "we utterly deny the power of congress to regulate, control, or in any manner to interfere with the States in determining what shall constitute crimes against the laws of the State, or the manner or extent of punishment." Echoing *Hairston*, the Indiana court agreed that marriage constituted a civil contract but viewed it as more than just a contract. Rather, marriage, "a public institution established by God himself," was "recognized in all Christian and civilized nations" and was "essential to the peace, happiness, and well-being of society." Society could not, in fact, function without marriage, "for upon it all the social and domestic relations are based." The sacred nature of marriage therefore meant that "The right in the States to regulate and control, to guard, protect and preserve this God-given, civilizing and Christianizing institution is of inestimable importance, and cannot be surrendered, nor can the States suffer or permit any interference therewith. If the Federal government can determine who may marry in a State, there is no limit to its power."[11] One of the strongest pronouncements against federal intervention in state marriage law—and originating in a nonsouthern court—*Gibson* thus affirmed that marriage was more than just a contract, it was a legal relationship with sacred meaning; also, it verified in a double sense the states' right to regulate marriage. The decision at once proclaimed the right of the secular state as opposed to that of any ecclesiastical institution, and the right of the independent state as opposed to the federal government.

State v. Gibson called upon the theology of separate races as well. While people in other states could opt to "permit a corruption of blood, and a mixture of races," the court maintained, the people of Indiana opposed the "intermixture of races, and all amalgamation." Until the legislature declared otherwise, this court would enforce the law, the judge declared. As its grand finale, the *Gibson* ruling then stated, "this subject is discussed with great ability, clearness, and force" by the Supreme Court of Pennsylvania, and proceeded to quote the entire *Philadelphia & Westchester R.R. Co. v. Miles* decision. The Indiana court then stated, "We fully concur in and indorse the doctrine above enunciated."[12] Far more explicitly than the *Lonas* ruling, *Gibson* affirmed a religion-based "doctrine" of race. The viewpoint represented here derived from a unique form of American Protestant biblicism, the theology of separate races that was most often, but not always, expressed by white southerners.

One of the most influential of nineteenth-century antimiscegenation cases was *Green v. State*. Appearing before the Alabama Supreme Court in 1877, just six years before the U.S. Supreme Court decision in *Pace v. Alabama*, the six-page *Green* decision decisively affirmed the civil understanding of marriage. In this case, an anonymous couple appealed their conviction for intermarriage on the grounds that Alabama's antimiscegenation statutes conflicted with the Civil Rights Act. In response to their argument, the court cited several cases that proclaimed the extracontractual nature of marriage and the "sovereign power of the State" to regulate and control marriage law.[13] In one of the most often cited passages in subsequent antimiscegenation cases, the court discussed how marriage constituted "the most interesting and important" societal institution, insofar as it was "through the marriage relation that the homes of a people are created." Indeed, the decision stated, "these homes, in which the virtues are most cultivated and happiness most abounds, are the true *officinae gentium*—the nurseries of the States. Who can estimate the evil of introducing into their most intimate relations, elements so heterogeneous that they must naturally cause discord, shame, disruption of family circles and estrangement of kindred? While with their interior administration the State should interfere but little, it is obviously of the highest public concern that it should, by general laws adapted to the state of things around them, guard them against disturbances from without" (742). The sanctity of the hearth and home both made marriage more than a mere contractual relation, and it thus demanded the states' legal protection. Altogether denying that antimiscegenation statutes violated anyone's constitutional rights, the court stated that the "amendments to the Constitution were evidently designed to secure to citizens, without distinction of race, rights of a civil or political kind only; not such as are merely social, much less those of a purely domestic nature.

The regulation of these belongs to the States" (744). *Green* thus affirmed the core assertion of the American understanding of marriage: the institution of marriage was to be subject to civil law.

The Alabama Supreme Court also emphasized the home's need for protection by the state and declared, "Hence it is, that, if not in every State of the Union, in all of them in which any considerable numbers of the negro race resided, statutes have been enacted prohibiting marriages between them and persons of the white race." The court then quoted an excerpt from *Philadelphia* as an explanation of the divine legitimacy of antimiscegenation statutes, affirming that God had made the races "dissimilar," and the "'natural law, which forbids their intermarriage and that amalgamation which leads to a corruption of races, is as clearly divine as that which imparted to them different natures'" (742). *Green* then went on at length to claim that homes and families needed the kind of protection afforded by antimiscegenation laws. "Surely," the Court maintained, "there cannot be any tyranny or injustice in requiring both alike to form this union with those of their own race only, whom God hath joined together by indelible peculiarities, which declare that He has made the two races distinct" (743). Just as *Philadelphia* and its explicit Protestant theology of race influenced subsequent cases, later cases frequently cited *Green*. The Protestant theology of race was thus perpetuated in cases that cited the race passages from precedents *Philadelphia* and *Green*.

The following year, in circumstances strangely parallel to those of Mildred and Richard Loving some eighty years later, a Virginia court upheld the 1878 conviction of an interracial couple for "lewdly and lasciviously associating and cohabiting together."[14] This case, *Kinney v. Commonwealth*, was Virginia's "major precedent regarding miscegenation cases in the late-nineteenth and twentieth centuries."[15] Andrew Kinney, a Negro man, and Mahala Miller, a white woman, left the state to get married in Washington, D.C. Upon returning to Virginia, they were indicted for cohabitation, for Virginia law deemed all interracial marriages absolutely void, regardless of where they had been contracted, and refused to grant any legitimacy to the Kinneys' marriage. The couple was thus subject to prosecution for fornication and cohabitation violations. Consequently, the constitutional question before Virginia's Court of Appeals differed from earlier cases; the court had to decide whether a marriage celebrated outside the state and in violation of state law could protect the couple from prosecution. Not surprisingly, the court unanimously held that their marriage afforded them no such protection. "There can be no doubt as to the power of every country to make laws regulating the marriage of its own subjects; to declare who they may marry, how they may marry, and what shall be the legal consequences of their marrying. The right to regulate the institution of marriage; to classify the parties and persons who may lawfully marry; to dissolve the relation by divorce; and to impose such restraints upon the relations as the laws of God, and the laws of propriety, morality and social order demand, has been exercised by all civilized governments in all ages of the world" (862). Rejecting the argument that "a marriage valid where celebrated is good everywhere," the court claimed there were certain exceptions to this rule, such as polygamous, incestuous, and interracial marriages. Antimiscegenation laws were valid expressions of public policy, "upon which social order, public morality, and the best interests of both races depend" (865). Such policy most definitely fell under the purview of the state. Marriage, "the most elementary of all [social relations]," the *Kinney* decision declared, "must be regulated and controlled by the sovereign power of the state" (869).

Kinney also cited Christian beliefs about race as a basis for both social and marital segregation. In another affirmation of the theology of separate races, the court declared: "The purity of public morals, the moral and physical development of both races, and the highest achievement of our cherished southern civilization, under which two distinct races are to work out and accomplish the destiny to which the Almighty has assigned them on this continent—all require that they should be kept distinct and separate, and that connections and alliances so unnatural that God and nature seem to forbid them, should be prohibited by positive law, and be subject to no evasion." The court thus depicted as unnatural and unholy the union of the interracial couple who had left the state of Virginia and married elsewhere in order to evade its antimiscegenation law. Such was the long-recognized "public policy of this state," which prevented the "intercommingling of the races by refusing to legitimate marriages between them" (869). If the couple desired "to maintain the relations of man and wife, they must change their domicile and go to some state or country where the laws recognize the validity of such marriages" (870). Like its other southern neighbors, Virginia thus accepted the Protestant theology of race as part of the basis for antimiscegenation statutes. And there is no indication in any of the court records that such a position was regarded as an exceptional or unusual explanation for legal prohibitions against interracial marriage.

The following year, the federal circuit court for Virginia's Eastern District received a petition for a writ of habeas corpus from another man named Kinney. African American Edmund Kinney had married a white woman,

Mary S. Hall, in Washington, D.C., in 1878, and then the couple returned to Virginia. Both were convicted of leaving the state to get married and both were sentenced to five years of hard labor. Filing the petition independently of Hall, Kinney requested that he be released from prison on the grounds that the state's antimiscegenation statutes violated his constitutional rights. In addition, Kinney's suit charged that Virginia was bound to recognize the marriage because "a marriage lawful in the District of Columbia is lawful everywhere in the United States, enabling those so married to live together as man and wife in any part of the United States, and that any state law forbidding them to do so is contrary to the constitution and void." Reiterating the authority of state over and against that of the federal government, the court ruled: "With the propriety, policy, or justice of such laws a court of the United States has nothing to do. . . . The fourteenth amendment gives no power to congress to interfere with the right of the state to regulate the domestic relations of its own citizens, and if a state enact such laws as those which have been quoted, the federal courts must respect them as they stand, without inquiring into the reasons of them." Congress, in fact, had established "no law relating to marriage." It had not done so, the decision continued, "simply because it has no constitutional power to make laws affecting the domestic relations and regulating the social intercourse of the citizens of a state. If it were to make such a law for the states, that law would be unconstitutional, and the federal courts would not hesitate to declare it so. It is the state which is endowed with the sovereign power of making such laws, and therefore only those contracts of marriage that are legal under state laws can be enforced or enjoyed within the jurisdiction of the state."[16] Refusing to give one inch toward Kinney's assertion that one state should recognize a marriage performed in another jurisdiction, lest such a position be construed as support for some kind of interstate and thus federally regulated marriage law, the court reasserted the state's authority to determine its own marriage law and denied Kinney's writ of habeas corpus.

In *Pace v. Alabama* (1883), the U.S. Supreme Court actually ruled antimiscegenation prohibitions constitutional, thereby setting a federal precedent. The Court held that statutes punishing interracial fornication more severely than intraracial fornication were constitutional because a) both black and white offenders were punished equally under antimiscegenation statutes, and b) antimiscegenation violations by definition pertained to an offense committed by a couple of different races. Therefore there was no legitimacy to the claim that the law was directed against persons because of their color or race. The unequal punishment for interracial offenses was "directed against the offense designated and not against the person of any particular color or race."[17] Until California set a new precedent with *Perez* in 1948, *Pace* remained the standard legal response to challenges alleging that antimiscegenation statutes were racially discriminatory and thus violated individuals' Fourteenth Amendment rights.

That same year, in *State v. Jackson*, the Supreme Court of Missouri also affirmed the states' duty to regulate marriage. The court testily asserted that it was "only by ascribing to that [fourteenth] amendment a force and scope expressly denied it by the Supreme Court of the United States that any ground exists for questioning" the validity of Missouri's antimiscegenation laws. In addition, it continued, it was not "one of the natural rights of man to marry whom he may choose. Under the Jewish dispensation persons nearly related by ties of blood intermarried, but in no Christian land are such marriages tolerated. The right to regulate marriage, the age at which persons may enter into that relation, the manner in which the rites may be celebrated, and the persons between whom it may be contracted, has been assumed and exercised by every civilized and Christian nation." It also asserted that while it "may interfere with the taste of negroes who want to marry whites, or whites who wish to intermarry with negroes," the state "has the same right to regulate marriages in this respect that it has to forbid the intermarriage of cousins or other blood relatives." Indeed, the decision proclaimed, "we know of no power on earth" that could prevent a state from enacting laws to preserve the racial purity of its citizens. "It is a matter of purely domestic concern. The 14th amendment to the Constitution of the United States, to which, by some, magical power is ascribed, has no such scope as seems to have been accorded to it by the Circuit Court." As if these statements had not adequately clarified its position, the Court again denied that the Constitution granted the individual the right to marry anyone "willing to wed him," and reiterated that the "power of each State to regulate and control marriages within its jurisdiction, is as unquestionable as State sovereignty."[18]

In 1890, a U.S. district court, in *State v. Tutty*, similarly refuted the applicability of the Fourteenth Amendment to Georgia's marriage law. Marriage legislation, the decision stated, "is not within the prohibition of the constitution of the United States against the impairment of a contract by such legislation."[19] Five years later, in *Dodson v. State*, the Supreme Court of Arkansas put a slightly different spin on the notion of the states' right to regulate marriage when it declared marriage to be "a social and domestic relation, subject to the exercise of the highest governmental power of the sovereign state,—the police power."[20] As Peter Wallenstein observes, in light of the U.S. Supreme Court decisions in *Pace* (1883) and *Maynard v. Hill* (1888), after this point, "miscegenation laws simply raised no constitutional issues that citizens could raise effectively in any quest to overturn them. Racial segregation in marriage and the family became just as central a part of American apartheid as did segregation in trains or in schools. From the 1880s into the 1960s, no state had to answer to federal authority for what it chose to do regarding the law of race and marriage."[21] Indeed, in case after case, courts affirmed the states' right to regulate marriage and to prohibit interracial marriage.

Twentieth-Century Cases

By the early twentieth century, the states' right argument formed one of the key legal defenses of antimiscegenation statutes. In *Kirby v. Kirby* (1922), for example, the Supreme Court of Arizona ruled that "The domestic relation, including the marriage and its dissolution by divorce or proceedings to annul, as well as the regulation of it during its continuance, is peculiarly a matter of state regulation."[22] In 1923 the Supreme Court of Oklahoma stated that "a state, in the exercise of its sovereign power, has the right to impose upon its citizens an incapacity to contract marriage by means of a positive policy of the state for the protection of the morals and good order of society against serious social evils."[23] The Supreme Court of Montana in 1942 similarly stated that the "control and regulation of marriage are matters of domestic concern within each state, and in the adoption of policies in respect thereto, which in its judgment are promotive of the welfare of its society and of the individual members thereof, the state is 'sovereign' and not subject to the control of the federal government or of the laws of any other state."[24]

During the twentieth century, whenever cases challenged the constitutionality of antimiscegenation statutes, court decisions continued to assert the states' right to regulate marriage as the basis for the statutes' legitimacy. *Stevens v. United States* in 1944 proffered that prohibiting interracial marriage fell "within the range of permissible adoption of policies deemed to be promotive of the welfare of society as well as the individual members thereof." According to the Tenth Circuit Court of Appeals, then, antimiscegenation statutes did not "contravene the Fourteenth Amendment."[25] Moreover, in 1944—toward the end of the extermination program in Germany and the beginning of the American civil rights movement—southern courts still viewed the Protestant theology of race as an acceptable justification for antimiscegenation laws.

That same year, in *Dees et al. v. Metts et al.*, the Supreme Court of Alabama heard a probate case involving a dispute between a black woman and the relatives of her white long-term lover, who had left his entire estate to her when he died. Although the court ultimately ruled in favor of the woman, it did address the immorality of interracial sexuality. "A universal public opinion prevalent in both races recognizes at least two grades of depravity in matters of illicit relationship. It is reprehensible enough for a white man to live in adultery with a white woman, thus defying the laws of both God and man, but it is more so, and a much lower grade of depravity, for a white man to live in adultery with a Negro woman." Although it is unclear if by "laws of God" the court intended to condemn interracial or intraracial extramarital affairs (or, more likely, both), the statement subtly underscores the theology of separate races. Quoting an earlier case with similar circumstances, the opinion reiterated its view that "Reclamation may be made of [the] one; but for the other, there little, if any, hope."[26] To the justices on the Alabama Supreme Court, an interracial couple living in adultery clearly symbolized a most heinous type of sin.

Eleven years later, on the heels of the momentous 1954 *Brown v. Board* ruling, the Supreme Court of Appeals of Virginia quite explicitly cited the Protestant theologies of marriage and race in *Naim v. Naim*. In 1955, a white woman asked the Supreme Court of Appeals of Virginia to annul her marriage to a Chinese man on the grounds of adultery.[27] Three years before, the couple had left Virginia to evade the state law and married in North Carolina.[28] A lower court had held the marriage to be void and therefore not subject to annulment. The woman, Ruby Elaine Naim, appealed the decision. The court of appeals affirmed the lower court's judgment in *Naim*, resurrecting the Protestant theology of race and upholding the states' right to establish marriage law. Quoting passages from Indiana's 1871 Gibson decision, which in turn quoted from *Philadelphia*, the court affirmed the Christian basis for prohibiting interracial marriage and amalgamation. "It was said in that case that the question [of the legitimacy of antimiscegenation statutes] was one of difference between the races, not of superiority or inferiority, and that the natural law which forbids their intermarriage and the social amalgamation which leads to a corruption of races is as clearly divine as that which imparted to them different natures" (84). The court did not indicate which case—*State v. Gibson* or *Philadelphia*—declared which view. In fact, it seems to have blurred the two cases into one. What is clear, however, is that in 1955 the justices on Virginia's highest court still viewed the religious beliefs expressed in 1860s legal precedents as reasonable, lawful bases for the state's antimiscegenation statutes.

In addition, the court declared the states' right to regulate marriage. "From the *Slaughterhouse Cases* (1873) . . . to *Brown v Board* (1954) and *Bolling v Sharpe*," it stated, "the Supreme Court has made no decision at variance with the holding in the *Stevens* case [1944]." Acknowledging that the U.S. Supreme Court had occasionally invoked the Fourteenth Amendment to invalidate state laws having to do with political and civil rights, the Virginia court insisted that the federal government had not refused the state's right to determine marriage law. "On the contrary," the decision stated, the nation's highest court "has been at pains to exclude that relation from the effects of its holdings" (86). With lingering bitterness over the *Brown* decision and the federal government's intervention with southern customs, the court laboriously discussed the state's right to regulate marriage. Reviewing scores of cases proclaiming this right, along with states' right to enact laws "'suppress[ing] what it is free to regard as a public evil,'" the decision stated that if "the prevention of miscegenetic marriages is a proper governmental objective," which "we hold it to be," then Virginia's antimiscegenation law was valid (88–89). In its penultimate paragraph, the court fiercely declared,

> We are unable to read in the Fourteenth Amendment to the Constitution, or in any other provision of that great document, any words or any intendment which prohibits the State from enacting legislation to preserve the racial integrity of its citizens, or which denies the power of the State to regulate the marriage relation so that it shall not have a mongrel breed of citizens. We find there no requirement that the State shall not legislate to prevent the obliteration of racial pride, but must permit the corruption of blood even though it weaken or destroy the quality of its citizenship. Both sacred and secular history teach that nations and races have better advanced in human progress when they cultivated their own distinctive characteristics and culture and developed their own peculiar genius. (90–91)

As if daring the Supreme Court to challenge this point, the court of appeals then closed the *Naim* case with a passionate appeal to the Tenth Amendment. Regulating marriage law, it stated, is "distinctly one of the rights guaranteed to the States and safe-guarded by that bastion of States' rights, somewhat battered perhaps but still a sturdy fortress in our fundamental law, the tenth section of the Bill of Rights, which declares: 'The powers not delegated to the United States by the Constitution, nor prohibited by it to the States, are reserved to the states respectively, or to the people'" (90). A defiant thumb-in-the-nose to the Warren Court and anyone else who dared intervene in southern racial customs, *Naim* called upon the timeworn but heretofore effective theologies of marriage and separate races to uphold Virginia's antimiscegenation statutes.

Four years later in 1959, the Supreme Court of Louisiana employed a similarly sassy strategy—minus the religion—in *State of Louisiana v. Brown and Aymond*. In this case, the court reversed the decision of a lower court that had convicted a couple of miscegenation, based upon a legal glitch, and sent them back to the district court for a new trial.[29] The court affirmed the right of states to enact antimiscegenation statutes, which, it claimed, "in no way violate[d]" guarantees of equal protection. It then provided a new reason for such laws, slyly using the Supreme Court's own logic in *Brown v. Board of Education*. An antimiscegenation statute, Justice Hawthorne wrote, "we think falls squarely within the police power of the state, which has an interest in maintaining the purity of the races and in preventing the propagation of half-breed children. Such children have difficulty being accepted by society, and there is no doubt that children in such a situation are burdened, as has been said in another connection, with a 'feeling of inferiority as to their status in the community that may affect their hearts and minds in a way unlikely ever to be undone.'"[30] The quoted passage was taken from *Brown v. Board of Education*, seemingly as a derisive means of justifying Louisiana law. Unlike Virginia's *Naim* ruling, the Louisiana Supreme Court decision had provided an argument for racial separation in marriage that did not call upon the theology of separate races.

Finally in 1964, the U.S. Supreme Court signaled the approaching end of religion-based arguments for antimiscegenation laws. In *McLaughlin v. Florida*, the Court declared unconstitutional Florida's prohibition against interracial cohabitation, which stated: "Any negro man and white woman, or any white man and negro woman, who shall habitually live in and occupy in the nighttime the same room shall each be punished by imprisonment not exceeding twelve months, or by fine not exceeding five hundred dollars."[31] Justice Byron White delivered the opinion of the Court. Florida's law, he stated, involved "an exercise of the state police power which trenches upon the constitutionality protected freedom from invidious official discrimination based on race. Such a law, even though enacted pursuant to a valid state interest, bears a heavy burden of justification . . . and will be upheld only if it is necessary, and not merely rationally related, to the accomplishment of a permissible state policy."[32] Although the decision applied only to Florida's law against interracial cohabitation and not to the law against marriage, it blasted an irreparable hole in the legal foundations of antimiscegenation law. After nearly one hundred years, the Fourteenth Amendment at last trumped the Tenth.

Three years later, Mildred and Richard Loving became the first couple in American history to have the nation's highest court rule in favor of an individual's free right to marry the person he or she loved of another race. With the *Loving* case, the legitimacy of the theology of separate races as a basis for antimiscegenation laws at last came to an end.

The Resistant South Upholds the Divine Law

If the connections between theologies of race and marriage are clear in antimiscegenation cases, they are less clear in actual post–Civil War statutes in the South and the West. Yet a regional comparison illustrates that the specifications of the laws differed greatly between the South and the West. While in the West such statutes included significantly more variety in the racial groups forbidden from marrying whites, western regions tended to repeal or drop altogether such laws far earlier than southern states. Moreover, western antimiscegenation laws tended to classify such violations as misdemeanors, whereas southern states usually deemed intermarriage a felony. Consequently, penalties for the crime were much less harsh in the western regions than in the formerly slaveholding South. While the history of the "peculiar institution" certainly influenced the tone of the South's antimiscegenation laws, the greater severity of the laws in the South also derives from the southern white Protestant theology of separate races.[33]

Historians have noted the differences between southern and western statutes in specifications of racial groups in antimiscegenation laws. With a few exceptions, southern antimiscegenation statutes tended to proscribe only marriages between whites and Negroes or mulattoes.[34] But in the West, prohibited racial categories were not so simple. Peggy Pascoe notes that antimiscegenation laws "were enacted first—and abandoned last—in the South, but it was in the West, not the South, that the laws became most elaborate. In the late nineteenth century, western legislators built a labyrinthine system of legal prohibitions on marriages between whites and Chinese, Japanese, Filipinos, Hawaiians, Hindus, and Native Americans, as well as on marriages between whites and blacks."[35] Indeed, at first glance, one of the most striking features of the statutes in the West is their exhaustive effort to enumerate each of the various races proscribed from marrying whites—a difference no doubt related to the increasingly more varied racial groups in the West. California, for example, in 1850 declared "all marriages of white persons with Negroes or mulattoes" as illegal and void.[36] Thirty years later "Mongolians" were added to the list of prohibited spouses for whites.[37] Following *Roldan v. Los Angeles County* (1933), the California legislature again amended the statute to include members of "the Malay race."[38] Arizona's statute included marriage between whites and "negroes, mulattoes, Indians or Mongolians" from its very inception in 1865, added "Hindus" and "Malays" in 1931, and deleted "Indians" in 1942.[39] In 1866 Oregon amended its 1862 statute, which had prohibited marriage between whites and "Negroes or persons of one-fourth or more Negro blood," to include "Negroes, Chinese, or persons having one-fourth or more Negro, Chinese, or Kanaka blood, or persons having more than one-half Indian blood." Montana outlawed in 1909 all marriages between whites and "Negroes, or persons of Negro blood, or in part Negro, Chinese, or Japanese."[40] Perhaps in an effort to be all-inclusive and legally foolproof, Nevada's revised statute of 1912 prohibited "marriage and cohabiting in fornication" between whites and "any persons of the Ethiopian or black race, Malay or brown race, Mongolian or yellow race, or American Indian or red race."[41]

Yet the greater variety of racial identities within western statutes is but one of the differences in southern and western antimiscegenation laws, and one not all that remarkable, considering the larger number of Asian immigrants in the West. In addition to differences in the racial groups prohibited from marrying whites, southern and western laws differed in another significant way: western states and territories tended to classify penalties for violations of antimiscegenation laws as misdemeanors, whereas southern states tended to designate such violations as felonies.[42] The more severe legal penalties for intermarriage in the South stemmed in part from the post–Civil War development of the Protestant theology of separate races. If God had deemed racial separation as a component of his divine plan, then violations of this plan constituted a direct affront to God himself. Penalties for infractions thus demanded severity.

In the 1860s immediately following the Civil War, southern states en-thusiastically enacted and amended antimiscegenation statutes. Deeply anxious about the potential hordes of formerly enslaved black men rush-ing to the altar to wed white women, white southerners viewed interracial unions, especially marriages, as something that needed to be prevented at all costs.[43] As W. J. Cash famously observed, in the "mind of the [white] South," intermarriage threatened the "South's palladium": white feminine virtue.[44] Historian Martha Hodes likewise notes that during the "wartime and Reconstruction climate of social upheaval in the American South, sex between white women and black men became a highly charged political issue, spurring whites to a level of public violence unknown under slavery." With the imminence of Emancipation, she contends, "southern whites who sought to maintain a racial hierarchy began systematically to invoke the idea that black men posed a grave sexual threat to white women."[45] To most white southerners, interracial marriage symbolized social and politi-cal equality between the races—the advocacy of which the state of Mis-sissippi actually made a misdemeanor in 1920 and against which white southerners, even a hundred years after the Civil War, cried, "Never!"[46] The combined result of postbellum white southerners' bewildered sense of loss, betrayal, and upheaval in the aftermath of the war, of their deep resistance to intermarriage and to black sociopolitical equality, and of their belief that black-white marriage violated God's will, antimiscegenation laws in south-ern states aimed to punish, sometimes severely, violators of the statutes.

As table 5-1 shows, in nine of the sixteen southern states, marriage be-tween whites and African Americans or descendants of African Americans was considered a felony. Alabama (1866), Florida (1881), Kentucky (1866), Mississippi (1865), Tennessee (1870), and Virginia (1878) treated intermar-riage as a felony immediately following the Civil War or shortly after the end of Reconstruction. Other southern states did not do so until after 1900: Louisiana and Oklahoma in 1908, and Georgia in 1927. In each of these states, violators faced the possibility of lengthy prison sentences. Alabama condemned interracially married couples to two to seven years in prison. In Florida, people convicted of intermarriage could be sentenced to up to ten years. Couples in Kentucky, Oklahoma, Tennessee, and Virginia could receive a sentence of up to five years. And in Mississippi in 1866, the state's Black Codes changed marriage between a white person and a Negro to warrant a life sentence, though this change was short-lived. In 1870 the U.S. Congress "took over the reins of power" and repealed the Codes, but in 1880 Mississippi's antimiscegenation law was restored and the penalty reduced to up to ten years imprisonment, up to a five-hundred-dollar fine, or both.[47] In addition, although South Carolina deemed the crime a misdemeanor in 1879, the penalty resembled a felony more than a misdemeanor, in that violators could receive a minimum prison sentence of one year.

In contrast, in the West no territory or state explicitly designated violations of antimiscegenation statutes as felonies. (See table 5-2.) In fact, Arizona, California, Colorado, Idaho, and Nevada deemed the crime of interracial marriage a misdemeanor. Interestingly, in the western states and territories where intermarriage was deemed a misdemeanor offense, violations carried felony-level penalties, a fact perhaps reflecting whites' increasing fears of black-white marriages or the migration of black southerners to western regions during and following the Civil War. In southern regions where intermarriage constituted a misdemeanor, such as Delaware, Oklahoma, and West Virginia, statutes merely specified fines ranging from $100 to $500 and prison terms of up to one year. But in Arizona, California, and Idaho (after 1867), couples could receive a $100–10,000 fine and/or three months to ten years in prison; prior to 1867 in Idaho married couples could receive one to two years in prison, and after 1913 Wyoming's statute called for a $100–1,000 fine and/or one to five years of imprisonment (but evidently only one couple was prosecuted for violating the statute). Colorado law specified a penalty of $50–500 and/or three months to three years of prison time. Moreover, Colorado exempted certain inhabitants from prosecution under its antimiscegenation statutes and allowed them to marry interracially. Its 1864 law forbade marriages between "whites and Negroes or mulattoes," yet it mysteriously specified that "nothing . . . shall be so construed as to prevent the people living in that portion of the Territory acquired from New Mexico, from marrying according to the custom of that country."[48] Colorado's exemption directly relates to the historical practice of intermarriage among Mexican Catholics of southern Colorado and the New Mexico Territory.

In contrast, in the South the emphasis on the protection of white womanhood and the disavowal of equality between whites and blacks was fueled by the southern white Protestant theology of separate races. The vehement tone of southern antimiscegenation laws and the harsh penalties violations merited thus were not merely about white womanhood, or even about the desire to socially emasculate black men. The statutes and penalties also derived from white southerners' perceptions of the biblical mandates for the

TABLE 5-1. Criminal Classifications and Penalties of Post-1865 Southern Antimiscegenation Statutes

State	Criminal Classification	Penalty
Alabama	Not specified [felony?]	1866—2–7 years of confinement in penitentiary or hard labor for county.
Arkansas	High misdemeanor	1838—Fine and/or imprisonment at discretion of jury/court. Penalty omitted as of 1884.
Delaware	Misdemeanor	1852—$100 fine for both races. 1911—$100 fine or up to 30 days of jail time.
Florida	Felony	1881—$50–$1,000 or 6 months–10 years of prison. 1903—Adultery/fornication, up to $500 fine or up to 1 year in prison; marriage, up to $1,000 fine or up to 10 years in prison.
Georgia	Not specified; felony (1927)	1852—White man up to $200 fine and/or up to 3 months in jail; no penalty for colored woman. 1861—White woman fined and imprisoned at discretion of court; Negro man imprisoned 1 week with 39 lashes given on 3 days during week. 1868—Up to $100 fine, 6 months in jail, up to 39 lashes, or up to 1 year on chain gang, or any combination thereof. 1927—Marriage a felony, 1–2 years in prison.
Kentucky	Felony	1866—Up to 5 years in prison. 1893—Marriage, $500–$5,000 fine. If parties continue to cohabit after conviction, 3–12 months in prison.
Louisiana*	Felony	1908—1–12 months in prison, with or without hard labor.
Maryland	Not specified; "infamous crime" (1884)	1860—Marriage: free Negro to be slave for life; whites and mulattoes born of white woman servant, 7 years of service. Bastardy: 18 months–5 years in prison for woman; Negro or mulatto man to be sold as slave for life and transported out of state. 1884—18 months–10 years in prison.
Mississippi	Felony	1865—Life imprisonment (repealed in 1870 by U.S. Congress). 1880—Up to $500 and/or up to 10 years in prison.
North Carolina	Not specified; "infamous crime" (1883)	1883—4 months–10 years in prison; could also be fined.
Oklahoma	Misdemeanor (1897); felony (1908)	1897—$100–$500 fine and/or 1–12 months in prison. 1908—Up to $500 fine and/or 1–5 years in prison.
South Carolina	Not specified; misdemeanor (1879)	1879—$500 minimum fine and/or minimum 1 year in prison.
Tennessee	Misdemeanor (1858); felony (1870)	1870—1–5 years in prison or fine and imprisonment in county jail, as court recommends.

Texas	High misdemeanor (1836)	1858—White offender, 2–5 years in prison. 1879—Both parties, 2–5 years in prison.
Virginia	Not specified [felony?] (1877)	1849—White offender, up to $100 fine and up to 1 year in prison. 1877–1878—White offender, 2–5 years in prison.
West Virginia	Not specified [misdemeanor?]	1882—White party only, up to $100 fine and up to 1 year in prison.

Source: Fowler, *Northern Attitudes.*

Note: For states that did not specify the statutes' criminal classification, I have provided a classification in brackets based upon its penalty and upon standard definitions of "misdemeanor" and "felony."

*Fowler indicates that, beginning in 1724, marriage was punished by an unspecified fine "and other arbitrary punishment" and that the white parties were also fined for any offspring resulting from the union (375). He notes no revisions to this policy until 1908, except from 1870 to 1894, when the law was not on the books. This information is fairly consistent with the findings of Franklin Johnson, who reported that he found no statutory prohibitions of intermarriage in Louisiana until 1894 (Johnson, *Development of State Legislation*).

TABLE 5-2. Criminal Classifications and Penalties of Post-1865
Western Antimiscegenation Statutes

State or Territory	Criminal Classification	Penalty
Arizona	Misdemeanor	$100–$10,000 fine and 3 months–10 years in prison.
California	Misdemeanor	1850—$100–$10,000 fine and/or 3 months–10 years in prison.
Colorado	Misdemeanor	$50–$500 fine and/or 3 months–3 years in prison.
Idaho	Misdemeanor (for marriage; cohabitation not specified)	1864—Marriage, 1–2 years in prison; cohabitation, $100–$500 fine and/or 6–12 months in jail. 1867—$100–$10,000 fine and/or 3 months–10 years in prison.
Montana	Not punished	
Nevada	Misdemeanor	1861—Marriage, 1–2 years in prison; cohabitation, $100–$500 fine and/or 1–6 months in jail. 1912—Marriage a gross misdemeanor, no penalty specified; cohabitation, same as 1861.
New Mexico	Not specified [felony?]	1857—2–3 years of hard labor for Negro man or white woman. 1866—Law of 1857 repealed entirely.
Oregon	Not specified [misdemeanor?]	1866—3–12 months in penitentiary or county jail.
Utah	Not specified [felony?]	1852—Whites subject to $500–$1,000 fine and up to 3 years in prison.
Washington	Provision stricken in 1866	
Wyoming	Not specified [felony?]	1913—$100–$1,000 fine and/or 1–5 years in prison.

Source: Fowler, *Northern Attitudes.*

marital segregation of the races as well as from beliefs purporting whites to be superior to people of color. The southern Protestant theology of separate races represented a divine mandate for racial separation in marriage and in all social relations. The weight of a biblically based injunction against intermarriage thus accounts in part for white southern opposition to repealing antimiscegenation laws.

TABLE 5-3. States Having Antimiscegenation Statutes in 1948

States Retaining Statutes until 1967 or After	States Dropping or Repealing Statutes, 1948–1965
Alabama*	Arizona (1962—repealed)
Arkansas	California (1959—repealed)
Delaware	Colorado (1957—repealed)
Florida*	Idaho (1959—dropped)
Georgia	Indiana (1965—repealed)
Kentucky	Montana (1953—repealed)
Louisiana	Nebraska (1963—dropped)
Maryland (March 1967, pre-*Loving*)	Nevada (1959—repealed)
Mississippi*	North Dakota (1955—repealed)
Missouri	Oregon (1951—repealed)
North Carolina*	South Dakota (1957—repealed)
Oklahoma	Utah (1963—dropped)
South Carolina*	Wyoming (1965—repealed)
Tennessee*	
Texas	
Virginia	
West Virginia	

Source: Fowler, *Northern Attitudes.*

*These six states included antimiscegenation provisions within the state constitution and consequently required state referenda in order to remove the provisions from the constitutions.

How the West Was Won, and How the South Was Lost . . . Again

During the seventeen years following *Perez* in 1948, Indiana plus every state west of the Mississippi that had had antimiscegenation statutes in place in 1948 either repealed them through the state legislatures or dropped them from the legal books.[49] By 1965—two years before the U.S. Supreme Court declared such statutes unconstitutional—no western state retained legal prohibitions against interracial marriage. By that time, only southern states upheld antimiscegenation laws. As table 5-3 shows, after *Perez*, Oregon was the first to abandon its antimiscegenation statutes in 1951, followed by Montana (1953), North Dakota (1955), Colorado and South Dakota (1957), California (which did not officially repeal its law until 1959, despite its invalidation by *Perez* in 1948), Idaho and Nevada (1959), Arizona

(1962), Nebraska and Utah (1963), and Indiana and Wyoming (1965).[50] Following the *Perez* decision of 1948, thirty states (including California, since the law still remained on the books at this point) had antimiscegenation laws. Of these, seventeen were in the South. Thirteen states repealed or dropped their laws by 1965, and of those, eight states—all in the West— dropped their laws by 1960, within twelve years of the *Perez* decision.

These data suggest that the eradication of antimiscegenation statutes in western and midwestern states between 1948 and 1965 related in some way to the *Perez* decision. As Randall Kennedy notes, factors such as a "growing respect for people of color" and the response to Nazi racism contributed much to civil rights reform. Moreover, Kennedy continues, the "reform movement gained momentum as every state that repealed a ban on interracial marriage made it easier for a sister state to do the same."[51] While certainly many factors influenced the differences in laws between the South and the West, the South's retention of antimiscegenation statutes relates not only to its history of slavery and segregation but also to the cultural givenness of the white Protestant theology of separate races. Similarly, the West's rapid abandonment of legal prohibitions against interracial marriage between 1948 and 1965 springs in part from the limited practice of African American slavery in the region as well as from the absence of a ubiquitous cultural commitment to the theology of separate races.

Christian, particularly white southern Protestant, beliefs about race and marriage left deep imprints upon antimiscegenation statutes and cases. Far from being a belief system advocated only from the isolated southern pulpit on Sunday mornings, the Protestant theology of marriage as a civilly regulated matter and the theology of separate races constituted a kind of cultural religion that permeated the hearts and minds of attorneys and judges throughout the courts of the South for a hundred years after the Civil War. Although both theologies threaded through the cases, the southern white Protestant theology of race legitimated and reinforced resistance to the desegregation of schools. Its perpetuation in antimiscegenation cases that cited the race passages from precedents *Philadelphia*, *Scott*, *Gibson*, and *Green* underscores the fact that it was not merely the backwoods perspective of an ill-educated minority, but a prominent doctrine that pervaded southern culture and even occasionally appeared elsewhere in the nation. Since no court was composed of merely one individual, these decisions represent the viewpoints of all the concurring judges on each court. Each judicial affirmation of the civil understanding of marriage and the southern Protestant theology of race thus indicates something more than a solitary voice in the southern judiciary. It represents a common cultural language of the white American South, shared by the most respected and most highly educated thinkers.

The theology of separate races was a lingua franca spoken outside courtrooms and legal offices. The massive resistance of southern whites to school desegregation, which at its core constituted a battle against the possibility of interracial marriage, underscores the ubiquity and enduring nature of such views. It is no surprise, then, that when faced with integration and legal efforts to ensure the social equality of African and Anglo Americans, the South stonewalled, while the West—though not without resistance to civil rights—tended to proceed with greater openness toward integration and racial equality. Believing integration and intermarriage to be grave sins against God, white southerners rallied against changes in the "antimiscegenation regime."

[6] The Southern Lingua Franca of Race Judge Leon M. Bazile and White Catholics

In February 1949, four months after the California Supreme Court validated their right to marry, Andrea Perez and Sylvester Davis exchanged wedding vows at St. Patrick's Catholic Church in Los Angeles, partaking of the Catholic sacrament of matrimony. True to the church's hopes for married couples, Andrea and Sylvester had a son and two daughters, the cherished prize of married life. Later the couple purchased a house in the racially mixed town of Pacoima, California, in the western end of the San Fernando Valley. Until his retirement Sylvester continued to work at Lockheed Aviation, where he had first met Andrea, and Andrea became a teacher's aide.[1] Thanks in part to Daniel Marshall's ingenious First Amendment strategy, Andrea and Sylvester won the legal right to marry and, moreover, to marry in the Catholic Church, as they wished. The couple's union triumphed over the prejudices against interracial marriage—first striking down California's antimiscegenation laws with their 1948 legal victory and then enduring against the odds for fifty-one years. Their marriage ended only with Andrea's death on 9 September 2000.

Nearly ten years after Andrea and Sylvester walked down the aisle together in their Catholic parish in Los Angeles, Virginia couple Mildred Jeter and Richard Loving got married in Washington, D.C. Soon after they returned home to Virginia, they were arrested for and convicted of having violated the state's laws against interracial marriage and against leaving the state to avoid that law. As the sentence for their crimes, the Lovings were prohibited from being in the state of Virginia together for twenty-five years. Ultimately exasperated with being unable to see their families together or to live together in the state, the couple filed a case challenging the constitutionality of their sentence and of Virginia's antimiscegenation laws. In early

1967, nearly ten years after the couple had married in Washington, the U.S. Supreme Court heard the Lovings' landmark case, *Loving v. Virginia*.

In the *Loving* decision—the final and most important of antimiscegenation cases—religion appeared in two seemingly insignificant places. In one instance, another Catholic—a southerner—took a stance opposite that of *Perez* attorney Daniel Marshall. Offering perhaps the most famous statement in American antimiscegenation history about God's mandates against interracial marriage, in 1965 Virginia's Roman Catholic judge Leon M. Bazile upheld the Lovings' sentences and explained the validity of the state's laws by attributing the separation of the races to God himself: "Almighty God created the races white, black, yellow, malay, and red, and he placed them on separate continents. And but for the interference with his arrangement there would be no cause for such marriages. The fact that he separated the races shows that he did not intend for the races to mix."[2] Perhaps more articulately than anyone before or since, this Catholic judge expressed the theology of separate races—the biblical hermeneutic of interracial marriage most commonly and most forcefully expressed by white southern Protestants.

In the following year, 1966, yet another Catholic Virginian—one in Judge Bazile's own diocese—acted in a manner more consistent with that of progressive Catholic attorney Daniel Marshall. Bishop John J. Russell, leader of the Diocese of Richmond, led a coalition of southern bishops and archbishops in filing a "friend of the court" brief on behalf of Richard and Mildred Loving. Echoing Marshall's argument from the 1940s, the brief stated that marriage was "a fundamental act of religion" and that it thus fell under the "Constitutionally-protected 'free exercise of religion.'" Moreover, it affirmed that the "importance of marriage as a religious act" pertained not merely to Catholics but to any person "committed to one or other of the major religious faiths in the United States."[3] While its tacit acknowledgment of the validity of Protestant and Jewish beliefs reflected the relaxed climate of the years following the Second Vatican Council, the brief's contentions about the individual's free right to marry the person of his or her choosing—and the religious right to marry—expressed the Catholic Church's position on marriage that dated at least as far back as last session of the Council of Trent in 1563. In addition, in its implicit rejection of religious rationales for racial segregation in marriage, the Catholic brief also conveyed what was by this time the Catholic "orthodoxy" of the unity and equality of the races.[4]

Thus far we have seen how Catholic and Protestant beliefs about marriage and race diverged; now we will examine the reasons for the profoundly different responses between Judge Leon M. Bazile—a lifelong Roman Catholic—and the coalition of Catholic bishops. Why did Bazile subscribe to the white southern Protestant theology of separate races? What motivated Bishop Russell and the other ordinaries to file the amicus curiae brief on behalf of the Lovings? And what do the answers to these questions suggest about the relationship between regional values and the historical American Catholic tensions over race? I contend that Judge Bazile's comment stemmed partly from his personal situation and partly from his cultural location: his marriage to a Southern Baptist woman, and his position as a white Catholic in the twentieth-century American South. The Protestant theology of separate races had so permeated southern culture that it even shaped the beliefs of white Catholics during slavery and during the century following the emancipation of African Americans. This fact reflects the historical ambiguity of southern white Catholics toward slavery and race, and it reflects the church's post–Civil War accommodation to the region's racial mores. At the same time, the fact that a group of southern Roman Catholic ordinaries dared to cosponsor the amicus curiae brief on behalf of the Lovings indicates the extent to which the Catholic theology of race had, by the 1960s, transformed the American hierarchy. Notable conflicts had grown between Vatican doctrine and the beliefs of white American Catholics sitting in the pews, and tensions had developed between the laity and hierarchy over race, in that ordinaries advanced the Lovings' cause rather than laypersons such as Daniel Marshall. And as we will see once again, the freedom to marry the person of one's choosing mattered to Roman Catholics more than to members of other faith traditions.

Judge Leon M. Bazile:
A Bible-Reading Southern White Catholic

Judge Leon M. Bazile has suffered decades of ridicule from scholars, legal analysts, and laypersons alike for his "almighty God" statement. Depicted by the northern press as a backwoods boor rather than as an erudite, well-respected, and accomplished statesman, the *New York Times* ran an article quoting the statement in 1966, after the U.S. Supreme Court agreed to hear the *Loving* case. The article led one irate New Yorker to mail the judge a letter in which the writer advised him to "take the first boat back to whichever continent [his] ancestors came from," or else "resign [his] office," for he was "not upholding the constitution but [his] own southern born bigotry." "Sir, for shame, for shame," the writer continued. "You surely did not mean what you said. Not in 1966; 1866 or 1766, yes, but not 1966. Don't you want to retract? You'll become the laughingstock of the country. Call the press and retract or deny; it's just too ludicrous."[5] The letter must have made an impression on the judge, for he kept it in his personal papers. But impressions of Judge Bazile based merely upon his famous statement conceal his other accomplishments and unfairly threaten to demarcate him as more racist than other white southerners of his era.

Born in 1890 in Hanover County, Virginia, Judge Bazile graduated first in his class from the T. C. Williams School of Law at the University of Richmond in 1910, at twenty years of age. He served as the assistant attorney general of the state of Virginia until his appointment in 1941 as judge of the Fifteenth Judicial Circuit, the position he held when he made the "almighty God" statement and which he occupied until his retirement in 1965. When Judge Bazile died in March 1967, just three months before the U.S. Supreme Court's decision in *Loving*, his obituary appeared on the front page of the *Richmond Times-Dispatch*. In appraising his life, the announcement depicted him as a "gentle and scholarly man, a devout Catholic, and a dedicated Virginia conservative." Like other well-educated white southerners of his generation, Judge Bazile earned a reputation as an outspoken critic of what he perceived as the federal government's usurpation of its authority following the *Brown* decision. When it became "apparent that racial bars would be lifted," the judge demanded the "repeal of Virginia's compulsory school attendance laws."[6] Indeed, several of the biographical sources on Bazile note his resistance to federal authority. One biographer states that the judge "mince[d] few words" on this topic.[7] Another asserts that he "deplored the encroachment of Federal authority upon the States."[8] In his notes on the *Brown* case, Bazile affirmed that he held "no prejudice against any person because of his race or his creed or his color." He also, "without reservation," affirmed the section of the Virginia Constitution that proclaimed "all men are by nature equally free and independent, and have certain inherent rights."[9] In the context of his notes, it is clear that Bazile took this statement to mean not that black and white persons should have social equality but, rather, that the Constitution bestowed upon white Virginians the right to view racial segregation as the preferred social arrangement. Judge Bazile's views on southern race relations and the desegregation of schools, then, were no more vociferous or bigoted than those of most other whites in the post-*Brown* South.

But the question remains: why did this Roman Catholic judge believe that God had separated the races, an idea that originated with white Protestants? Discovering the reasons for an individual's private beliefs is difficult and by nature speculative. We must piece together these reasons based upon the available evidence: biographical materials, Bazile's personal letters and papers, and what we know about the Protestant theology of separate races and about the history of white Roman Catholics in the American South. Taken together, the evidence suggests that Judge Bazile's belief derived from both a personal and a broader cultural ethic of Protestant biblicism. The judge, it seems, was an avid Bible reader. In his work on Catholics in the Old South, historian Randall Miller notes that antebellum white Catholics occasionally turned to the Bible as a source of social conservatism. "Like the dominant Protestant churches of the Old South," he writes, "the Catholic church endorsed the racial and social values of its white parishioners by applying biblical justifications for slavery and a conservative social order."[10] Although Miller's focus is on antebellum Catholics, his observation functions to explain Judge Bazile's statement: from the years following the Civil War, to the tempestuous decades of the civil rights movement, the ubiquitous presence of southern Protestant biblicism led some white Catholics such as Judge Bazile—through personal relationships with Protestants and through the broader influences of culture—to adopt a regard for the Bible that was out of keeping with their Catholic upbringing. In other words, Judge Bazile developed what might be best described as a Protestant orientation to the Bible.

In the Virginia State Bar Association's "memorials to deceased members," the entry on Judge Bazile offers a first clue as to why Bazile reverenced the Bible and how it influenced his social views. According to the biographer, Bazile "believed with a sincere and abiding faith that the spiritual concepts and doctrines as enunciated in the Bible and the basic principles of the law of man are the solidifying forces which hold together the fabric of our society." His "love," the article continued, was "the law of God and the law of man."[11] The seemingly immaterial detail that the judge perceived in the Bible the "basic principles of the law of man" is significant, for it provides an initial inkling of the judge's un-Catholic—indeed, one might say a decidedly Protestant—approach to faith. As American Studies scholar Paul Gutjahr notes, "canon law emanating from the 1546 Council of Trent (which had declared the 'Pre-eminence of the Latin Vulgate') forbade Catholics from reading any biblical translation that was not based on the Latin Vulgate."[12] The question thus arises of what led Judge Bazile to turn to the Bible? Although he may have begun reading the Bible following

Pius XII's 1943 encyclical *Divino afflante Spiritu*, which permitted Catholic scholars to use, with some restrictions, the biblical critical method in their studies, since this encyclical was primarily directed toward scholars, it does not seem likely that Bazile's interest in the Bible originated there.[13] Indeed, the evidence points to much earlier, and far more earthly, origins for his curiosity about the Christian scriptures.

During the 1910s, while serving as Virginia's assistant attorney general, Judge Bazile met Virginia Hamilton Bowcock. The daughter of a Southern Baptist minister, Bowcock was likewise an ardent Southern Baptist and had attended the Baptist Seminary in Louisville, Kentucky (now known as Southern Baptist Theological Seminary).[14] Recognizing her as his intellectual equal, Bazile soon fell in love with Bowcock, though it was not to be an easy romance. Bowcock remained resolute about the correctness of her Baptist beliefs (and the errors of the Roman faith), and she armed herself with texts that demonstrated her learning and challenged Bazile's beliefs. During their courtship, she shared her books with him, and the young couple wrote lengthy letters to each other, struggling together with the merits of their respective faith traditions as well as with the question of whether to marry a person of another faith. They affectionately referred to the matter of their religious differences as "Our Problem." At several points in their relationship, Bowcock decided, much to Bazile's disappointment, that they "could only be friends," and she once declared that she was "sure that [they] can never find a common ground unless [he] could accept [her] faith," and she advised him to "forget all about [her]."[15]

After much agonizing, the couple finally decided to marry in January 1918, though not before Bazile agreed in writing to several conditions. In a note handwritten on the letterhead of the Office of the Attorney General of the State of Virginia and dated 25 January 1918, the day before their nuptials, Bazile made several promises to his fiancée. He promised to never coerce or interfere with Bowcock's religious practices; to attend church with her "except on 2nd Sundays and on special occasions"; to allow their children to be taught the catechism, and to not "coerce them against their will as to religious matters" or require his wife to attend the children's baptism; also, in the event of her death, he agreed to respect her wishes in who assisted him in the children's upbringing. Further, he "recognized the fact that every person who reaches the age of discretion has the right to make such choice as his conscience dictates"; thus he remained open to the possibility that his children might grow up to be Southern Baptists. Bazile signed the statement, noting that he had done so "in consideration of [Bowcock] having agreed to marry [him]." Rather progressive for a southern Catholic man of the 1910s, Leon Bazile loved and respected Virginia Hamilton Bowcock enough to engage with her in lengthy and difficult theological questions and enough to desire her to be her own person—even if that person was a stubborn Southern Baptist.

In their correspondence on Christian doctrines, we begin to glimpse some of the judge's inspiration for reading the Bible. In July 1917 Bazile informed Bowcock that he had already commenced to study the Baptist faith, "realizing [his] inability to intelligently discuss with [her] the points of difference between [them] unless [he] understood just what [her] belief was." He admitted that "heretofore [he] ha[d] been content enough to take religion as a matter of course[,] believing what [he] ha[d] been taught and making no private investigations to confirm what [he] believed." Recognizing the central place of the Bible in the Southern Baptist faith, Bazile observed that Baptists viewed "this book [as] (1) sufficient, (2) certain, and (3) authoritative," and quoting from one of the theological books Bowcock had given him, he reiterated the Southern Baptist belief that "'the Scriptures speak with authority.' (Mullins p 12)."[16] Thus acknowledging Baptists' recognition of the Bible as the only real source of spiritual authority, Bazile delved into biblical study as a means of meeting Bowcock on her home turf. In order to find a specific place to launch into a discussion of such a "big subject" as theology, he began with an analysis of the Catholic doctrine of transubstantiation, or the "real presence" of the body and blood of Christ in the Eucharist, which the Southern Baptists deny. Employing his training as a lawyer, Bazile turned to the Bible to assess the evidence for both the Catholic and Baptist positions on this doctrine. Intellectual curiosity, combined with a desire to speak intelligently about a topic dear to the woman he loved, thus initially piqued Bazile's interest in the Bible and led him along a spiritual path uncharacteristic of most Roman Catholics of his era.

Judge Bazile's affirmation of divinely separated races—an idiosyncratic southern white Protestant interpretation of biblical stories—thus seems to have derived partly from the love for the Bible he developed as a result of his relationship with the Southern Baptist woman who would become his wife. For Virginia Bowcock Bazile, the judge developed a deep interest in the Bible, which presumably led him to conclude that somewhere in its pages was the story of God separating the races. His adoption of the theology of separate races also stemmed simply from being born a white southerner during the late nineteenth century. Residing in a culture where the biblical hermeneutic of separate races functioned as the white southern lingua franca of race, Judge Bazile, like many other white southern Catholics and Protestants, espoused the white South's foremost religious explanation for racial difference, inequality, and segregation. In one of his 1917 love letters to Bowcock, he promised that he "shall ever value the little Testament" that she had sent him "as one of [his] dearest treasures."[17] Over the years, reading the Bible became important to Bazile not merely because biblical study had brought him and his wife together but also because he learned to appreciate it on its own. Although Bazile was equally Catholic and southern, his southern identity left deep imprints on his Catholicism and shaped his racial beliefs, ultimately cultivating within him a Protestant appreciation for and orientation toward scripture. As a result, the cultural prevalence of an idea—that the Bible taught that God had separated the races and intended them to remain that way—penetrated his consciousness and provided the interpretive paradigm for making sense of interracial marriage and segregation. This interpretative paradigm shaped Judge Bazile's thinking as he sat in the pews of his parish as well as on the bench of his courtroom, where he interpreted the law.

White Southern Catholics and Accommodation to Racial Ideologies

The adoption of American racial beliefs by white southern *and* northern Catholics long preceded Judge Bazile. Historians trace white Catholic accommodation to racial mores to the years preceding the Civil War. Iver Bernstein, for example, explores Irish Catholics' long-standing race prejudice toward African Americans as a driving force behind the New York City draft riots of 1863.[18] Randall Miller notes an even earlier clash in the South between church teachings and southern Catholic practice with regard to slave marriages. Although the church taught that marriage was a sacrament and that slave owners were not to violate its holy bond by separating enslaved husbands and wives, the southern church capitulated in the face of resistance from slaveholders. "Rather than force the issue," Miller contends, "the southern church quietly accepted the verdicts of individual masters who refused to abide by church teaching on marriages and the family." As debates among pro- and antislavery forces heated up after 1830, the southern church's position on slavery increasingly tended to adapt to local practices and values, especially in communities were the church keenly perceived its "minority status."[19] Antebellum American bishops viewed slavery "as a political and social issue rather than a moral one" and thus attempted to steer clear of conflict by relegating discussion of slavery to politicians. According to historian Stephen Ochs, the bishops "left the question of slavery up to politicians and individual Catholics" because they wished to "avoid all purely political-social issues for fear of provoking nativist hysteria."[20] And southern white parishioners did not respond well if they perceived a bishop to take a political stance in a sermon. In one instance, Baltimore parishioners left the cathedral in reaction against Archbishop Francis Kenrick's wartime prayer that the nation "be preserved in union."[21]

White southern Catholics persisted in their accommodation to white American racial ideology after the Civil War ended. As historian I. A. Newby observes, "non-Protestants in the South, notably Catholics and Jews, generally acquiesced in Jim Crow policies of the majority, although without giving them the Protestant's vociferous endorsement. . . . [T]he attitudes and practices of Catholics toward Negroes did not materially differ from those of Protestants. Indeed there was a substantial parallel between the two groups." Moreover, Newby notes that while "theoretically" Catholic doctrines "recognized no distinctions between races," in practice, "racial equality was in the sight of God only and not in the sight of man or the Church on earth."[22] Southern black Catholics "attended segregated churches and schools or found themselves relegated to church galleries. They approached the communion rail after whites and confessed their sins in segregated confessionals."[23] Most Catholic colleges and seminaries would not admit African American students. "Acutely aware of their church's minority status in much of the South and of the suspicion and hostility harbored by many Bible-belt southerners toward Catholicism," Stephen Ochs maintains, southern white Catholics "avoided challenge to the region's system and instead accommodated themselves, and the institution they guided, to existing racial ideology and practices. Moreover, most Catholics, northern and southern, lay and cleric, absorbed the widespread racism of American society and regarded Afro-Americans as their intellectual and moral inferiors."[24]

Indeed, in the North, white Catholics were just as likely as their southern counterparts to treat African Americans as lower-class citizens. The northern urban context, in fact, led white Catholics to adopt racism as a means of protecting and proving themselves. The mass immigration of European Catholics—one million per decade between 1880 and 1920, and more than two million from 1901 to 1910—into northern cities during the late nineteenth and early twentieth centuries created an identity crisis for the American church and for individual Catholics alike.[25] Always suspected of possessing more allegiance to Rome than to the U.S. government, recent immigrants and long-term Catholic Americans alike experienced challenges from Protestants who doubted their capacity for patriotism. Moreover, with the increase of U.S. nationalism during the Spanish-American War of 1898 and during the years leading up to World War I, American Protestants became even more antagonistic toward Catholics. "In the face of strident nationalism," one writer asserts, American Catholics "had still to lay claim to an identity as citizens and to legitimate their existence on the American political and religious scene."[26] As one means of proving themselves as true Americans, it seems, some Catholic immigrants learned to adopt the racist ideology that characterized the thinking of other white Americans of this era, and in time there were violent consequences. During and after World War I, northern cities erupted in riots as white residents, many of whom were Catholic, resisted the presence in their neighborhoods of southern black families that had migrated north in search of a better life.

In the context of over a century of white Catholic accommodation to the racial beliefs, discriminatory practices, and racial hierarchy of the dominant culture, the Vatican's post–World War II emphasis on racial unity thus met with considerable resistance, and it signaled that the Vatican was out of step with most white American Catholics. As racial tensions mounted and as the Vatican issued encyclicals on human unity and racial equality in the years following the war, American Catholic leaders began, grudgingly at times, to proclaim a Catholic theology of race rooted in notions of racial and religious unity. During the 1940s, "Detroit's Cardinal Mooney eagerly endorsed plans to make St. Leo's a model of integration and showered praise upon priests working in the African-American community. In Chicago, Cardinal Stritch placed increasing pressure on Catholic schools to accept African-American applicants and quickly, if privately, eliminated dissent among the clergy."[27] Prelates in the South also urged changes in local church policies. Archbishops Joseph Ritter of St. Louis and Patrick O'Boyle of Washington, D.C., integrated the Catholic schools in their archdioceses in 1947 and 1948. Bishop Vincent Waters of Raleigh ordered an end to segregation in the North Carolina church in 1953.[28] Ten days before the U.S. Supreme Court released its decision in *Brown*, Bishop Peter L. Ireton of Richmond announced that Richmond's Catholic high schools would be open to black students that fall.[29] In 1951, 1953, and again in 1956, New

Orleans archbishop Joseph Rummel appealed for segregation to end in the church and, much to the chagrin of local officials, declared that segregation was sinful in 1956.[30] Catholic leaders thus took measures to bring the laity and lower-level clergy into compliance with post-1945 Vatican teachings.

But the laity proved recalcitrant. Many white Catholics were not at all open to what they perceived as "new" church doctrine, and as John Mc-Greevy observes of Catholics in the urban North, "appeals to universalist theological principles often fell upon rocky soil." While some readily endorsed integration and racial equality, "other Catholics invoked different 'Catholic' traditions as they persistently refused African-Americans admission to particular neighborhoods, schools, and churches."[31] In the South, some white Catholics mounted a protest against desegregation. Indeed, white southern Catholics numbered among the staunchest of segregationists. A couple of years after New Orleans archbishop Rummel's 1953 appeal for segregation to end, intractable members of the laity "who were not ready to embrace this new social order within or without the church" challenged desegregation "on the grounds that segregation was a social rather than moral issue."[32] They organized the Association of Catholic Laymen in 1956 in open defiance of Archbishop Rummel's calls for an end to segregation, proposing to investigate and study "the problem of compulsory integration of the black and white races."[33] Louisiana Jesuit Sam Hill Ray urged his fellow Jesuits to continue segregation.[34] By 1958, when American bishops signed and published their letter "Discrimination and the Christian Conscience," the hierarchy's conflict with the laity and with the religious was well under way, and it was still far from clear that white lay Catholics in the American North or South would ever embrace the notion that segregation constituted a religious and moral problem.

Clearly, racist ideologies infiltrated the white southern Catholic Church, and indeed, the Americanization of the church in the South appears to have virtually demanded the espousal of white supremacist beliefs. In his study of Catholic interracialism in New Orleans, R. Bentley Anderson observes that for most of its history, the American Catholic Church had been a "predominately southern institution," and that twentieth-century white Catholics in New Orleans "differed little from either their co-religionists in other parts of the country or their Protestant brethren regarding racial attitudes."[35] Given the ubiquity of white southern racial values, it was therefore reasonable for some southern white Catholics to conclude that God separated the races and frowned on interracial marriage and, further, that these notions originated in the Bible. The conservative Protestant tendency to locate explanations for social customs in the Bible, it seems, transmuted the southern white Catholic conscience.

Southern Catholic Ordinaries and the Amicus Curiae Brief

To other mid-twentieth-century white southern Catholics, and particularly to those charged with shepherding the flock of Christ, racial segregation and the theology of separate races stood in utter conflict with Catholic doctrine. If Christ and even the testy St. Paul perceived no distinctions between human groups, then neither could the church affirm racial distinctions. Church leaders could therefore admit no legitimate theological reason for laws preventing marriages between whites and persons of color. While the church might find justifiable *social* reasons to advise against intermarriage, such as the potential ostracism of the couple's children or strain on the marriage, it could not square the notion of God having separated the races at the marriage altar with Catholic theology.

In November 1966, as Mildred and Richard Loving waited to hear whether or not the U.S. Supreme Court would hear their case, Bishop John J. Russell of the Richmond Diocese prepared to put this belief into practice to help the Lovings. First, the bishop created a list of the thirty-six ordinaries "of all the Sees in the twenty states with antimiscegenation statutes."[36] Then he mailed the prelates a letter informing them that the Diocese of Richmond was "prepared to support an amicus curiae brief on behalf of the Lovings since we feel that the issue involved is an important concern for all religious leaders." Bishop Russell's letter invited the ordinaries to join the brief if they felt the matter "deserve[d] [their] support." After describing the couple's legal situation, he explained that if the U.S. Supreme Court agreed to hear the case, the National Catholic Conference on Interracial Justice would file the brief, which was to be written by Reverend William Lewers, faculty member of the Notre Dame University Law School. While the Lovings' attorneys would focus on Fourteenth Amendment issues, the bishop continued, "it is Father Lewers' intent" to emphasize "the violation of the liberty or freedom of religion," for First Amendment rights "should include the freedom to participate in the sacraments of the Church, including the Sacrament of Matrimony."[37]

Over the next six weeks, Bishop Russell and Father Lewers received response letters from the ordinaries. In all, fifteen southern prelates signed on as amici curiae: Lawrence Cardinal Shehan of Baltimore; Archbishop

Paul A. Hallinan of Atlanta; Archbishop Philip M. Hannan of New Orleans; Archbishop Robert E. Lucey of San Antonio; Bishop Joseph B. Brunini of Natchez-Jackson; Bishop Lawrence M. DeFalco of Amarillo; Joseph A. Dirick, apostolic administrator of Galveston-Houston; Bishop Thomas K. Gorman of Dallas–Fort Worth; Bishop Joseph H. Hodges of Wheeling; John L. Morkovsky, apostolic administrator of Galveston-Houston; Bishop Victor J. Reed of Oklahoma City and Tulsa; Bishop L. J. Reicher of Austin; Bishop Thomas Tschoepe of San Angelo; Bishop Vincent S. Waters of Raleigh; and Bishop Ernest L. Unterkoeffler of Charleston. In addition, the National Catholic Conference for Interracial Justice and the National Catholic Social Action Conference joined the brief.[38] A January letter from Lewers to Russell noted that one prelate, Bishop Robert E. Tracy of Baton Rouge, a native of Louisiana, declined to join the brief on the grounds that "the exclusion of the parties from the Sacrament of Matrimony is but an indirect effect of the law and not included in the legislative intent."[39] Another Louisiana bishop, Charles Pasquale Greco of Alexandria, also did not join, though he did request a copy of the brief. And Bishop Hubert H. Newell of Wyoming declined to join because the state legislature had repealed its antimiscegenation law during the previous term.

Father Lewers prepared the brief and mailed Bishop Russell a copy in February 1967. Quoting from the Second Vatican Council's December 1965 "Pastoral Constitution of the Church in the Modern World," Lewers began with the assertion that "these bishops, as pastors of their respective dioceses, are committed to the proposition that 'with regard to the fundamental rights of the person, every type of discrimination, whether social or cultural, whether based on sex, race, color, social condition, language or religion, is to be overcome and eradicated as contrary to God's intent.'"[40] Lewers's brief advanced two main contentions: first, that antimiscegenation statutes prohibited the free exercise of religion, insofar as marriage constituted "a fundamental act of religion" (934), and second, that such statutes unconstitutionally denied the right to bear children. Following Daniel Marshall's arguments in *Perez*, Lewers contended that antimiscegenation statutes prohibited interracial couples' free exercise of religion, insofar as marriage constituted "a fundamental act of religion" (934). In the spirit of the Second Vatican Council, Lewers devoted several pages to other religious traditions and organizations, including the Eastern Orthodox and Anglican churches, Judaism, and the World Council of Churches, strengthening his argument for the religious right to marry by demonstrating that antimiscegenation statutes impeded the religious freedom of members of several faith traditions. Then, turning to U.S. Supreme Court rulings that deemed racial classifications "constitutionally suspect," he argued that the "preservation of a racially segregated society is not an interest which the state may *lawfully* protect" (943, Lewers's emphasis). "To uphold the validity of a statute prohibiting or invalidating marriages simply because of a difference in the race of the spouses," he continued, "would be to permit the racial views of third persons to determine one of the most personal and sensitive of human decisions. In the absence of any grave danger to the lawful interests of the state, this is a decision that belongs solely to the man and woman contemplating marriage" (944). Then quoting several passages from the 1948 *Perez* decision, Lewers reiterated California Supreme Court justice Roger Traynor's assertion that if California's antimiscegenation statutes were unconstitutional and discriminatory, then they restricted two fundamental human liberties: religious freedom and the freedom to marry (945).

Lewers then briefly turned to an issue that Daniel Marshall had not addressed at length in *Perez*: the implications of antimiscegenation laws for interracial couples' right to have children. He claimed that bans on interracial marriage denied couples the right to bear children. By making race the "test of whether a man and woman may marry," he argued, antimiscegenation statutes "bar[red] those who cannot meet this racial test from one of the chief lawful rights in marriage, the having of children." Further, and especially critical from a religious perspective, any children born of such unions would thus legally be deemed illegitimate, unable to inherit property from their parents, and forever marked as bastards. Virginia's antimiscegenation statutes thus "clearly contravene[d] a fundamental liberty"—the couple's right to bear legitimate children—and moreover, such laws implicitly denied the children of such couples inheritance rights and the legal status of "legitimate."

When Lewers filed the brief with the U.S. Supreme Court in mid-February 1967, it made the local news. A *Richmond Times-Dispatch* headline announced that "Catholic Clergymen Hit Mixed Marriage Laws," explaining that sixteen clerics had "allied themselves with a mixed Protestant couple" to challenge Virginia's antimiscegenation statutes, "and, by implication, similar laws in 17 other states." Walking a fine line between journalistic objectivity and insinuations of Catholics' fondness for racial integration, the writer reported that the prelates claimed "states may restrain the free exercise of religion, including marriage, only on a showing of 'grave and immediate danger to interests which the state may lawfully protect. The preservation of a racially segregated society' is not such an interest, they said." In addition, the article continued, the clergymen asserted that "so long as antimiscegenation laws remain valid the children in such families are forced to suffer the penalty of being 'legally denominated as bastards.'"[41]

The article led at least one Richmond resident to complain to Bishop Russell. The writer, who was apparently untroubled by the illegitimate status conferred upon interracial children by virtue of antimiscegenation laws, lamented the social burdens mixed-race children would face. Bishop Russell wrote back, careful to reiterate that he did not "favor" interracial marriage per se; in fact, he stated that he would "certainly do all [he] could to discourage a couple from entering into such a marriage" due to the social burdens the couple and their children would face. Yet, the bishop continued, he "indeed fe[lt] that a law which makes illegal such a union deprives the two persons of their freedom." An interracial couple has "a right to marry if they wish and no law should prevent them [from] exercising their freedom of choice."[42] Similarly, on 16 June 1967, just four days after the Supreme Court issued its ruling in *Loving*, the *Catholic Virginian*, the official newspaper of the Diocese of Richmond, printed the bishop's statement on the ruling. Claiming to be "delighted" with the court's decision, Russell nevertheless declared that he would not "wish to encourage such marriages, anymore than [he] would encourage persons of different religions to marry, but because [he] sincerely believe[d] in the inherent right of a person to marry another person who happens to be a member of a different race." He continued on, repeating once again that although he would "discourage couples from entering into an interracial marriage because of many difficulties for the husband and wife, their future children and other relations," he believed that if the couple was "willing to accept all the annoyances and difficulties [then] they have a right to marry[,] and [he] [was] glad that the laws of Virginia no longer deprive citizens of this right."[43]

Three months later, in September 1967, Bishop Russell reiterated these sentiments yet one more time. In an article about him in the *Virginia Record*, the author observed, "now that the Supreme Court has ruled unanimously in accordance with the petition of Bishop Russell and his associates, he explains that he certainly does not wish to encourage interracial marriages, 'any more than I would encourage people of different religions to marry.'" Yet as in his previous statements, Bishop Russell insisted that he believed "'in the inherent right of a person to marry another person who happens to be a member of a different race.'"[44] Despite his affirmations of the inherent right to marry a person of another race, it seems that the bishop was not comfortable unequivocally endorsing interracial marriage. It remains unclear whether his reservations reflected savvy politics—perhaps the effort to retain the support of his parishioners—or lingering personal ambivalence about interracial marriage. While his actions in enlisting support for the amicus curiae brief demonstrate his willingness to take a public stance against prevailing white southern views on interracial marriage, his reticence suggests a far less enthusiastic level of commitment to the issue than that of California's Daniel Marshall.

Yet it is clear that Bishop Russell, like Marshall, believed that an interracial couple's right to marry derived from Catholic theologies of marriage and race. Likewise, it is also clear that this theological position stood in marked contrast to that of many white southern Protestants as well as to that of some white Catholics, such as Judge Leon M. Bazile. Moreover, the fact that fifteen ordinaries joined the brief with Bishop Russell while no Protestant denominations or organizations submitted a similar brief on behalf of the Baptist Lovings underscores the contention that Roman Catholics perceived a theological importance in the freedom to marry the person of one's choosing that members of other faith traditions did not. Antimiscegenation laws' combined assault on doctrines involving marriage, race, and reproductive rights presented particularly objectionable violations of human freedom. Catholic teachings on marriage and race significantly elevated the importance of the fundamental liberty to marry a beloved person—regardless of his or her race—and to have legitimate children with that individual.

Ambivalent though the Catholic commitment to interracial marriage may have at times been, the ordinaries' amicus curiae brief was the *only* response elicited by any religious group in support of the Lovings. It was deeply rooted in long-standing Catholic doctrines on marriage and in less entrenched yet critically important doctrines on race. Also, it stood in stark contrast to the racial beliefs that had resulted in the genocide of some six million Jewish people in Europe and to white southern Protestants' assertions of divinely separated races. Yet the brief went virtually unnoticed by the attorneys and the justices in the case, as well as by most of the public. As with the majority of California justices in the *Perez* case, in the eyes of the Court, the real legal issue was whether or not antimiscegenation laws violated the due process and equal protection clauses of the Fourteenth Amendment. For most of the people concerned with the Lovings' rights, such statutes' infringements on religious freedom were incidental to their violation of other fundamental liberties.

Free at Last, Thank God Almighty:
Loving v. Virginia, 12 June 1967

In early March 1967, two weeks before Hanover County's Judge Leon Bazile quietly passed away in his home following a long illness, the *New York Times* reported that the Maryland legislature had passed a bill to abolish the state's 306-year-old antimiscegenation law. Maryland's governor, Spiro T. Agnew, had already announced that he favored the repeal and that he would sign the bill. A brief article buried on page 15 of the *Times*, it nonetheless served both as the epitaph of the nation's oldest ban on interracial marriages and as the portent of things to come.[45] If Maryland, the first region in the United States to enact bans on black-white marriages—and the first southern state to make an about-face in its interracial marriage policy—was about to repeal its antimiscegenation statute, then surely the U.S. Supreme Court would likewise rule such laws unconstitutional.

As expected, three months later on Monday, 12 June 1967, Mildred and Richard Loving finally heard the words they had waited nearly nine years to hear. Delivering the unanimous *Loving v. Virginia* decision, Chief Justice Earl Warren stated that Virginia's antimiscegenation statutes "cannot stand consistently with the Fourteenth Amendment."[46] The Court asserted that "restricting the freedom to marry solely because of racial classifications violates the central meaning of the Equal Protection Clause" and affirmed marriage as

one of the "basic civil rights of man," fundamental to our very existence and survival. . . . To deny this fundamental freedom on so unsupportable a basis as the racial classifications embodied in these statutes, classifications so directly subversive of the principle of equality at the heart of the Fourteenth Amendment, is surely to deprive all the State's citizens of liberty without due process of law. The Fourteenth Amendment requires that the freedom of choice to marry not be restricted by invidious racial discriminations. Under our Constitution, the freedom to marry, or not marry, a person of another race resides with the individual, and cannot be infringed by the State.[47]

After three centuries of laws prohibiting marriages across the color line, the United States of America at last affirmed the individual's right to marry a person of another race. With the *Loving* decision, a federal court—for the first time in U.S. history—deemed the individual's right to marry superior to the states' right to regulate marriage law. Richard and Mildred Loving were overjoyed by the ruling. As Richard later reported, "When we got the word we'd won, I just stood there, frozen with happiness. For the first time, I could put my arm around 'Baby' and call her my wife in Virginia."[48]

Newspapers around the country announced the court's ruling. "Justices Upset All Bans on Interracial Marriage," the front page of the *New York Times* proclaimed. The African American *Los Angeles Sentinel* chirped, "Interracial Love Gets Supreme Court O.K." Richmond-area papers achieved a more stoic tone: the *Virginian-Pilot* simply stated, "Intermarriage Bans Held Unconstitutional," while its competitor, the *Times-Dispatch* declared, "Miscegenation Ban Is Ended by High Court." The *Times-Dispatch* ran an additional story, "State Couple 'Overjoyed' by Ruling," focusing on Richard and Mildred Loving's victory.[49] Norfolk's African American newspaper, the *Journal and Guide*, announced, "Top Court Junks Marriage Bars." An editorial in the same issue of *Journal and Guide* offered perhaps the most pointed commentary on the court's decision: "What makes this Supreme Court decision so desirable," the writer observed, "is that it lifts an onerous and brutalizing stigma from Negro Virginians by knocking down that psychological barrier which, in effect, told them and the world that no Negro is good enough to be the husband or wife of a white Virginian."[50]

For all the drama the specter of interracial marriage had produced following the court's 1954 *Brown* decision, the public and media responses to *Loving* were rather subdued. Contrary to the theatrical declarations of some white supremacists during the mid-1950s, fire and brimstone had not rained down when the South's schools were desegregated, nor did a lightning bolt zap the justices when they reached their decision in *Loving*. Indeed, an event in Atlanta, casually depicted in a small photograph in a newspaper, encapsulates the profound change that had swept through the South since 1954. Five days after the Court's ruling, Norfolk's *Journal and Guide* reported that the Georgia Klan was "on the march again," though the parade did not appear to have any relation to *Loving*. A photograph showed a small group of African Americans smiling at the stern-faced, white-robed Klansmen as they marched through Atlanta's black neighborhood. The caption noted, "If the Kluxers paraded through the 'Negro section' to frighten residents, they failed miserably. Colored citizens simply had a good laugh."[51] No longer having the power to strike terror into the hearts of black people, the Klan had become a source of amusement. Like the white South's tepid response to *Loving*, black Georgians' reaction to the Klan parade served as an indication that white southern racism appeared to be crumbling, its public expression relegated to a few laughable extremists.

The responses to *Loving* and to the Klan parade suggest that, as in 1865, a sense of defeat had settled over the white South. Agitating outsiders had once again relentlessly pecked away at southern racial values until they fell more into line with those of the broader culture. White racism was far from dead, but the paralyzing fear and hopelessness that had once gripped the hearts of southern blacks was fading away.

Richard and Mildred Loving, together with their three children, Sidney, Peggy, and Donald, returned home to Central Point, Virginia, known to local residents as "the passing capital of America." According to a September 1967 article about the Lovings in *Ebony* magazine, Central Point was an area in which "hundreds of young men and women have migrated to cross racial lines, later marrying and working as whites in cities throughout the country." In this context of racial tolerance and mixing, the Lovings found a supportive community that quietly cheered them on through the long days during which they awaited their legal fate. One "prominent Caroline County leader" asserted, "we have a community of our own. . . . Our mores only apply here. We've done more integrating than in any other part of the U.S." A farmer who knew Richard Loving remarked, "There has been plenty mingling across races for years and nobody griped or tried to legalize it. Negroes got kind of slick and passed and fooled outsiders. Rich just wasn't that type. What he wanted, he wanted on paper and legal. As a result, he broke up the system."[52] In Caroline County, long before their experience in the U.S. Supreme Court in Washington, D.C., Mildred and Richard Loving found a community that recognized a different kind of justice than the one that court officials sought to impose, one that recognized the possibility of different expressions of love, including love across the color line.

THE STORIES BEHIND the *Perez* and *Loving* cases illustrate that Christian beliefs were centrally important to the motivations of lawyers and judges on both sides of the contentious issue of interracial marriage. For attorney Daniel Marshall and Bishop John Russell, the *religious* right to marry a person of another race served as a centrally significant matter, and for Marshall especially, Catholic teachings on human unity provided an equally important basis for his position on interracial marriage and for challenging antimiscegenation laws. For Judge Bazile and a significant number of white southerners, on the other hand, the mixing of races in alleged violation of God's plan for humanity constituted a deep ideological basis for their opposition to intermarriage. From even before the Civil War, a theological idiosyncrasy had appeared among white southerners emphasizing the ideas that God had separated the races, that God therefore frowned upon the social and marital equality of black and white persons, and that these views were located in the Bible.

The theology of separate races, coupled with the Protestant tradition of the state exercising control over marriage law, appeared in volumes of American legal cases "establishing" and "proving" the validity of antimiscegenation laws—a tautological system in which attorneys and judges "knew" the laws were constitutional because previous judges had ruled so, and those judges had ruled so because they "knew" their interpretations of the law to be correct. This racial worldview, combined with the European-American valuation of the fixedness of "truth" within texts, created a situation in which couples such as Mildred and Richard Loving faced the challenge of asserting that such established religious and legal "truths" were not, in their eyes, true, and that they "knew" a different reality.

Issues of truth and knowledge—how one "knows" and how one "knows what one knows" about a text, how we claim to "know" more generally, the sociopolitical consequences of such knowledge, and the differences between social conservatives and progressives in "knowing" the meanings of texts such as the U.S. Constitution or the Bible—are issues still to be examined. Reflecting on the differences between, for example, Daniel Marshall and Judge Bazile, Catholics and Protestants, and progressives and conservatives—between epistemological paradigms—reveals some of the crucial lessons of the history explored in this book: how "knowledge" is produced, and how epistemologies mobilize to advance political viewpoints.[53] More important, it reminds us that basing one's beliefs about racial hierarchy or about the constitutionality of segregation, for example, in something as variable as a text—open, as texts are to multiple interpretations—paves the way for the demise of interpretations that we sometimes take as "certain." As historian Paul Harvey astutely observes, the so-called biblical bases of racism and segregation ultimately led to the dismantling of the southern theology of separate races, "in part through a reimagination of the same Christian thought that was part of its creation."[54] In other words, other readers came along and perceived different meanings in the biblical texts that white supremacists claimed as the basis for the separate races theology, just as the Warren Court perceived a different meaning of the U.S. Constitution in regard to racial segregation than did the Fuller court of the 1890s. The intellectual relationships between texts, interpretation, knowledge, and politics point to the significant lessons that may be learned from the cultural history of American antimiscegenation law.

Epilogue A Postmodernist's Reflections on History and Knowledge

Ignorance more frequently begets confidence than does knowledge.
—Charles Darwin, *The Descent of Man*, 1871

On 12 June 2007, Mildred Loving, widowed for thirty-two years from the man she had fought so hard to wed legally, released a statement commemorating the fortieth anniversary of the *Loving* decision.[1] Titled "Loving for All," the statement recounted the circumstances by which she and Richard "took [their] case for the freedom to marry all the way to the Supreme Court." Quoting Judge Leon M. Bazile's "almighty God" statement, Mrs. Loving observed that many people in her generation had believed "it was God's plan to keep people apart and that the government should discriminate against people in love." Not a "day goes by," she continued, "that I don't think of Richard and our love, our right to marry, and how much it meant to me to have that freedom to marry the person precious to me, even if others thought he was the 'wrong kind of person' for me to marry. I believe all Americans, no matter their race, no matter their sex, no matter their sexual orientation, should have that same freedom to marry. Government has no business imposing some people's religious beliefs over others. Especially if it denies people's civil rights. . . . I support the freedom to marry for all. That's what *Loving*, and loving, are all about."[2]

Mrs. Loving, an active member of St. Stephen's Baptist Church in Central Point, did not come to support same-sex marriage easily. A few months before the fortieth anniversary of the court's ruling, a Christian gay rights organization called Faith in America approached her, asking if she might be willing to endorse a statement of support for same-sex couples at an event commemorating the *Loving* decision. At first Mrs. Loving hedged on giving the group an answer. "I just don't know," she told them. According to the *New York Times*, she "listened sympathetically, a worn Bible on her end table, as the group's founder, the furniture entrepreneur Mitchell Gold, told her of his own struggles as a teenager to accept that society would never let him marry someone he loved." But she was not yet sure how she felt about marriage for same-sex couples. After the members of the group departed, Mrs. Loving struggled with her decision, discussing the issue with neighbors and family. Finally, after much reflection, she agreed to allow Faith in America to read a statement in her name at the celebration commemorating the *Loving* decision. A member of the organization asked Mrs. Loving if she was sure she understood what she was agreeing to. "'You understand that you're putting your name behind the idea that two men or two women should have the right to marry each other?' 'I understand it,' Loving said, 'and I believe it.'"[3]

Faith in America, founded to end religious bigotry against lesbian, gay, bisexual, and transgender people, wrote the "Loving for All" statement endorsed by Mrs. Loving. In its mission statement, the organization cites a number of historical precedents for discrimination against LGBT people, including "violence, intolerance, and inequity toward women, people of color, and people with religious traditions different from those of the majority." Moreover, Faith in America contends that today, most Americans view such attitudes as wrong. The group believes that "to end the persecution of gay people engendered by religion-based bigotry, its common link with these historical precedents must be acknowledged."[4] Keenly noting the role of religion in opposition to both interracial and same-sex marriage, Faith in Action and the "Loving for All" statement that the group created draw attention to what many scholars have failed to analyze: just as religious beliefs imbue the arguments of some contemporary opponents of same-sex marriage, they also profoundly influenced historical antagonism to interracial marraige.

For most twenty-first-century thinkers, the idea that God created racial groups whom he intended should never marry is so ludicrous as to be dismissed without another thought. Yet for much of the late nineteenth and twentieth centuries, this belief prevailed among many white Americans, particularly southerners. Although nondominant religious beliefs sometimes occasioned the demise of unjust practices, as the actions of Daniel Marshall demonstrate, at other times religious beliefs reinforced the status quo, as segregationists' beliefs illustrate. The dominant strains of American Christianity—those that have echoed through centuries of racist, sexist, heterocentric, and colonialist policies at home and abroad, from the New England pulpit to the halls of the U.S. Congress—have most often consolidated power in the hands of the already-powerful, masking inequality in the language of natural law, and making hierarchy the operative paradigm for human relations.

To understand the historical bases and contemporary significance of why and how white Americans of earlier generations affirmed biblical justifications for racial inequality and how their beliefs changed despite their conviction that racial separation was an immutable social reality created by God, these final pages address what I see as the lessons of *Almighty God Created the Races*. For a moment I will step out of my comfort zone as a historian and venture to articulate a *theory* of history, insofar as my book, in its most expansive sense, offers a history of the production of knowledge and the effects of that knowledge. As I see it, *Almighty God* documents a history of meaning making and the usage of those meanings in order to regulate bodies and identities: how Roman Catholics and Protestants looked to their respective traditions to understand marriage and race; how they "knew" their beliefs and their interpretations of texts to be correct; how those beliefs were subsequently encoded into laws that regulated human behaviors; and even how love has been, and continues to be, culturally (and religiously) constructed. My book points both to the constructedness of meanings as well as to the consequences of these meanings for human lives—the effects of laws and beliefs that determined what Americans could believe, how they could live, and who they could love.

The Twentieth-Century Legacies of the European Reformation

It is important, first, to explain why white American beliefs about interracial marriage fragmented historically along Catholic and Protestant lines. Catholic and Protestant theologies of marriage and race clearly reflect what historian Jaroslav Pelikan deems the critical "line of demarcation" between the two faiths during the sixteenth century: "the sole authority of the Bible."[5] The Roman Catholic Church, claiming its right by the direct authority of Saint Peter to proclaim doctrine and administer salvation, took issue with Protestant reformers such as Martin Luther, who asserted that the Bible, rather than the church and its traditions, formed the wellspring of authority on matters of faith. The sixteenth-century Catholic Church claimed sole authority to understand and interpret the Bible and to proclaim doctrines. Consequently its centralized authority disseminated top-down, from pope to clerics to the faithful. In contrast, Protestant reformers emphasized the "priesthood of all believers"—the view that God endowed individual believers with the ability to discern scriptural truths and that the faithful required no mediator or priest to explain the message of the Gospel, but only the guidance of the Holy Spirit within the context of a faith community. And because there were many Protestant faith communities that disagreed specifically on matters of biblical interpretation, Protestantism created as many congregations as there were interpretations of the Bible. Thus Protestants, by definition, ultimately exhibited multiple locations of congregational authority, all of which claimed to derive from the Bible.

The division we see specifically between Catholics-at-large and *American* Protestants over theologies of marriage and race also thus underscores the larger division over the universal nature of Catholic faith and the localized nature of Protestantism. The divergent theologies of marriage and race mirror the Catholic tradition of centralized authority extending to the faithful versus the Protestant tradition of decentralized authority and the autonomy of local congregations. Whereas the Vatican issued official statements on race in an effort to bring the American faithful into line with ecclesiastical teachings on human unity, white southern Protestants identified a biblical hermeneutic of racial hierarchy and separation that squared with their local mores. For Protestants, spiritual authority is local, confined to its own membership and subject to its own interpretive paradigm. On the other hand, Catholics, whatever their national origin, possess a self-identity that springs from a sense of a larger connection to Rome. In contrast, while American Protestant believers might share in some way in an international faith community, such as Episcopalians and the Church of England, more often they are either linked to an American denomination, such as the United Methodist Church, or they belong to local congregations that have little or no affiliation with a larger group. Although several of the mainstream denominations have made significant strides toward ecumenicalism within the last century, many conservative American Protestants, and particularly white southerners, participate in a rather insular and individualistic religious self-identity that often demonstrates little regard for unity with other Christian believers and, on the contrary, tends to assert the exclusive correctness of its own doctrines. As Pelikan describes it, the Protestant "rule of the sole authority of Scripture meant in practice the unquestioned authority of this or that particular interpretation of Scripture as it was characteristic of this or that church body."[6]

In addition, because several groups of American Protestants suffered schisms as a result of nineteenth-century disagreements over slavery and secession from the union, they shared distinct regional views on slavery and race *and* fragmented along regional lines. The differences between, for example, mid-nineteenth-century southern and northern Methodists were both cultural and doctrinal. Northern and southern Methodists struggled to regain denominational unity after the Civil War and into the twentieth century, and like their Catholic counterparts in the North and South, they located that unity both in religious practice—reuniting in 1939—and in racial segregation. As Peter C. Murray observes,

> Methodists, and other predominantly white denominations, operated in an area defined by American society and culture regarding civil rights and race relations. Through these various racial structures they condoned, if not embraced, racial inequality. The Gospel came second to the degraded status assigned African Americans by white Americans, although most white Americans seldom juxtaposed the two in their minds. Most white Methodists accepted a Jim Crow church as easily as they accepted the Declaration of Independence and de jure discrimination.[7]

And as the civil rights movement accelerated following the *Brown* decision, denominational unity between Methodists and Baptists decreased when white northern Protestants who became active in the civil rights movement did so precisely because they perceived white southerners' racial segregation to be an egregious violation of Christian belief.

White southern conservative Protestants turned to the Bible to create their theology of race, while American Catholics ultimately received their doctrines on race from the church in Rome, though some white southern Catholics, steeped in a culture that exalted both individualism and the certainty of truths purportedly based in the immutable words of the Good Book, made sense of racial difference through the southern lingua franca of separate races. As we have seen, this seemingly unremarkable and perhaps self-evident fact that each faith tradition derived its spiritual authority from different sources hearkens back to the origins of Protestant and Catholic differences in the early sixteenth century. In navigating the churning seas of race and segregation in the twentieth century, it only made sense for each group to apply its most tried-and-true methods to locate a safe harbor from which it could address the most difficult issues of the day. The Catholic Church asserted its universal authority to proclaim the sacramental character of marriage, which in turn necessarily demanded that the church itself determine rules regarding marriage, especially those involving marital impediments. Similarly, when it became clear after the extermination of some six million Jewish people in Germany that proclamations about racial superiority possessed terrible consequences, the church again asserted a Catholic doctrine that refuted all racial teachings affirming racial separation and hierarchy and declared the unity of the human family.

In the American South, on the other hand, the biblically inflected racial culture acquired new intensity during the century following the Civil War, and the development of the separate races theology mandated racial segregation in marriage. Indeed, the Protestant theology of separate races required legal action: if God had deemed racial separation as the divine plan, then humans must enact in law rules to prevent any violation of that plan. Failure to uphold God's plan constituted a direct affront to God. Antimiscegenation statutes therefore functioned as the legal by-product of the white southern Protestant theology of separate races.

How Do We "Know" What We Know?
Cultural Epistemology and Hermeneutics

The theological differences between Catholic and Protestant believers presented in *Almighty God Created the Races* reflect historically situated conflicts involving authority—the authority of the Roman Catholic Church versus the authority of the Bible. Reflecting upon the role of authority in their respective traditions raises questions about epistemology (how a person knows; what constitutes knowledge) and hermeneutics (how one interprets texts, such as biblical passages or the amendments to the U.S. Constitution). How does one person "know," for example, Catholic teachings to be authoritative, while another person "knows" the Bible as the source of spiritual authority? Or how does one come to "know" that matrimony is a sacrament, and another that marriage is sacred but not a sacrament? By what means does a person "know" one biblical interpretation to be correct and another incorrect? Or, to offer a different example, how does a judge "know" that racial segregation in public facilities is a constitutional or unconstitutional interpretation of the Fourteenth Amendment? While I do not claim to be able to answer these questions satisfactorily, I do want to suggest and explore the ways that one's cultural and epistemological location (the position from which one "knows") influences one's hermeneutics (the way in which one interprets), and how these two factors mutually reinforce one another.

The work of two very different historians sheds light on the relationship between epistemology and hermeneutics and on the ways that transformative paradigm shifts occur in text-based worldviews: Michael Klarman's *From Jim Crow to Civil Rights* and Mark Noll's *The Civil War as a Theological Crisis*.[8] Klarman's study provides us with a model from constitutional law and race politics for making sense of the roles of epistemology and hermeneutics. In his survey of U.S. Supreme Court cases from the 1896 *Plessy* ruling to the 1954 *Brown v. Board of Education* decision, Klarman explores the variety of historical factors that shaped changes in American "racial attitudes and practices" during that era. Specifically, he analyzes the historical issues that explain how the Supreme Court issued contradictory decisions in *Plessy* and *Brown* and how the court construed the equal protection clause so differently in these two cases. Klarman argues that legal and political issues jointly influence judicial decisions, depending upon which factors judges prioritize in their legal interpretations. "Because constitutional law is generally quite indeterminate," Klarman asserts, "constitutional interpretation almost inevitably reflects the broader social and political context of the times. 'Equal protection of the laws' does not plainly condemn school segregation, and the Fifteenth Amendment's ban on race-based qualifications to the suffrage does not plainly prohibit race-neutral voter qualifications that disparately affect blacks. In the absence of determinate law, constitutional interpretation necessarily implicates the values of the judges, which themselves generally reflect broader social attitudes."[9] According to Klarman, then, the Court's rulings in *Plessy* and *Brown*—and, by extension, in all of the Court's decisions on important social issues—reflect predominant social attitudes in addition to current beliefs about which legal interpretations are indeed "constitutional."

In attempting to explain the justices' constitutional interpretations in these cases, Klarman emphasizes the idea that while contemporary scholars and analysts tend to "vilify the Court for its performance during the [*Plessy*] era" and for contributing to the vicious spread of white supremacist notions, in fact the *Plessy* Court's racial cases "were not blatant nullifications of post–Civil War constitutional amendments designed to secure racial equality." "On the contrary," Klarman maintains, "*Plessy*-era race decisions were plausible interpretations of conventional legal sources: text, original intent, precedent, and custom." We may critique such decisions today, but not, Klarman insists, "on the grounds that they butchered clearly established law or inflicted racially regressive results on a nation otherwise inclined to favor racial equality."[10] Just as the *Brown* decision fifty-eight years later, *Plessy* was a legitimate constitutional interpretation. Both rulings had legitimate legal bases. What changed, however, was the cultural basis: by 1954, the Court no longer viewed racial segregation as a legitimate cultural perspective; the justices consequently interpreted the law to reflect that new viewpoint.

Judges' interpretations thus invariably and necessarily derive in part from their social location—from the views prevalent in their culture and from their personal values, which may or may not contradict those views. Particularly in areas of constitutional interpretation in which the law is "indeterminate," judges have to rely upon nonlegal factors as aids in their interpretations. Drawing our attention to the socially constructed nature of race within American law, Klarman's argument thus highlights the socially constructed nature of constitutional interpretation. While the law may be "determinate" on certain issues, cases such as *Plessy* and *Brown* as well as the cases I have presented here in *Almighty God* illustrate the extent to which critical aspects of constitutional law remain open to vastly different interpretive schema. Moreover, these schema change and are subject to— and in fact are completely influenced by—human biases, interests, and hermeneutical paradigms stemming from the interpreter's cultural location. To reiterate, despite what "strict constructionists" may claim, constitutional law does not possess static, objectively discernible meaning. Every text is subject to interpretation; there *is* no literal interpretation or "strict constructionism."

As with my book, the issue at the heart of Klarman's analysis, then, is that of cultural epistemologies and hermeneutics: how did late nineteenth-century Supreme Court justices "know" that racial segregation constituted a legitimate legal objective? Likewise, how do contemporary Americans— judges as well as the populace at large—"know" that the *Brown* ruling was "right" and the *Plessy* ruling was "wrong"? Why are we so certain today that we "know" that race-based slavery and segregation were "wrong," that interracial couples possess the right to marry, and that same-sex couples possess (or do not possess) that same right? And most specifically for our purposes here, how do we determine and "know" legal and social "truths" based on (religious and constitutional) texts and established (religious and legal) doctrines?

Without using the term "epistemology," Klarman perceives that constitutional interpretations stem from the interpreter's sociocultural and epistemological location. "Whether the traditional sources of constitutional law are thought to plainly forbid a particular practice," he contends, "depends on the personal values of the interpreter and on the social and political context." In Klarman's view, a judge's legal and personal understanding shapes her or his constitutional interpretation. When judges' "preferences are strong, [they] may reject even relatively determinate law, because they are unable to tolerate the result it indicates. In 1954, most of the justices considered racial segregation—the doctrine that Hitler preached—to be evil, and they were determined to forbid it, regardless of whether conventional legal sources sanctioned that result."[11] As the historical circumstances changed, American judges began to rethink previously held epistemologies of race. No longer could racial hierarchies inscribed in law be deemed just, consistent with the clauses of the Fourteenth Amendment. The American judicial epistemology of race and of constitutional interpretation began to shift in favor of a new conceptual paradigm of racial equality.

We see a similar situation arising in historical materials involving religion. In his analysis of how the Civil War presented Americans with a "theological crisis," historian Mark Noll contends that "the American Civil War generated a first-order theological crisis over how to interpret the Bible, how to understand the work of God in the world, and how to exercise the authority of theology in a democratic society." Noll's book deftly explores how abolitionists' exegeses of biblical passages failed to gain widespread support because they were too subtle—or one might say "academic"—to be accessible to most Americans. The simpler, less-nuanced biblical arguments of proslavery advocates tended to make more sense to the average citizen. Because antislavery biblical arguments "did not feature intuition, republican instinct, and common sense readings of individual texts, they were much less effective in a public arena that had been so strongly shaped by intuitive, republican, and commonsensical intellectual principles." According to Noll, abolitionists' "nuanced biblical attacks on American slavery faced rough going precisely because they were nuanced. . . . It demanded that sophisticated interpretive practice replace a commonsensically literal approach to the sacred text."[12]

True to their traditions, nineteenth-century American Protestants turned to the Bible to explain and offer guidance on the critical issues of the day. Just as with many contemporary Christians, they believed the Bible to enlighten and guide the faithful in all matters. But what is significant here is that many believers then as now adopted a "commonsensical" or "plain" understanding of scripture and rejected more sophisticated interpretations that required deeper reflection on the possible meanings of the text. As Noll discusses elsewhere in the book, the Protestant belief that the Bible should be accessible to, and that it was (with the guidance of the Holy Spirit) comprehensible to, any reader shaped Americans' understanding of how they read the text. They did not, in other words, perceive that their reading was an "interpretation"; rather, they viewed their reading simply as reading—that it did not entail anything but common sense and a plain understanding, that it did not import meaning from within the reader. Their belief that the biblical text possessed "determinate meaning" necessarily shaped their interpretations of the Bible.

As Klarman's analysis demonstrates the social construction of constitutional jurisprudence, Noll's insights call attention to the social construction of biblical hermeneutics, particularly of "literalism." In Noll's book, nineteenth-century Americans' fondness for "literal" biblical interpretations blinded them to seeing their interpretations qua interpretations, which inclined them (as with contemporary conservative Bible readers) to believe they were merely reading the "plain" text. This is similar to "strict constructionism," which legal scholar David O'Brien defines as the notion that judges can and should restrict their constitutional interpretations to the "literal language of the text in the Constitution."[13] Yet following Kathleen Boone, I would argue that literalism is in fact an epistemological orientation rather than an unadulterated approach to reading a text.[14] If a reader "knows" a text to be "true" and her reading of it to be "literal," this preconceived paradigm for viewing the text in fact shapes that "literal" interpretation. And if this "knowledge" coincides with the reader's conviction that her brand of faith provides epistemological certainty about matters of faith—her God, her soul, and so forth—then this also shapes the way she "literally" interprets the text. As Noll observes of the Civil War–era Americans, "when the prevalence of religious conviction was added to widespread self-confidence in the powers of human perception, assessment, and interpretation, the result was a flourishing of providential reasoning. Americans thought they could clearly see what the world was like, what God was like, what factors drove the world, who was responsible for events, and how the moral balance sheet should be read."[15] Religious conviction shaped and reinforced nineteenth-century Protestant Americans' sense of epistemological certainty, which in turn shaped and reinforced their biblical hermeneutics. Conversely, epistemology and hermeneutics shaped and reinforced their religious convictions, resulting in an insulated, self-perpetuating, tautological system for making sense of the world and of change. This insulated hermeneutical paradigm informed the theology of separate races, and today it undergirds contemporary biblical hermeneutics on the "abomination" of homosexuality. The means by which we evaluate what we "know" shapes the ways we interpret—texts, our experience, and the world at large. The more confidence we have in the certainty of what we "know" as "truth," the more likely we perceive that we can and do interpret texts "literally."

Religious Belief and the Right to Marry a Person of the Same Sex: Lessons from the American History of Interracial Marriage

Understanding how white judges and segregationists of bygone eras identified a textual basis for racial segregation in the U.S. Constitution or in the Bible and then came to abandon their view is instructive for contemplating how some Christians today read select biblical passages as "proof" of God's hatred of homosexuality. Despite the fierceness with which the Christian Right decries the "homosexual agenda" today (which echoes white segregationists' exclamations of "Never!" during the 1950s and 1960s), based upon what we have witnessed with southern segregationists of the past, it seems possible that they may one day forsake these claims. Current disagreements between conservative Christians and proponents of same-sex marriage, just like those between segregationists and integrationists during the last century, center on the seemingly insurmountable differences wrought by polarized cultural epistemologies. One group perceives the existence of fixed and immutable absolutes, while the other emphasizes contingencies, relativities, and the role of context. These epistemological differences in turn shape each side's approach to interpreting religious, legal, and cultural texts.

In contrast to those claiming to present an "unchanging" and "biblical" conception of same-sex relations, *Almighty God Created the Races* reveals that, far from there being an eternal or static standard of biblical interpretation, hermeneutics do in fact change. Notions of God's "unchanging" will change. And even though the words on the page of a text may remain the same over time, how people understand those words change. These change because people, not God, *interpret* the passages. People, not God, make claims about what is "God's" will, based upon what they think they "know." Not all people in all times and all places will read biblical passages in the same way, even if they claim to read "literally." As with interpreters of constitutional law or any other text, Bible readers do, in fact, read their historical context and personal values into their interpretations. Where at one time the biblical justifications for the enslavement of African peoples rang as clear as a church bell, such notions shifted during the nineteenth century such that, by the twentieth century, all but the most recalcitrant fringes of white America regarded slavery as a moral evil to be uniformly rejected. Where at one time, it seemed perfectly reasonable to interpret Genesis 10–11 as the "historical" explanation for racial groups existing on separate continents, and thus as proof of God's command for legalized segregation, such ideas now seem preposterous. And where, presently, the conservative Christians assert that the "unchanging" word of God, or the "unchanging" teachings of the Catholic Church, have forever prohibited the ordination of women, or loving relationships between same-sex partners, Americans are beginning to see that their interpretations of select biblical passages in fact reflect the same historically contingent and self-interested hermeneutical paradigms.[16]

The question remains, then, of what hope is there for American Christians to alter their views and recognize the sanctity of same-sex unions on an equal basis with heterosexual relationships. Although Catholic theology proved beneficial for interracial couples in the American past, it promises little hope for today's same-sex couples. The Roman Catholic sacramental theology of marriage—with its implicit connection to original sin and sanctification through procreation—which enabled and ultimately demanded openness toward interracial marriage, is precisely what hampers this church from openness toward same-sex marriage and civil unions. Unless the church deems nonprocreative sexuality as divine, and/or the children acquired through adoption and surrogacy and through in vitro fertilization and other medical technologies, as theologically valid means of fulfilling the doctrinal goal of sanctification of the couple, the Roman Catholic Church will not sanction same-sex unions. And although Protestant theology proved detrimental for interracial couples in the American past, the hope for a religious sanction of same-sex couples may lie in its theology of the future. The possibility of a denomination creating its own theological imperative for same-sex couples—marriage as a sacrament, for example—exists among Protestants and other religious traditions in a way that unfortunately eludes Catholics. It seems, then, that in the case of same-sex marriage, it will be up to other religious groups—Protestant and non-Christian alike—to develop a theology of marriage that mandates these couples' religious right to marry.

As long as religious groups continue to view their theological beliefs and biblical interpretations as absolutes, rather than recognizing that we each create our own truth, we will continue to have biblical hermeneutics that affirm absolutism, that separate and divide rather than unite the human family. In order for the same-sex marriage controversy to be legally resolved, a sufficient majority of the American populace must affirm that all adults in consensual, loving relationships possess the right to marry and to determine the terms of their intimate relationships. And we must recognize that efforts to make "truth" absolute entails flailing toward a certainty that constantly and consistently eludes precisely *because* it is not there.

Charles Darwin's assertion, cited at the beginning of this chapter, that "confidence more frequently begets certainty than does knowledge," suggests that epistemological certainty by definition renders people confident in their pronouncements about "truth," while "knowledge" makes a person more tentative and, ideally, more humble about what constitutes "truth." Because religion often aims to comfort people in the existential crises rendered by epistemological uncertainty, conservative religious belief tends to create psychological certainty, rather than enabling people to come to terms with *un*certainty or to recognize that "knowledge" is unstable, a product of the fleeting "truths" and interpretive paradigms that inform every historical era. We would do better to hold opinions that challenge systemic oppression and inequalities while maintaining the humility to recognize that those opinions—and that "knowledges," legal, religious, historical— are far more relative than certain, and they are more the consequences of our historical moment and personal interpretive paradigm than of any absolute truth.

Notes

Abbreviations of Manuscript and Archival Collections

JLP John LaFarge, S.J., Papers, Georgetown University Special Collections, Washington, D.C.

JRP Bishop John J. Russell Papers, Box 7: Miscegenation, Archives of the Diocese of Richmond, Richmond, Virginia.

LBP Judge Leon M. Bazile Papers, General Correspondence File, 1963–1966, Virginia Historical Society, Richmond, Virginia.

LCF *Loving* Case File. Commonwealth of Virginia, *County of Caroline v. Richard Loving and Mildred Jeter*. Central Rappahannock Heritage Center, Fredericksburg, Virginia.

PCF *Perez v. Moroney* (sub. nom. *Perez v. Lippold*). L.A. No. 20305. Supreme Court Case Files, California State Archives, Office of the Secretary of the State, Sacramento, California.

Introduction

1 The racial descriptions of the Lovings and the details of the events preceding their arrests come from an essay by Robert A. Pratt, who grew up in Central Point and who had played with the Lovings' children when he was a child. Mildred Loving agreed to be interviewed by him in 1994. See Pratt, "Crossing the Color Line," 234–35.

2 Volume 4 of Virginia's 1950 Codes on intermarriage, quoted in "Jurisdictional Statement," In the Matter of the Application of Richard Perry Loving and Mildred Delores Jeter Loving, in Kurland and Casper, *Landmark Briefs and Arguments*, 694–95.

Code 20–54 stipulates:

"Intermarriage prohibited; meaning of term 'white persons.'—It shall hereafter be unlawful for any white person in this State to marry any save a white person, or a person with no other admixture of blood than white and American Indian. For the purpose of this chapter, the term 'white person' shall apply only to such persons as has no trace whatever of any blood other than Caucasian; but persons who have one-sixteenth or less of the blood of the American Indian and have no other non-Caucasic blood shall be deemed to be white persons. All laws heretofore passed and now in effect regarding the intermarriage of white and colored persons shall apply to marriages prohibited by this chapter." (Kurland and Casper, *Landmark Briefs and Arguments*, 695.)

Code 20-58 stipulates:

"Leaving State to evade law.—If any white person and colored person shall go out of this State, for the purpose of being married, and with the intention of returning, and be Married out of it, and afterwards return to and reside in it, cohabiting as man and wife, they shall be punished as provided in [Code] 20-59, and the marriage shall be governed by the same law as if it had been solemnized in this State. The fact of their cohabitation here as man and wife shall be evidence of their marriage." (Ibid., 694.)

3   Quote taken from Arrest Warrants for Richard Loving and Mildred Delores Jeter, 11 July 1958, *Loving* Case File, Commonwealth of Virginia, *County of Caroline v. Richard Loving and Mildred Jeter*, Central Rappahannock Heritage Center, Fredericksburg, Va. Hereinafter cited as LCF.

4   According to Byron Curti Martyn, the couple had planned to plead not guilty, but upon the judge's promises of leniency, they waived the jury trial and pleaded guilty. See Martyn, "Racism in the United States," 1300–301.

5   A motion to vacate is a brief asking the judge to invalidate an earlier judgment.

In 1964 Cohen and Hirschkop also filed a class action suit with the U.S. District Court for the Eastern District of Virginia, enjoining the judges to declare Virginia's antimiscegenation laws unconstitutional and to prevent state officials from enforcing the Lovings' sentences. The U.S. District Court refused to decide on the legality of Virginia's antimiscegenation laws but granted a temporary order allowing the Lovings to reside in Virginia until the matter was resolved.

6   "Order Denying the Defendants' Motion to Vacate Judgment and Set Aside Sentence," 22 January 1965, LCF.

7   The case took Richard Loving's name, as the lower courts did not recognize Mildred as Mrs. Loving and thus referred to her by her maiden name.

8   Quoted in "Oral Arguments," in Kurland and Casper, *Landmark Briefs and Arguments*, 971.

9   *Loving v. Virginia*, 388 U.S. 1, 12 (1967).

10 Several other organizations, including the Japanese American Citizens' League, also filed amicus curiae briefs on behalf of the couple, but the Catholic brief was the only one to address the right to marry as a specifically religious right.

11 Dara Orenstein provides many of the details of the couple's courtship and life together in her fine essay "Void for Vagueness." See also Peggy Pascoe's much-anticipated book, *What Comes Naturally*, 205–23. Many thanks to Professor Pascoe for having shared the page proofs with me.

12 The couple's case was originally called *Perez v. Moroney*, later became *Perez v. Sharp*, and was subsequently published as *Perez v. Lippold*, the title that I employ throughout this book. The changes in the name of the case correspond to the changes in

name of the person holding the title of Los Angeles County Clerk. Over the course of the year that the case was active, Clerk Joseph Moroney was replaced by Clerk W. G. Sharp, and Earl O. Lippold later replaced Sharp.

13 On the connections between interracial and same-sex marriage, see, for example, Pascoe, "Sex, Gender, and Same-Sex Marriage."

14 Anthropologist Verena Martinez-Alier devotes one chapter of her 1974 book to the influence of Catholic doctrine on civil policies toward interracial marriage in nineteenth-century Cuba. Patricia Seed also investigates a shift in the Catholic Church's perspective on parental choice over marriage partners in sixteenth- and seventeenth-century Mexico. Neither book, however, examines laws on interracial marriage in the United States or compares Catholic and Protestant beliefs. See Martinez-Alier, *Marriage, Class, and Colour*, especially 42–56; and Seed, *To Love, Honor, and Obey*.

Of *Tell the Court I Love My Wife*, Peter Wallenstein's fine analysis of race, marriage, and law in antimiscegenation history, notes that during the 1960s prior to the *Loving* decision, "various religious figures, together with groups of church people, voiced a growing opposition to laws and attitudes that would ban interracial marriages" (203). Wallenstein discusses the "rise of religious opposition to miscegenation laws" but does not analyze these activities in depth, consider religion prior to the 1960s, or explore religious opposition to intermarriage.

On pages 205–23 of her forthcoming monograph *What Comes Naturally*, Pascoe examines in some depth the role of *Perez* attorney Daniel Marshall's religious freedom arguments, taking a different approach from her 1996 essay, "Miscegenation Law, Court Cases, and Ideologies of 'Race' in Twentieth-Century America."

Nancy Cott and Kathleen M. Brown address the interplay of gender, race, and religious beliefs in American marriage history in their scholarship, yet while each writer does address religion, it is not the focal point of either book. See Kathleen M. Brown, *Good Wives*, 194–98; and Cott, *Public Vows*, 3.

15 Historian Jane Dailey is the only scholar to devote attention specifically to the relationship between conservative white southern Protestantism and views on interracial marriage. She published a wonderful essay exploring this topic, though she does not consider the roles of Catholic beliefs in antimiscegenation cases, or extend her analysis back into the early years of the Protestant Reformation or even into the period immediately following the Civil War. See Dailey, "Sex, Segregation, and the Sacred." Other scholars note the connections between white southern Protestantism and opposition to intermarriage but do not analyze the issue in depth. See, for example, Haynes, *Noah's Curse*, 3–4, 15–18, 99–101, 103; and Bill J. Leonard, "Theology for Racism."

16 I employ the term "antimiscegenation" only for laws and cases that occur after 1863, when the term was coined. I refer to bans and restrictions that occurred prior to 1863 as "laws against interracial sex and marriage." For the origins of the term "antimiscegenation," see Chapter 5.

Also, when speaking of racial categories generally, I tend to interchange the terms "black" and "African American," and "white" and "Anglo American," except when referring to a particular document or historical moment, at which times I employ the terms used in the document, such as "mulatto," "Caucasian," "Negro," or "colored."

17 For a book-length analysis of the role of "Noah's curse" in justifications for American slavery, see Haynes, *Noah's Curse.*

18 Noll, *Civil War as a Theological Crisis,* 18.

Chapter One

1 Verge, "Daily Life," 16.

2 Franklin D. Roosevelt, "Executive Order 8802," <http://www.eeoc.gov/abouteeoc/ 35th/thelaw/eo-8802.html>. 3 January 2009. FDR's willingness to establish the FEPC came only after a long battle with Randolph, Walter White of the NAACP, and other groups, and the administration refused to touch many other issues of importance to African Americans, including lynching. For analyses of racial policies in FDR's administration, see Patricia Sullivan, *Days of Hope,* and McMahon, *Reconsidering Roosevelt.*

3 *Morgan v. Virginia,* 328 U.S. 373 (1946); *Shelley v. Kraemer,* 334 U.S. 1 (1948). On restrictive housing covenants, see Clement E. Vose, *Caucasians Only.*

4 These figures given in Kevin Allen Leonard, "In the Interest," 311–12.

5 Kevin Allen Leonard, "'Brothers under the Skin'?" 192.

6 Verge, "Daily Life," 18, 20.

7 According to Mark Brilliant, Governor Warren's bill functioned mostly as a symbolic act, for earlier in 1947 the Ninth Circuit Court of Appeals in San Francisco had struck down de jure segregation policies. See Brilliant, "Color Lines," 73. Chapter 3 of Brilliant's dissertation, "*Mendez v. Westminster,*" analyzes the case at length.

8 *Oyama v. State of California,* 332 U.S. 633 (1948). For a fine analysis of the Oyama case, see Brilliant, "Color Lines," 95–127.

9 "Couple to Marry as Court Voids Interracial Ban," [Los Angeles] *Tidings,* 17 December 1948, 6.

10 The bride's whiteness is a matter of some dispute. As Orenstein argues, Andrea Perez identified as Mexican rather than as white, and Mexican Americans historically occupied a liminal space on the American racial landscape. Indeed, in California during the three decades following the Mexican Revolution of 1910, Mexican students attended segregated schools and sometimes "white" schools. (Brilliant observes that the "lines dividing students of Mexican descent from their 'Anglo' counterparts were often porous" ["Color Lines," 75].) Orenstein notes that while the Los Angeles County Clerk deemed Perez "white" in 1947, when she died in 2000, her death certificate listed her as "Caucasian" and "Mexican American." See Orenstein, "Void for Vagueness," 405. David A. Hollinger discusses similar issues and includes a photograph of Andrea Perez in his essay "Amalgamation and

Hypodescent." Other helpful analyses of the case include Brilliant, "Color Lines," 128–53; Pascoe, "Miscegenation Law"; and Pascoe, *What Comes Naturally*, 205–23.

11   McWilliams, "Critical Summary," 194.

12   Engh, *Frontier Faiths*, xiii.

13   Figures on Mexican Americans taken from Sanchez, *Becoming Mexican American*, 90, 92. I added the general population figures to contextualize the numbers of nonwhites in Los Angeles. Population figures for 1920 available in the Bureau of the Census, *Fourteenth Census, 1920*, <http://www.census.gov/prod/www/abs/decennial/1920.htm>. Population figures for 1930 available in the Bureaus of the Census, *Fifteenth Census, 1930*, <http://www.census.gov/prod/www/abs/decennial/1930.htm>. 6 June 2008.

14   These figures given in Kevin Allen Leonard, "In the Interest," 312.

15   Ibid., 315.

16   LeFlore, "Important Decade," 63.

17   In 1936 the Monterey–Los Angeles Diocese advanced to archdiocese. At this time, the boundaries of the see, which had stretched from the Mexican border to regions of Santa Cruz, Santa Clara, and Merced Counties—a region totaling roughly 80,000 square miles—were redrawn.

18   In newspaper clippings found in LeFlore, "Important Decade."

19   LeBerthon, "Council of All Races," 152.

20   Quoted in Francis J. Weber, *John Joseph Cantwell*, 101; Ochs, *Desegregating the Altar*, 291.

21   Ochs, *Desegregating the Altar*, 291. Ochs describes Cantwell as a "liberal on race questions."

22   Francis J. Weber, *John Joseph Cantwell*, 123, 104, 117, 121, 128.

23   LaFarge founded the New York Catholic Interracial Council in 1934, but councils later sprang up in several American cities, mainly in the North. There were only a few—usually small and short-lived—in cities west of the Mississippi, including, Denver, St. Louis, San Antonio, and Minneapolis, in addition to Los Angeles. Except for St. Louis and San Antonio, there were no councils south of the Mason-Dixon line. On LaFarge, see Southern, *John LaFarge*.

24   "Ted LeBerthon to Mathew Ahmann, 10 August 1959." I am grateful to Father Michael Engh of Loyola-Marymount University, Los Angeles, for having shared this document with me.

25   Ibid.

26   LeBerthon, "Council of All Races," 150.

27   The Los Angeles CIC approached its mission far more stridently than LaFarge's own New York council, which aimed merely to "Promote in every practicable way, relations between the races based on the Christian principles of Interracial justice and charity which uphold the God-given dignity and destiny of every person, [and] to promote integral justice and charity by creating a better understanding in the public as to the capacities, situation and progress of the Negro group in America."

"Constitution as accepted at the annual meeting of the Catholic Interracial Council, November 26, 1940," John LaFarge, S.J., Papers, Georgetown University Special Collections, Washington, D.C. Hereinafter cited as JLP.

28 LeBerthon, "Council of All Races," 150.

29 Ibid.

30 Ibid., 151.

31 "Whites Try to Evict Catholic Indian Family," in Press Release, Catholic Interracial Council of Los Angeles Collection, Center for the Study of Los Angeles, Loyola-Marymount University, Los Angeles (hereinafter cited as Press Release). The document gives no additional information as to the meaning of "Indian"—whether the family was East Indian or Native American. I am grateful to Mark Brilliant for having shared this document with me.

32 Marshall to LaFarge, 23 January 1950, JLP, Box 17, Folder 29; LaFarge to Marshall, 14 August 1950, JLP, Box 17, Folder 29.

33 LeBerthon to LaFarge, 20 May 1949, in JLP, Box 17, Folder 29.

34 "Proposition No. 11 Called Communistic by Tenney," 4. Interestingly, Kevin Starr notes that Senator Jack B. Tenney also took issue with advocates of interracial marriage during this same time period. Tenney clashed quite publicly with Carey McWilliams over the issue. According to Starr, the 1947 Tenney Report "castigated McWilliams for advocating the marriage of blacks and whites," which was "'part of the Communist philosophy . . . of breaking down the races.'" "This playing of an anti-inter-racial marriage race card," Starr writes, "represented the most ugly line of attack ever taken by the intemperate inquisitor from Los Angeles County [Tenney]." See Starr, *Embattled Dreams*, 305–6.

35 Marshall to LaFarge, 23 May 1949, in JLP, Box 17, Folder 29.

36 Marshall to LaFarge, 23 January 1950, in JLP, Box 17, Folder 29.

37 LeBerthon, "Council of All Races," 152. In his 1959 letter to Mathew Ahmann, LeBerthon cited the priest's name as Father Rinaldo Bereamo (though in the "Council of All Races" article he spelled the name Reynald Bergamo, 152). But an article by Msgr. Francis J. Weber, ostensibly representing the official record of the Los Angeles Archdiocese, named the priest as Joseph Della Torre. See Weber, "Black Enrichment," 901.

38 Krebs, "Church of Silence," 474.

39 Orenstein, who interviewed many of the principal figures involved in the Perez case, includes many of the details of how the couple connected with Marshall in her essay "Void for Vagueness." The documents alone do not adequately clarify or harmonize the dates or the exact sequence of events that brought Perez and Davis into contact with Marshall, or even agree upon the name of their priest. See also Pascoe, *What Comes Naturally*, 209–11. Both Orenstein's and Pascoe's summations of these events differ slightly from mine.

40 The release does not indicate its author, to whom the statement would be released, or if it was in fact released.

41 The statement did not name the case, but as will be demonstrated later in this

chapter, it was *West Virginia State Board of Education v. Barnette*, 319 U.S. 624 (1943), one of the key cases upon which Marshall constructed his arguments in *Perez*.

42 "Interracial Marriage Ban to Be Attacked," in Press Release.

43 Ibid.

44 Marshall's letter to McGucken (dated 23 April 1947) is attached to a letter Marshall sent to LaFarge on 6 November 1947, JLP, Box 17, Folder 29.

45 LeBerthon to Mathew Ahmann, 10 August 1959.

46 Marshall to Aux. Bishop Joseph McGucken, 23 April 1947, JLP, Box 17, Folder 29.

47 As it turned out, Bishop McGucken was never required to testify on Marshall's doctrinal interpretation. In a letter from Marshall to Father LaFarge in November 1947, Marshall mentioned that he had been "able to arrange the case so that the anticipated issue was not raised forcibly enough to require such testimony." In this same letter Marshall also explained to LaFarge that he "did not regard the Bishop's letter as a command that [he] should not file the suit," and that Marshall "did follow the suggestion of consulting older heads," though he was "highly selective" as to whom he did contact. Daniel Marshall to John LaFarge, 6 November 1947, JLP, Box 17, Folder 29.

48 McGucken to Marshall, 26 April 1947, JLP, Box 17, Folder 29.

49 In a letter to LaFarge in 1950, Marshall remarked that the "Chancery Office has never been entirely satisfied with my motivation in the interracial marriage case." Because the letter contained no other references to the *Perez* case, it is unclear what exactly his comment meant, although the fact that this sentence followed the one about being summoned to see McIntyre in order to save Marshall from the Marxists, suggests perhaps that the archdiocese, like other conservative organizations of this era, associated the advocacy of interracial marriage with Communism. Marshall to John LaFarge, 23 January 1950, JLP, Box 17, Folder 29.

50 Delaney, *Dictionary of American Catholic Biography*, 371.

51 LeBerthon bitterly recalled years later, "the Chancery Office took a dim view of us as 'crackpots,' 'lunatic fringe,' starry-eyed idealists,' and worse, as 'Reds.'" LeBerthon to Ahmann, 2, 5.

52 Ibid. (LeBerthon's emphasis.)

53 Ibid.

54 In 1950, two years after the *Perez* ruling, and shortly after a scandal involving an award that the CIC presented to a Catholic and allegedly Communist businessman, Archbishop McIntyre unofficially disbanded the council. LeBerthon contended that McIntyre dissolved the CIC because such groups "gave Communists and left-wingers in general an opportunity 'to beat the Catholic Church over the head with the charge that she is doing virtually nothing to improve race relations.'" McIntyre purportedly asserted that he did not believe "the bringing together of a fanatical few of the various races was the best way to promote interracial fraternization." LeBerthon to Ahmann, 6.

55 Marshall to LaFarge, 6 November 1947, JLP, Box 17, Folder 29.

56 California's antimiscegenation laws originated in 1850, at which time marriages between whites and "Negroes or mulattoes" were banned. In 1880, the legislature amended the statutes to include marriages between whites and Chinese persons, and in 1905 whites and "Mongolians," by which the State meant persons of Chinese or Japanese heritage. Following *Roldan v. Los Angeles County et al.* (1933), a case involving a marriage between a white woman and a man of Filipino descent, the statutes were once again amended to include "Malays" among the list of groups prohibited from marrying whites. On *Roldan*, see Volpp, "American Mestizos."

57 Petition for Writ of Mandamus, *Perez v. Lippold*. L.A. 20305, 3, 4. California Supreme Court Case Files, California State Archives, Sacramento, California. Hereinafter cited as PCF.

58 Although the petition explicitly argued for the unconstitutionality of section 69, it also implicated section 60, without which section 69 would have no basis.

59 Petition for Writ of Mandamus, *Perez v. Lippold*, L.A. 20305, 3, PCF.

60 Petitioners' Reply Brief, *Perez v. Lippold*, L.A. 20305, 20, PCF.

61 Petition for Writ of Mandamus, 2–3, PCF.

62 Indeed, this doctrine formed a significant area of disagreement between Catholics and Protestants during the sixteenth century. In Chapter 4, I discuss Protestant as well as Catholic theologies of marriage in detail and explain the meaning of sacramental theology.

63 U.S. Constitution, Fourteenth Amendment, sec. 1. For a helpful analysis of the events of the Civil Rights Act of 1866 and the Fourteenth Amendment, see Earl M. Maltz, *Civil Rights, the Constitution, and Congress*, especially chapters 5 and 6.

64 The Fourteenth Amendment sought "in part to put into the Constitution the central provisions of the Civil Rights Act" of 1866, against which white southerners, as well as many northerners, chafed, and which President Andrew Johnson had vetoed. Wallenstein, *Tell the Court*, 69.

65 Ibid., 59.

66 Lesser-known Reconstruction-era cases that ruled antimiscegenation statutes unconstitutional include: 1) *Hart v. Hoss and Elder* (26 La. 90), in which the Supreme Court in Louisiana upheld in 1874 the validity of a marriage between a white man and a "colored" woman and determined that their children could inherit their father's estate; 2) *Bonds v. Foster* (36 Tex. 68), in which the Texas Supreme Court ruled in 1872 that a white man regarded his former slave as his wife and that she could therefore inherit his estate, based upon the antimiscegenation laws' violation of the Fourteenth Amendment; and 3) *Honey v. Clark* (37 Tex. 686), in which the Texas Supreme Court determined in 1873 that a black woman could legally inherit her husband's property when he died, although because the man had died before the enactment of either the Civil Rights Act or the Fourteenth Amendment, the court based its decision on the 1869 Texas State Constitution, which newly recognized the marriages of those couples who were prevented from marrying under slave laws as legally married and recognized their children as legitimate.

Furthermore, during Reconstruction four additional southern states (Mississippi, Florida, South Carolina, and Arkansas) briefly suspended their antimiscegenation laws via constitutional conventions, legislative majorities, or a simple omission from the law books. All told, then, of the eleven states of the former Confederacy, seven had no antimiscegenation laws at one time or another during the roughly thirty years after the Civil War. The four other states—Georgia, North Carolina, Tennessee, and Virginia—retained their laws throughout Reconstruction. On this history, see Wallenstein, *Tell the Court*, 81–93.

67 See *Burns v. State*, 48 Ala. 195 (1872); *Ellis v. State*, 42 Ala. 525 (1868); and *Green v. State*, 29 Am. Rep. 739 (1877). On these cases, see Novkov, *Racial Union*, 29–67.

68 This fact probably accounts for why Daniel Marshall did not emphasize *Burns* and the other post–Civil War cases in which antimiscegenation laws were declared unconstitutional in his arguments in the *Perez* case. And although Marshall did cite *Burns*, neither Charles Stanley nor the California Supreme Court justices addressed it. Indeed, as Wallenstein astutely observes, given Marshall's attention to *Burns*, "the [*Perez*] dissenters' claim that no court had ever declared a miscegenation statute unconstitutional was not merely wrong on the facts but, one gathers, willfully misleading." Wallenstein, *Tell the Court*, 198. Moreover, Wallenstein notes that "subsequent writers (on both sides of the issue)" perpetuated this error (286 n. 25).

69 Narrow interpretation of the due process and equal protection clauses during this era also mirrors the contentiousness of the ratification process that the Fourteenth Amendment faced in Congress, and it highlights the cross-regional opposition to civil rights for African Americans.

70 *Butchers' Benevolent Association v. Crescent City Live-Stock Landing and Slaughter-House Co. (The Slaughter-House Cases)*, 83 U.S. 16, 78 (1873). Michael A. Ross's essay on the *Slaughter-House Cases* and Justice Samuel Freeman Miller's opinion therein offers a nuanced and compelling analysis of the decision, contending that Miller's narrow rendering of the Fourteenth Amendment did not in fact derive from a "conscious attempt to end Reconstruction and to undermine black freedom," but rather from an effort to "affirm the authority of the biracial government of New Orleans, and to thwart conservatives . . . who hoped to defeat state regulation of private property." See Ross, "Justice Miller's Reconstruction," 62.

71 Civil Rights Act of 1875. *U.S. Statutes at Large*, Volume XVIII, 335–37.

72 U.S. Constitution, Fourteenth Amendment, sec 5.

73 O'Brien, *Constitutional Law and Politics*, 2:1290.

74 *Pace v. Alabama*, 106 U.S. 583, 584 (1883). On *Pace*, see Wallenstein, *Tell the Court*, 110–31, and Novkov, *Racial Union*, 58–64.

75 *Pace v. Alabama*, 106 U.S. 583, 585.

76 Wallenstein, *Tell the Court*, 103. In this same period, Wallenstein observes, northern states began to repeal their antimiscegenation statutes, "so that such laws were becoming more and more a regional phenomenon." He does not mention the proliferation of antimiscegenation laws in western states during this same period.

77 Indeed, the issue of whether or not the First Amendment, and the Bill of Rights

more generally, applied to the states has a long history. For a detailed analysis of this question as it relates to the Fourteenth Amendment, see Amar, "Bill of Rights"; and O'Brien, *Constitutional Law and Politics*, 2:304–12.

78 O'Brien offers a helpful and concise historical overview of the developments in U.S. Supreme Court jurisprudence on the incorporation of the Bill of Rights and the intensification of the debates over incorporation that emerged with the ratification of the Fourteenth Amendment. See O'Brien, *Constitutional Law and Politics*, 2:304–12.

79 *Barron v. The Mayor and City Council of Baltimore*, 32 U.S. 251 (1833).

80 O'Brien, *Constitutional Law and Politics*, 2:304.

81 U.S. Constitution, Tenth Amendment.

82 O'Brien, *Constitutional Law and Politics*, 2:306.

83 Ibid., 2:307. On developments of the freedom of speech clause, see Kalven, *Worthy Tradition*. Thanks to Paul Passavant for bringing this book to my attention. On historical context leading up to the *Meyer v. Nebraska, Pierce v. Society of Sisters*, and *Farrington v. Tokushige* decisions, see William G. Ross's wonderful book, *Forging New Freedoms*.

84 Witte, *Religion and the American Constitutional Experiment*, 135. According to Witte, a number of other cases between *Meyer* and *Cantwell* contributed to this standard of "fundamental religious liberty," including *Pierce* (1925), *Hamilton v. Board of Regents* (1934), *Palko v. Connecticut* (1937), *Lovell v. City of Griffin* (1938), and *Schneider v. Town of Irvington* (1939), but I am highlighting only *Meyer* and *Cantwell* here, since Daniel Marshall explicitly cited these cases in his petition for the writ of mandate.

85 *Meyer v. Nebraska*, 262 U.S. 390, 401 (1923). In *Skinner v. Oklahoma* (1942) and *Buck v. Bell* (1927) the Court also included the rights to marry and procreate as fundamental human liberties. *Skinner* observed that "Marriage and procreation are fundamental to the very existence and survival of the race." 316 U.S. 535, 541 (1942). On *Skinner*, see Nourse, *In Reckless Hands*. Two recent books also contextualize eugenics, the *Buck* decision, and southern history: see Gregory Michael Dorr, *Segregation's Science*; and Lombardo, *Three Generations*. Thanks to Peter Wallenstein for bringing these books to my attention.

86 Witte, *Religion and the American Constitutional Experiment*, 126. The Court again applied the Fourteenth to the First Amendment three years later in *Murdock v. Commonwealth of Pennsylvania and Seven Other Cases*, 319 U.S. 105 (1943).

87 *Cantwell v. Connecticut*, 310 U.S. 296, 304 (1940).

88 Witte, *Religion and the American Constitutional Experiment*, 149. As Witte explains it, the test for a "heightened level of scrutiny" is as follows: A challenged law will be upheld if 1) "it is in pursuit of an *important* or significant *governmental interest*, and 2) it is *substantially related* to that interest." In contrast, in a "high level scrutiny" case, the Court "will uphold the challenged law if: 1) it is in the pursuit of a *legitimate* governmental interest, and 2) it is *reasonably related* to that interest" (147, Witte's emphases).

89 *U.S. v. Carolene Products Co.,* 304 U.S. 144, 156 n. 4 (1938).

90 O'Brien, *Constitutional Law and Politics,* 2:1278, 1279, 1282.

91 *Korematsu v. United States,* 323 U.S. 214, 217 (1944).

92 By way of contrast, in *U.S. v. Carolene Products Co.,* Justice Stone had observed that for cases not involving individual rights and liberties, "the existence of facts supporting the legislative judgment is to be presumed, for regulatory legislation affecting ordinary commercial transactions is not to be pronounced unconstitutional unless . . . it is of such a character as to preclude the assumption that it rests upon some rational basis." *U.S. v. Carolene Products Co.,* 304 U.S. 144, 152 (1938).

93 *Meyer v. Nebraska,* 262 U.S. 390, 401 (1923). William G. Ross notes that *Meyer* marked the "first time that the Court had declared that the federal Constitution protects civil liberties against infringements by states involving matters other than racial discrimination and the enactment of economic regulations." Ross, *Forging New Freedoms,* 5.

94 *West Virginia State Board of Education v. Barnette,* 319 U.S. 624, 639 (1943).

95 *Busey et al. v. District of Columbia,* 138 F.2d 592, 595 (1943).

96 Petition for Writ of Mandamus, 5, PCF.

97 "Impediment" is the term used in Catholic canon law to refer to conditions that the church recognizes as prohibiting a couple from marrying. There are two types of impediments: prohibitory and diriment. According to the online version of the 1910 *Catholic Encyclopedia,* "The chief division is that which distinguishes between prohibitory and diriment impediments, the former rendering the marriage illicit, the latter making it void. They have been divided according to their juridical cause: some arise from natural law, as the different forms of defective consent, impotency, relationship in direct ascending or descending line; others arise from Divine law, which demands unity and perpetuity of marriage, thus forbidding polygamy and marriage after divorce; others, finally, while suggested by natural and Divine law have been created by ecclesiastical law. A distinction must be made between absolute and relative impediments. The former forbid any marriage of the person on whom the impediment falls, for instance, impotency, Holy orders, etc., the latter forbid the marriage with certain definite persons only." <http://www.new advent.org/cathen/09707a.htm>. 17 February 2007. I analyze these issues at length in Chapter 3.

98 Marshall made this assertion in the Petition for Writ of Mandamus, 3, PCF.

99 Quoted in Respondent's Return by Way of Answer, 3, PCF.

100 Return by Way of Demurrer, 1, PCF. Subsequent page references are noted parenthetically.

101 *Cantwell v. Connecticut,* 310 U.S. 296, 303 (1940).

102 Daniel Marshall to John LaFarge, 19 September 1947, JLP, Box 17, Folder 29.

103 John LaFarge to Daniel Marshall, 26 September 1947, JLP, Box 17, Folder 29.

104 Ibid.

105 Though the documents do not indicate who began the arguments, due to Stanley's reference to Hitler and not wanting to be associated with him, I have concluded

that Marshall initiated the debate. Marshall closed his remarks by quoting *Mein Kampf*, so Stanley must have mentioned Hitler in response to Marshall's quotation.

106 Oral Argument in Support of Petition, *Perez*, PCF. Subsequent page references are noted parenthetically.

107 The excerpt that Marshall read was actually a passage from *Tutty* that quoted an earlier case from Georgia, *Scott v. State*, 39 Ga. 323 (1869).

108 Quoted in Oral Argument in Support of Petition, 11, *Perez*, PCF.

109 Oral Argument on Behalf of Respondent, 1, PCF. The "clear and present danger" rule refers to Justice Oliver Wendell Holmes's 1919 statement in *Schenck v. United States* that the way to determine the constitutionality of free speech and press cases is to assess "whether the words used are used in such circumstances and are of such a nature as to create a clear and present danger that they will bring about the substantive evils that Congress has a right to prevent." *Schenck v. United States*, 249 U.S. 47, 48 (1919). Technically, the rule applied to the First Amendment freedoms of speech and of the press, rather than to the freedom of religion. See O'Brien, *Constitutional Law and Politics*, 2:382–88. Both Marshall and Stanley refer to this rule in the oral arguments; I suspect that one of them used the phrase in error, and that they both then continued to employ the term throughout their arguments.

110 Briefly, in *Reynolds v. United States* (1878), the U.S. Supreme Court denied that Latter-day Saints were protected under the First Amendment to marry multiple wives as part of their religious system. I discuss this case in Chapter 3.

111 U.S. Constitution, art. IV, sec. 1, which provides that the "Citizens of each State shall be entitled to all Privileges and Immunities of Citizens in the several States," effectively prohibiting states from enacting laws that restrict the rights and immunities that they are guaranteed as U.S. citizens.

112 Oral Argument on Behalf of Respondent, PCF.

113 As Pascoe notes, with this exchange, "Justice Traynor's questions gave Dan Marshall the kind of gift no lawyer had ever before received in a miscegenation case: judicial willingness to question the entire enterprise of race classification." Pascoe, *What Comes Naturally*, 218.

114 Oral Argument on Behalf of Respondent, PCF.

115 In his written opinion, Traynor addressed at length the issue of alleged health differences between members of different races. He concluded that "generalizations based on race are untrustworthy in view of the great variations among members of the same race." Further, the statute "condemns certain races as unfit to marry with Caucasians on the premise of a hypothetical racial disability, regardless of the physical qualifications of the individual concerned. If this premise were carried to its logical conclusion, non-Caucasians who are now precluded from marrying Caucasians on physical grounds would also be precluded from marrying among themselves on the same grounds. The concern to prevent marriages in the first category and the indifference about marriages in the second reveal the spuriousness of the

contention that intermarriage between Caucasians and non-Caucasians is socially dangerous on physical grounds." *Perez v. Lippold*, 198 P.2d 17, 24 (1948).

116 Oral Argument on Behalf of Respondent, PCF.

117 In August 1946, the *Buffalo (N.Y.) Star* sensationally reported such a case. A seventy-eight-year-old white man and a forty-five-year-old black woman, both from San Francisco, traveled to Albuquerque, New Mexico, to legalize their relationship. The "romance," the article claimed, had begun thirty years before and had resulted in a daughter, who witnessed the ceremony. The groom stated that they had married in order to "get a birth certificate for the child" and because "it was the only honorable thing to do." The bride gave no statements to reporters, and instead screamed, "leave me alone," and "hurled dishpans of water" at the journalists who attempted to interrogate her. "Interracial Marriage Clippings and Letters, 1939–1961" file, JLP, Box 5, Folder 17.

118 *Green v. State*, 58 Ala. 190 (1877), quoted in Oral Argument on Behalf of Respondent, 9, PCF. As discussed earlier in this chapter, *Green* was a very influential decision in antimiscegenation cases, especially in its claims for the state's right to regulate marriage laws.

119 Kennedy, *Interracial Intimacies*, 259.

120 *Perez v. Lippold*, 198 P.2d 17, 19, 21 (1948). Subsequent references to the decision are parenthetically cited.

121 Field, "Justice Roger Traynor," 59.

122 Grace E. Simons, "California Kills Ban on Intermarriage," *Los Angeles Sentinel*, 7 October 1948, V, 1. According to legal historian and Traynor biographer Benjamin Thomas Field, as novel as Traynor's opinion was, the tendency within law to reject or devalue the judicial activist approach was still strong and accounts for the subdued response among legal scholars. Together, the majority and dissenting opinions in *Perez* illustrate the developing tension between approaches that favored or rejected "activism" in judicial opinions and that culminated in *Brown v. Board of Education* (1954). Field points out that Justice John Wesley Shenk, author of the dissenting opinion, "held an anti-activist's view of the role of the courts and legislature." Traynor, on the other hand, during his thirty years as a California Justice, led the Court in legal reform and "embraced the role of judge as policy maker." Traynor "viewed judicial activism as a necessity in a fast changing world, and many of his 892 opinions and 75 law review articles offered a justification for judicial activism. Few if any theorists of judicial decision-making have so resolutely advocated activism. Even among the great judicial innovators, such as Lemuel Shaw and Benjamin Cardozo, Traynor was remarkable for his fervent advocacy of judicial policy-making. His judicial philosophy stands out in the intellectual history of judging as an extreme, yet many of his most innovative opinions gained widespread acceptance and generated surprisingly little controversy." Field, "Justice Roger Traynor," vii.

123 *Perez v. Lippold*, 198 P.2d 17, 32 (1948).

124 Kennedy, *Interracial Intimacies*, 266.

125 Shenk, of course, was wrong about *Perez* being the first case to declare antimiscegenation laws unconstitutional. See notes 66 and 68 above.

126 *Perez v. Lippold*, 198 P.2d 17, 35 (1948).

127 Field, "Justice Roger Traynor," 59.

Chapter Two

1 For a brief overview of antimiscegenation laws in a global context, see Kennedy, *Interracial Intimacies*, 241–43; and Wallenstein, *Tell the Court*, 255–56. During the 1930s under Mussolini, Italy also banned marriage between "Aryans" and "non-Aryans." I discuss this history at the end of Chapter 4.

2 An English translation of the Nuremberg Laws is available at <http://web.jjay.cuny.edu/~jobrien/reference/ob14.html>. 11 July 2006.

3 Quoted in Higginbotham and Kopytoff, "Racial Purity," 139 n. 245. Seventeen thousand South Africans were prosecuted for violating the law between 1949 and its repeal in 1985. See "South Africa Drops a Barrier."

4 In 1638 while under Dutch colonial rule, New Netherlands enacted an ordinance stipulating that "each and every one must refrain from Fighting, Adulterous intercourse with Heathens, Blacks, or other persons, Mutiny, Theft, False Swearing, Calumny and other Immoralities, as in all this the Contraveners shall, according to the circumstance of the case, be corrected and punished, as an example to others." *Laws and Ordinances of New Netherland, 1638–1674*, 12. Yet because the ordinance never reappeared in subsequent statutory books during Dutch or British rule, and because it did not prescribe a penalty for its violation, scholars do not treat it as the first antimiscegenation law and instead regard Maryland's 1661 ban as the more significant "first" legal restriction on interracial marriage.

5 Legally speaking, "fornication" was usually defined to mean sex between partners who were not married to each other. "Adultery" meant sex between partners of whom one or both was married; thus, any couple guilty of adultery was also guilty of fornication, but the reverse was not necessarily true. "Bastardy" signified the birth of a child to parents who were not married or whose marriage was not legally valid, and a child's status as a "bastard" prevented the child from inheriting the parents' estate. Another legal category was "concubinage," which meant an unmarried couple who cohabited.

6 Delaware fined those who solemnized marriage ceremonies beginning in 1807; Georgia enacted a similar law in 1866 just after the Civil War. South Carolina did not punish celebrants until 1879.

7 According to historian Peter Wallenstein, this law lasted only five years. Wallenstein, *Tell the Court*, 81–82.

8 See Thorpe, *Constitutions, Colonial Charters, and Other Organic Laws*, Alabama (1:124); Florida (2:758); Mississippi (4:2125); North Carolina (5:2843); South Carolina (6:3317); and Tennessee (6:3469).

9   Even though the laws remained on the books in Alabama and South Carolina until 2000 and 1998 respectively, the statutes were unenforceable, due to the 1967 *Loving* ruling.

10   One cannot discuss the development of racial slavery without referencing Winthrop D. Jordan's classic analysis, *White over Black*, and particularly 3–98. Jordan astutely observes that British perceptions about African "heathenness" contributed to the development of racial slavery, insofar as the English seem to have associated heathenism "with the condition of slavery," and that Africans' religiosity was "initially of greater importance than color" to English colonists (91, 98). I explore the reasons for the association of specifically African peoples and slavery in Chapter 4.

    For a concise overview of the relationship between American slavery and bans on interracial sex and marriage, see Kennedy, *Interracial Intimacies*, 41–69. On the development of slavery more generally, see David Brion Davis, *Problem of Slavery*. On the historic relationship between Christianity and slavery, see Glancy, *Slavery in Early Christianity*. For cross-cultural analyses, see Degler, "Slavery in Brazil and the United States: An Essay in Comparative History," and *Neither Black nor White*; and Tannenbaum, *Slave and Citizen*.

11   Due to indentured servitude, even the assumption that all "English" colonists were "free" was laden with difficulties.

12   Jordan, *White over Black*, 178.

13   Kathleen M. Brown notes that "after the 1660s, courts focused more exclusively on the monetary damages owed to masters by female servants and their lovers than on the moral nature of the sexual transgression." Brown, *Good Wives*, 191. Indeed, protecting the financial investments of slave owners and masters of indentured servants constitutes one of the most fundamental prima facie causes of American laws on interracial marriage and sexual unions.

14   While Maryland's early relationship to Catholicism might initially seem to contradict my claims that Catholic doctrine tended to place Catholics in opposition to laws banning or punishing interracial marriage, it seems to me that perceptions of Maryland as a "Catholic" colony are somewhat misplaced, and thus the early enactment of a ban on intermarriage does not refute my argument that Catholic regions tended to tolerate intermarriage more than Protestant regions. On colonial Maryland's Catholicism, see Dolan, *American Catholic Experience*, 72–75; Hennesey, *American Catholics*, 36–45; and Duncan, "Catholics and the Church," 77.

15   *Proceedings and Acts of the General Assembly of Maryland*, 533–34.

16   According to Martha Hodes, white legislators in Maryland soon realized that "such a law legally encouraged masters to force marriages between servant women and slave men in order to gain more slaves for themselves," so they revised the law in 1681. See Hodes, *White Women, Black Men*, 29. Hodes also notes that Maryland's 1692 revision of the law "penalized all liaisons between blacks and whites without regard to gender" (222 n. 27).

17   Hening, *Statutes at Large*, 2:170.

18 On "race mixture," see Fredrickson, *White Supremacy*, especially 94–135. On the role of religion in the making of "race," see Fredrickson, *Racism*, especially chapter 1.

19 Hening, *Statutes at Large*, 3:86–66. As Kathleen M. Brown notes, this marks the "first use of the term 'white' in the Virginia statutes." Brown, *Good Wives*, 198.

20 It is important to note, however, that church courts punished women and men alike for interracial adultery and fornication, as well as for bastardy. See Kathleen M. Brown, *Good Wives*, 188–92.

21 As Kennedy observes about a later era, the "paucity of antebellum cases featuring black female victims of sex crimes is in itself eloquent testimony to the extreme vulnerability of black women." Kennedy, *Interracial Intimacies*, 176. See also Hodes, *White Women, Black Men*, 162–213.

22 Kathleen M. Brown, *Good Wives*, 181.

23 Woodson, "Beginnings of Miscegenation," 337, 338.

24 David Brion Davis notes, for example, that "while Latin America was by no means immune from racial prejudice, even against freemen of mixed blood, there was a gradual acceptance of racial intermixture and a willingness to accept each stage of dilution as a step toward whiteness. In the British colonies . . . there was never any tolerance of racial blending." See Davis, "Comparative Approach," 66. On racial mixing among the Spanish and Portuguese, see Kingsley Davis, "Intermarriage," 390–92; Degler, *Neither Black nor White*; Love, "Marriage Patterns"; Seed, "Social Dimensions," 569; Siegel, "Race Attitudes," 163; Stolcke, *Marriage, Class, and Colour*; Landers, *Black Society*, 107, 111; Wesley, "Negro in the West Indies," 52. More recent is Skidmore, "Racial Mixture and Affirmative Action." The evidence suggests that a Catholic-sanctioned tradition of interracial marriage also existed in the American Southwest. See Gutierrez, *When Jesus Came*; and Mitchell, "Accomplished Ladies." For evidence of Catholic intermarriage during the twentieth century, see Karen Isaksen Leonard, *Making Ethnic Choices*, especially chapter 4.

25 Peabody, "*There Are No Slaves*," 11.

26 *Le Code Noir de Louisiane* (1724), article 6. The full text reads: "We forbid our white subjects of either sex from contracting marriage with blacks on pain of punishment and arbitrary penalty; and [we forbid] all vicars, priests, or regular or secular missionaries, and even ship chaplains, from marrying them. We also prohibit said white subjects and even emancipated or free-born blacks from living in concubinage with slaves; we require those who have had one or more children from such a union, together with the masters who have suffered them, each to be condemned to a penalty of three hundred livres, and if they are the masters of the slave who has had said children we require the additional penalty that they be deprived of the slave and the children, and that they be presented to a hospital without the power ever to be freed. Nevertheless we do not intend that the present article be applied when the man is a free black who is not legitimately married during his concubinage with his slave, and if he will marry her in the form prescribed by the church said slave will be freed by this means, and the children rendered free and

legitimate." Translation mine. French text available at <http://www.centenary.edu/french/codenoir.htm>. 14 July 2006.

27 "Decree on the Reformation of Marriage," Council of Trent, Twenty-fourth Session, <http://history.hanover.edu/texts/trent/ct24.html>. 8 June 2008.

28 Stolcke, *Marriage, Class, and Colour*, 12–13. Stolke remarks that the Sanción was not widely enforced in the colonies and that the penalty did not adequately serve to dissuade couples from marriage, as most had little to inherit in the first place.

29 Quoted in Mörner, *Race Mixture*, 38–39. Mörner notes that in Mexico, however, government officials "recommended that 'special orders be given to the parish priests so that, in case some Indian wants to contract marriage with a person belonging to those Castas, both he and his parents . . . will receive a warning and explanation of the serious harm . . . that such unions will cause to themselves, their families and villages, besides making the descendants incapable of obtaining municipal positions of honor in which only pure Indians are allowed to serve'" (39).

30 Seed, *To Love, Honor, and Obey*, 24.

31 Quoted in Stolcke, *Marriage, Class, and Colour*, 12–13.

32 On marriage in colonial Mexico and its regulation by the church, see Seed, *To Love, Honor, and Obey*, chapter 5.

33 Scholars know of the story of Irish Nell and Negro Charles not because the couple was prosecuted under any law against intermarriage, but because two of their enslaved descendants petitioned for their freedom during the 1760s, claiming that they had descended from a white woman, Irish Nell. Hodes also notes that the Lord Baltimore subsequently had the 1664 statute revised to ensure that masters might not compel women like Nell to marry enslaved men in order to benefit from acquiring their enslaved offspring. See Hodes, *White Women, Black Men*, 19–38.

34 Gayarré, *Louisiana*, 214. Gilbert C. Din also cites Gayarré's anecdote. See Din, *Spaniards, Planters, and Slaves*, 40. Gayarré's reference to canon or ecclesiastical law is somewhat difficult to explain and may indicate his assumption that canon law would correspond precisely to civil law. As we will see later in this chapter, no canon law or church-sanctioned regulations on marriage ever prohibited interracial marriage. However, an interracial marriage could be prohibited on the basis of one of the parties not being Catholic.

35 O'Neill, *Church and State*, 248. On church-state conflict over marriage between French men and Native American women, see 92–94, 107–9, and especially 246–55. This particular example of white-Native marriage did not contravene Louisiana law, yet it does demonstrate the willingness on the part of some Catholic priests to celebrate marriages across the color line.

36 Castañeda, "Pobladores y Presidarias," 286.

37 Unfortunately, Castañeda does not elaborate upon this "tradition" in this study. She does, however, cite Mörner, *Race Mixture*. On Mörner, see note 45 below.

38 Interestingly, another scholar observes that "Spanish policy was not to remove and exterminate the Indian people (as in the United States), but to assimilate and exploit them." See Moreno, "Here the Society Is United," 10.

39 Castañeda, *Pobladores y Presidarias*, 101. Albert Hurtado confirms the joint Chris-
tianization and Hispanicization strategy of California missionaries, observing
that "the reformation of Indian sexual behavior was an important part of [priests']
endeavor to Christianize and Hispanicize native Californians" and that "in order
to convert Indians, the Franciscans had to uproot other aspects of the normative
sexual system that regulated Indian sexuality and marriage. At the very least, missionaries meant to restructure Indian marriage to conform to orthodox Catholic
standards of monogamy, permanence, and fidelity." Hurtado, *Intimate Frontiers*,
2, 8.

40 Castañeda, *Pobladores y Presidarias*, 255.

41 I discovered a copy of this letter in Father John LaFarge's papers at the Georgetown
University Library. Letter to John LaFarge from Joseph Francis Doherty, 30 April
1948, JLP, Box 5, Folder 17. Translation mine. Thanks to May Farnsworth, Hobart
and William Smith Colleges, for correcting my translations.

42 Tannenbaum, *Slave and Citizen*, viii.

43 See, for example, Herb Aptheker's review of the book in *American Historical Review*
52, no. 4 (July 1947): 755–57; or that of John Hope Franklin, *William and Mary
Quarterly*, 3rd ser., 4, no. 4 (October 1947): 544–46. Also, David Brion Davis offers
a substantive critique in "Comparison of British and Latin America," 70–71 n. 1.

44 Tannenbaum, *Slave and Citizen*, 52, 53, 82. I want to emphasize that Tannenbaum's
focus on legal statutes, in contrast to documents chronicling the actual treatment
of enslaved persons and/or behavior of slaveholders, enables him to overlook the
ample evidence that contradicts his claims. While there are many flaws in his
analysis, what is valuable for my project is his recognition that theological differences between Catholics and Protestants had a considerable effect on underlying
perceptions of human being that were written into law, whether or not in practice
theological doctrines actually influenced behaviors. Doctrines influenced the ideas
behind law, but not necessarily the enforcement or practice of law, or the behaviors
of slaveholders toward their slaves.

   Moreover, while recognizing the merits of Tannenbaum's analysis, I am of the
opinion that his overall argument crumbles in the face of the historical evidence on
the actual treatment of slaves (as opposed to the laws purporting to regulate that
treatment). As such, the implications of his claims—namely that Latin America
produced a less brutal form of slavery while the U.S. and British colonies, lacking
Catholic doctrine's insights on the moral value of human being, cultivated a particularly harsh slave system—are also unsupportable. I want to reiterate that my
argument is about the influence of theological doctrines on laws rather than on
behaviors, and I am not positing here any arguments about the severity of slave
systems in Latin or North America.

45 Cutter, *Legal Culture*, 7. Swedish scholar Magnus Mörner confirms the occasionally
difficult relationship between church and state in the Spanish Americas, specifically with regard to intermarriage. He contends that interracial marriage held "a
key position within the 'racial policy' of the Spanish Crown." According to Mörner,

though the Crown tolerated marriages between Spaniards and noble Native Americans, it "on the whole opposed intermarriage with the African element." As in the British colonies, the Spanish government frowned upon such marriages because it wanted to prevent slaves from obtaining freedom either for themselves or their children through marriage to a free person. The church and state disapproved of interracial concubinage, but by 1650 or so, in some regions of the Americas, concubine relationships were "so frequent as to be considered completely normal," even by priests and friars. "For all the efforts of state and Church," Mörner contends, "concubinage continued to provide the normal form of interethnic sexual relations." Mörner, *Race Mixture in the History of Latin America*, 36, 38, 40.

46   Stolcke, *Marriage, Class, and Colour*, 13.

47   Seed, *To Love, Honor, and Obey*, 190, 188, 193, 195. It should be noted that Seed's analysis is not on interracial marriage per se, though as noted earlier, as a result of Spanish conceptions of nobility and social hierarchy, and the "tripartite division within colonial [Mexican] society of Spaniard, Indian and black echoed the peninsular division of status among nobles, plebeians, and slaves" (24).

48   Chapter 9, "Decree on the Reformation of Marriage," Council of Trent, Twenty-fourth Session, <http://history.hanover.edu/texts/trent/ct24.html>. 8 June 2008.

Chapter Three

1   Marshall to McGucken, 23 April 1947, JLP, Box 17, Folder 29. Emphasis added. Though he did not acknowledge it, Marshall had taken this entire passage verbatim from the 1910 Catholic Encyclopedia entry on moral and canonical aspects of marriage. See "Moral and Canonical Aspect of Marriage," sec. 2, E, <http://www.newadvent.org/cathen/09699a.htm>. 1 December 2008.

2   "Respondent's Brief in Opposition to Writ of Mandate," 56, PCF.

3   This translation is from the Douay-Rheims version of the Bible, which prior to Vatican II was the foremost American Catholic version. <http://www.scriptours.com/bible/bible.cgi?oldbook=56&book+56&chapteer=5&x=14&y=6&reference>. 21 January 2007. More recently, the New American and Revised New American versions have supplanted the Douay-Rheims, but I use the latter here in order to be consistent with the usage by twentieth-century American Catholics prior to the Second Vatican Council.

4   The King James Version of Ephesians 5:32 reads: "This is a great mystery: but I speak concerning Christ and the church." <http://etext.lib.virginia.edu/kjv.browse.html>. 18 February 2007.

5   According to Catholic doctrine, Jesus raised marriage to the level of a sacrament, insofar as in several Gospel passages he spoke strongly against divorce and called for a return to lifelong monogamy, as mentioned in Genesis 2. See Matthew 19:3ff.; Mark 10:2ff.; and Luke 16:18ff. See also I Corinthians 7:12ff. For a concise overview of the Catholic theology of marriage, see Witte, "Transformation of Marriage Law," 60–68.

6 "Sacraments," *Catholic Encyclopedia*, <http://www.newadvent.org/cathen/13295a .htm>. 18 February 2007. The *Encyclopedia* was first published between 1907 and 1917, and I refer to it because it explicated the theology of marriage prior to the Second Vatican Council. Marriage doctrine remained in flux through the 1960s, and current Church teachings are significantly different than pre–Vatican II doctrine.

The Catholic Church recognizes seven sacraments—Baptism, Confirmation, Holy Eucharist, Penance, Extreme Unction, Orders, and Matrimony—which, through rites administered by a priest, confer God's grace to baptized individuals. The first five sacraments are necessary for all Christians; the last two—religious vows or ministry, and marriage—represent two options between which Catholic Christians must decide, although celibacy without taking religious vows constitutes a third option.

7 "Marriage, Sacrament of," sec. 1; sec. 4(3)(c) *Catholic Encyclopedia*, <http://www .newadvent.org/cathen/09707a.htm>. 18 February 2007.

8 "Original Sin," sec. 1, *Catholic Encyclopedia*, <http://www.newadvent.org/cathen/ 11312a.htm>. 18 February 2007. I include the entry at length here because it clearly explains the meaning of sacrament, how matrimony is a sacrament, and how the sacrament of marriage relates to the doctrine of original sin. According to the writer, original sin "is the privation of sanctifying grace in consequence of the sin of Adam . . . one man has transmitted to the whole human race not only the death of the body, which is the punishment of sin, but even sin itself, which is the death of the soul. As death is the privation of the principle of life, the death of the soul is the privation of sanctifying grace which according to all theologians is the principle of supernatural life. Therefore, if original sin is the death of the soul, it is the privation of sanctifying grace" (sec. 6). The writer then goes on to explain the connection between Original Sin and the sacramental theology of marriage: "Since Adam transmits death to his children by way of [sexual] generation when he begets them mortal, it is by generation also that he transmits to them sin" (sec. 3). "The original marriage [between Adam and Eve], and consequently marriage as it was conceived in the original plan of God before sin, was to be the means not merely of the natural propagation of the human race, but also the means by which personal supernatural sanctity should be transmitted to the individual descendents of our first parents. It was, therefore, a great mystery, intended not for the personal sanctification of those united by the marriage tie, but for the sanctification of others, i.e. of their offspring. But this Divinely ordered sanctity of marriage was destroyed by original sin. The effectual sanctification of the human race, or rather of individual men, had now to be accomplished in the way of redemption through the Promised Redeemer, the Son of God made Man. In place of its former sanctity, marriage retained only the significance of a type feebly representing the sanctity that was thenceforth to be acquired; it foreshadowed the Incarnation of the Son of God, and the close union which God was thereby to form with the human race. It was reserved for Christian marriage to symbolize this higher supernatural

union with mankind, that is, with those who unite themselves to Christ in faith and love, and to be an efficacious sign of this union."

For a contemporary feminist scholarly assessment of St. Augustine's conception of original sin and its relationship to sex, see Pagels, *Adam, Eve, and the Serpent*, 109–14.

9   "Marriage, Moral and Canonical Aspect," *Catholic Encyclopedia*, <http://www .newadvent.org/cathen/09699a.htm>. 18 February 2007. Emphasis added.

10 In his 1938 draft of the unissued encyclical *Humani Generis Unitas* (discussed in Chapter 4 below), Father John LaFarge similarly notes the "melancholy heritage of original sin": "every time parents, even those who possess sanctifying grace, exercise their holy function of awakening new life, since they are themselves bearers of this stream of life [that is, the blood stream, through which sin is carried], their very act inevitably endows the child with membership in a community subject to supernatural death." *Humani Generis Unitas*, August 1938, sec. 73, printed in Passelecq and Suchecky, *Hidden Encyclical*, 213–14.

11 John Witte contends that even as early as the eleventh through fifteenth centuries, the church regarded marriage as a "created, natural institution," a sacrament, and a contract. See Witte, "Transformation of Marriage Law," 62. Significantly, Witte remarks that the increased efforts of the church to regulate the institution resulted in conceiving of marriage as a legal relationship, subject to ecclesiastical law and authority (64). See also Witte, *From Sacrament to Contract*.

12 Doherty, *Moral Problems*, 38.

13 Nau, *Manual on the Marriage Laws*, 13.

14 *Casti Connubii*, Encyclical of Pope Pius XI On Christian Marriage, 31 December 1930, sec. 6, <www.vatican.va/holy_father/pius_xi/encyclicals/documents/hf_p-xi _enc_31121930_casti-co nnubii_en.html>. 12 March 2005.

15 Doherty, *Moral Problems*, 40. Subsequent references are cited parenthetically.

16 Doherty acknowledges that the "right to marry is not a right that is as absolute as that of life itself," and that the church does recognize some restrictions upon it. "Some rights," he contends, "must be allowed untrammeled action because of their supreme position in the hierarchy of rights [which, he claims, include the right to live, good name, and marriage]. Marriage is not such a right, but must be so exercised that the good of one's immortal soul might be not hindered, that the rights of one's intended mate be not infringed, that the demands of life in the community be not passed over, that the valid demands of the institution of marriage be not ignored. When each one of these rights is respected by the prospective spouse, and his entrance into marriage is so governed, then he may be said properly to be exercising his right to marry." Ibid., 43–44.

17 The Catholic Church does recognize the right of the state to "make just laws affecting the civil effects of the marriage contract" for both baptized and unbaptized parties. Nau, *Manual on the Marriage Laws*, 17.

18 Council of Trent, 24th session, "Decree on the Reformation of Marriage," and "On

the Sacrament of Matrimony." <http://history.hanover.edu/texts/trent/ct24.html>. 12 March 2005.

19 *Arcanum*, Encyclical of Pope Leo XIII on Christian Marriage, 10 February 1880, in *Papal Encyclicals*, vol. 2, secs. 7, 17, 33, 20–21, 33. Hereinafter cited as *Arcanum*.

20 Nau, *Manual on the Marriage Laws*, 14; see also 12–17. Numerous other sources confirm Nau's statement. Rene Metz offers the following assessment: "The Church claims exclusive competence in laying down the law of marriage properly so-called, in such matters as impediments, the exchange of consent, its effects and the causes of nullity. She recognizes in the state only the right to decide about the purely civil effects, in the law of property, for example. The Church makes these claims because according to Catholic teaching the contract and the sacrament are not separable." See Metz, *What Is Canon Law?* 145.

21 Nau, *Manual on the Marriage Laws*, 14. Two kinds of matrimonial impediments exist in canon law: prohibiting impediments "render a marriage unlawful but not invalid," while diriment impediments "make a marriage invalid." Prohibiting impediments involve vows that are incompatible with marriage, such as vows of virginity, chastity, receiving Holy Orders, or entering a religious order. Diriment impediments invalidate a marriage that might otherwise have existed; these impediments include age, impotence, an existing/previous marriage, marriage with an unbaptized party, sacred orders, and certain degrees of relationship (i.e., marriage between certain family members). See *Pius XI's Latest Word on Marriage*, in Cohausz, *Pope and Christian Marriage*, 103, 104. See also part 5, sec. 3, "Impediments in General," in Bouscaren and Ellis, *Canon Law*, 481–95. For a concise secondary source offering an overview of marital impediments, see Witte, "Transformation of Marriage Law," 65–67.

22 Bouscaren and Ellis, *Canon Law*, 481. Nau also states the ostensibly traditional Catholic perspective: "Freedom to marry is an inalienable personal right of the physically and mentally fit for this state in life. Hence, for such only relative hindrances can be placed, namely, lest this person marry this other person. All ecclesiastical impediments are relative in this sense." Nau, *Manual on the Marriage Laws*, 14.

Bouscaren and Ellis specify: "The natural law itself forbids marriage to persons who are incapable of the act which is the object of the contract, or who lack the mental capacity to understand in a suitable manner the object of the contract." Bouscaren and Ellis, *Canon Law*, 481.

23 *Rerum Novarum*, Encyclical of Pope Leo XIII on Capital and Labor, 15 May 1891, in *Papal Encyclicals*, 2:243–44.

24 *Arcanum*, sec. 19.

25 Bouscaren and Ellis, *Canon Law*, 460–61.

26 Council of Trent, 24th session, "On the Sacrament of Matrimony," Canon XII, <www.intratext.com/IXT/ENG0432/_P2B.HTM>. 12 March 2005.

27 Witte, *From Sacrament to Contract*, 5. George Elliott Howard's classic *History of Matrimonial Institutions* similarly affirms that the "dogma of its [matrimony's] sac-

ramental character was abandoned throughout the Protestant world." Howard, *History of Matrimonial Institutions*, 1:386. Likewise, in his entry "Marriage" in the *Oxford Encyclopedia of the Reformation*, Thomas Max Saffley states that most Protestant reformers adopted Luther's view that marriage constituted "a holy estate but not a sacrament; all [Protestants] valued it as a hospital for the soul, unable to resist its own predilection to sin; and all rejected clerical celibacy as contrary to God's will and human nature." Saffley, "Marriage," 20.

Early Protestants discussed many other elements of marriage as well, such as clerical marriage, the idea that celibacy was not superior to matrimony, and Henry VIII's many marriages and subsequent break with the Roman Church over these issues. My focal point, however, is on the nonsacramental aspect, since it impinged most directly on the legal jurisdiction of marriage.

28 Luther, "Babylonian Captivity," 220, 224.

29 Calvin, *Institutes of the Christian Religion*, book IV, chapter xix, sec. 34, 2:766.

30 Eric Carlson notes that in 1536 the Ten Articles, the "first official doctrinal statement of the new dispensation, quietly dropped matrimony (along with confirmation, holy orders and extreme unction) from the list of sacraments" (42). It should be emphasized, however, that in England the shift toward civil regulation of marriage was exceedingly slow and complicated. For a concise overview of the transformations in theological views of marriage among sixteenth-century English thinkers, see Carlson, *Marriage and the English Reformation*, 37–49.

31 Howard, *History of Matrimonial Institutions*, 2:128. Contemporary scholars of the American history of marriage, likewise, rarely mention the civil regulation of marriage and its relationship between church and state. Cott briefly describes the Catholic Church's authority over marriage in pre-Reformation Europe. She states simply that "because the United States established no national church, but said it would separate church and state and observe religious tolerance, state control [over marriage] flourished." However, she does not address how the colonies negotiated that control. Cott, *Public Vows*, 6. Michael Grossberg's work notes that "domestic relations during [this] era was the province of the states," but his brief description of family life during the colonial period makes no mention of religion or of the development of the civil regulation of marriage. Grossberg, *Governing the Hearth*, ix.

32 Howard, *History of Matrimonial Institutions*, 2:125, 126, 127, 130, 131. Indeed, Howard observed that the "zeal with which the Pioneers of Plymouth and Massachusetts Bay proscribed the ceremonies and usages of the Roman and Anglican churches has had much to do with the character of civil institutions in the United States," including probate law, the jurisdiction over chanceries, and the regulation of children's education.

According to Howard, in 1653 after England's civil wars, Parliament transferred authority over marriage from church courts to local magistrates, effectively making marriage a civil institution. The Civil Marriage Act stipulated that all "'matters and controversies touching contracts and marriages, and the lawfulness and unlawful-

ness thereof; and all exceptions against contracts and marriages, and the distribution of forfeiture within this act, shall be in the power, in each county, city, or town
corporate . . .' as the 'parliament shall hereafter appoint.'" Ibid., 1:420. The act—an
unpopular piece of legislation that was repealed a mere seven years later—also
made illegal all other forms of marriage, most especially religious ceremonies involving either church or minister.

33 Ibid., 2:228–29, 248–49.

34 Ibid., 2:262–63.

35 Ibid., 2:267, 312.

36 In their wonderful analysis of the Christian bases that inform American notions
of sexuality, morality, and marriage, Janet R. Jakobsen and Ann Pellegrini also observe a purportedly secularized American Protestant rhetoric undergirding these
ideas. "In a fundamental sense," they argue, "the secular state's regulation of the
sexual life of its citizens is actually religion by other means." Moreover, "the assumptions that underlie sexual regulation are so deeply embedded that people no
longer recognize them as being derived from religious thought." Critically, the
authors identify the Christian bases of American beliefs about sexual morality as
"specifically Protestant." Jakobsen and Pellegrini, *Love the Sin*, 19, 21, 22.

37 Quoted in *Mormon Church v. United States*, 136 U.S. 1, 20 (1890).

38 Cott, *Public Vows*, 112, 113. Cott provides a concise overview of the circumstances
surrounding the polygamy debate and its relation to federal interest in marriage;
see pages 111–20. For an excellent, book-length analysis of the complicated relationship between church and state, religious freedom, and polygamy in the polygamy controversy, see Gordon, *Mormon Question*.

39 *Reynolds v. United States*, 98 U.S. 145, 152 (1878).

40 *Reynolds v. United States*, 98 U.S. 145, 166 (1878).

41 Cott, *Public Vows*, 118, 119.

42 *Mormon Church v. United States*, 136 U.S. 1, 50 (1890). The polygamy issue was
largely resolved in 1890, when the church issued a statement ordering the Saints
to comply with all state marriage laws.

43 Wallenstein, *Tell the Court*, 114.

44 *Maynard v. Hill*, 125 U.S. 190, 205 (1888).

45 Yet attorneys and judges arguing for the constitutionality of antimiscegenation
laws clearly overlooked or deliberately obfuscated the definitions of "state" in the
precedents. For example, they cited *Reynolds* and *Maynard* as precedents for the
states' authority to impose antimiscegenation statutes. In these cases Congress
had proclaimed the right not of the state or territorial government, but of the federal government, to regulate marriage. So proponents of antimiscegenation statutes who cited such precedents as authority for their cases essentially interpreted
"state" or "government" in a way that served their arguments, rather than in a way
that acknowledged the federal authority proclaimed in *Reynolds* and *Maynard*.

46 *Reynolds v. United States*, 98 U.S. 145, 165 (1878).

47 Doherty, *Moral Problems*, ix, 47–48, xi. Considerably more conservative than Nau,

Doherty, or even LaFarge, Francis Gilligan's 1928 dissertation in sacred theology admitted that although the church "earnestly urg[es] her members to respect and reverence the civil law," it nevertheless "does not regard as invalid properly solemnized marriages between Negroes and whites who are subject to her jurisdiction. Of that fact there is no question" (93–94). Gilligan did argue, however, that the "social separation [of whites and colored persons] is justifiable and compatible with Christianity." Inexplicably, he simultaneously maintained that segregation "undoubtedly stands in stark opposition to the ideals of Christ and to the ideal of the brotherhood of man." Gilligan, *Morality of the Color Line*, 106, 110.

48 Doherty, *Moral Problems*, 101.

49 Ibid., 36; see also 155.

50 With regard to Christian and non-Christian marriage, Doherty stated that "laws forbidding interracial marriage between baptized persons are unjust because of the lack of competence of the State to legislate on such matters for the baptized. Considering the lack of competence of the State to legislate, laws forbidding interracial marriages between a baptized person and an unbaptized person are more probably unjust." He also maintained that antimiscegenation laws "are in general unjust" and that they should be repealed. Elsewhere Doherty mentioned that his views should not be "understood as an unqualified advocacy of miscegenation, but merely as a statement of the transcendency of personal rights in this particular situation." Ibid., 155, xi. It seems safe to conclude, then, that he regarded intermarriage prohibitions as unjust for all people, whether baptized or unbaptized.

51 Ibid., 53, 60.

52 Quoted in ibid., 33, 34. Doherty apparently translated the statement from Italian, which he included in his footnotes.

53 Ibid., 34. The bracketed word is included in the excerpt in Doherty's book. According to Doherty, the statement did not exactly constitute an "official document of the Church," insofar as it appeared in *L'Osservatore Romano*, "the approved newspaper of Vatican City." Yet he reiterated that it had "high authoritative standing," by virtue of the fact that it was printed in a paper approved by the church.

Gene Bernardini offers an insightful analysis of racial anti-Semitism in Fascist Italy. He contends that during this era the Catholic Church perceived religious anti-Semitism as consistent with church doctrine, but that racial anti-Semitism (which he describes as anti-Semitism rooted in beliefs about the biology of Jewish peoples)—and racism more generally—were not compatible with Catholic beliefs. See Bernardini, "Origins and Development," 431–53.

54 The church's reasons for protesting Italy's laws may not have been entirely beneficent, altruistic, or free from self-serving political scheming. In *Hidden Encyclical*, Passelecq and Suchecky discuss the Vatican's reaction to the Italian government's enactment of anti-Semitic laws during the fall of 1938. They contend that until the bans on Aryan–non-Aryan marriages were enacted in November, the church, and Pius XI in particular, remained fairly quiet about the new laws. Other than one statement in September, in which Pius explicitly stated that "anti-Semitism

is inadmissible," the pontiff "made no explicit statement regarding the new discriminatory legislation" (139). But according to Passelecq and Suchecky when the antimarriage laws went into effect, Pius "wrote personally to the head of the government and to the king" (144). Passelecq and Suchecky speculate that the pope's confrontation of the government may have derived from the implied curtailment of the church's authority over marriage, and the government's violation of the 1929 Lateran Concordat, of which article 34 stated, "The Italian State, wishing to restore to the institution of matrimony, which is the foundation of the family, that dignity which is conformable with the Catholic traditions of its people, recognizes the civil effects of the Sacrament of matrimony regulated by Canon Law." (Text of Lateran Concordat available at <http://www.aloha.net/~mikesch/treaty.htm>. 12 June 2008.) In *L'Osservatore Romano*'s statement, the writer admits that it was a "painful surprise" to see "a commitment made in the Concordat weakened," and indeed, that "the *vulnus* [wound] inflicted on the Concordat [by the legislation] is unparalleled" (146). The excerpt from the *L'Osservatore Romano* statement that Doherty included in *Moral Problems* omitted the part about the Concordat. Passelecq and Suchecky conclude that "more than the future condition of Italian Jews, it is the *vulnus* inflicted on the Lateran Concordat that seems to have particularly attracted the ecclesiastical institution's attention." Passelecq and Suchecky, *Hidden Encyclical*, 147.

55 For an excellent analysis of black Catholic priests and the difficulties they faced in gaining admittance to Catholic colleges and seminaries (as well as in being ordained), see Ochs, *Desegregating the Altar*. On the response of urban white Catholics to African Americans in their neighborhoods and parishes, see McGreevy's fine book *Parish Boundaries*.

Chapter Four

1 Respondent's Brief in Opposition to Writ of Mandate, *PCF*, 115–16. The biblical passages Stanley quoted were Genesis 24:3–4 and Nehemiah 13:23–28.

2 Petitioners' Reply Brief, PCF, 51, 51–52. Marshall's emphasis. Here Marshall quoted from the *Green* case, which itself quoted from *Philadelphia & West Chester R.R. Co. v. Miles* (1867). I discuss both cases at length in the next chapter.

3 I Corinthians 12:12–14.

4 Noll, *Civil War as a Theological Crisis*, 18.

5 For a discussion of how Genesis 9–11 function in the hermeneutical history of race, see Haynes, *Noah's Curse*, especially 3–6, 15–19, 23–61. On biblical influences on notions of race more generally, see also Kidd, *Forging of Races*.

6 All biblical quotes are taken from the King James Version unless otherwise noted.

7 In addition to the Haynes and Kidd books mentioned above, several other sources have been particularly helpful in shaping my depiction here, including Freedman, *Images of the Medieval Peasant*, 86–104; Goldenberg, *Curse of Ham*; and Braude,

"Sons of Noah." Other relevant scholarship on the Genesis stories also includes Fredrickson, *Racism*, 29, 43–47; Haynes, "Original Dishonor"; Sylvester Johnson, *Myth of Ham*; Jordan, *White over Black*, 17–20, 35–37; and Peterson, *Ham and Japheth*.

8   Flavius Josephus, *Antiquities of the Jews*, 1.6.3, <http://www.sacred-texts.com/jud/josephus/ant-1.htm>. 8 June 2008.

9   Haynes, *Noah's Curse*, 26. The last examples are cited in Haynes.

10 Augustine, *City of God*, 16.2. <http://www.ccel.org/fathers2/NPNF1-02/npnf1-02-22.htm#P2731_1531545>. 27 January 2007.

11 Haynes, *Noah's Curse*, 29.

12 Justin Martyr, "Dialogue with Trypho," chap. 138, <http://www.ccel.org/fathers2/ANF-01/anf01-48.htm#P4043_787325>. 27 January 2007. Origen similarly compared Noah's ark to Christ's sepulcher, as did medieval poet Dante in *The Inferno*.

13 Augustine, *City of God*, 16.2, <http://www.ccel.org/fathers2/NPNF1-02/npnf1-02-22.htm#P2731_1531545>. 15 February 2007.

14 Haynes, *Noah's Curse*, 29.

15 Ibid., 34.

16 "Subdivision of the three portions amongst the grandchildren," Charles, *Book of Jubilees*, 75 n. 1. The writer of *The Book of Jubilees* ends this chapter by stating that Noah bound his sons to their lands by an oath, "imprecating a curse on everyone that sought to seize the portion which had not fallen (to him) by his lot" (78).

17 Goldenberg, *Curse of Ham*, 178; Freedman, *Images of the Medieval Peasant*, 88. According to Freedman, however, no Jewish commentators linked blackness and slavery before the eleventh century; nothing within the Talmud, he contends, posited blackness as a "hereditary taint" or connected "black skin and Canaan or servitude."

18 Haynes, *Noah's Curse*, 24.

19 Goldenberg, *Curse of Ham*, 141. Indeed, Goldenberg claims that the most likely reason for the persistent association of Ham and blackness has to do with the name "Ham," which is related to the Hebrew word for "black" or "brown" (143).

20 On Peyrère, see Kidd, *Forging of Races*, 62–64, and Popkin, *Isaac La Peyrère*.

21 Jordan, *White over Black*, 18. Jordan observes that the "extraordinary persistence of this idea in the face of centuries of incessant refutation was probably sustained by a feeling that blackness could scarcely be anything but a curse and by the common need to confirm the facts of nature by specific reference to Scripture" (19). He concludes with the insight that the Negro's color set him radically apart from the English, and "served as a highly visible label identifying the natives of a distant continent which for ages Christians had known as a land of men radically defective in religion" (20).

22 Willard, "Sermon CLXXIX, 24 August 1703," 614.

23 Weld, *Bible against Slavery*, 95.

24 H. Shelton Smith, *In His Image*, 130; Hughes and Allen, *Illusions of Innocence*. See also Peterson, *Ham and Japheth*.

25 Haynes, *Noah's Curse*, 13. Haynes is not the first to offer this observation. See, for example, Hughes and Allen, *Illusions of Innocence*, 200–201. I. A. Newby also stated that "religious authority has been used to buttress discriminatory and repressive policies—slavery at first, and later segregation." Newby, *Jim Crow's Defense*, 84.

26 Some biblical rationales for white supremacy became increasingly sinister, and fanatical, after the Civil War. Picking up the "pre-Adamite" theories of Isaac de la Peyrère, nineteenth-century proponents of British-Israelism, and the related twentieth-century Christian Identity movement, posited that Cain—whom they regarded as the ancestor of black peoples—was the offspring of Eve and Satan (or Eve and one of Satan's minions). See Barkun, *Religion and the Racist Right*. In this very disturbing interpretive tradition, Cain was perceived as part of an evildoing, satanic bloodline that included Ham as well as Jewish people and all other non-whites. On contemporary pagan white supremacist movements, see Gardell, *Gods of the Blood*.

27 Stringfellow, "Bible Argument."

28 Quoted in Peterson, *Ham and Japheth*, 42.

29 Mauss, *All Abraham's Children*, 214.

30 Peterson, *Ham and Japheth*, 45.

31 Mark Twain's 1894 *Pudd'nhead Wilson* also mentioned the Ham story, as did—not surprisingly—Thomas Dixon's *The Leopard's Spots*, upon which the 1915 film *Birth of a Nation* was based.

32 Peterson, for example, offers several examples of black preachers who believed Ham to be their ancestor. See Peterson, *Ham and Japheth*, 46–47.

33 Priest, *Slavery as It Relates to the Negro*, 39.

34 Nott, "Types of Mankind," 126.

35 Horsman, *Race and Manifest Destiny*, 137; Cartwright, "Prognathous Species of Mankind," 139, 147.

36 Sloan, *Great Question Answered*, 190. Sloan's emphases.

37 Baldwin, *Dominion*, 134, 233.

38 Robinson, *Pictures of Slavery*, 18, 20, 30, 231.

39 Ariel [Buckner Payne], *Negro*, 30. Payne's emphases.

40 Ibid., 41–42. Payne's emphases.

41 *Harper's Weekly*, 29 November 1873, 1062.

42 *Harper's Weekly*, 10 September 1887, 643.

43 On Carroll, see Newby, *Jim Crow's Defense*, pages 93–96, and Barkun, *Religion and the Racist Right*, 158–60. Hardly deserving of the energy it took to refute them, Carroll's ideas strongly influenced the virulently white supremacist Christian Identity movement of the 1960s but had little bearing on mainstream southern white Protestantism.

44 Armistead, *Negro Is a Man*, 85, 36. Subsequent references are parenthetically cited, and all emphases are Armistead's.

45 Rev. William Montgomery Brown, *Crucial Race Question*, xxvii, xxiv, xxv.

46 Ibid., 12.

47 Bratton, "Christian South," 297.

48 Culp, "Past and the Future," 790.

49 "The Ku Klux Kreed," in *Kloran: Knights of the Ku Klux Klan*, 2. Although the imprint page offers no publishing date, a greeting signed by "His Majesty, William Joseph Simmons, Imperial Wizard," indicates that he "decreed" the sacredness of the Kloran in the "Imperial City of Atlanta," on June 26, 1916.

50 *Congressional Record*, 55th Cong., 3d sess., 1899, 32:1424.

51 "James Thomas Heflin," *American National Biography Online*.

52 *Congressional Record*, 71st Cong., 2d sess., 7 February 1930, 3234.

53 Simpson, "Non-Segregation," 6.

54 Ibid., 7. Simpson's emphases.

55 Gillespie, "Christian View," 9, 8. For an insightful and detailed analysis of Gillespie's pamphlet, see Chappell, "Religious Ideas," 245–48; and Chappell, *Stone of Hope*, 112–13.

56 Kinney, "Segregation Issue," 9. In 1965 as the *Loving* case was still circulating through Virginia's courts, Reverend Dr. C. E. McLain similarly conflated separation and segregation—seemingly speaking for God himself—even bracketing the terms "segregated" to clarify the meaning of the word "separated" in Deuteronomy 32:8 ("When the most High divided to the nations their inheritance, when he separated the sons of Adam, he set the bounds of the people according to the number of the children of Israel"). McLain quoted the verse as follows, stating God "the Most High, divided to the nations their inheritance, when He separated [segregated] the sons of Adam." McLain, *Place of Race*, 15. McLain's brackets.

57 Daniel, *God the Original Segregationist.*

58 "Truman Opposes Biracial Marriage," *New York Times*, 12 September 1963, 30. The separate races theology also continued to shape the views of more conservative politicians, such as Senator Robert C. Byrd of Virginia. In a 1964 hearing on the Civil Rights Act, Senator Byrd dredged up a number of biblical passages to oppose the passage of the bill. Because the "distinguished majority whip" had sought support for the bill in the Bible, Byrd turned to scriptures to support his view, fighting fire with fire. Byrd quoted numerous passages (though Genesis 11 and Acts 17 were not among them), asserting "God's statutes, therefore, recognize in the natural order, the separateness of things." *Congressional Record*, 88th Cong., 2d sess., 1964, 110:13206.

59 Chappell, "Religious Ideas," 239.

60 "Many Support Wiping Out Mixed-Race Marriage Ban," *Spartanburg (S.C.) Herald-Journal*, 7 February 1998, 1 and A10.

61 "Profile: Interracial Marriages," National Public Radio, 15 April 1999. Bill Merrell, spokesperson for the Southern Baptist Convention, also stated in the program that "God never said, 'Thou shall not race mix.'" This represents, of course, a recent shift in Southern Baptist theology.
      Martin also interviewed Professor Alan Callahan of the Harvard Divinity School for the program. In response to Littlejohn's remark that his views derived from his

Southern Baptist heritage, Callahan stated that these beliefs in fact constitute a "complex doctrine that can't be isolated in any one denominational strain"; rather, these notions "circulate within American evangelical religion generally."

62 Newby, *Jim Crow's Defense*, 103.

63 McGreevy, *Parish Boundaries*, 43, 90.

64 The development of the Catholic theology of race is, it seems, yet another chapter in story of the historic tension between the American church and the Church at Rome. Although I do not address this issue fully here, McGreevy examines some of the tensions pertaining to race in chapters 2 and 3 of *Catholicism and American Freedom*, 43–90. While not examining racial issues per se, on conflicts between Rome and American Catholics, see also D'Agostino, *Rome in America*; and Fogarty, *Vatican and the American Hierarchy*.

65 On Slattery and his work with the Josephites, see Ochs, *Desegregating the Altar*, 49–134.

66 Slattery, "Catholic Church and the Colored People," 379. Interestingly, in 1906 Slattery publicly renounced Catholicism, in part because of its disingenuous stance toward black peoples. "If anything in this world is certain," he wrote, "it is that the stand of the Catholic Church toward the negro is sheer dishonesty." Quoted in Ochs, *Desegregating the Altar*, 133.

67 *In Plurimis*, Encyclical of Pope Leo XIII on the Abolition of Slavery, 5 May 1888, secs. 3, 4. Subsequent references are parenthetically cited. <http://www.vatican .va/holy_father/leo_xiii/encyclicals/documents/hf_l-xiii_enc_05051888_in- plurimis_en.html>. 17 February 2007.

68 Quotations in this section are taken from the Douay-Rheims Version, unless otherwise noted. Galatians 3:26–28: "For you are all the children of God by faith, in Jesus Christ. For as many of you as have been baptized in Christ, have put on Christ. There is neither Jew, nor Greek; there is neither bond, nor free; there is neither male nor female. For you are all one in Christ Jesus."

Colossians 3:11: "Where there is neither Gentile nor Jew, circumcision nor uncircumcision, barbarian nor Scythian, bond nor free. But Christ is all and in all."

1 Corinthians 12:13: "For in one Spirit were we all baptized into one body, whether Jews or Gentiles, whether bond or free; and in one Spirit we have all been made to drink."

69 *Rerum Novarum* (1891) was another of Leo's encyclicals that contributed to the Catholic theology of race, but because its emphasis is on human rights and charity, rather than on theological anthropology and doctrines of human being and human unity, I have chosen not to analyze it here.

70 O'Connell, *John Ireland*, 265–85.

71 Ireland, "Let There Be No Barrier," 91. On Ireland and his views on race, see Moynihan, *Life of Archbishop John Ireland*, 228–29; O'Connell, *John Ireland*, 268–69; and Reardon, *Catholic Church*, 263–68.

72 *Mit brennender Sorge*, Encyclical of Pope Pius XI on the Church and the German Reich, 14 March 1937, in *Papal Encyclicals*, 4:527, 528.

73 "Symposium to be Published on 'Race: Nation, Person,'" *Interracial Review* 17 (May 1944): 78.

74 Passelecq and Suchecky, *Hidden Encyclical*, x. LaFarge's 1937 book, *Interracial Justice*, asserted that the "Christian religion has never ceased to lay stress upon the fact that all men are brothers, as descendants from a common earthly ancestor and as children of the same Heavenly Father. Flowing from this community of origin, as well as from our need of one another in the task of fulfilling our temporal and eternal destiny, are those obligations of the natural law which are characterized as human rights. Far from destroying or ignoring this natural unity of mankind, the supernatural unity of the Kingdom of God perfects and transforms natural unity into a corporate spiritual communion." LaFarge, *Interracial Justice*, 102. Thus, in sharp contrast to the theology of separate races emanating from white southern Protestants, LaFarge highlighted the key elements of the Vatican's theology of race: common descent through Adam and Eve, and human unity.

75 Passelecq and Suchecky, *Hidden Encyclical*, sec. 130, p. 245–46.

76 *Humani Generis Unitas* should not be confused with the 1950 encyclical, *Humani Generis*.

77 Jim Castelli, "Unpublished Encyclical Attacked Anti-Semitism," *National Catholic Reporter* 9 (15 December 1972): 1, 15.

78 Passelecq and Suchecky, *Hidden Encyclical*, 67–68. As Passelecq and Suchecky emphasize, for all its positive content, *Humani Generis Unitas* expressed some disturbingly anti-Semitic ideas, stating, for example, that the church's position on human unity does not "blind her to the spiritual dangers to which contact with Jews can expose souls, or make her unaware of the need to safeguard her children against spiritual contagion" (sec. 142, p. 252). Moreover, "the Church leaves to the powers concerned the solution of these problems [involving 'Jews of different countries']", though the church "insists that no solution is the true solution if it contradicts the very demanding laws of justice and charity" (sec. 148, pp. 256–57).

79 Ibid., 82, 166.

80 It must be noted that Pius XII is a terribly complicated figure in Catholic history, particularly in regard to the practical application of church teachings on human unity. Deemed by one Catholic writer "Hitler's Pope," Pius XII remained silent on both the war and the human atrocities in Germany. Popular authors and scholars alike have attempted to discern the reasons for his silence—fear, anti-Semitism, personal ambition. See Cornwell, *Hitler's Pope*; Falconi, *Silence of Pius XII*; and Peter C. Kent's more scholarly analysis, "Tale of Two Popes."

81 *Summi Pontificatus*, Encyclical of Pope Pius XII on the Unity of Human Society, 20 October 1939, in *Papal Encyclicals*, 4:10. Subsequent references are parenthetically cited.

82 Romans 12:4–5: "For as in one body we have many members, but all the members have not the same office: So we being many, are one body in Christ, and every one members one of another."

83 *Mystici Corporis Christi*, Encyclical of Pope Pius XII on the Mystical Body of Christ,

29 June 1943, secs. 15, 5, 95–96 <http://www.vatican.va/holy_father/pius_xii/
encyclicals/documents/hf_p-xii_enc_29061943_mystici-corporis-christi
_en.html>. 10 February 2007.

84 *Humani Generis,* Encyclical of Pope Pius XII, "Concerning Some False Opinions
Threatening to Undermine the Foundations of Catholic Doctrine," 12 August 1950,
in *Papal Encyclicals,* vol. 4, sec. 37.

85 For a concise discussion emphasizing different aspects of the doctrinal development of Catholic teachings on race, see McGreevy, *Parish Boundaries,* 50–52. For
a lengthier treatment on this topic, see Martensen, "Region, Religion, and Social
Action" (1978), 1–20.

86 "Discrimination and Christian Conscience," 507–8.

87 McGreevy, *Parish Boundaries,* 90–91.

88 See, for example, "Catholic Heads Urge Integration," *Washington Post and Times
Herald,* 14 November 1958, A1; and "Papal Stand Cited," *New York Times,* 14 November 1958, 1.

89 Quoted in *Pastoral Letters of the American Hierarchy, 1792–1970,* 442.

90 Quoted in McGreevy, *Parish Boundaries,* 55.

91 Ireland, "Let There Be No Barrier," 92.

92 Slattery, "Is the Negro Problem Becoming Local?" 313.

93 The Sacred Congregation for the Propagation of the Faith (Sacra Congregation de
Propaganda Fide), or the Propaganda, was an office of the Roman Curia entrusted
with the responsibility to administer all missionary organizations and activities.

94 Anciaux, letter of 27 August 1902, "Plain Facts for Fair Minds," 1, 3, Slattery Papers,
31-G-16, Josephite Fathers Archives, Baltimore.

95 "Mgr. Belford Urges Church Color Line," *New York Times,* 8 October 1929.

96 "Cardinal Hayes's View on Color Line Sought," *New York Times,* 9 October 1929.

97 "Cardinal Opposes Exclusion of Negro," *New York Times,* 18 October 1929.

98 Nau, *Manual on the Marriage Laws,* 15. "Noe" and "Cham" are the Latin spellings of
"Noah" and "Ham."

99 Perbal, "La Race Nègre," 157, 159. Translation mine.

100 Ibid., 167. It appears that Cardinal Lavigerie, founder of two missionary societies
in Africa, proposed the postulatum at the council. The prayer translates from Latin
as follows: "Let us pray for the most unhappy people of Africa, that God almighty
may finally at some time remove the curse of Ham from their hearts and grant
them a blessing to be gained uniquely in Jesus Christ our Lord. Let us pray, Lord
Jesus Christ, unique Savior of the human race, who are now Lord from sea to sea
and from the river as far as the ends of the earth, in your favor open your Most
Sacred Heart to the most unhappy souls of Africa also, who still dwell in darkness
and the shadow of death, so that, through the intercession of the most loving Vir-
gin Mary and her Spouse, the most glorious saint Joseph, the Africans may abandon their idols and fall before you and become members of your holy Church. . . .
An indulgence of 300 days is granted each and every time this prayer is recited,

and, if it is recited each day, a Plenary Indulgence each month." Translation from Quintus' Latin Translation Service, <http://www.latin.fsbusiness.co.uk/>.

101 Perbal, "La Race Nègre," 176, 177.

102 McNeil, "Collapse of the Canard," 135.

103 Ibid., 136, 137.

104 Friedel, "Is the Curse of Cham?" 450.

105 Ibid., 450–51, 452, 453.

106 On Catholic organizations that resisted desegregation, see Anderson, *Black, White, and Catholic*, 142–89.

107 Rev. William Montgomery Brown, *Crucial Race Question*, 153.

108 On segregation in Louisiana parishes during this same period, see Labbé, *Jim Crow Comes to Church*.

109 *Congressional Record*, 71st Cong., 2d sess., 7 February 1930: 3235, 3236, 3237. See also "Hot Talk in Senate over Heflin letter," *New York Times*, 8 February 1930, 32.

110 Archbishop Jannsen's action noted in Ochs, *Desegregating the Altar*, 68.

111 As mentioned in the previous chapter, Nau stated that antimiscegenation laws "can affect only marriage when both parties are unbaptized." He also disputed whether such laws were "just and reasonable" and asserted that "the purpose of the laws is to protect financially and politically the domination of the whites." See Nau, *Manual on the Marriage Laws*, 15. Though far less progressive than Nau, Gilligan similarly concluded that the church did "not regard as invalid properly solemnized marriages between Negroes and whites who are subject to her jurisdiction. Of that fact there is no question." See Gilligan, *Morality of the Color Line*, 93–94.

112 John A. Ryan, "Black Patterns of White America," 53.

113 Peterson, *Ham and Japheth*, 8.

Chapter Five

1 I follow the U.S. Census Bureau's regional definitions, according to which the "South" is that area encompassing Alabama, Arkansas, Delaware, Florida, Georgia, Kentucky, Louisiana, Maryland, Mississippi, North Carolina, Oklahoma, South Carolina, Tennessee, Texas, Virginia, West Virginia, and the District of Columbia; and the "West" is composed of Alaska, Arizona, California, Colorado, Hawaii, Idaho, Montana, Nevada, New Mexico, Oregon, Utah, Washington, and Wyoming. "Census Regions and Divisions of the United States," <http:www.eia.doe.gov/cneaf/solar.renewables/page/rea_data/figb1.html>. 2 May 2009.

2 Croly and Wakeman, *Miscegenation*, 14.

3 For a well-researched synopsis, see Kaplan, "Miscegenation Issue."

4 As noted in Chapter 1, the concept of due process derived from clauses in the Fifth and Fourteenth Amendments providing that neither federal nor state governments unfairly "deprive any citizen of life, liberty, or property, without due process of law." The Fourteenth Amendment declared African Americans citizens

and aimed to establish a principle of fairness for black citizens in the postwar South. The equal protection provision guaranteed citizens, and particularly African Americans, the right to be treated equally in both the procedures and principles of law, such that the government must treat every person the same as it treats other persons in similar circumstances.

5 For details on those three cases, see note 66 in Chapter 1.

6 *Philadelphia & West Chester R.R. Co. v. Miles*, 2 Am. Law Rev 358, 358–59 (1867). Subsequent references are from this source.

7 *Scott v. State*, 39 Ga. 321, 322 (1869). Subsequent references are parenthetically cited. See also Wallenstein, *Tell the Court*, 96ff.

8 As noted in Chapter 1, the Alabama Supreme Court ruled in 1868 that the state's antimiscegenation statute did not violate the couple's right to make contracts (i.e., a marriage contract) guaranteed in the 1866 Civil Rights Act. See *Ellis v. State*, 42 Ala. 525 (1868). Four years later, a Republican-led court pronounced the same law unconstitutional thus overturning *Ellis*. See *Burns v. State*, 48 Ala. 195 (1872). At the end of Reconstruction when southern Democrats resumed the bench, they restored Alabama's antimiscegenation statutes in *Green v. State*.

9 *State v. Hairston*, 63 N.C. 439, 441 (1869). See also Wallenstein, *Tell the Court*, 98.

10 *Lonas v. State*, 3 Heisk. 287, 296 (1871). Subsequent references are parenthetically cited. See also Wallenstein, *Tell the Court*, 97.

11 *State v. Gibson*, 10 Am. Rep. 42, 53 (1871). See also Wallenstein, *Tell the Court*, 63–64.

12 *State v. Gibson*, 10 Am. Rep. 42, 54–55 (1871).

13 *Green v. State*, 29 Am. Rep. 739, 741 (1877). Subsequent references to this case are parenthetically cited. See also Wallenstein, *Tell the Court*, 75–77.

14 *Kinney v. the Commonwealth*, 71 Va. 858 (1878). Subsequent references to this case are parenthetically cited.

15 Wallenstein, *Tell the Court*, 152.

16 *Ex parte Kinney*, 14 Fed Cas 602, 603, 605, 606 (1879). See also Wallenstein, *Tell the Court*, 109–10.

17 *Pace v. Alabama*, 106 U.S. 583, 585 (1883). See also Wallenstein, *Tell the Court*, 110–14.

18 *State v. Jackson*, 50 A.R. 499, 502, 500, 501, 502 (1883). See also Wallenstein, *Tell the Court*, 101–2. The decision closed by reiterating a common nineteenth-century myth: "It is stated as a well authenticated fact that if the issue of a black man and a white woman, and a white man and a black woman intermarry, they cannot possibly have any progeny, and such a fact sufficiently justifies those laws which forbid the intermarriage of blacks and whites, laying out of view other sufficient grounds for such enactments" (503).

19 *State v. Tutty*, 41 Fed 753, 758 (1890).

20 *Dodson v. State*, 31 SW 977 (1895).

21 Wallenstein, *Tell the Court*, 120.

22 *Kirby v. Kirby*, 206 Pac. 405, 406 (1922). See also Hardaway, "Unlawful Love."

23 *Blake et al. v. Sessions et al.*, 220 P. 876 (1923).

24 *In re Shun T. Takahashi's Estate*, 129 P.2d 217, 218 (1942).

25 *Stevens v. United States*, 146 F.2d 120, 123 (1944).

26 *Dees et al. v. Metts et al.*, 245 Ala. 370, 373 (1944).

27 See Gregory Michael Dorr, "Principled Expediency," 119.

28 North Carolina did not prohibit marriage between whites and Chinese persons, whereas in Virginia it was "unlawful for any white person in the state to marry any save a white person or a person with no other admixture of blood than white and American Indian." *Naim v. Naim*, 197 Va. 80 (1955). Subsequent references to this case are parenthetically cited.

29 The court's decision was apparently based on someone having improperly filed (or having neglected to file) a bill of exception, which is a statement containing all the objections or exceptions with the trial court, plus the grounds upon which these exceptions are based. *Black's Law Dictionary*, 67.

30 *State of Louisiana v. Brown and Aymond*, 236 La. 562, 567 (1959).

31 *McLaughlin v. Florida*, 85 S.Ct. 283, 284 (1964).

32 *McLaughlin v. Florida*, 85 S.Ct. 283, 291 (1964).

33 The corollary position—the idea that Catholic theology of race influenced western antimiscegenation statutes—cannot be proven in a way that satisfies my thinking.

34 According to Fowler, most of the southern states that proscribed additional races from marrying whites did not add them until after 1900. Arkansas added "Mongolians" in 1901 (348). In 1927 Georgia law criminalized marriage between "whites and any persons not white" (362). Louisiana included "persons of the aboriginal Indian race of America" in 1920 (378). Mississippi was the only state to include Asians prior to 1900; it added "Mongolians or persons with one-eighth or more Mongolian blood" to its list of prohibited marriage partners for whites in 1892 (393). North Carolina included "Indians" in 1715 (403); "Croatan Indians" were specified in 1887, and in 1912 this term was replaced by "Indians of Robeson County," which in turn was replaced the following year by "Cherokee Indians of Robeson County" (408–9). Virginia law included "Indians" in 1691 and omitted them in 1753 (431–32). Fowler, *Northern Attitudes*. Maryland added "Malays" to the list of races forbidden from marrying whites in 1935. Martyn, "Racism in the United States," 1062.

In 1924, the year in which Virginia enacted its Racial Integrity Act, the law was amended to declare it unlawful for "any white person . . . to marry any save a white person, or a person of no admixture of blood other than white and American Indian." The act specified further that the phrase "white person" signified only those persons having "no trace whatsoever of any blood other than Caucasian; but persons who have one-sixteenth or less of the blood of the American Indian and have no other non-caucasic blood shall be deemed to be white persons." See "The Virginia Act to Preserve Racial Integrity of 1924," <http://www.eugenicsarchive .org/eugenics/image_header.pl?id=1240&printable=1&detailed=0.> 8 June 2008.

35 Pascoe, "Race, Gender, and Intercultural Relations," 6.

36 *Laws of the State of California, Passed 22 April 1850*, chapter 140, sec. 3, 424,

37 *The Acts Amendatory to the Codes of California, 1880*, chapter 41, sec. 69.

38 *Statutes of California, 1933*, chapter 105, sec. 69. *Roldan v. Los Angeles County* was a 1933 case involving Solvador Roldan, a Filipino man, who applied to the Los Angeles county clerk for a marriage license to marry a white woman. The clerk refused to grant the license on the ground that Filipinos were included under "Mongolians" in the state antimiscegenation statute. Roldan took the county to court, contending that Filipinos were not Mongolians. The California Supreme Court ruled in Roldan's favor and compelled the clerk to issue the couple a marriage license. *Roldan v. Los Angeles County et al.*, 129 Cal. App. 267 (1933). Within weeks after the court issued its decision, state legislators amended the antimiscegenation statute to read: "no license must be issued authorizing the marriage of a white person with a negro, mulatto, Mongolian or member of the Malay race." *Statutes of California, 1933*, chapter 105, sec. 69, 561. For 1930s-era views on intermarriage between whites and Asians in California, see *California Law Review* 22 (1933), and Nellie Foster, "Legal Status of Filipino Intermarriages in California" (1932), both reprinted in McClain, *Asian Indians*, 2–18.

39 Hardaway, "Unlawful Love."

40 Fowler, *Northern Attitudes*, 414, 397.

41 The 1912 statute replaced the 1866 version, which proscribed marriage and cohabitation between whites and "Negroes, mulattoes, Indians or Chinese." In 1919, "American Indians" were removed from the statute. Ibid., 400.

42 *Black's Law Dictionary* defines a misdemeanor as a "crime that is less serious than a felony and is usu. punishable by fine, penalty, forfeiture, or confinement (usu. for a brief term) in a place other than a prison (such as a county jail)" (451). In contrast, a felony is a "serious crime usu. punishable by imprisonment for more than one year or by death" (281).

43 There is a vast literature on the southern obsession with white womanhood and the relationship between antimiscegenation laws and gender. See, for example, Kathleen M. Brown, *Good Wives*; Cash, *Mind of the South*, 86; Lisa Lindquist Dorr, "Arm in Arm," 144; Edwards, "Politics of Marriage"; Godshalk, "William J. Northen's Public and Personal Struggles," esp. 146–49; Jordan, *White over Black*; Pascoe, "Race, Gender, and the Privileges of Property," and "Race, Gender, and Intercultural Relations"; Cott, *Public Vows*; D'Emilio and Freedman, *Intimate Matters*; Grossberg, *Governing the Hearth*; and Woodson, "Beginnings of Miscegenation."

44 Cash, *Mind of the South*, 86. For a wonderful study of unions among white women and black men in the South during the nineteenth century, see Hodes, *White Women, Black Men*. Against conventional wisdom, Hodes argues that prior to the Civil War, white southerners in fact tolerated interracial relationships between white women and black men. It was only after Emancipation that white attitudes

against these unions hardened, resulting in white violence toward black men during the post–Civil War era.

45 Hodes, "Wartime Dialogues," 230, 231.

46 Martin, *Deep South Says "Never."*

47 Wallenstein, "Reconstruction, Segregation, and Miscegenation," 59.

48 *General Laws, and Joint Resolutions, Memorials, and Private Acts, passed at the 3rd Session of the Legislative Assembly of the Territory of Colorado*, 108. In and of itself, the provision suggests that a unique tolerance for intermarriage existed among the Mexicans not only of southern Colorado but also of "New Mexico"—the territory which in 1861 encompassed what is today New Mexico, Arizona (including the 1853 Gadsden Purchase), and a section of Colorado south of the Arkansas River. In light of New Mexico's strong adherence to Catholicism, the law also hints at a Catholic as well as a Spanish-Mexican tradition of intermarriage. Arguably the most Catholic acquisition of the Mexican-American War—even as late as 1890, 95.1 percent of the territory's residents identified as Catholic—New Mexico and southern Colorado were also well-known for their tolerance of interracial mixing.

In addition, the phrase "custom of the country," or "*mariage à la façon du pays*," was a term deriving from the seventeenth and eighteenth centuries and referred to the commonly accepted practice of interracial common-law marriages between Native American women and French and Spanish traders. See Van Kirk, *Many Tender Ties*; and Jennifer S. H. Brown, *Strangers in Blood*. See also Perry, *On the Edge of Empire*.

49 According to Hardaway, Arizona and Wyoming both repealed their statutes (Hardaway, "Unlawful Love," 388, and "Prohibiting Interracial Marriage," 59). Nevada also repealed its law (Earl, "Nevada's Miscegenation Laws," 15), as did Oregon, Montana, North Dakota, Colorado, and South Dakota (Martyn, "Racism in the United States," 1210, 1211, 1213, 1216). Idaho, Nebraska, and Utah removed the prohibitions from their statute books but did not officially repeal them (Martyn, "Racism in the United States," 1217, 1222, 1223).

50 Martyn states that the "California legislature did not get around to repealing the state intermarriage prohibitions until eleven years after" the *Perez* case (that is, 1959), for reasons that are a "mystery" (Martyn, "Racism in the United States," 1216).

51 Kennedy, *Interracial Intimacies*, 258, 259. In 1965 attorney William D. Zabel similarly observed that the western states that repealed their antimiscegenation laws since 1951 (when Oregon became the first state to repeal its statutes) acted "at least partially in response to the Negro social revolution." See Zabel, "Interracial Marriage," 57.

Chapter Six

1 Orenstein provides these personal details in "Void for Vagueness," 404, 405.
2 "Order Denying the Defendants' Motion to Vacate Judgment and Set Aside Sentence," 22 January 1965, LCF.
3 "Brief Amicus Curiae, Urging Reversal, on Behalf of: John J. Russell et al.," in Kurland and Casper, *Landmark Briefs and Arguments*, 934.
4 The concept of interracial "orthodoxy" is one I borrow from McGreevy, *Parish Boundaries*, 90, 222.
5 Letter from Harold S. French, 14 December 1966, Judge Leon M. Bazile Papers, General Correspondence File, 1963–1966, Virginia Historical Society, Richmond. Hereinafter cited as LBP. On 13 December 1966, the day before Mr. French sent his letter to Judge Bazile, the *Times* ran a story announcing that the Court had decided to hear the Lovings' case, though this article made no mention of the "almighty God" statement.
6 "Judge Bazile Dies at 76 in Hanover," *Richmond Times-Dispatch*, 19 March 1967, 3.
7 Layne, "Leon Maurice Bazile," 83.
8 "Leon M. Bazile," 275. Biographical information on Judge Bazile includes entries in *Portraits in the Historic Hanover County Courthouse*, 23; *Virginia Lives*, 60; *History of Virginia*, vol. 4, 133–34; *Virginia Democracy*, 392–93; *The General Assembly of the Commonwealth of Virginia, 1919–1939*, 211; and *The General Assembly of the Commonwealth of Virginia, 1940–1960*, 500. These sources are all available at the Virginia Historical Society, Richmond.
9 Notes on *Brown v. Board of Education*, Public School Desegregation, 1954–1959, Box 6, LBP.
10 Randall Miller, "Slaves and Southern Catholicism," 130.
11 "Leon M. Bazile," *Virginia State Bar Association Proceedings*, 275.
12 Gutjahr, *American Bible*, 126. On the differences and the history between nineteenth-century American Protestants and Catholics on the use of the Bible, see ibid., 113–42.
13 According to historian Jaroslav Pelikan, *Divino afflante Spiritu* (1943) brought about a "dramatic upsurge in Roman Catholic biblical study." Pelikan, *Whose Bible?* 179. *Divino afflante Spiritu* replaced Leo XIII's (1893) *Providentissimus Deus*, which described the errors of biblical criticism and explained how Catholic seminaries should teach scripture. Some twenty years after the publication of *Divino afflante Spiritu*, the Second Vatican Council (1962–1965) further loosened the church's restrictions on the laity's access to the Bible. *Dei verbum* (1965) declared that "easy access to Sacred Scripture should be provided for all the Christian faithful" and that "the study of the sacred page, is, as it were, the soul of sacred theology," though the task of "instruction in the right use of divine books" continued to fall upon the clergy (secs. 22, 24, 25). *Dei verbum*, 18 November 1965, <http://www.vatican.va/archive/hist_councils/ii_vatican_council/documents/vat-ii_const_19651118_dei-verbum_en.html>. 27 November 2008.

14 According to the seminary Web site, the institution "began admitting women to Seminary classes in the 1900s, though they could not register as official students." Presumably Bowcock thus attended, but did not graduate from, the institution. <http://archives.sbts.edu/CC/article/0,,PTID325566|CHID717898|CIID1979694,00.html>. 28 November 2008.

15 Leon M. Bazile to Virginia Hamilton Bowcock, 2 July 1917, and Virginia Hamilton Bowcock to Leon M. Bazile, 31 July 1917, both in General Correspondence, Box 4 (June–August 1917), LBP.

16 Leon M. Bazile to Virginia Hamilton Bowcock, 1 July 1917, General Correspondence, Box 4 (June–August 1917), LBP. The "Mullins" to whom Bazile refers is most likely Edgar Young Mullins, who served as the fourth president of the Baptist Seminary when Bowcock attended.

17 Leon M. Bazile to Virginia Hamilton Bowcock, 2 July 1917, General Correspondence, Box 4 (June–August 1917), LBP. One more clue provides another possible explanation for Judge Bazile's embrace of the theology of separate races. Mrs. Bazile taught Sunday school for a number of years, and among her papers is a Sunday school lesson for children on the Genesis 9–11 stories. It does not go into great detail, but her notes allude to the idea of separation, noting that "each family should have their home *apart*, living close to God," for there was "less danger of sin then" (Mrs. Bazile's emphasis). 11 August 1926, Virginia (Bowcock) Bazile Papers, Sunday School Lessons, 1926, 1933–1934, Box 24, Virginia Historical Society, Richmond. While Mrs. Bazile's notes made no mention of racial separation, the fact that she emphasized separation by underlining the word "apart" indicates that she associated separation with the Genesis stories. Given the prevalence of the theology of separate races among white southern Protestants and Mrs. Bazile's upbringing in Alabama and education in Southern Baptist theology, she was surely familiar with the biblical rationales for segregation deriving from these stories.

18 Bernstein, *New York City Draft Riots*, 27–31, 119–23.

19 Randall Miller, "Slaves and Southern Catholicism," 138–39, 130.

20 Ochs, *Desegregating the Altar*, 31.

21 Quoted in Fogarty, *Commonwealth Catholicism*, 146. For a narrative of Catholics and the circumstances leading up to and during the Civil War in Virginia, see Fogarty, chapters 7–9. As Robert Emmett Curran notes, "Catholics easily accommodated themselves to slavery. The traditional moral theology of the Church held that slavery was not in itself evil so long as the natural rights and duties of slaveholder and slave were respected." Curran, "Rome, the American Church, and Slavery," 33.

22 Newby, *Jim Crow's Defense*, 105.

23 Hennesey, *American Catholics*, 193.

24 Ochs, *Desegregating the Altar*, 2.

25 Figures from Hennesey, *American Catholics*, 171. On immigration, see, for example, Ignatiev, *How the Irish*; and Jacobson, *Whiteness*. Ignatiev does not adequately assess the role of Catholic identity in the Americanization of Irish immigrants,

but his book is helpful otherwise. Billington, *Protestant Crusade* is very good on anti-Catholic sentiment. John Higham's classic *Strangers in the Land* remains my favorite explanation for nineteenth- and early twentieth-century white American xenophobia.

26 Hennesey, *American Catholics*, 196. Hennesey offers a nice analysis of the related Americanist controversy of the late nineteenth century, 184–203.

27 McGreevy, *Parish Boundaries*, 89.

28 Anderson, *Black, White, and Catholic*, 245 n. 15.

29 "A Moral, Religious Problem," *Catholic Virginian* 29, no. 28 (14 May 1954): 8.

30 Anderson, *Black, White, and Catholic*, 112.

31 McGreevy, *Parish Boundaries*, 91, 101.

32 Anderson, *Black, White, and Catholic*, 142. Similarly, David Chappell observes that Protestant segregationists' efforts to rationalize their position "coalesced around opposition to social and political preaching" (Chappell, *Stone of Hope*, 122). Douglas Hudgins, Southern Baptist pastor of the First Baptist Church of Jackson, Mississippi, for example, explained his opposition to the Southern Baptist Convention's decision in 1954 to support the *Brown* ruling by declaring that he perceived the Court's decision as "a purely civic matter" rather than a religious one (quoted in Marsh, *God's Long Summer*, 100). As during the days of slavery, throughout the post-*Brown* South, some white Protestant prosegregationist ministers refused to speak publicly about segregation, charging that churches had no business in worldly affairs such as race relations. Southern white Catholics were thus in good company to adopt antipolitical, prosegregation positions and to criticize the church for its increasing involvement in protests and sit-ins and for meddling in political matters.

33 Quoted in Anderson, *Black, White, and Catholic*, 167.

34 On Sam Hill Ray, S.J., see ibid., 82–84, 89–91, 115–16.

35 Ibid., 1, 10.

36 At this point, there were actually only seventeen states still having antimiscegenation statutes, but apparently Russell or the lawyer advising him was unaware of this fact. Also, it is unclear from Bishop Russell's papers if he actually sent the letter to each person on his list.

37 Letter to Ordinaries from Bishop of Richmond, 28 November 1966, Bishop John J. Russell Papers, Box 7: Miscegenation, Archives of the Diocese of Richmond, Va. Hereinafter cited as JRP.

38 Letter to Father William Lewers from John P. Sisson (of the National Catholic Conference for Interracial Justice), copied to Bishop Russell, 14 February 1967, JRP.

39 Rev. William M. Lewers to Bishop John J. Russell, 18 January 1966, JRP.

40 "Brief Amicus Curiae, Urging Reversal, on Behalf of John J. Russell et al.," in Kurland and Casper, *Landmark Briefs and Arguments*, 930. Subsequent references are parenthetically cited.

41 "Catholic Clergymen Hit Mixed Marriage Laws," *Richmond Times-Dispatch*, 13 February 1967.

42 Letter to William P. Harrison, 21 February 1967, JRP.

43 *Catholic Virginian* 43, no. 33 (16 June 1967): 1.

44 Dabney, "Bishop Russell Story," 11.

45 "Maryland Governor Gets a Bill to Abolish Miscegenation Ban," *New York Times*, 4 March 1967, 15.

46 *Loving v. Virginia*, 388 U.S. 1 (1967).

47 *Loving v. Virginia*, 388 U.S. 1, 12 (1967).

48 Quoted in Booker, "Couple That Rocked," 82.

49 "Justices Upset All Bans on Interracial Marriage," *New York Times*, 13 June 1967, 1; Joe Bingham, "Interracial Love Gets Supreme Court O.K.," *Los Angeles Sentinel*, 15 June 1967, A1; "Intermarriage Bans Held Unconstitutional," *Virginian-Pilot*, 13 June 1967, 1; "Miscegenation Ban Is Ended by High Court," *Richmond Times-Dispatch*, 13 June 1967, 1; "State Couple 'Overjoyed' by Ruling," *Richmond Times-Dispatch*, 13 June 1967, B1.

50 "Top Court Junks Marriage Bars," *Norfolk (Va.) Journal and Guide*, 17 June 1967, 1; "Freedom of Choice at the Altar," *Norfolk (Va.) Journal and Guide*, 17 June 1967, 6.

51 "Georgia Klan on the March Again," *Norfolk (Va.) Journal and Guide*, 17 June 1967, 8.

52 Booker, "Couple That Rocked," 79, 80.

53 To be clear, by "epistemology" I mean: "that branch of philosophy concerned with the nature of knowledge, its possibilities, and general basis" (D. W. Hamlyn, "Epistemology, history of," in *The Oxford Companion to Philosophy*, ed. Ted Honderich (Oxford: Oxford University Press, 1995), 242.

54 Harvey, *Freedom's Coming*, 2. Moreover, as many other scholars also argue, some white Protestants, southern as well as northern, actively resisted the theology of separate races. In 1942 two white Baptist ministers, for example, founded Georgia's Koinonia Farm as a communal space in which blacks and whites could live and work and where black sharecroppers could become economically independent. See K'Meyer, *Interracialism and Christian Community*. On Protestant interracialism, see Harvey, *Freedom's Coming*, as well as Chappell, *Stone of Hope*; and Charles Marsh, *God's Long Summer*.

Epilogue

1 Mrs. Loving became a widow in June 1975, when Richard was killed in an automobile accident involving a drunk driver. In this accident, her sister was also injured, and Mrs. Loving lost an eye. See "Victim Figured in Historic Suit," *Richmond Times-Dispatch*, 1 July 1975; Richard P. Loving Obituary, *Washington Post*, 30 June 1975; "1967 Race Law Ruling Just a Memory," *Richmond Times-Dispatch*, 11 February 1979, B1; and Pratt, "Crossing the Color Line," 241. Mrs. Loving, sixty-eight, passed away in her Central Point, Virginia, home on 2 May 2008. "Mildred Loving Obituary," *New York Times*, 6 May 2008.

2 Mildred Loving, "Loving for All," 12 June 2007. National Gay and Lesbian Task Force, <http://www.thetaskforce.org/press/releases/PR_050708> 4 September 2008.

3 Susan Dominus, "The Color of Love," *New York Times*, 23 December 2008.

4 From Faith in America's Mission Statement, <http://www.faithinamerica.info/mission.php>. 3 January 2009.

5 Pelikan, *Whose Bible?* 166.

6 Ibid., 167.

7 Peter C. Murray, *Methodists and the Crucible of Race*, 52. On Southern Baptists during this era, see Newman, *Getting Right with God*, 20–34.

8 John T. Noonan Jr. explores similar issues in his book on change in the Catholic tradition. He asks how the church, representing a tradition that purports not to change its doctrines, reversed its teachings on moral issues such as slavery, religious freedom, and usury. See Noonan, *Church That Can*.

9 Klarman, *From Jim Crow*, 5–6.

10 Ibid., 9–10.

11 Ibid., 447.

12 Noll, *Civil War as a Theological Crisis*, 162, 40, 49.

13 O'Brien, *Constitutional Law and Politics*, 2:77. O'Brien's chapter "The Politics of Constitutional Interpretation" is very insightful on this issue of whether or not judges "interpret" the constitution. See pp. 2:69–99.

14 Kathleen Boone's wonderfully insightful deconstruction of fundamentalism illustrates—among other things—the fallaciousness of the very concept of "literalism," highlighting the discrepancies between those who claim to interpret the Bible literally yet who fail to arrive at an identical interpretation of the very same text. See Boone, *Bible Tells Them*, 39–60. The irony of the idea of literalism in terms of the "separate races" theology is, of course, that the notion of "race," much less of "separate races," is not "literally" found in the biblical text.

15 Noll, *Civil War as a Theological Crisis*, 75.

16 For evidence of a historical tradition of same-sex relationships sanctioned by the church, see Boswell, *Christianity, Social Tolerance, and Homosexuality*, and for a broad overview of the American history of marriage in debates over gay equality, see Chauncey, *Why Marriage?*

Bibliography

Manuscript and Archival Collections

Bazile, Judge Leon M. Papers. General Correspondence File, 1963–1966, Virginia Historical Society, Richmond.

Bazile, Virginia (Bowcock). Papers. Sunday School Lessons, 1926, 1933–1934, Box 24. Virginia Historical Society, Richmond.

LaFarge, John. Papers. Georgetown University Special Collections, Washington, D.C.

LeBerthon, Ted, to Michael Ahmann, 10 August 1959. National Catholic Conference for Interracial Justice Records. In the collection of Fr. Michael Engh, Santa Clara University, Santa Clara, Calif.

LeFlore, John. "The Important Decade: The Black Catholics in California in the 1940s: A Study in Art, Culture, and Religion." December 1987. Archival Center, Archdiocese of Los Angeles, Mission Hills, Calif.

Loving Case File. Commonwealth of Virginia, *County of Caroline v. Richard Loving and Mildred Jeter.* Central Rappahannock Heritage Center, Fredericksburg, Va.

Perez v. Moroney (sub. nom. *Perez v. Lippold*). L.A. No. 20305. Supreme Court Case Files, California State Archives, Office of the Secretary of the State, Sacramento.

Richmond Times-Dispatch News Clippings File: Marriage, Interracial #1, 1937–1963. *Richmond Times-Dispatch* Archives, Richmond, Va.

Russell, Bishop John J. Papers. Box 7: Miscegenation, Archives of the Diocese of Richmond, Richmond, Va.

Legal Materials

Individual Cases

Barron v. The Mayor and City Council of Baltimore, 32 U.S. 251 (1833).

Blake et al. v. Sessions et al., 220 P. 876 (1923).

Bonds v. Foster, 36 Tex. 68 (1871–1872).

Buck v. Bell, 274 U.S. 200 (1927).

Burns v. State, 48 Ala. 195 (1872).

Busey et al. v. District of Columbia, 138 F.2d 592 (1943).

Butchers' Benevolent Association v. Crescent City Live-Stock Landing and Slaughter-House Co. (The Slaughter-House Cases), 83 U.S. 16 (1873).

Cantwell v. Connecticut, 310 U.S. 296 (1940).

The Civil Rights Cases, 109 U.S. 3 (1883).

Dees et al. v. Metts et al., 245 Ala. 370 (1944).

Dodson v. State, 31 SW 977 (1895).

Ellis v. State, 42 Ala. 525 (1868).

Ex parte Kinney, 14 Fed Cas 602 (1879).

Farrington v. Tokushige, 273 U.S. 284 (1927).

Green v. State, 29 Am. Rep. 739 (1877).

Hamilton v. Board of Regents of the University of California, 293 U.S. 245 (1934).

Hart v. Hoss and Elder, 26 La. 90 (1874).

Honey v. Clark, 37 Tex. 686 (1873).

In re Shun T. Takahashi's Estate, 129 P.2d 217 (1942).

Kinney v. the Commonwealth, 71 Va. 58 (1878).

Kirby v. Kirby, 206 Pac. 405 (1922).

Korematsu v. United States, 323 U.S. 214 (1944).

Lonas v. State, 3 Heisk. 287 (1871).

Lovell v. City of Griffin, 303 U.S. 444 (1938).

Loving v. Virginia, 388 U.S. 1 (1967).

Maynard v. Hill, 125 U.S. 190 (1888).

McLaughlin v. Florida, 85 S.Ct. 283 (1964).

Meyer v. Nebraska, 262 U.S. 390 (1923).

Minersville School District v. Gobitis, 310 U.S. 586 (1940).

Morgan v. Virginia, 328 U.S. 373 (1946).

Mormon Church v. United States, 136 U.S. 1 (1890).

Murdock v. Commonwealth of Pennsylvania, 319 U.S. 105 (1943).

Naim v. Naim, 197 Va. 80 (1955).

Oyama v. State of California, 332 U.S. 633 (1948).

Pace v. Alabama, 106 U.S. 583 (1883).

Palko v. Connecticut, 302 U.S. 319 (1937).

Perez v. Lippold, 198 P.2d 17 (1948).

Philadelphia & West Chester R.R. Co. v. Miles, 2 Am. Law Rev 358 (1867).

Pierce v. Society of Sisters, 268 U.S. 510 (1925).

Reynolds v. United States, 98 U.S. 145 (1878).

Roldan v. Los Angeles County et al., 129 Cal. App. 267 (1933).

Schenck v. United States, 249 U.S. 47 (1919).

Schneider v. Town of Irvington, 308 U.S. 147 (1939).

Scott v. State, 39 Ga. 323 (1869).

Shelley v. Kraemer, 334 U.S. 1 (1948).

Skinner v. Oklahoma, 316 U.S. 535 (1942).

State v. Tutty, 41 Fed. 753 (1890).

State v. Gibson, 10 Am. Rep. 42 (1871).

State v. Jackson, 50 A.R. 499 (1883).

State v. Hairston, 63 N.C. 439 (1869).

State of Louisiana v. Brown and Aymond, 236 La. 562 (1959).

Stevens v. United States, 146 F.2d 120 (1944).

Testa v. Katt, 330 U.S. 386 (1947).

United States v. Carolene Products, 304 U.S. 144 (1938).

West Virginia State Board of Education v. Barnette, 319 U.S. 624 (1943).

Collections of Legal Documents

The Acts Amendatory to the Codes of California Passed at the Twenty-Third Session of the Legislature, 1880. Sacramento, Calif.: State Office, J. D. Young, Sup't. State Printing, 1880. California State Archives, Office of the Secretary of State, Sacramento.

General Laws, and Joint Resolutions, Memorials, and Private Acts, passed at the 3rd Session of the Legislative Assembly of the Territory of Colorado, begun at Golden City, February 1, 1864, Adjourned to Denver, February 6, 1864. Colorado State Archives, Denver.

Kurland, Philip B., and Gerhard Casper, eds. Landmark Briefs and Arguments of the Supreme Court of the U.S.: Constitutional Law. Arlington, Va.: University Publications of America, 1975: 687–1007.

Laws of the State of California, Passed 22 April 1850. California State Archives, Office of the Secretary of State, Sacramento.

Laws and Ordinances of New Netherland, 1638–1674. Comp. and trans. Edmund Bailey O'Callaghan. Albany, N.Y.: Weed, Parsons, 1868.

Proceedings and Acts of the General Assembly of Maryland. Vol. 1. Baltimore: Maryland Historical Society, 1883–1947.

Statutes of California, 1933. Sacramento: California State Printing Office, 1933. California State Archives, Office of the Secretary of State, Sacramento.

Primary and Secondary Materials

Aaron, David H. "Early Rabbinic Exegesis on Noah's Son Ham and the So-called Hamitic Myth." Journal of the American Academy of Religion 63 (1995): 721–59.

Abell, Aaron I. "Origins of Catholic Social Reform in the United States: Ideological Aspects." Review of Politics 11, no. 3 (July 1949): 294–309.

Alberigo, Giuseppe. A Brief History of Vatican II. Translated by Matthew Sherry. Maryknoll, N.Y.: Orbis Books, 2006.

Almaguer, Tomás. Racial Fault Lines: The Historical Origins of White Supremacy in California. Berkeley: University of California Press, 1994.

Alpert, Jonathan L. "The Origin of Slavery in the United States: The Maryland Precedent." American Journal of Legal History 14, no. 3 (July 1970): 189–221.

Amar, Akhil Reed. "The Bill of Rights and the Fourteenth Amendment." Yale Law Journal 101, no. 6 (April 1992): 1193–284.

Anciaux, Joseph. Letter of 27 August 1902, "Plain Facts for Fair Minds," Slattery Papers, 31-G-16, Josephite Fathers Archives, Baltimore, Md.

Anderson, R. Bentley. Black, White, and Catholic: New Orleans Interracialism, 1947–1956. Nashville, Tenn.: Vanderbilt University Press, 2005.

Ariel [Buckner Payne]. The Negro: What Is His Ethnological Status; Is He the Progeny of

Ham? Is He a Descendant of Adam and Eve? Has He a Soul? Or Is He a Beast in God's Nomenclature? What Is His Status as Fixed by God in Creation? What Is His Relation to the White Race? 2nd ed. Cincinnati, Ohio: Published for the Proprietor, 1867.

Armistead, W. S. *The Negro Is a Man: A Reply to Professor Charles Carroll's Book, "The Negro Is a Beast; or, In the Image of God."* 1903. Reprint, Miami, Fla.: Mnemosyne Publishing, 1969.

Ayers, Edward. *The Promise of the New South: Life after Reconstruction.* New York: Oxford University Press, 1993.

Ayrinhac, Rev. H. A. *Marriage Legislation in the New Code of Canon Law.* Revised edition. New York: Benziger Brothers, Printers to the Holy Apostolic See, 1932.

Baldwin, James. *The Fire Next Time.* New York: Vintage International, 1993.

Baldwin, Samuel Davies. *Dominion; or, The Unity and Trinity of the Human Race with the Divine Political Constitution of the World, and the Divine Rights of Shem, Ham, and Japheth.* Nashville, Tenn.: E. Stevenson and F. A. Owen, 1858.

Barkan, Elazar. *The Retreat of Scientific Racism: Changing Concepts of Race in Britain and the United States between the World Wars.* New York: Cambridge University Press, 1992.

Barkun, Michael. *Religion and the Racist Right: The Origins of the Christian Identity Movement.* Chapel Hill: University of North Carolina Press, 1994.

Bederman, Gail. *Manliness and Civilization: A Cultural History of Gender and Race in the United States, 1880–1917.* Chicago: University of Chicago Press, 1996.

Bellitto, Christopher M. *Renewing Christianity: A History of Church Reform from Day One to Vatican II.* New York: Paulist Press, 2001.

Berlin, Ira. *Slaves without Masters: The Free Negro in the Antebellum South.* New York: Norton, 1976.

Berman, Harold J., and John Witte Jr. "The Transformation of Western Legal Philosophy in Lutheran Germany." *Southern California Law Review* 62 (September 1989): 1573–660.

Bernardini, Gene. "The Origins and Development of Racial Anti-Semitism in Fascist Italy." *Journal of Modern History* 49, no. 3 (September 1977): 431–53.

Bernstein, Iver. *The New York City Draft Riots: Their Significance for American Society and Politics in the Age of the Civil War.* New York: Oxford University Press, 1990.

Bickel, Alexander M. "The Original Understanding and the Segregation Decision." *Harvard Law Review* 69, no. 1 (November 1955): 1–65.

Billington, Ray Allen. *The Origins of Nativism in the United States, 1800–1844.* New York: Arno Press, 1974.

———. *The Protestant Crusade, 1800–1860: A Study of the Origins of American Nativism.* 1938. Reprint, Chicago: Quadrangle Books, 1964.

Blackburn, Robin. "The Old World Background to European Colonial Slavery." *William and Mary Quarterly* 54, no. 1 (January 1997): 65–102.

Black's Law Dictionary. 2nd pocket ed. St. Paul, Minn.: West Publishing, 2001.

Blee, Kathleen. *Women of the Klan: Racism and Gender in the 1920s.* Berkeley: University of California Press, 1992.

Blum, Edward J. *Reforging the White Republic: Race, Religion, and American Nationalism, 1865–1898.* Baton Rouge: Louisiana State University Press, 2005.

Blumin, Stuart M. *The Emergence of the Middle Class: Social Experience in the American City, 1760–1900.* New York: Cambridge University Press, 1998.

Boles, John B. *Masters and Slaves in the House of the Lord: Race and Religion in the American South, 1740–1870.* Lexington: University Press of Kentucky, 1988.

———. *The South through Time: A History of an American Region.* 3rd ed. Englewood Cliffs, N.J.: Prentice-Hall, 2003.

Bonfield, Lloyd. "Developments in European Family Law." In *Family Life in Early Modern Times, 1500–1789,* vol. 1 of *The History of the European Family,* edited by David I. Kertzer and Marzio Barbagli, 87–124. New Haven, Conn.: Yale University Press, 2001.

Booker, Simeon. "The Couple That Rocked the Courts." *Ebony,* September 1967, 78–84.

Boone, Kathleen C. *The Bible Tells Them So: The Discourse of Protestant Fundamentalism.* Albany: State University of New York Press, 1989.

Boswell, John. *Christianity, Social Tolerance, and Homosexuality: Gay People in Western Europe from the Beginning of the Christian Era to the Fourteenth Century.* Chicago: University of Chicago Press, 1980.

Bouscaren, Lincoln T., S.J., and Adam C. Ellis, S.J. *Canon Law: A Text and Commentary.* 2nd rev. ed. Milwaukee, Wis.: Bruce Publishing, 1953.

Bratton, Bp. Theodore. "The Christian South and Negro Education." *Sewanee Review* 16 (July 1908): 290–97.

Braude, Benjamin. "Ham and Noah: Race, Slavery, and Exegesis in Islam, Judaism, and Christianity." *Annales: Histoires, Sciences Sociales* (March 2002): <www.bc.edu/bc_org/research/rapl/events/braude_abstract.html>.

———. "The Sons of Noah and the Construction of Ethnic and Geographical Identities in the Medieval and Early Modern Periods." *William and Mary Quarterly* 54, no. 1 (January 1997): 103–42.

Bredbenner, Candice Lewis. *A Nationality of Her Own: Women, Marriage, and the Law of Citizenship.* Berkeley: University of California Press, 1998.

Brilliant, Mark. "Color Lines: Civil Rights Struggles on America's Racial Frontier, 1945–1975." Ph.D. diss., Stanford University, 2002.

Bringhurst, Newell. *Saints, Slaves, and Blacks: The Changing Place of Black People within Mormonism.* Westport, Conn.: Greenwood Press, 1981.

Brooks, James F. *Captives and Cousins: Slavery, Kinship, and Community in the Southwest Borderlands.* Chapel Hill: University of North Carolina Press, 2002.

Brown, Callum G. *Postmodernism for Historians.* Harlow, England: Pearson Education, 2005.

Brown, Jennifer S. H. *Strangers in Blood: Fur Trade Company Families in Indian Country.* Vancouver: University of British Columbia Press, 1980.

Brown, Kathleen M. *Good Wives, Nasty Wenches, and Anxious Patriarchs: Gender, Race, and Power in Colonial Virginia.* Chapel Hill: University of North Carolina Press, 1996.

Brown, Wendy. *Regulating Aversion: Tolerance in the Age of Identity and Empire.* Princeton, N.J.: Princeton University Press, 2006.

Brown, Rev. William Montgomery. *The Crucial Race Question; or, Where and How Shall the Color Line Be Drawn?* Little Rock, Ark.: Arkansas Churchman's Publishing, 1907.

Browning, James. R. "Anti-Miscegenation Laws in the United States." *Duke Bar Journal* 1, no. 1 (March 1951): 26–41.

Brundage, James A. *Law, Sex, and Christian Society in Medieval Europe.* Chicago: University of Chicago Press, 1987.

Cady, Daniel. "Southern California: Southern Whites in Greater Los Angeles, 1914–1930." Ph.D. diss., Claremont Graduate University, 2005.

Calvin, John. *Institutes of the Christian Religion.* 7th ed. Translated by John Allen. Philadelphia, Pa.: Presbyterian Board of Christian Education, 1936.

———. *Commentaries on the First Book of Moses Called Genesis.* Vol. 1. Grand Rapids, Mich.: Eerdmans, 1948.

Carlen, Claudia, ed. *The Papal Encyclicals.* 5 vols. Wilmington, N.C.: McGrath Publishing, 1981.

Carlson, Eric Josef. *Marriage and the English Reformation.* Oxford: Blackwell Publishers, 1994.

Cartwright, Samuel. "The Prognathous Species of Mankind." In *Slavery Defended: The Views of the Old South,* edited by Eric L. McKitrick, 139–47. Englewood Cliffs, N.J.: Prentice-Hall, 1963.

Cash, W. J. *The Mind of the South.* New York: Alfred A. Knopf, 1941.

Castañeda, Antonia I. "Presidarias y Pobladores: Spanish-Mexican Women in Frontier Monterey, California," Ph.D. diss., Stanford University, 1990.

Catholic Bishops of the South. Concluding message, read at the biennial convention of the Catholic Committee of the South, Richmond, Virginia, April 21–25, 1953. Reprinted in "The Church in the South," *Catholic Mind* 51 (August 1953): 510–12.

Chalmers, David M. *Hooded Americanism: The History of the Ku Klux Klan.* New York: F. Watts, 1981.

Chappell, David L. "Religious Ideas of the Segregationists." *Journal of American Studies* 32, no. 2 (1998): 237–62.

———. *A Stone of Hope: Prophetic Religion and the Death of Jim Crow.* Chapel Hill: University of North Carolina Press, 2004.

Charles, R. H., trans. *The Book of Jubilees; or, The Little Genesis.* London: Adam and Charles Black, 1902.

Charles, Rodger, S.J., and Drostan Maclaren, O.P. *The Social Teaching of Vatican II: Its Origin and Development.* San Francisco: Ignatius Press, 1982.

Chauncey, George. *Why Marriage? The History Shaping Today's Debate over Gay Equality.* New York: Basic Books, 2005.

Clinton, Catherine, and Nina Silber, eds. *Divided Houses: Gender and the Civil War.* New York: Oxford University Press, 1992.

Cocke, Emmett W., Jr. "Luther's View of Marriage and Family." *Religion in Life* 42, no. 1 (Spring 1973): 103–15.

Cohausz, Otto. *The Pope and Christian Marriage.* Trans. George D. Smith. New York: Benziger Brothers, 1933.

Coleman, John A., S.J. *One Hundred Years of Catholic Social Thought: Celebration and Challenge.* Maryknoll, N.Y.: Orbis Books, 1991.

Coontz, Stephanie. *Marriage, a History: From Obedience to Intimacy, or How Love Conquered Marriage.* New York: Viking Press, 2005.

Cornwell, John. *Hitler's Pope: The Secret History of Pius XII.* New York: Penguin Books, 1999.

Cott, Nancy. *Public Vows: A History of Marriage and Nation.* Cambridge, Mass.: Harvard University Press, 2000.

Craver, Rebecca McDowell. *The Impact of Intimacy: Mexican-Anglo Intermarriage in New Mexico, 1821–1846.* El Paso: Texas Western Press, 1982.

Creel, Margaret Washington. *A Peculiar People: Slave Religion and Community-Culture among the Gullahs.* New York: New York University Press, 1988.

Croly, David Goodman, and George Wakeman. *Miscegenation: The Theory of the Blending of the Races, Applied to the White Man and the Negro.* New York: H. Dexter, Hamilton, 1864.

Crowther, Edward R. "Holy Honor: Sacred and Secular in the Old South." *Journal of Southern History* 58, no. 4 (November 1992): 619–36.

Culp, D. W. "The Past and the Future of the American Negro." *Arena* 21 (April 1899): 786–99.

Curran, Robert Emmett. "Rome, the American Church, and Slavery." In *Building the Church in America: Studies in Honor of Monsignor Robert F. Trisco on the Occasion of His Seventieth Birthday,* edited by Joseph C. Linck, C.O., and Raymond J. Kupke, 30–49. Washington, D.C.: Catholic University of America Press, 1999.

Cutter, Charles R. *The Legal Culture of Northern New Spain, 1700–1810.* Albuquerque: University of New Mexico Press, 1995.

Dabney, Virginius. "The Bishop Russell Story." *Virginia Record* 89, no. 9 (September 1967): 7–13, 60–61.

D'Agostino, Peter R. *Rome in America: Transnational Catholic Ideology from the Risorgimento to Fascism.* Chapel Hill: University of North Carolina Press, 2004.

Dailey, Jane. "Sex, Segregation, and the Sacred after *Brown.*" *Journal of American History* 91, no. 1 (June 2004): 119–44.

Daniel, Rev. Carey. *God the Original Segregationist and Seven Other Segregation Sermons.* N.p.: [1956?].

David, Timothy, Kevin R. Johnson, and George A. Martínez. *A Reader on Race, Civil Rights, and American Law: A Multiracial Approach.* Durham, N.C.: Carolina Academic Press, 2001.

Davis, David Brion. "The Comparative Approach to American History: Slavery." In *Slavery in the New World: A Reader in Comparative History.* Edited by Laura Foner and Eugene D. Genovese, 60–68. Englewood Cliffs, N.J.: Prentice-Hall, 1969.

———. "A Comparison of British and Latin America." In *Slavery in the New World: A Reader in Comparative History*. Edited by Laura Foner and Eugene D. Genovese, 69–83. Englewood Cliffs, N.J.: Prentice-Hall, 1969.

———. "Constructing Race: A Reflection." *William and Mary Quarterly* 54, no. 1 (January 1997): 7–18.

———. *The Problem of Slavery in Western Culture*. Ithaca, N.Y.: Cornell University Press, 1966.

———. "Some Themes of Counter-Subversion: An Analysis of Anti-Masonic, Anti-Catholic, and Anti-Mormon Literature." In *From Homicide to Slavery: Studies in American Culture*, 137–65. New York: Oxford University Press, 1986.

Davis, Kingsley. "Intermarriage in Caste Societies." *American Anthropologist*, n.s., 43, no. 3 (July/September 1941): 390–92.

Davis, Peggy Cooper. *Neglected Stories: The Constitution and Family Values*. New York: Hill and Wang, 1997.

Dawidoff, Robert. *The Education of John Randolph*. New York: W. W. Norton, 1979.

Dayton, Cornelia Hughes. *Women before the Bar: Gender, Law, and Society in Connecticut, 1639–1789*. Chapel Hill: University of North Carolina Press, 1995.

Degler, Carl N. *Neither Black nor White: Slavery and Race Relations in Brazil and the United States*. New York: Macmillan, 1971.

———. "Slavery in Brazil and the United States: An Essay in Comparative History." *American Historical Review* 75, no. 14 (April 1970): 1004–28.

Delaney, John J. *Dictionary of American Catholic Biography*. Garden City, N.J.: Doubleday, 1984.

D'Emilio, John, and Estelle Freedman. *Intimate Matters: A History of Sexuality in America*. New York: Harper and Row, 1988.

Demos, John. *A Little Commonwealth: Family Life in Plymouth Colony*. Oxford: Oxford University Press, 1970.

Dickens, A. G. *The English Reformation*. New York: Schocken Books, 1964.

Din, Gilbert C. *Spaniards, Planters, and Slaves: The Spanish Regulation of Slavery in Louisiana, 1763–1803*. College Station: Texas A&M University Press, 1999.

"Discrimination and Christian Conscience." In *Pastoral Letters of the American Hierarchy, 1792–1970*, edited by Hugh J. Nolan, 201–6. Huntington, Ind.: Our Sunday Visitor, 1971.

Doherty, Joseph Francis. *The Moral Problems of Interracial Marriage*. Washington, D.C.: Catholic University of America, 1949.

Dolan, Jay P. *The American Catholic Experience: A History from Colonial Times to the Present*. Garden City, N.J.: Doubleday, 1985.

Dorr, Gregory Michael. "Principled Expediency: Eugenics, *Naim v. Naim*, and the Supreme Court." *American Journal of Legal History* 42, no. 2 (April 1998): 119–59.

———. *Segregation's Science: Eugenics and Society in Virginia*. Charlottesville: University of Virginia Press, 2008.

Dorr, Lisa Lindquist. "Arm in Arm: Gender, Eugenics, and Virginia's Racial Integrity Acts of the 1920s." *Journal of Women's History* 11, no. 1 (Spring 1999): 143–66.

Douglas, Mary. *Purity and Danger: An Analysis of the Concepts of Pollution and Taboo.* 1966. Reprint, New York: Routledge, 1991.

Drinnon, Richard. *Facing West: The Metaphysics of Indian-Hating and Empire-Building.* Minneapolis: University of Minnesota Press, 1980.

Dubow, Saul. "Afrikaner Nationalism, Apartheid, and the Conceptualization of 'Race.'" *Journal of African History* 33, no. 2 (1992): 209–37.

Duncan, Richard R. "Catholics and the Church in the Antebellum Upper South." In *Catholics in the Old South: Essays on Church and Culture.* Edited by Randall M. Miller and Jon L. Wakelyn. Macon, Ga.: Mercer University Press, 1999: 77–98.

Du Toit, Andre. "No Chosen People: The Myth of the Calvinist Origins of Afrikaner Nationalism and Racial Ideology." *American Historical Review* 88, no. 4 (October 1983): 920–52.

Dvorak, Katharine L. *African-American Exodus: The Segregation of the Southern Churches.* Brooklyn, N.Y.: Carlson Publishing, 1991.

Earl, Phillip I. "Nevada's Miscegenation Laws and the Marriage of Mr. & Mrs. Harry Bridges." *Nevada Historical Society Quarterly* 37, no. 1 (1994): 1–18.

Edwards, Laura F. *Gendered Strife and Confusion: The Political Culture of Reconstruction.* Urbana: University of Illinois Press, 1997.

———. "The Politics of Marriage and Households in North Carolina during Reconstruction." In *Jumpin' Jim Crow: Southern Politics from Civil War to Civil Rights,* edited by Jane Dailey, Glenda Elizabeth Gilmore, and Bryant Simon, 7–27. Princeton, N.J.: Princeton University Press, 2000.

Elkins, Stanley. *Slavery: A Problem in American Institutional and Intellectual Life.* Chicago: University of Chicago Press, 1959.

Engh, Michael E., S.J. *Frontier Faiths: Church, Temple, and Synagogue in Los Angeles, 1846–1888.* Albuquerque: University of New Mexico Press, 1992.

Esguerra, Jorge Canizares. "New World, New Stars: Patriotic Astrology and the Invention of Indian and Creole Bodies in Colonial Spanish America, 1600–1650." *American Historical Review* 104, no. 1 (February 1999): 33–68.

Ezell, Humphrey K. *The Christian Problem of Racial Segregation.* New York: Greenwich Book Publishers, 1959.

Falconi Carlo. *The Silence of Pius XII.* Translated by Bernard Wall. Boston: Little, Brown, 1970.

Fanon, Frantz. *Black Skin, White Masks.* Translated by Charles Lam Markmann. New York: Grove Press, 1967.

———. *The Wretched of the Earth.* Translated by Constance Farrington. New York: Grove Press, 1963.

Faragher, John Mack. "The Custom of the Country: Cross-Cultural Marriage in the Far Western Fur Trade." In *Western Women: Their Land, Their Lives.* Edited by Lillian Schlissel, Vicki L. Ruiz, and Janice Monk, 199–215. Albuquerque: University of New Mexico Press, 1988.

Faulkner, William. *Absalom, Absalom!* New York: Vintage, 1991.

Faust, Drew Gilpin. *Mothers of Invention: Women of the Slaveholding South in the American Civil War.* Chapel Hill: University of North Carolina Press, 1996.

———. *Southern Stories: Slaveholders in Peace and War.* Columbia: University of Missouri Press, 1992.

Felder, Cain Hope. *Race, Racism, and the Biblical Narratives.* Minneapolis, Minn.: Augsburg Fortress Press, 2002.

Feldman, Glenn, ed. *Before Brown: Civil Rights and White Backlash in the Modern South.* Tuscaloosa: University of Alabama Press, 2004.

Fenton, Elizabeth. "Birth of a Protestant Nation: Catholic Canadians, Religious Pluralism, and National Unity in the Early U.S. Republic." *Early American Literature* 41, no. 1 (March 2006): 29–57.

Ferrell, Lori Anne. *The Bible and the People.* New Haven, Conn.: Yale University Press, 2008.

Fessenden, Tracy. "The Convent, the Brothel, and the Protestant Woman's Sphere." *Signs: Journal of Women in Culture and Society* 25, no. 2 (Winter 2000): 451–78.

———. *Culture and Redemption: Religion, the Secular, and American Literature.* Princeton, N.J.: Princeton University Press, 2007.

Fett, Sharla M. *Working Cures: Healing, Health, and Power on Southern Slave Plantations.* Chapel Hill: University of North Carolina Press, 2002.

Field, Benjamin Thomas. "Justice Roger Traynor and His Case for Judicial Activism." Ph.D. diss., University of California, Berkeley, 2000.

Finkelman, Paul. "The Ten Commandments on the Courthouse Lawn and Elsewhere." *Fordham Law Review* 73 (2005): 1477–520.

———, ed. *Slavery and the Law.* Madison, Wis.: Madison House, 1997.

Flamming, Douglas. *Bound for Freedom: Black Los Angeles in Jim Crow America.* Berkeley: University of California Press, 2005.

Flynt, J. Wayne. *Alabama Baptists: Southern Baptists in the Heart of Dixie.* Tuscaloosa: University of Alabama Press, 1998.

Fogarty, Gerald P., S.J. *Commonwealth Catholicism: A History of the Catholic Church in Virginia.* Notre Dame, Ind.: University of Notre Dame Press, 2001.

———. *The Vatican and the American Hierarchy from 1870 to 1965.* Wilmington, Del.: Michael Glazier, 1985.

Foley, Neil. *The White Scourge: Mexicans, Blacks, and Poor Whites in Texas Cotton Culture.* Berkeley: University of California Press, 1997.

Foner, Eric. *Forever Free: The Story of Emancipation and Reconstruction.* New York: Vintage, 2006.

———. *Free Soil, Free Labor, Free Men: The Ideology of the Republican Party before the Civil War.* Oxford: Oxford University Press, 1995.

———. *Reconstruction: America's Unfinished Revolution, 1863–1877.* New York: Harper and Row, 1988.

Foner, Laura, and Eugene D. Genovese. *Slavery in the New World: A Reader in Comparative History.* Englewood Cliffs, N.J.: Prentice-Hall, 1969.

Foster, Gaines M. *Ghosts of the Confederacy: Defeat, the Lost Cause, and the Emergence of the New South*. New York: Oxford University Press, 1987.

———. *Moral Reconstruction: Christian Lobbyists and the Federal Legislation of Morality, 1865–1920*. Chapel Hill: University of North Carolina Press, 2002.

Foucault, Michel. *Power/Knowledge: Selected Interviews and Other Writings, 1972–1977*. Edited by Colin Gordon. New York: Pantheon Books, 1980.

Fowler, David. *Northern Attitudes towards Interracial Marriage: Legislation and Public Opinion in the Middle Atlantic and the States of the Old Northwest, 1780–1930*. New York: Garland Publishing, 1987.

Franchot, Jenny. *Roads to Rome: The Antebellum Protestant Encounter with Catholicism*. Berkeley: University of California Press, 1994.

Franklin, John Hope. *From Slavery to Freedom: A History of American Negroes*. 4th ed. New York: Knopf, 1974.

Fredrickson, George M. *The Black Image in the White Mind: The Debate on Afro-American Character and Destiny, 1871–1914*. New York: Harper and Row, 1972.

———. *Racism: A Short History*. Princeton, N.J.: Princeton University Press, 2002.

———. *White Supremacy: A Comparative Study in American and South African History*. New York: Oxford University Press, 1981.

Freedman, Paul. *Images of the Medieval Peasant*. Stanford, Calif.: Stanford University Press, 1999.

Freehling, William W. *The Road to Disunion: Secessionists at Bay, 1776–1854*. Oxford: Oxford University Press, 1990.

Friedel, Lawrence M. "Is the Curse of Cham on the Negro Race?" *American Ecclesiastical Review* 106, no. 6 (June 1942): 447–53.

Friedman, Lawrence M. *A History of American Law*. New York: Simon and Schuster, 1973.

Friend, Craig Thompson, and Lorri Glover, eds. *Southern Manhood: Perspectives on Masculinity in the Old South*. Athens: University of Georgia Press, 2004.

Gardell, Mattias. *Gods of the Blood: The Pagan Revival and White Separatism*. Durham, N.C.: Duke University Press, 2003.

Gaustad, Edwin S., and Philip L. Barlow. *New Historical Atlas of Religion in America*. Oxford: Oxford University Press, 2001.

Gayarré, Charles Étienne Arthur. *Louisiana: Its Colonial History and Romance*. New York: Harper and Brothers, 1851–1852.

Genovese, Eugene. *Roll, Jordan, Roll: The World the Slaves Made*. New York: Vintage, 1975.

Gillard, John T. *Colored Catholics in the United States*. Baltimore: Josephite Press, 1941.

Gillespie, Rev. G. T., D.D. "A Christian View on Segregation." Winona, Miss.: Association of Citizens' Councils, 1954.

Gilligan, Francis. *The Morality of the Color Line: An Examination of the Right and the Wrong of the Discriminations against the Negro in the United States*. 1928. Reprint, New York: Negro Universities Press, 1969.

Gilman, Sander. *Freud, Race, and Gender.* Princeton, N.J.: Princeton University Press, 1995.

Gilmore, Glenda Elizabeth. *Gender and Jim Crow: Women and the Politics of White Supremacy in North Carolina, 1896–1920.* Chapel Hill: University of North Carolina Press, 1996.

Giraud, Marcel. *A History of French Louisiana.* Vol. 5, *The Company of the Indies, 1723–1731.* Translated by Brian Pearce. Baton Rouge: Louisiana State University Press, 1991.

Glancy, Jennifer A. *Slavery in Early Christianity.* Oxford: Oxford University Press, 2002.

Godshalk, David F. "William J. Northen's Public and Personal Struggles against Lynching." In *Jumpin' Jim Crow: Southern Politics from Civil War to Civil Rights,* edited by Jane Dailey, Glenda Elizabeth Gilmore, and Bryant Simon, 140–61. Princeton, N.J.: Princeton University Press, 2000.

Goldenberg, David M. *The Curse of Ham: Race and Slavery in Early Judaism, Christianity, and Islam.* Princeton, N.J.: Princeton University Press, 2003.

Gordon, Sarah Barringer. *The Mormon Question: Polygamy and Constitutional Conflict in Nineteenth-Century America.* Chapel Hill: University of North Carolina Press, 2002.

Gossett, Thomas F. *Race: The History of an Idea in America.* Dallas, Tex.: Southern Methodist University Press, 1963.

Gregg, Josiah. *The Commerce of the Prairies by Josiah Gregg.* Edited by Milo Milton Quaife. Chicago: Lakeside Press, 1926.

Grossberg, Michael. *Governing the Hearth: Law and the Family in Nineteenth-Century America.* Chapel Hill: University of North Carolina Press, 1985.

———. "Guarding the Altar: Physiological Restrictions and the Rise of State Intervention in Matrimony." *American Journal of Legal History* 26, no. 3 (July 1982): 197–226.

Guterl, Matthew Pratt. *The Color of Race in America, 1900–1940.* Cambridge, Mass.: Harvard University Press, 2001.

Gutierrez, Ramon. *When Jesus Came the Corn Mothers Went Away: Marriage, Sexuality, and Power in New Mexico, 1500–1846.* Stanford, Calif.: Stanford University Press, 1991.

Gutjahr, Paul. *An American Bible: A History of the Good Book in the United States, 1777–1880.* Stanford, Calif.: Stanford University Press, 1999.

Gutman, Herbert G. *The Black Family in Slavery and Freedom, 1750–1925.* New York: Vintage, 1976.

Haigh, Christopher. *English Reformations.* New York: Oxford University Press, 1993.

Hale, Grace Elizabeth. *Making Whiteness: The Culture of Segregation in the South, 1890–1940.* New York: Pantheon Books, 1998.

Hamburger, Philip. *Separation of Church and State.* Cambridge, Mass.: Harvard University Press, 2002.

Haney López, Ian F. *White by Law: The Legal Construction of Race.* New York: New York University Press, 1996.

Hannaford, Ivan. *Race: The History of an Idea in the West*. Baltimore: Johns Hopkins University Press, 1996.

Hardaway, Roger D. "Prohibiting Interracial Marriage: Miscegenation Laws in Wyoming." *Annals of Wyoming* 52, no. 1 (Spring 1980): 55–60.

———. "Unlawful Love: A History of Arizona's Miscegenation Law." *Journal of Arizona History* 27, no. 4 (1986): 377–90.

Hartog, Hendrik. *Man and Wife in America: A History*. Cambridge, Mass.: Harvard University Press, 2000.

Harvey, Paul. *Freedom's Coming: Religious Culture and the Shaping of the South from the Civil War through the Civil Rights Era*. Chapel Hill: University of North Carolina Press, 2005.

———. "God, Negroes, and Jesus and Sin and Salvation: Racism, Racial Interchange, and Interracialism in Southern History." In *Religion in the American South: Protestants and Others in History and Culture*, edited by Beth Barton Schweiger and Donald G. Mathews, 283–329. Chapel Hill: University of North Carolina Press, 2004.

———. *Redeeming the South: Religious Cultures and Racial Identities among Southern Baptists, 1865–1925*. Chapel Hill: University of North Carolina Press, 1997.

Haw, Reginald. *The State of Matrimony: An Investigation of the Relationship between Ecclesiastical and Civil Marriage in England after the Reformation, with a Consideration of the Laws Relating Thereto*. London: S.P.C.K., 1952.

Haynes, Stephen R. *Noah's Curse: The Biblical Justification of American Slavery*. Oxford: Oxford University Press, 2002.

———. "Original Dishonor: Noah's Curse and the Southern Defense of Slavery." *Journal of Southern Religion* vol. 3 (2000): <http://jsr.as.wvu.edu/honor.htm>.

Helmholz, R. H. *Marriage Litigation in Medieval England*. London: Cambridge University Press, 1974.

Hening, William W. *The Statutes at Large; Being a Collection of All the Laws of Virginia, from the First Session of the Legislature in the Year 1619*. Vol. 2. Richmond, Va.: Franklin Press, 1819–1823.

Hennesey, James J. *American Catholics: A History of the Roman Catholic Community in the United States*. New York: Oxford University Press, 1981.

Heyrman, Christine Leigh. *Southern Cross: The Beginnings of the Bible Belt*. Chapel Hill: University of North Carolina Press, 1998.

Higginbotham, A. Leon, Jr. *In the Matter of Color: The Colonial Period*. Vol. 1 of *Race and the American Legal Process*. Oxford: Oxford University Press, 1978.

Higginbotham, A. Leon, Jr., and Barbara A. Kopytoff. "Racial Purity and Interracial Sex in the Law of Colonial and Antebellum Virginia." *Georgetown Law Journal* 77, no. 6 (1989): 1967–2029.

Higham, John. *Strangers in the Land: Patterns of American Nativism, 1869–1925*. 1955. Reprint, New York: Atheneum, 1963.

Hill, Samuel S. "Fundamentalism in Recent Southern Culture: Has It Done What the Civil Rights Movement Couldn't Do?" *Journal of Southern Religion* 1, no. 1 (1998).

———. *The South and the North in American Religion*. Athens: University of Georgia Press, 1980.

———. "Southern Protestantism and Racial Integration." *Religion in Life* 33, no. 3 (Summer 1964): 421–29.

Hodes, Martha. "Wartime Dialogues on Illicit Sex: White Women and Black Men." In *Divided Houses: Gender and the Civil War*, edited by Catherine Clinton and Nina Silber, 230–42. Oxford: Oxford University Press, 1992.

———. *White Women, Black Men: Illicit Sex in the Nineteenth-Century South*. New Haven, Conn.: Yale University Press, 1997.

Hodges, Graham Russell. "The Pastor and the Prostitute: Sexual Power among African Americans and Germans in Colonial New York." In *Sex, Love, Race: Crossing Boundaries in North American History*, edited by Martha Hodes, 60–71. New York: New York University Press, 1999.

Hofstadter, Richard. *Anti-Intellectualism in American Life*. New York: Alfred A. Knopf, 1962.

———. *The Paranoid Style in American Politics, and Other Essays*. New York: Alfred A. Knopf, 1965.

Hollinger, David A. "Amalgamation and Hypodescent: The Question of Ethnoracial Mixture in the History of the United States." *American Historical Review* 108, no. 5 (December 2003): 1363–90.

Horsman, Reginald. *Race and Manifest Destiny: The Origins of American Racial Anglo-Saxonism*. Cambridge, Mass.: Harvard University Press, 1981.

Howard, George Elliott. *A History of Matrimonial Institutions*. 2 vols. Chicago: University of Chicago Press, 1904.

Hughes, Richard T., and C. Leonard Allen. *Illusions of Innocence: Protestant Primitivism in America, 1630–1875*. Chicago: University of Chicago Press, 1988.

Hurd, John Codman. *The Law of Freedom and Bondage in the United States*. Vol. 1. 1858. Reprint, New York: Negro Universities Press, 1968.

Hurtado, Albert. *Intimate Frontiers: Sex, Gender, and Culture in Old California*. Albuquerque: University of New Mexico Press, 1999.

Ignatiev, Noel. *How the Irish Became White*. New York: Routledge, 1995.

Ingram, Martin. *Church Courts, Sex and Marriage in England, 1570–1640*. Cambridge: Cambridge University Press, 1987.

Ireland, John. "Let There Be No Barrier against Mere Color." *Interracial Review* 21, no. 6 (June 1948).

Isaac, Rhys. *The Transformation of Virginia, 1740–1790*. Chapel Hill: University of North Carolina Press, 1982.

Jabour, Anya. *Marriage in the Early Republic: Elizabeth and William Wirt and the Companionate Ideal*. Baltimore: Johns Hopkins University Press, 1998.

Jacobson, Matthew Frye. *Whiteness of a Different Color: European Immigrants and the Alchemy of Race*. Cambridge, Mass.: Harvard University Press, 1998.

Jakobsen, Janet R., and Ann Pellegrini. *Love the Sin: Sexual Regulation and the Limits of Religious Tolerance*. New York: New York University Press, 2003.

Johnson, Franklin. *The Development of State Legislation concerning the Free Negro.* 1919. Reprint, Westport, Conn.: Greenwood Press, 1979.

Johnson, J. Edward. *History of the Supreme Court Justices of California.* Vol. 2. San Francisco: Bender-Moss, 1963.

Johnson, Sylvester A. *The Myth of Ham in Nineteenth-Century American Christianity: Race, Heathens, and the People of God.* New York: Palgrave Macmillan, 2004.

Jordan, Winthrop. *White over Black: American Attitudes toward the Negro, 1550–1812.* Chapel Hill: University of North Carolina Press, 1968.

Kalven, Harry, Jr. *A Worthy Tradition: Freedom of Speech in America.* New York: Harper and Row, 1988.

Kaplan, Sidney. "The Miscegenation Issue in the Election of 1864." *Journal of Negro History* 34, no. 3 (July 1949): 274–343.

Kennedy, Randall. *Interracial Intimacies: Sex, Marriage, Identity, and Adoption.* New York: Pantheon Books, 2003.

Kent, Peter C. "A Tale of Two Popes: Pius XI, Pius XII, and the Rome-Berlin Axis." In *Journal of Contemporary History* 23 (1988): 589–608.

Kerber, Linda K. *Women of the Republic: Intellect and Ideology in Revolutionary America.* Chapel Hill: University of North Carolina Press, 1980.

Kidd, Colin. *The Forging of Races: Race and Scripture in the Protestant Atlantic World, 1600–2000.* New York: Cambridge University Press, 2006.

Kinney, Kenneth R. "The Segregation Issue." *Baptist Bulletin,* October 1956, 9–10.

Klarman, Michael J. *From Jim Crow to Civil Rights: The Supreme Court and the Struggle for Racial Equality.* Oxford: Oxford University Press, 2004.

Kloran: Knights of the Ku Klux Klan. 5th ed. Atlanta, Ga.: Knights of the Ku Klux Klan, 1916.

Kloran; or, Ritual Women of the Ku Klux Klan. Denver, Colo.: Imperial Headquarters, Women of the Ku Klux Klan, John F. Sass Printing [1924?]. Senter Collection, Box 49, Western History Division, Denver Public Library, Denver, Colorado.

K'Meyer, Tracy E. *Interracialism and Christian Community in the Postwar South.* Charlottesville: University of Virginia Press, 1997.

Kolchin, Peter. *A Sphinx on the American Land: The Nineteenth-Century South in Comparative Perspective.* Baton Rouge: Louisiana State University Press, 2003.

Koppelman, Andrew. *Same Sex, Different States: When Same-Sex Marriages Cross State Lines.* Ann Arbor, Mich.: Sheridan Books, 2006.

Krebs, A. V. "A Church of Silence." *Commonweal* 80, no. 16 (10 July 1964): 467–76.

Labbé, Dolores Egger. *Jim Crow Comes to Church: The Establishment of Segregated Catholic Parishes in South Louisiana.* New York: Arno Press, 1978.

LaFarge, John. *Interracial Justice: A Study of the Catholic Doctrine of Race Relations.* New York: America Press, 1937. Reprinted as *The Race Question and the Negro.* New York: Longmans, Green, 1943.

Lambert, Frank. *The Founding Fathers and the Place of Religion in America.* Princeton, N.J.: Princeton University Press, 2003.

Landers, Jane. *Black Society in Spanish Florida*. Urbana: University of Illinois Press, 1999.

Larson, Robert. *New Mexico's Quest for Statehood, 1846–1912*. Albuquerque: University of New Mexico Press, 1968.

Lay, Shawn, ed. *The Invisible Empire in the West: Toward a New Historical Appraisal of the Ku Klux Klan of the 1920s*. Urbana: University of Illinois Press, 2003.

Layne, John Edward, III. "Leon Maurice Bazile." In *Legal Education in Virginia, 1779–1979: A Biographical Approach*, edited by W. Hamilton Bryson, 82–86. Charlottesville: University Press of Virginia, 1982.

LeBerthon, Ted. "Council of All Races." *Interracial Review* 18, no. 10 (October 1945): 150–52.

Leonard, Bill J. "A Theology for Racism: Southern Fundamentalists and the Civil Rights Movement." In *Southern Landscapes*, edited by Tony Badger, Walter Edgar, and Jan Nordby Gretlund, in cooperation with Lothar Hönnighausen and Christoph Irmscher, 165–81. Tübingen, Germany: Stauffenburg, 1996.

Leonard, Karen Isaksen. *Making Ethnic Choices: California's Punjabi Mexican Americans*. Philadelphia, Pa.: Temple University Press, 1992.

Leonard, Kevin Allen. "'Brothers under the Skin'? African Americans, Mexican Americans, and World War II in California." In *The Way We Really Were: The Golden State in the Second Great War*, edited by Roger W. Lotchin, 187–214. Urbana: University of Illinois Press, 2000.

———. "'In the Interest of All Races': African Americans and Interracial Cooperation in Los Angeles during and after World War II." In *Seeking El Dorado: African Americans in California*, edited by Lawrence B. de Graaf, Kevin Mulroy, and Quintard Taylor. Los Angeles: Autry Museum of Western Heritage in Association with University of Washington Press, 2001.

"Leon M. Bazile." *Virginia State Bar Association Proceedings*. Vol. 78. Richmond: Virginia State Bar Association, 1967.

Levine, Lawrence W. *Black Culture and Black Consciousness: Afro-American Folk Thought from Slavery to Freedom*. Oxford: Oxford University Press, 1977.

Litwack, Leon F. *Been in the Storm So Long: The Aftermath of Slavery*. New York: Vintage, 1980.

———. *Trouble in Mind: Black Southerners in the Age of Jim Crow*. New York: Knopf, 1998.

Loescher, Frank. *The Protestant Church and the Negro: A Pattern of Segregation*. 1948. Reprint, Westport, Conn.: Negro Universities Press, 1971.

Lofgren, Charles. *The Plessy Case: A Legal-Historical Interpretation*. New York: Oxford University Press, 1987.

Lombardo, Paul A. "Miscegenation, Eugenics, and Racism: Historical Footnotes to *Loving v. Virginia*." *University of California–Davis Law Review* 21, no. 2 (Winter 1988): 421–52.

———. *Three Generations, No Imbeciles: Eugenics, the Supreme Court, and Buck v. Bell*. Baltimore: Johns Hopkins University Press, 2008.

Love, Edgar F. "Marriage Patterns of Persons of African Descent in a Colonial Mexico City Parish." *Hispanic American Historical Review* 51, no. 1 (February 1971): 79–91.

Luker, Ralph E. *The Social Gospel in Black and White: American Racial Reform, 1885–1912.* Chapel Hill: University of North Carolina Press, 1991.

Luther, Martin. "The Babylonian Captivity of the Church." In *Three Treatises*, 2nd rev. ed., translated by Charles M. Jacobs, 123–260. Philadelphia, Pa.: Fortress Press, 1970.

———. "Lectures on Genesis, Chapters 6–14." In *Luther's Works*, vol. 2. edited by Jaroslav Pelikan and Daniel E. Poellot. St. Louis, Mo.: Concordia Publishing House, 1960.

———. "On Marriage Matters." In *Luther's Works*, American ed., vol. 46, edited by Walter I. Brandt. Philadelphia, Pa.: Muhlenberg Press, 1962.

———. "Temporal Authority: To What Extent It Should Be Obeyed." In *Luther's Works*, American ed., vol. 45, edited by Walter I. Brandt. Philadelphia, Pa.: Muhlenberg Press, 1962.

Maltz, Earl M. *Civil Rights, the Constitution, and Congress, 1863–1869.* Lawrence: University Press of Kansas, 1990.

Mangum, Charles S., Jr. *The Legal Status of the Negro.* Chapel Hill: University of North Carolina Press, 1940.

"Many Support Wiping Out Mixed-Race Marriage Ban." *Spartanburg (S.C.) Herald-Journal*, 7 February 1998, 1, A10.

Mardsen, George M. *Fundamentalism and American Culture: The Shaping of Twentieth-Century Evangelicalism, 1870–1925.* Oxford: Oxford University Press, 1980.

———. *Understanding Fundamentalism and Evangelicalism.* Grand Rapids, Mich.: William B. Eerdmans Publishing, 1991.

Marsh, Charles. *God's Long Summer: Stories of Faith and Civil Rights.* Princeton, N.J.: Princeton University Press, 1999.

Martensen, Katherine. "Region, Religion, and Social Action: The Catholic Committee of the South, 1939–1956." *Catholic Historical Review* 68, no. 2 (April 1982): 249–67.

Martin, John Bartlow. *The Deep South Says "Never."* New York: Ballantine Books, 1957.

Martinez, Maria Elena. *Genealogical Fictions: Limpieza de Sangre, Religion, and Gender in Colonial Mexico.* Stanford, Calif.: Stanford University Press, 2008.

Martinez-Alier, Verena. *Marriage, Class, and Colour in Nineteenth-Century Cuba: A Study of Racial Attitudes and Sexual Values in a Slave Society.* London: Cambridge University Press, 1974.

Martyn, Byron Curti. "Racism in the United States: A History of the Anti-Miscegenation Legislation and Litigation." Ph.D. diss., University of Southern California, 1979.

Mason, Alpheus Thomas. "Judicial Activism: Old and New." *Virginia Law Review* 55, no. 3 (April 1969): 385–426.

Mathews, Donald G. *Religion in the Old South.* Chicago: University of Chicago Press, 1977.

Matsumoto, Valerie J., and Blake Allmendinger, eds. *Over the Edge: Remapping the American West.* Berkeley: University of California Press, 1999.

Mauss, Armand L. *All Abraham's Children: Changing Mormon Conceptions of Race and Lineage.* Urbana: University of Illinois Press, 2003.

May, Geoffrey. *Marriage Laws and Decisions in the United States: A Manual.* New York: Russell Sage Foundation, 1929.

Mazar, Benjamin. "The Historical Background of the Book of Genesis." *Journal of Near Eastern Studies* 28, no. 2 (April 1969): 73–83.

McCarthy, Timothy G. *The Catholic Tradition: Before and after Vatican II, 1878–1993.* Chicago: Loyola University Press, 1998.

———. *The Catholic Tradition: The Church in the Twentieth Century.* 2nd ed. Chicago: Loyola University Press, 1998.

McClain, Charles, ed. *Asian Indians, Filipinos, Other Asian Communities, and the Law: Historical and Contemporary Perspectives.* New York: Garland, 1994.

McGreevy, John T. *Catholicism and American Freedom: A History.* New York: W. W. Norton, 2003.

———. *Parish Boundaries: The Catholic Encounter with Race in the Twentieth-Century Urban North.* Chicago: University of Chicago Press, 1996.

———. "Racial Justice and the People of God: The Second Vatican Council, the Civil Rights Movement, and American Catholics." *Religion and American Culture* 4 (Summer 1994): 221–54.

McKivigan, John. *The War against Proslavery Religion: Abolitionism and the Northern Churches, 1830–1865.* Ithaca, N.Y.: Cornell University Press, 1984.

McLain, C. E., D.D. *Place of Race.* New York: Vantage Press, 1965.

McMahon, Kevin J. *Reconsidering Roosevelt on Race: How the Presidency Paved the Road to Brown.* Chicago: University of Chicago Press, 2004.

McManus, Edgar J. *A History of Negro Slavery in New York.* Syracuse, N.Y.: Syracuse University Press, 1966.

McMillen, Neil R. *Dark Journey: Black Mississippians in the Age of Jim Crow.* Urbana: University of Illinois Press, 1977.

McNeil, Harry. "Collapse of the Canard of Cham." *Interracial Review,* September 1940, 135–37.

McWilliams. Carey. "Critical Summary." *Journal of Educational Sociology* 19, no. 3 (November 1945): 187–97.

Mellinkoff, Ruth. *The Mark of Cain.* Berkeley: University of California Press, 1981.

Menchaca, Martha. *Recovering History, Constructing Race: The Indian, Black, and White Roots of Mexican Americans.* Austin: University of Texas Press, 2001.

Merk, Frederick. *Manifest Destiny and Mission in American History: A Reinterpretation.* New York: Vintage Books, 1963.

Metz, Rene. *What Is Canon Law?* Translated by Michael Derrick. New York: Hawthorn Publishers, 1960.

Miller, Darlis. "Cross-Cultural Marriages in the Southwest: The New Mexico Experience, 1846–1900." *New Mexico Historical Review* 57 (1982): 335–59.

Miller, Randall. "The Failed Mission: The Catholic Church and Black Catholics in the Old South." In *Catholics in the Old South: Essays on Church and Culture*, edited by Randall Miller and Jon Wakelyn, 149–70. Macon, Ga.: Mercer University Press, 1999.

———. "Slaves and Southern Catholicism." In *Masters and Slaves in the House of the Lord: Race and Religion in the American South, 1740–1870*, edited by John B. Boles, 127–52. Lexington: University Press of Kentucky, 1988.

Miller, Robert Moats. *American Protestantism and Social Issues, 1919–1939*. Chapel Hill: University of North Carolina Press, 1958.

———. "The Protestant Churches and Lynching, 1919–1939." *Journal of Negro History* 42, no. 2 (April 1957): 118–31.

Miller, Steven P. "From Politics to Reconciliation: *Katallagete*, Biblicism, and Southern Liberalism." *Journal of Southern Religion* 7 (November 2004).

Mitchell, Pablo. "Accomplished Ladies and *Coyotes*: Marriage, Power, and Straying from the Flock in Territorial New Mexico, 1880–1920." In *Sex, Love, Race: Crossing Boundaries in North American History*, edited by Martha Hodes, 331–51. New York: New York University Press, 1999.

Moore, Andrew S. "Anti-Catholicism, Anti-Protestantism, and Race in Civil Rights Era Alabama and Georgia." *Journal of Southern Religion* 8 (December 2005).

Moore, Leonard J. "Historical Interpretations of the 1920s Klan: The Traditional View and Recent Revisions." In *The Invisible Empire in the West: Toward a New Historical Appraisal of the Ku Klux Klan of the 1920s*, edited by Shawn Lay, 17–38. Champaign: University of Illinois Press, 1992.

Moreno, Deborah. "'Here the Society Is United': 'Respectable' Anglos and Intercultural Marriage in Pre–Gold Rush California." *California History* 80, no. 1 (Spring 2001): 2–17.

Morgan, Edmund S. *American Slavery, American Freedom: The Ordeal of Colonial Virginia*. New York: Norton, 1975.

———. *The Puritan Family: Religion and Domestic Relations in Seventeenth-Century New England*. New York: Harper and Row, 1966.

Mörner, Magnus. *Race Mixture in the History of Latin America*. Boston: Little, Brown, 1967.

Moynihan, James H. *The Life of Archbishop John Ireland*. New York: Harper and Bros., 1953.

Mueller, William A. *Church and State in Luther and Calvin: A Comparative Study*. Nashville, Tenn.: Broadman Press, 1954.

Mumford, Kevin. "After Hugh: Statutory Race Segregation in Colonial America, 1630–1725." *American Journal of Legal History* 43, no. 3 (July 1999): 280–305.

Murray, Pauli. *States' Laws on Race and Color, and Appendices Containing International Documents, Federal Laws and Regulations, Local Ordinances and Charts*. Cincinnati, Ohio: Women's Division of Christian Service, Methodist Church, 1951.

Murray, Peter C. *Methodists and the Crucible of Race, 1930–1975*. Columbia: University of Missouri Press, 2004.

Myrdal, Gunnar. *An American Dilemma: The Negro Problem and Modern Democracy.* 1944. Reprint, New York: Harper and Row, 1962.

Nau, Rt. Rev. Louis J. *Manual on the Marriage Laws of the Code of Canon Law.* 2nd revised ed. New York: Frederick Pustet, 1934.

Newbeck, Phyl. *Virginia Hasn't Always Been for Lovers: Interracial Marriage Bans and the Case of Richard and Mildred Loving.* Carbondale: Southern Illinois University Press, 2004.

Newby, I. A. *Jim Crow's Defense: Anti-Negro Thought in America, 1900–1930.* Baton Rouge: Louisiana State University Press, 1965.

Newman, Mark. *Getting Right with God: Southern Baptists and Desegregation, 1945–1995.* Tuscaloosa: University of Alabama Press, 2001.

Nickels, Marilyn Wenzke. *Black Catholic Protest and the Federated Colored Catholics, 1917–1933: Three Perspectives on Interracial Justice.* New York: Garland Publishing, 1988.

Noll, Mark A. "The Bible and Slavery." In *Religion and the American Civil War,* edited by Randall M. Miller, Harry S. Stout, and Charles Reagan Wilson, 43–73. New York: Oxford University Press, 1998.

———. *The Civil War as a Theological Crisis.* Chapel Hill: University of North Carolina Press, 2006.

Noonan, John T., Jr. *A Church That Can and Cannot Change.* Notre Dame, Ind.: University of Notre Dame Press, 2005.

Norton, Mary Beth. *Founding Mothers and Fathers: Gendered Power and the Forming of American Society.* New York: Vintage, 1997.

Nott, Josiah A. "Types of Mankind." In *Slavery Defended: The Views of the Old South,* edited by Eric L. McKitrick, 126–38. Englewood Cliffs, N.J.: Prentice-Hall, 1963.

Nourse, Victoria F. *In Reckless Hands: Skinner v. Oklahoma and the Near Triumph of American Eugenics.* New York: W. W. Norton, 2008.

Novick, David. *That Noble Dream: The "Objectivity Question" and the American Historical Profession.* Cambridge: Cambridge University Press, 1988.

Novkov, Julie. *Racial Union: Law, Intimacy, and the White State in Alabama, 1865–1954.* Ann Arbor: University of Michigan Press, 2008.

Obituary of Joseph Cardinal Ritter. *Richmond Times-Dispatch* 11 June 1967, C-16.

O'Brien, David M. *Constitutional Law and Politics.* 2 vols. New York: W. W. Norton, 2000–2003.

Ochs, Stephen J. *Desegregating the Altar: The Josephites and the Struggle for Black Priests, 1871–1960.* Baton Rouge: Louisiana State University Press, 1990.

O'Connell, Marvin R. *John Ireland and the American Church.* St. Paul: Minnesota Historical Society Press, 1988.

O'Neill, Charles Edwards. *Church and State in French Colonial Louisiana: Policy and Politics to 1732.* New Haven, Conn.: Yale University Press, 1966.

Orenstein, Dara. "Void for Vagueness: Mexicans and the Collapse of Miscegenation Law in California." *Pacific Historical Review* 74 (2005): 367–408.

Orsi, Robert. "The Religious Boundaries of an In-between People: Street Feste and the Problem of the Dark-Skinned Other in Italian Harlem, 1920–1990." *American Quarterly* 44, no. 3 (September 1992): 313–47.

Ownby, Ted. *Subduing Satan: Religion, Recreation, and Manhood in the Rural South, 1865–1920.* Chapel Hill: University of North Carolina Press, 1990.

Pagels, Elaine. *Adam, Eve, and the Serpent.* New York: Vintage Books, 1989.

The Papal Encyclicals, 1740–1981. 5 vols. Edited by Claudia Carlen. Wilmington, N.C.: McGrath Publishing, 1981.

Parrish, Michael E. "Earl Warren and the American Judicial Tradition." *American Bar Foundation Research Journal* 7, no. 4 (Autumn 1982): 1179–88.

Parry, J. H. *The Spanish Theory of Empire in the Sixteenth Century.* Cambridge: Cambridge University Press, 1940.

Pascoe, Peggy. "Miscegenation Law, Court Cases, and Ideologies of 'Race' in Twentieth-Century America." *Journal of American History* 8, no. 1 (June 1996): 44–69.

———. "Race, Gender, and Intercultural Relations: The Case of Interracial Marriage." *Frontiers* 12, no. 1 (1991): 5–18.

———. "Race, Gender, and the Privileges of Property: On the Significance of Interracial Marriage in the U.S. West." In *Over the Edge: Remapping the American West,* edited by Valerie J. Matsumoto and Blake Allmendinger, 215–30. Berkeley: University of California Press, 1999.

———. "Sex, Gender, and Same-Sex Marriage." In *Is Academic Feminism Dead? Theory in Practice,* edited by the Social Justice Group at the Center for Advanced Feminist Studies, University of Minnesota, 86–129. New York: New York University Press, 2000.

———. *What Comes Naturally: Miscegenation Law and the Making of Race in America.* Oxford: Oxford University Press, 2009.

Passelecq, George, and Bernard Suchecky. *The Hidden Encyclical of Pius XI.* New York: Harcourt, Brace, 1997.

Patterson, Sara M. "Divine Revelations/Delusions Revealed: Historical Understandings of Revelation in Debates over Mormonism." Ph.D. diss., Claremont Graduate University, 2005.

Peabody, Sue. *"There Are No Slaves in France": The Political Culture of Race and Slavery in the Ancien Régime.* New York: Oxford University Press, 1996.

Pearce, Roy Harvey. *Savagism and Civilization: A Study of the Indian and the American Mind.* 1953. Reprint, Baltimore: Johns Hopkins University Press, 1967.

Pelikan, Jaroslav. *Whose Bible Is It? A History of the Scriptures through the Ages.* New York: Viking Penguin Publishing, 2005.

Perbal, Albert. "La Race Nègre et la Malédiction de Cham." *Revue de l'Université d'Ottawa* 10, no. 2 (April–June 1940): 156–77.

Perry, Adele. *On the Edge of Empire: Gender, Race, and the Making of British Columbia, 1849–1871.* Toronto: University of Toronto Press, 2001.

Peterson, Thomas V. *Ham and Japheth in America: The Mythic World of Whites in the Antebellum South.* Metuchen, N.J.: American Theological Library Association, 1978.

Pittman, R. Carter. "The Fourteenth Amendment: Its Intended Effect on Anti-Miscegenation Laws." *North Carolina Law Review* 43 (1964–1965): 92–109.

Popkin, Richard H. *Isaac La Peyrère (1596–1675): His Life, Work, and Influence.* Leiden, Netherlands: Brill Press, 1987.

Pratt, Robert A. "Crossing the Color Line: A Historical Assessment and Personal Narrative of *Loving v. Virginia.*" *Howard Law Journal* 41, no. 2 (1998): 229–44.

Press Release, Catholic Interracial Council of Los Angeles Collection, Center for the Study of Los Angeles, Loyola-Marymount University, Los Angeles [n.d.].

Priest, Josiah. *Slavery as It Relates to the Negro, or African Race, Examined in the Light of Circumstances, History, and the Holy Scriptures; With an Account of the Origin of the Black Man's Color, Causes of His State of Servitude, and Traces of His Character as Well in Ancient Times as in Modern Times: With Strictures on Abolitionism.* 1843. Reprint, New York: Arno Press, 1977.

"Proposition No. 11 Called Communistic by Tenney." *Los Angeles Times*, October 30, 1946, 4.

Prucha, Francis Paul. *American Indian Policy in Crisis: Christian Reformers and the Indian, 1865–1900.* Norman: University of Oklahoma Press, 1964.

Raboteau, Albert. *Canaan Land: A Religious History of African Americans.* New York: Oxford University Press, 2001.

———. *Slave Religion: The "Invisible Institution" in the Antebellum South.* New York: Oxford University Press, 1978.

Reardon, James Michael. *The Catholic Church in the Diocese of St. Paul, from Earliest Origin to Centennial Achievement.* St. Paul, Minn.: North Central Publishing, 1952.

Rice, Marilyn Hooke. *American Catholic Opinion in the Slavery Controversy.* New York: Cornell University Press, 1944.

Robinson, John Bell. *Pictures of Slavery and Anti-Slavery: Advantages of Negro Slavery and the Benefits of Negro Freedom, Morally, Socially, and Politically Considered.* 1863. Reprint, Miami, Fla.: Mnemosyne Publishing, 1969.

Roediger, David R. *The Wages of Whiteness: Race and the Making of the American Working Class.* New York: Verso, 1991.

Ross, Michael A. "Justice Miller's Reconstruction: The Slaughter-House Cases, Health Codes, and Civil Rights in New Orleans, 1861–1873." *Journal of Southern History* 64, no. 4 (November 1998): 649–76.

Ross, William G. *Forging New Freedoms: Nativism, Education, and the Constitution, 1917–1927.* Lincoln: University of Nebraska Press, 1994.

Russett, Cynthia Eagle. *Sexual Science: The Victorian Construction of Womanhood.* Cambridge, Mass.: Harvard University Press, 1989.

Ryan, John A. "The Black Patterns of White America." *Negro Digest* 1 (April 1943).

Ryan, Stephen P. "The Church and the New South." *Catholic World* 177 (September 1953): 416–22.

Saffley, Thomas Max. *Let No Man Put Asunder: The Control of Marriage in the German Southwest: A Comparative Study, 1550–1600.* Kirksville, Mo.: Sixteenth Century Journal Publishers, 1984.

————. "Marriage." In *The Oxford Encyclopedia of the Reformation*, vol. 3, edited by Hangs J. Hillerbrand, 18–25. Oxford: Oxford University Press, 1993.

Sanchez, George J. *Becoming Mexican American: Ethnicity, Culture, and Identity in Chicano Los Angeles, 1900–1945*. New York: Oxford University Press, 1993.

Sanders, Edith R. "The Hamitic Hypothesis: Its Origin and Functions in Time Perspective." *Journal of African History* 10, no. 4 (1969): 521–32.

Schechter, Patricia A. *Ida B. Wells-Barnett and American Reform, 1880–1930*. Chapel Hill: University of North Carolina Press, 2001.

Scott, Anne Firor. *The Southern Lady: From Pedestal to Politics, 1830–1930*. Chicago: University of Chicago Press, 1970.

Scott, Joan Wallach. "Gender: A Useful Category for Historical Analysis." *American Historical Review* 91, no. 5 (December 1986): 1053–75.

Seed, Patricia. "Social Dimensions of Race: Mexico City, 1753." *Hispanic American Historical Review* 62, no. 4 (November 1982): 569–606.

————. *To Love, Honor, and Obey in Colonial Mexico: Conflicts over Marriage Choice, 1574–1821*. Stanford, Calif.: Stanford University Press, 1988.

Shattuck, Gardiner H., Jr. *Episcopalians and Race: Civil War to Civil Rights*. Lexington: University Press of Kentucky, 2000.

Sides, Josh. *L.A. City Limits: African American Los Angeles from the Great Depression to the Present*. Berkeley: University of California Press, 2003.

Siegel, Morris. "Race Attitudes in Puerto Rico." *Phylon* 14, no. 2 (2nd quarter 1953): 163–78.

Simpson, Rev. J. David. "Non-Segregation Means Eventual Inter-Marriage." *Southern Presbyterian Journal* (15 March 1948): 6–7.

Skidmore, Thomas E. "Racial Mixture and Affirmative Action: The Cases of Brazil and the United States." *American Historical Review* 108, no. 5 (December 2003): 1391–96.

Slattery, John. "The Catholic Church and the Colored People." *Catholic World* 37 (April–September 1883): 374–84.

————. "Is the Negro Problem Becoming Local?" *Catholic World* 44 (October–March 1886–1887): 309–18.

Sloan, James A. *The Great Question Answered; or, Is Slavery a Sin in Itself? (Per Se?) Answered According to the Teaching of the Scriptures*. Memphis, Tenn.: Avalanche Southern Book and Job Office, Hutton, Gallaway, 1857.

Smith, H. Shelton. *In His Image, but . . . : Racism in Southern Religion, 1780–1910*. Durham, N.C.: Duke University Press, 1972.

Smith, John David, ed. *The "Ariel" Controversy: Religion and "The Negro Problem."* New York: Garland Publishing, 1993.

Snay, Mitchell. *Gospel of Disunion: Religion and Separatism in the Antebellum South*. New York: Cambridge University Press, 1993.

Sollors, Werner, ed. *Interracialism: Black-White Intermarriage in American History, Literature, and Law*. Oxford: Oxford University Press, 2000.

"South Africa Drops a Barrier to Relations between Races." *New York Times*, 21 April 1985: E2.

Southern, David. *John LaFarge and the Limits of Catholic Interracialism, 1911–1963*. Baton Rouge: Louisiana State University Press, 1996.

Stampp, Kenneth. *The Peculiar Institution: Slavery in the Ante-bellum South*. New York: Alfred A. Knopf, 1956.

Stanley, Amy Dru. *From Bondage to Contract: Wage Labor, Marriage, and the Market in the Age of Slave Emancipation*. Cambridge: Cambridge University Press, 1998.

Stanton, William R. *The Leopard's Spots: Scientific Attitudes toward Race in America*. Chicago: University of Chicago Press, 1960.

Starr, Kevin. *Embattled Dreams: California in War and Peace, 1940–1950*. Oxford: Oxford University Press, 2002.

Stepan, Nancy Leys. *"The Hour of Eugenics": Race, Gender, and Nation in Latin America*. Ithaca, N.Y.: Cornell University Press, 1991.

Stephenson, Gilbert Thomas. *Race Distinctions in American Law*. New York: AMS Press, 1969.

Stocking, George W. *Race, Culture, and Evolution: Essays in the History of Anthropology*. Chicago: University of Chicago Press, 1982.

Stolcke, Verena. *Marriage, Class, and Colour in Nineteenth-Century Cuba: A Study of Racial Attitudes and Sexual Values in a Slave Society*. London: Cambridge University Press, 1974.

Stokes, Mason. "Someone's in the Garden with Eve: Race, Religion, and the American Fall." *American Quarterly* 50, no. 4 (1998): 718–44.

Stone, Lawrence. *Uncertain Unions: Marriage in England, 1660–1753*. Oxford: Oxford University Press, 1992.

Stowell, Daniel W. *Rebuilding Zion: The Religious Reconstruction of the South, 1863–1877*. New York: Oxford University Press, 1998.

Stringfellow, Thornton. "The Bible Argument; or, Slavery in the Light of Divine Revelation." In *Cotton Is King, and Pro-Slavery Arguments: Comprising the Writings of Hammond, Harper, Christy, Stringfellow, Hodge, Bledsoe, and Cartwright on This Important Subject*. 1860. Reprint, New York: Johnson Reprint, 1968.

Sullivan, Patricia. *Days of Hope: Race and Democracy in the New Deal Era*. Chapel Hill: University of North Carolina Press, 1996.

Sullivan, Winnifred Fallers. *Paying the Words Extra: Religious Discourse in the Supreme Court of the United States*. Cambridge, Mass.: Harvard University Press, 1994.

Sundquist, Eric J. "Mark Twain and Homer Plessy." *Representations* no. 24, special issue: *America Reconstructed, 1840–1940* (Autumn 1988): 102–28.

Swartley, Willard M. *Slavery, Sabbath, War, and Women: Case Issues in Biblical Interpretation*. Scottsdale, Pa.: Herald Press, 1983.

Takaki, Ronald T. *Iron Cages: Race and Culture in Nineteenth-Century America*. New York: Alfred A. Knopf, 1979.

Tannenbaum, Frank. *Slave and Citizen: The Negro in the Americas*. New York: Alfred A. Knopf, 1946.

Taylor, William Robert. *Cavalier and Yankee: The Old South and American National Character*. New York: G. Braziller Press, 1961.

Thorpe, Francis Newton, ed. *Constitutions, Colonial Charters, and Other Organic Laws of the States, Territories, and Colonies.* Washington, D.C.: Government Printing Office, 1909.

Tise, Larry. *A History of the Defense of Slavery in America, 1701–1840.* Athens: University of Georgia Press, 1987.

Van Kirk, Sylvia. *Many Tender Ties: Women in Fur-Trade Society, 1670–1870.* Norman: University of Oklahoma Press, 1983.

Verge, Arthur. "Daily Life in Wartime California." In *The Way We Really Were: The Golden State in the Second Great War,* edited by Roger W. Lotchin, 13–29. Urbana: University of Illinois Press, 2000.

Volpp, Leti. "American Mestizos: Filipinos and Antimiscegenation Laws in California." *U.C. Davis Law Review* 33 (Summer 2000): 795–835.

Vose, Clement E. *Caucasians Only: The Supreme Court, the NAACP, and the Restrictive Covenant Cases.* Berkeley: University of California Press, 1959.

Wadlington, Walter. "The *Loving* Case: Virginia's Anti-Miscegenation Statute in Historical Perspective." *Virginia Law Review* 52 (1966): 1189–223.

Wallace, Les. *The Rhetoric of Anti-Catholicism: The American Protective Association, 1887–1911.* New York: Garland Publishing, 1990.

Wallenstein, Peter. "Law and the Boundaries of Place and Race in Interracial Marriage: Interstate Comity, Racial Identity, and Miscegenation Laws in North Carolina, South Carolina, and Virginia, 1860s–1960s." *Akron Law Review* 32 (1999): 557–76.

———. "Native Americans Are White, African Americans Are Not: Racial Identity, Marriage, Inheritance, and the Law in Oklahoma, 1907–1967." *Journal of the West* 39, no. 1 (January 2000): 55–65.

———. "Race, Marriage, and the Supreme Court from *Pace v. Alabama* (1883) to *Loving v. Virginia* (1967)." *Journal of Supreme Court History* 2 (1998): 65–86.

———. "Reconstruction, Segregation, and Miscegenation: Interracial Marriage and the Law in the Lower South, 1865–1900." *American Nineteenth Century History* 6, no. 1 (March 2005): 57–76.

———. *Tell the Court I Love My Wife: Race, Marriage, and Law—An American History.* New York: Palgrave Macmillan, 2002.

Waring, Luther Hess. *The Political Theories of Martin Luther.* 1910. Reprint, Port Washington, N.Y.: Kennikat Press, 1968.

Watt, Jeffrey R. "The Impact of the Reformation and Counter-Reformation." In *Family Life in Early Modern Times, 1500–1789.* Vol. 1 of *The History of the European Family,* edited by David I. Kertzer and Marzio Barbagli, 125–54. New Haven, Conn.: Yale University Press, 2001.

———. *The Making of Modern Marriage: Matrimonial Control and the Rise of Sentiment in Neuchâtel, 1550–1800.* Ithaca, N.Y.: Cornell University Press, 1992.

———. "The Marriage Laws Calvin Drafted for Geneva." In *Calvinus Sacrae Scripturae Professor: Calvin as Confessor of Holy Scripture,* 245–55. Grand Rapids, Mich.: Eerdmans, 1994.

Weber, David J. "'Scarce More Than Apes': Historical Roots of Anglo-American

Stereotypes of Mexicans." In *New Spain's Far Northern Frontier: Essays on Spain in the American West, 1540–1821*, 293–307. Dallas, Tex.: Southern Methodist University Press, 1979.

Weber, Francis J. "Black Enrichment of Los Angeles." In *Encyclopedia of California's Catholic Heritage, 1769–1999*. Mission Hills, Calif.: Saint Francis Historical Society and Arthur H. Clark, 2001: 900–901.

———. *John Joseph Cantwell: His Excellency of Los Angeles*. Hong Kong: Cathay Press, 1971.

Weitzman Lenore. *The Marriage Contract: Spouses, Lovers, and the Law*. New York: Free Press, 1981

Weld, Theodore Dwight. *The Bible against Slavery; or, An Inquiry into the Genius of the Mosaic System, and the Teachings of the Old Testament on the Subject of Human Rights*. 1837. Reprint, Detroit, Mich.: Negro History Press, 1970.

Wesley, Charles H. "The Negro in the West Indies, Slavery and Freedom." *Journal of Negro History* 17, no. 1 (January 1932): 51–66.

White, Richard. *"It's Your Misfortune and None of My Own": A New History of the American West*. Norman: University of Oklahoma Press, 1991.

White, Shane. *Somewhat More Independent: The End of Slavery in New York City, 1770–1810*. Athens: University of Georgia Press, 1991.

Wiesner-Hanks, Merry E. *Christianity and Sexuality in the Early Modern World: Regulating Desire, Reforming Practice*. London: Routledge, 2000.

Willard, Samuel. "Sermon CLXXIX, 24 August 1703." In *A Compleat Body of Divinity in Two Hundred and Fifty Expository Lectures on the Assembly's Shorter Catechism*, 613–17. Reprint, Boston: B. Eliot and D. Henchman, 1726.

Williams, Oscar. *African Americans and Colonial Legislation in the Middle Colonies*. New York: Garland Publishing, 1998.

Williamson, Joel. *The Crucible of Race: Black/White Relations in the American South since Emancipation*. New York: Oxford University Press, 1984.

———. *New People: Miscegenation and Mulattoes in the United States*. New York: Free Press, 1980.

Wilson, Charles Reagan. *Baptized in Blood: The Religion of the Lost Cause, 1865–1920*. Athens: University of Georgia Press, 1980.

Witte, John, Jr. *From Sacrament to Contract: Marriage, Religion, and Law in the Western Tradition*. Louisville, Ky.: Westminster John Knox Press, 1997.

———. "Moderate Religious Liberty in the Theology of John Calvin." *Calvin Theological Journal* 31 (1996): 359–403.

———. *Religion and the American Constitutional Experiment*. 2nd ed. Boulder, Colo.: Westview Press, 2005.

———. "The Transformation of Marriage Law in the Lutheran Reformation." In *The Weightier Matters of the Law: Essays on Law and Religion: A Tribute to Harold J. Berman*, edited by John Witte Jr. and Frank S. Alexander, 57–97. Atlanta, Ga.: Scholars Press, 1988.

Woodson, Carter G. "The Beginnings of Miscegenation of the Whites and Blacks." *Journal of Negro History* 3, no. 4 (October 1918): 335–53.

Woodward, C. Vann. *American Counterpoint: Slavery and Racism in the North-South Dialogue*. Boston: Little, Brown, 1971.

———. *The Strange Career of Jim Crow*. New York: Oxford University Press, 1966.

Wyatt-Brown, Bertram. *Honor and Violence in the Old South*. New York: Oxford University Press, 1986.

Zabel, William D. "Interracial Marriage and the Law." In *Interracialism: Black-White Intermarriage in American History, Literature, and Law*, edited by Werner Sollors, 54–61. Oxford: Oxford University Press, 2000.

Zachernuk, Philip S. "Of Origins and Colonial Order: Southern Nigerian Historians and the 'Hamitic Hypothesis,' c. 1870–1970." *Journal of African History* 35, no. 3 (1994): 427–55.

Index

163–66, 187–89; and Leon Bazile,
161–66; in southern culture, 163,
165–66; Catholic relationship with,
163–64, 165, 166, 181; authority of, for
Protestants, 165, 181–82; and constitutional interpretation, 178, 184–89;
authority of, as dividing line between
Catholicism and Protestantism, 181–
84. *See also* Acts 17:26; Babel, Tower
of; Canaan; "Dispersion" story; Genesis, Book of; Ham, biblical story of;
Hermeneutics; Noah
Bonds v. Foster (1871–72), 200 (n. 66)
Brown v. Board of Education (1954), 8, 12,
109, 145, 147, 230 (n. 9); and judicial
activism, 46, 205 (n. 122); and judicial
paradigm shift since *Plessy*, 185–87
Burns v. State (1872), 26–27, 201 (n. 68)
Busey et al. v. District of Columbia (1943),
33, 37, 48
*Butchers' Benevolent Association v. Crescent
City* (1873). See *Slaughter-House Cases*

Cain, 93, 96, 99, 220 (n. 26)
Canaan (son of Ham), 7, 91, 94, 95, 126,
219 (n. 17)
Canon law, 74–76, 77, 89
Cantwell v. Connecticut (1940): and "strict"
scrutiny, 31–32; and Marshall, 31–34;
and Stanley, 35; in Edmonds's opinion,
47–48
Casti Connubii (1930), 73–74
Catholic Church: in conflict with colonial
governments in Americas, 66–68; and
conflict with civil governments over
marriage laws, 69, 74–78; opposes
Italy's racial restrictions on marriage,
88–90; conflict with American laity
over race, 122–23, 161, 168–69; in
South, 166–70; and Lovings' case,
170–74; and authority of Bible, 181–82;
authority of, under St. Peter, 181–82;
and same-sex marriage, 190
Catholic Interracial Council, Los Angeles,
4, 13, 16–18, 19, 20–22

Catholics: and freedom to choose marriage partner, 61, 74–78, 170–74; and
interracialism, 61–65, 111, 123, 161; and
resistance to antimiscegenation laws,
62–65, 86–90, 114, 170–74; and authority of church, 63–65, 66–68, 74–
78; affirm right to regulate marriage,
69, 74–78; and individual's consent
to marry, 75–77; pronounce "separate
races" as un-Catholic, 89–90, 97–98,
114–18, 120–26; and ambivalence of
Americans toward race, 89–90, 112,
122–23, 161, 173–74; American vs.
Vatican, on race, 90, 122, 168–69, 182;
progressive attitudes on race, 112–14;
and responses to "separate races," 112–
20, 120–26; deemed "race-mixers,"
120, 127–28; as supporters of "separate
races," 120–26, 169–70; racism of, 121,
166–70; in urban North, 122, 166–69;
and prosegregation, 122–23; request
that "curse of Ham" be lifted, 124, 126,
224–25 (n. 100); role of, in *Loving*,
160, 166–70, 170–74; southern white,
161–70; Bible and, 163–64, 166; and
slavery, 166–67; immigration of, 167–
68; as only religious group to support
Lovings, 174. *See also* Bazile, Leon M.;
LaFarge, John; Marshall, Daniel G.
Church-state conflict, 86–90; in French
Louisiana and Spanish colonies, 66–
68; and Catholic-Protestant disagreements, 67–68; and Catholic marriage,
73–78
Civil Rights Act: of 1964, 2, 110; of 1866,
26, 27, 126, 132, 226 (n. 8); of 1875,
28
Civil Rights Cases (1883), 28, 30
Civil War: effects on Protestant theology
of race, 7, 99–101; effects on antimiscegenation statutes, 150–51; Catholic Church and, 166–67; interpretation, 187–89
"Clear and present danger" rule, 38, 42,
48, 204 (n. 109)

Davis, Sylvester, 3, 4, 15–16, 25, 29, 31, 34, 41, 47, 49, 198 (n. 39); marriage of, 13, 159; Marshall takes case of, 19–20

Dees et al. v. Metts et al. (1944), 145

Desegregation, 8; linked to interracial marriage, 108–10; Catholics accused of endorsing, 126, 127–28; of southern Catholic schools, 128; and Catholic resistance to, 128–29, 168–69

"Discrimination and the Christian Conscience" (1958), 119–20, 169

"Dispersion" story (Genesis 11), 94, 96, 98; antebellum interpretations of, 99, 101, 103, 111; meaning of for Catholics, 117. *See also* Babel, Tower of; Bible; Genesis, Book of; Ham, biblical story of; Noah

Dodson v. State (1895), 143–44

Due process, 132; origins of, 26; and states' Tenth Amendment rights, 29; and First Amendment, 29, 30–33; and fundamental liberties, 30–33; includes right to marry, 32; and "rational basis" test, 32, 33, 48; in *Perez*, 41, 42, 47; antimiscegenation laws as deprivation of, 175. *See also* Equal protection; Fourteenth Amendment; "Judicial activism"; "Strict scrutiny" standard

Edmonds, Douglas L., 36, 41; as Christian Scientist, 42; and role of religious freedom in *Perez* ruling, 47–49

Ellis v. State (1868), 136

Equality, racial, 9, 11–12; in *Perez*, 42, 44; and white Catholics, 88, 166–70; Protestants interpret Bible as opposed to, 100–106, 135, 136; as Catholic doctrine, 112, 114, 119, 167–68; Protestants accused Catholics of endorsing, 126, 127–28; interracial marriage equated with, 132, 134–36, 150; as basis of *Loving* decision, 175

Equal protection, 25, 32, 35, 47, 147; narrow interpretation of, 26–29, 201 (n. 69); and *The Civil Rights Cases*, 28–

29; and constitutionality of antimiscegenation laws, 28–29, 132; and racial classifications, 32, 172, 175; in *Perez*, 38, 41–44; in *Loving*, 172, 175; construal of, in *Plessy* and *Brown*, 185–87. *See also* Due process; Fourteenth Amendment; "Judicial activism"; "Strict scrutiny" standard

Ex parte Kinney (1878), 141–42

Faith in America (Christian gay rights organization), 179, 180

First Amendment: as first impression argument in *Perez*, 24; relation to Fourteenth Amendment, 29–33; and application to state laws, 30–31; Traynor on, 42–43; Edmonds on, 42, 47–48; in *Loving* amicus curiae brief, 170, 171–72. *See also Cantwell v. Connecticut*; Due process; Freedom; Liberties, fundamental

First impression: *Perez* as case of, 24

Fourteenth Amendment: as basis of challenges to antimiscegenation laws, 26–29, 37, 175; history of, in relation to antimiscegenation cases, 26–29, 132–33, 200 (n. 66), 225–26 (n. 4); vs. states' rights to enact law, 27–29, 133, 138–39; narrow readings of, 27–29, 201 (nn. 69, 70); and "strict scrutiny," 31–32; in relation to *Cantwell* and *Barnette*, 31–34; application to state laws denied by southern courts, 138, 139, 142, 143–48; in *Loving*, 175. *See also* Due process; Equal protection; "Judicial activism"; "Strict scrutiny"

Freedom:
—of religion: in *Perez*, 20, 37, 41–49; and Bill of Rights, 29–33; as fundamental liberty protected under Fourteenth Amendment, 30–33; and "strict scrutiny," 29–32; incorporated into due process clause, 30–31; role of in *Loving*, 160, 170–74
—to choose marriage partner: as Catholic

doctrine, 25, 61, 66–68, 73–75, 87–88; as contested legal issue, 43–44, 48–49, 136, 137, 143
See also First Amendment; Liberties, fundamental

Gender, 56–60, 64, 105; and post–Civil War antimiscegenation laws, 150, 151
Genesis, Book of: cited in antimiscegenation cases, 91–92; chapter eleven, 92–93, 97, 102, 108; chapter four, 93; chapter ten, 94, 96, 97, 101, 105; and pre-Adamite theories of race, 96; as explanation for origins of race and slavery, 97, 98; as justification for racial segregation, 97, 98, 108–11; and hermeneutical differences between Catholics and Protestants, 97–98, 123–26; chapter six, 102–3; chapter one, 117; racial readings of chapters, 9–11, 98–101. See also Bible; Cain; Canaan, son of Ham; Genesis, book of; Noah
—chapter 9, 97, 98, 101, 109, 190; Jewish interpretations of, 94–95; early Christian interpretations of, 95; Catholics on, 120–26;
Green v. State (1877): overturned Burns, 26–27; Supreme Court's construal of Fourteenth Amendment in, 27–28; Stanley on, 40–41; affirms divinely separated races, 91, 140, 156; affirms state's right to regulate marriage law, 139–40;

Ham, biblical story of: as account of slavery's origins, 94–96; as explanation for enslavement of African peoples, 95–97; cited by American proslavery advocates, 97, 98–99, 100–101; significance of, for white American Protestants, 97, 124–25; idea of Ham's blackness rejected by Catholics, 123–26; and Catholics request that "curse of Ham" be lifted, 124, 126. See also Bible; Cain; Canaan; Genesis, Book of; Noah

Hart v. Hoss and Elder (1874), 200–201 (n. 66)
Hermeneutics, 8, 178; of Genesis, 9–11, 93–97; and shift from Genesis 9 to Genesis 10–11 to justify racial segregation, 97, 98, 101; and white southern Protestants, 103–10; similarities between biblical and constitutional, 178, 184–89; defined, 184; role of personal values in judicial, 185–86; explored in shift from Plessy to Brown, 185–87; social attitudes as influence on judges, 185–87; as socially constructed concept, 186, 188; derived from personal values and socio-historical context, 186–88, 189–91; and change, 189–91. See also Bible; Ham, biblical story of; Genesis, Book of; Interpretation
Hitler, Adolph, 11, 38, 45, 51, 88, 114–15, 187
Honey v. Clark (1873), 200–201 (n. 66)
Humani Generis (1950), 118
Humani Generis Unitas, 116, 223 (n. 78)

In Plurimus, 113–14
In re: Shun T. Takahashi's Estate (1942), 144
Interpretation:
—biblical: confused with "the Bible," 8, 129; "plain" or "literal" vs. "nuanced," 187–88; "literalism" not perceived by some Christians as hermeneutical method, 188; "literalism" as tautological interpretive method, 188; and antigay rhetoric, 189–91
—constitutional: and narrow readings of Fourteenth Amendment, 27–29, 201 (nn. 69, 70); and fixedness of legal rulings, 45; role of text, intent, precedent, custom in, 185; role of judge's personal values in, 185–87; and "indeterminate" laws, 186; as socially constructed, 186
See also Bible; Ham, biblical story of; Hermeneutics; "Judicial activism"
Ireland, John (archbishop), 88, 114, 120–21

90, 170–74; as impediment to same-
sex unions, 190. *See also* Canon law;
Sacramental theology
— interracial: and parallels to same-sex
marriage, 5, 179–80; legality of, contracted in other states, 27, 142; and
"dangers" to state, 32–33, 39, 43, 46,
47–49, 172; linked to polygamy, 35, 48,
49; recognition of, in other states, 40–
41, 140–41, 142; banned in Nazi Germany, 51–52; and race-based slavery,
56–60; and English hostility toward,
56–61; tolerance for, among Catholics,
60, 108, 114, 128, 172; and French
colonies, 60–61; and Spanish colonies,
61–65; as tool of Spanish colonial-
ism, 63–64; in Cuba, 64; children of,
64, 91, 132, 170, 172, 173; and church-
state conflict, 65–68, 70; opposition
toward, located in "the Bible," 110, 129,
178; perceptions of God's disapproval
of, 110–11; Abp. John Ireland on, 114;
reluctance of Catholic hierarchy to
address, 119–20; Protestants accuse
Catholics of endorsing, 127–28; as
"unnatural," 134, 135, 137, 141, 145; and
Catholic doctrine, 170, 174. *See also*
Antimiscegenation laws; Miscegenation; "Race-mixing"; Sex, interracial
— Protestant theology of: and civil regulation, 78–79; historical origins of,
78–79; as nonsacramental, 78–79; as
hidden influence on American law,
79, 81–82, 215 (n. 31); influence of on
colonial American law, 79–82; as secular theology of marriage, 81–82, 133,
216 (n. 36); and conflict with Mormon
faith, 82–84. *See also* States' right to
regulate marriage
— same-sex: and historical parallels with
interracial marriage, 5, 8, 179–80; and
role of religion in future, 189–91
Marry, right to: as religious right, 3, 9,
23–25, 31, 76–77, 86–90, 170–74,
189–91; as constitutionally protected

fundamental liberty, 32–33, 41, 76–77,
171–72, 175–76; interracially, 86–90,
170–74; subordinate to states' right to
regulate marriage, 137–43; as Catholic
doctrine, 160, 174; protected under
equal protection clause, 175; Mildred
Loving on, 179–80; of same-sex
couples, 189–91
Marshall, Daniel G., 86, 159–61, 172, 174,
177, 178; as civil rights activist, 16–17,
18–19, 86; and Catholic Interracial
Council, 16–18; and conflicts with Sen.
Jack B. Tenney, 18–19, 198 (n. 34); and
religion strategy, 20, 23–26, 29, 31–34,
42; perceived non-Catholic theology of
race, 90, 91–92; arguments of, echoed
in *Loving* amicus curiae brief, 171–72
Maynard v. Hill (1888), 84–85, 144
McGucken, Joseph (auxiliary bishop),
20–21, 69, 199 (n. 47)
McLaughlin v. Florida (1964), 131, 147–48
Meyer v. Nebraska (1923), 31–32, 202
(n. 84), 203 (n. 93)
Minersville School District v. Gobitis (1940),
32
Miscegenation: cited as cause of biblical
flood, 102–3; prevention of, as basis
of Jim Crow policies, 104–11; origins
of term, 132. *See also* Marriage — interracial; "Race-mixing"; Sex, interracial
Mit brennender Sorge (1937), 114–15, 119
Mormon Church v. United States (1890),
48, 84
Mystici Corporis Christi (1943), 117–18

Naim v. Naim (1955), 145–47
Native Americans, 14, 52, 124, 198 (n. 31),
209 (nn. 29, 35, 38), 210 (n. 39),
210–11 (n. 45), 211 (n. 47); included in
some regions' antimiscegenation laws,
59–61, 149, 193 (n. 2), 227 (nn. 28, 34),
228 (n. 41), 229 (n. 48); in French and
Spanish Americas, 61–64
Noah, 7, 93–98, 109–11, 114, 129; and
American notions of slavery, 97–99;

religious basis for antimiscegenation laws, 129, 177; in antimiscegenation cases, 131, 133–35, 137–39, 140–41, 145; in antimiscegenation statutes, 148–55; imbuing white southern culture, 158–59, 161, 163, 169; influence on southern white Catholics, 161–66, 169–79; akin to anti-gay biblical hermeneutics, 188–89. *See also* Bible; Ham, biblical story of; Noah

"Race-mixing," 37, 39, 91–92; antimiscegenation laws to prevent, 56–60, 143; as "unnatural," 103, 134, 135, 137, 141, 145; as contrary to God's plan, 103, 106, 108, 111; and theology of separate races, 106; states' right to prevent, 146, 147. *See also* Marriage—interracial; Miscegenation; Sex, interracial

Races, theology of separate. *See* Race—Protestant theology of

Races, unity of, 92, 93, 120, 160, 182; and Acts 17:26, 100–101, 109; as basis of Catholic theology of race, 112; and unity in Christ, 113, 117–18; John Ireland on, 114; and Nazi racial doctrines, 115, 118, 183–84; John LaFarge on, 115–16; Pius XII on, 116–17, 118; Protestants recognize as Catholic doctrine, 127; resisted by American laity, 168–69. *See also* Race—Catholic theology of

Racism: and antimiscegenation laws, 56–60; within American Catholic hierarchy, 89; Vatican rejects, 89, 114–17, 125; of white Catholics, 89–90, 128–29, 166–70; Marshall cites, as basis of antimiscegenation laws, 92; of white Protestants, 120–26, 129, 151, 154, 156–57. *See also* Ku Klux Klan; Race—Protestant theology of; Segregation; Slavery

Rape, 59–60; of Native American women, 63–64; as crime of black men toward white women, 105, 150

"Rational basis" test, 32–33, 48, 203 (n. 92)

Reconstruction: and overturning of antimiscegenation laws, 26–27, 201 (n. 68); and Supreme Court's narrow reading of Fourteenth Amendment, 27–29

Regional values: and Protestant localism, 8–9, 182–84; in *Perez*, 13–22; and British colonies, 56–60; in Spanish Catholic colonies, 60–66; role of, in antimiscegenation statutes, 148–57; and religious views on race, 156–57, 161, 166–70; and Bible in South, 163, 165–66; and Catholic identity in North, 166, 167–69; and Catholic identity in South, 166–70; and antebellum churches, 182–83; and segregation in churches, 183

Reynolds v. United States (1878), 82–84, 85; and analogy between polygamy and interracial marriage, 35, 37, 41, 48, 216 (n. 45); Stanley on, 35, 38, 41; Edmonds on, 48; and states' rights, 216 (n. 45). *See also* Polygamy

Right to marry. *See* Marry, right to

Right, of states to regulate marriage. *See* States' right to regulate marriage

Roldan v. Los Angeles County et al. (1933), 149, 200 (n. 56), 228 (n. 38)

Russell, John J., 160–61, 170–74, 177, 232 (n. 36)

Sacramental theology: definition of, 6, 70–72, 212 (n. 5), 213 (n. 6); Protestants and, 214–15 (n. 27), 215 (n. 30). *See also* Marriage—Catholic theology of

Sacramental theology of marriage. *See* Marriage—Catholic theology of

Schenk v. United States (1919), 48, 204 (n. 109)

Scott v. State (1869), 135, 156, 204 (n. 7)

Segregation, 6–8, 12–13, 144; and Los Angeles Catholic Interracial Council, 16–18; biblical justifications of, 97, 98; and Protestant theology of race, 103; in Protestant churches, 106, 127; linked to "dispersion" story, 108, 109–11, 129;

Catholic bishops oppose, 119–20, 172–73; and Catholics link separate races to Protestants, 120–26; and white American Catholics, 122, 126, 127, 169; in North, 122, 168–69; and Protestant churches, 122–23, 127; in Catholic churches, 123; Protestants charge Catholics with opposing, 127–28; endorsed by Catholics, 128–29, 168–69; as "right" of state, 162; deemed "political" issue, 169; demise of, 190. See also *Brown v. Board of Education*; Desegregation; "Dispersion" story; Noah; *Plessy v. Ferguson*; "Race-mixing"

Sex, interracial, 28–29, 51–52; and slavery, 56–60; nonconsensual in Spanish missions, 63–64; in antimiscegenation cases, 135, 145; between white women and black men, 150. See also Marriage—interracial; Miscegenation; "Race-mixing"

Shenk, John W., 36, 42, 45–47, 205 (n. 122), 206 (n. 125)

Slaughter-House Cases (1873), 28–29, 146

Slavery: and antimiscegenation laws, 56–60; Latin American vs. U.S., 65–66, 113; and Bible, 94–97; biblical justifications for racial, 97, 98; Leo XIII on, 113–14; Catholic Church and, 166–67. See also Bible; Ham

Stanley, Charles, 34, 46, 70; denies Marshall's religious freedom argument, 35; and *Reynolds*, 35, 48; uses LaFarge's writings, 35; oral arguments of, 38–41; and biblical rationales for antimiscegenation laws, 91–92, 218 (n. 1)

States' right to regulate marriage: vs. individual's right to marry, 2–3, 86–90, 133; affirmed by post-Reconstruction courts, 27–29; in *Perez*, 45, 70; and *Reynolds*, 48–49, 82–84; contrasted with Catholic doctrine, 75–78; Protestant theological basis of, 78–82; in British colonies, 79–82; vs. federal authority, 82–84, 138, 139, 142–48; in

Reynolds and *Maynard*, 85; as theme in antimiscegenation cases, 133, 135–48; subordinated to individual's right to marry in *Loving*, 175–76

State v. Brown and Aymond (1959), 147

State v. Gibson (1871), 138–39, 145, 156

State v. Hairston (1869), 136, 138

State v. Jackson (1883), 143

State v. Tutty (1890), 40, 144–45; Marshall on, 37–38, 204 (n. 107)

Stevens v. United States (1944), 144, 146

"Strict scrutiny" standard, 202 (n. 88); and Marshall's religion strategy, 25, 29–33; origins of, 31–32; and *Cantwell*, 31, 47–48; and *Korematsu*, 32, 45; and fundamental liberties, 32–33; Stanley on, 34, 35, 38; in *McLaughlin*, 147–48. See also "Judicial activism"; "Rational basis" test

Summi Pontificatus (1939), 117, 118

Tenth Amendment, 27, 29–30, 137, 146, 148. See also States' right to regulate marriage

Traynor, Roger J., 38–41, 46, 204–5 (n. 115); written opinion of, 41–44; on judicial activism, 205 (n. 122)

Trent, Council of, 63, 67, 73, 78, 160; on marriage, 71–72, 75–76

United States v. Carolene Products (1938), 32, 203 (n. 92)

Vatican, 123, 126, 183; and Italian ban on interracial marriage, 88–90; and racial "orthodoxy," 111, 118, 119, 160, 230 (n. 4); on race as a marital impediment, 115–16; presses American church to proclaim racial equality, 168

Vatican Council, First (1869–70), 124, 126

Vatican Council, Second (1962–65), 71, 72, 160, 171

West Virginia v. Barnette (1942), 32–37, 47, 48, 198–99 (n. 41)